The MICHELIN Guide

Chicago

RESTAURANTS

2014

Michelin Travel Partner
Société par actions simplifiées au capital de 11 288 880 EUR
27 Cours de l'Ile Seguin - 92100 Boulogne Billancourt (France)
R.C.S. Nanterre 433 677 721

Dépôt légal octobre 2013

Printed in Canada - septembre 2013
Printed on paper from sustainably managed forests

Compogravure : Nord Compo à Villeneuve d'Ascq (France)
Impression et Finition : Transcontinental (Canada)

Our editorial team has taken the greatest care in writing this guide and checking the information in it. However, practical information (administrative formalities, prices, addresses, telephone numbers, Internet addresses, etc) is subject to frequent change and such information should therefore be used for guidance only. It is possible that some of the information in this guide may not be accurate or exhaustive as of the date of publication. Before taking action (in particular in regard to administrative and customs regulations and procedures), you should contact the appropriate official administration. We hereby accept no liability in regard to such information.

Dear Reader

We are thrilled to present the fourth edition of our MICHELIN Guide to Chicago.

Our dynamic team has spent this year updating our selection to reflect the rich diversity of Chicago's restaurants. As part of our meticulous and highly confidential evaluation process, our inspectors have anonymously and methodically eaten through all of the city's neighborhoods and suburbs to compile the finest in each category for your enjoyment. While the inspectors are expertly trained food industry professionals, we remain consumer driven and provide comprehensive choices to accommodate your comfort, tastes, and budget. Our inspectors dine, drink, and lodge as 'regular' customers in order to experience and evaluate the same level of service and cuisine you would as a guest.

We have expanded our criteria to reflect the more current and unique elements of the city's dining scene. Don't miss the tasty "Small Plates" category, highlighting places with a distinct style of service, setting, and menu; and the comprehensive "Under $25" list which includes an impressive choice at great value.

Additionally, you may also follow our Inspectors on Twitter @MichelinGuideCH as they chow their way around town. They usually tweet daily about their unique and entertaining food experiences.

Our company's founders, Édouard and André Michelin, published the first MICHELIN Guide in 1900, to provide motorists with practical information about where they could service and repair their cars, find quality accommodations, and a good meal. Later in 1926, the star-rating system for outstanding restaurants was introduced, and over the decades we have developed many new improvements to our guides. The local team here in Chicago eagerly carries on these traditions.

We truly hope that the MICHELIN Guide will remain your preferred reference to the city's restaurants.

Contents

© MICHELIN

Contents

The MICHELIN Guide

"This volume was created at the turn of the century and will last at least as long".

This foreword to the very first edition of the MICHELIN Guide, written in 1900, has become famous over the years and the Guide has lived up to the prediction. It is read across the world and the key to its popularity is the consistency in its commitment to its readers, which is based on the following promises.

→ Anonymous Inspections

Our inspectors make anonymous visits to hotels and restaurants to gauge the quality offered to the ordinary customer. They pay their own bill and make no indication of their presence. These visits are supplemented by comprehensive monitoring of information—our readers' comments are one valuable source, and are always taken into consideration.

→ Independence

Our choice of establishments is a completely independent one, made for the benefit of our readers alone. Decisions are discussed by the inspectors and the editor, with the most important decided at the global level. Inclusion in the guide is always free of charge.

→ The Selection

The Guide offers a selection of the best hotels and restaurants in each category of comfort and price. Inclusion in the guides is a commendable award in itself, and defines the establishment among the "best of the best."

How the MICHELIN Guide Works

→ Annual Updates

All practical information, the classifications, and awards, are revised and updated every year to ensure the most reliable information possible.

→ Consistency & Classifications

The criteria for the classifications are the same in all countries covered by the Michelin Guides. Our system is used worldwide and is easy to apply when choosing a restaurant or hotel.

→ The Classifications

We classify our establishments using XXXXX-X and ⌂⌂⌂⌂⌂-⌂ to indicate the level of comfort. The ✿✿✿-✿ specifically designates an award for cuisine, unique from the classification. For hotels and restaurants, a symbol in red suggests a particularly charming spot with unique décor or ambiance.

→ Our Aim

As part of Michelin's ongoing commitment to improving travel and mobility, we do everything possible to make vacations and eating out a pleasure.

How to Use This Guide

The Michelin Distinctions for Good Cuisine

Stars for good cuisine

⚹⚹⚹ Exceptional cuisine, worth a special journey
⚹⚹ Excellent cuisine, worth a detour
⚹ A very good restaurant in its category

Bib Gourmand

Inspectors' favorites for good value

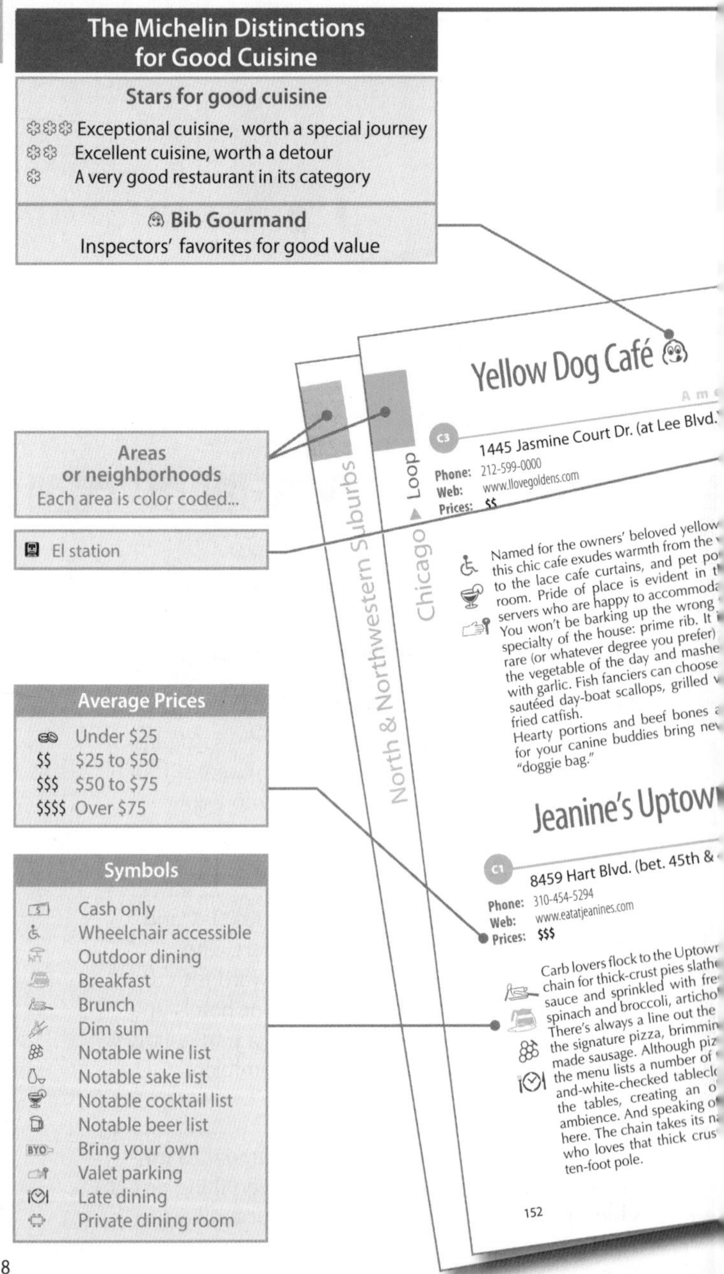

Areas or neighborhoods
Each area is color coded...

El station

Average Prices

⊜	Under $25
$$	$25 to $50
$$$	$50 to $75
$$$$	Over $75

Symbols

- Cash only
- Wheelchair accessible
- Outdoor dining
- Breakfast
- Brunch
- Dim sum
- Notable wine list
- Notable sake list
- Notable cocktail list
- Notable beer list
- BYO Bring your own
- Valet parking
- Late dining
- Private dining room

Restaurant Classifications by Comfort

More pleasant if in red

✗	Comfortable
✗✗	Quite comfortable
✗✗✗	Very comfortable
✗✗✗✗	Top class comfortable
✗✗✗✗✗	Luxury in the traditional style
	Small plates

Map Coordinates

Sonya's Palace

Italian

B5 100 Reuther Pl. (at 30th Street)

Dinner daily
LaSalle/Van Buren

Phone: 415-867-5309
Subway: 14th St - 8 Av
Web: www.sonyasfabulouspalace.com
Prices: $$$

David Buffington/Getty Images

Home cooked Italian never tasted so good than at this unpretentious little place. The simple décor claims no big-name designers, and while the Murano glass light fixtures are chic and the velveteen-covered chairs are comfortable, this isn't a restaurant where millions of dollars were spent on the interior.

Instead, food is the focus here. The restaurant's name may not be Italian, but it nonetheless serves some of the best pasta in the city, made fresh in-house. Dishes follow the seasons, thus ravioli may be stuffed with fresh ricotta and herbs in summer, and pumpkin in fall. Most everything is liberally dusted with Parmigiano Reggiano, a favorite ingredient of the chef.

For dessert, you'll have to deliberate between the likes of creamy tiramisu, ricotta cheesecake, and homemade gelato. One thing's for sure: you'll never miss your nonna's cooking when you eat at Sonya's.

Chicago ▸ Loop

153

Where to Eat

Chicago

Andersonville, Edgewater & Uptown

Lincoln Square · Ravenswood

This rare and diverse collection of spirited neighborhoods in Chicago's north side is like a real-world Epcot theme park, with visitors easily flitting from one immigrant ethnic tradition to the next, and all the while sampling international cuisines, but without a passport. Lauded as one of the most bewitching neighborhoods in the Windy City, Andersonville also struts a plethora of quaint "Places to Stay" including a host of popular bed-and-breakfasts and charming hotels. A food mecca of sorts, the **Andersonville Farmer's Market** (held every Wednesday) houses a cluster of bakeries, fresh farm produce, and Asian fruit orchards.

Swedish Spreads

From the art on the lamppost banners to the Swedish American Museum Center, you can see the influence of Andersonville's historical roots upon arrival on Clark Street. Happily, much of that can be explored with your taste buds, starting the day at **Svea Restaurant**. This well-known hangout is also home to the hearty Viking breakfast that may unveil Swedish-style pancakes, sausages, roasted potatoes, and toasted *limpa* bread (to name a few of the offerings).

Meanwhile, **Wikström's Gourmet Foods** is one of the last standing Swedish emporiums of packaged and prepared favorites, still stocked with everything needed for a traditional smörgåsbord, from homey Swedish meatballs and herring, to lingonberry preserves.

Locals yearning for additional authentic baked goods eagerly take a number and wait in line at the **Swedish Bakery**. Many of its venerable baked treats are available in individual sizes, as well as larger portions perfect for those looking to entertain. For more instant gratification, scout a seat at the counter by the window and enjoy that miniature yet exquisite coconut-custard coffeecake right away, perhaps with a complimentary cup of steaming coffee. Finally, Andersonville also caters to its worldly community with the well-tread **Middle East Bakery & Grocery**. Make a massive meze feast from spreads, breads, olives, and an impressive range of hummus among other goodies available in the deli. Or, choose to stock up on dried fruits, spices, rice, rosewater, nuts, and teas from the grocery section. Either way, you will have ample options for a magnificent Middle Eastern menu.

All Italia

As if named solely for the Italian community, **Sauce and Bread Kitchen** is largely coveted for its first-rate sauces and equally delicious, fresh-baked breads. This locally minded Edgewater eatery comes fresh from Co-op Sauce and Crumb Bread, the two beloved producers and farmers' market experts. Naturally, their the storefront brings heaven on earth for breakfast fiends (maybe with a maple sausage breakfast sandwich?), lunch clientele (applewood-smoked turkey sandwiches anyone?) as well as condiment lovers who are sure to fall instantly for their house-made cider vinegars, tomato sauce, pickles, and other sumptuous hot sauces—imagine a creamy plate of *mole* and you will start to get the drift. Then move on over to **The Coffee Studio** for a cup of joe prepared by what critics have named one of the country's best boutique coffee shops. Superlatives aside, take home a pretty little green box of chocolate-dipped *glacée* fruits to devour all by yourself.

An Asian Affair

Further uptown, Argyle Street is renowned for being a pocket of intermixed East Asian culture—even the Argyle Red Line El stop is thematically decorative. A terrific concentration of Chinese, Thai, and Vietnamese delis, as well as bakeries, herbalists, noodle shops, and restaurants line these streets; and there is endless tasting to be done along these blocks. Speaking of which, **Sun Wah BBQ** is a forever-cherished spot for Cantonese cuisine. Walk in and be greeted by their glistening selection of bronzed meats. These are offered on their own or over rice for a complete meal. The real draw in Edgewater is its art deco architecture, especially evident along Bryn Mawr Avenue and Lake Michigan's beaches. This neighborhood also boasts a vibrant community that convenes at **The Metropolis Café**, an offshoot of Chicago's lauded Metropolis Coffee Company. Watch a crowd of students, professionals, and locals gulp down oodles of their creative coffee quenchers.

Hot Dog Haven

This is Chicago, so there's always a good hot dog nearby, and one of the best red-hots uptown is as thrilling as it is easy to spot. Just look for the iconic pitchfork piercing a sausage over the name **Wolfy's**, and know that you have arrived. Try the classic dog, but know that by the time the limitless listing of toppings are piled on, the meat will be invisibly buried beneath piccalilli, pickles, peppers, and other impossibly colored yet divine condiments.

Lincoln Square and Ravenswood

Evidence of the German immigrants who helped develop Lincoln Square still lingers in this quaint expanse. Highlights may include a century-old apothecary as well as new, yet Old World-inspired butchers and specialty items that abound at **Gene's Sausage Shop**. For a fine menu of chops, steaks, free-range poultry, smoked sausages, and bacon in its many glorious forms, plan to sample the wares of **Lincoln Quality Meat Market**. The **Lincoln Square Farmer's Market** has long been loved and frequented (on Tuesdays). They now showcase a Thursday evening market, replete with live music alongside a medley of fruits, vegetables, and flowers, which remains a draw for locals with day jobs.

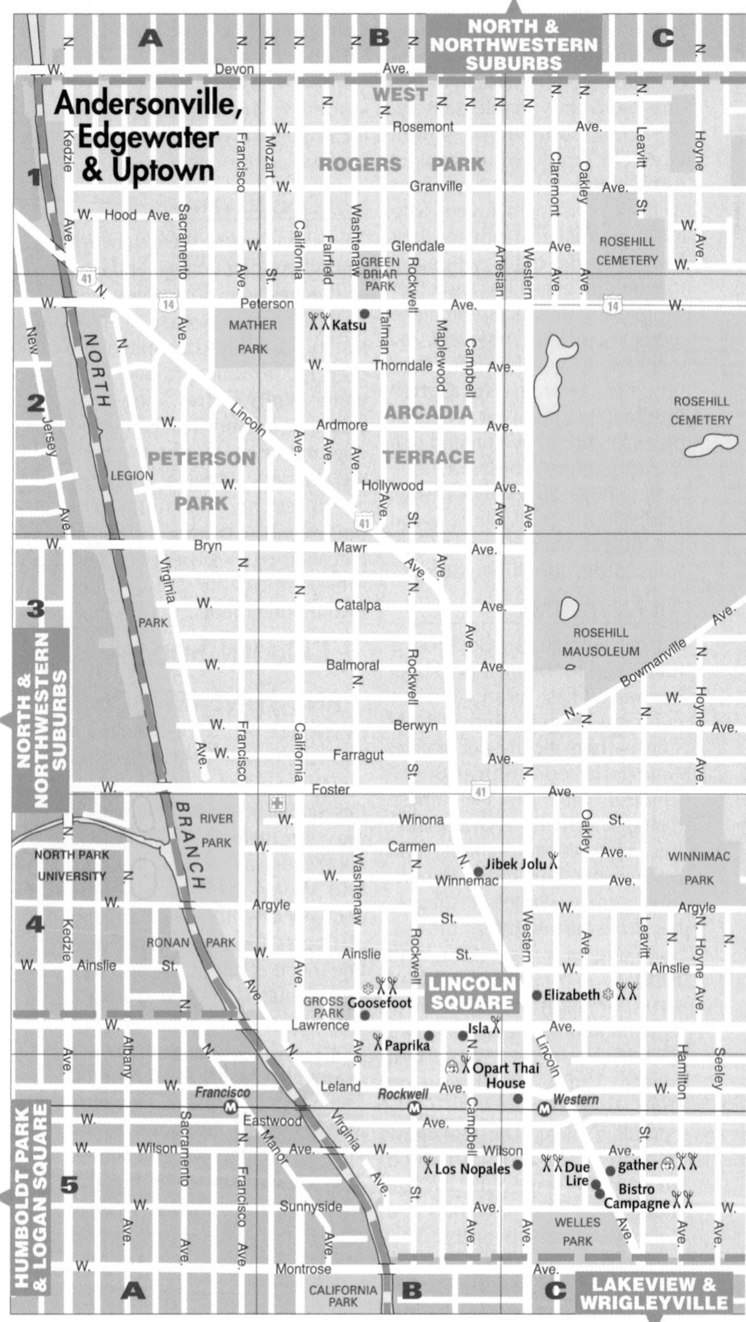
Andersonville, Edgewater & Uptown
NORTH & NORTHWESTERN SUBURBS
HUMBOLDT PARK & LOGAN SQUARE
LAKEVIEW & WRIGLEYVILLE
WEST ROGERS PARK
PETERSON PARK
ARCADIA TERRACE
LINCOLN SQUARE
ROSEHILL CEMETERY
ROSEHILL MAUSOLEUM
MATHER PARK
GREEN BRIAR PARK
LEGION PARK
RIVER PARK
NORTH PARK UNIVERSITY
RONAN PARK
GROSS PARK
WINNIMAC PARK
WELLES PARK
CALIFORNIA PARK
NORTH BRANCH
Katsu
Jibek Jolu
Goosefoot
Elizabeth
Isla
Paprika
Opart Thai House
Los Nopales
Due Lire
gather
Bistro Campagne
Francisco
Rockwell
Western
Devon Ave.
Rosemont
Granville
Hood Ave.
Glendale
Peterson
Thorndale
Ardmore
Hollywood
Bryn Mawr
Catalpa
Balmoral
Berwyn
Farragut
Foster
Winona
Carmen
Winnemac
Argyle
Ainslie
Lawrence
Leland
Eastwood
Wilson
Sunnyside
Montrose
Lincoln
Bowmanville
Virginia Manor
Kedzie
Francisco
Mozart
California
Fairfield
Washtenaw
Talman
Rockwell
Maplewood
Campbell
Artesian
Western
Claremont
Oakley
Leavitt
Hoyne
Sacramento
New Jersey
Albany
Hamilton
Seeley
A
B
C
1
2
3
4
5

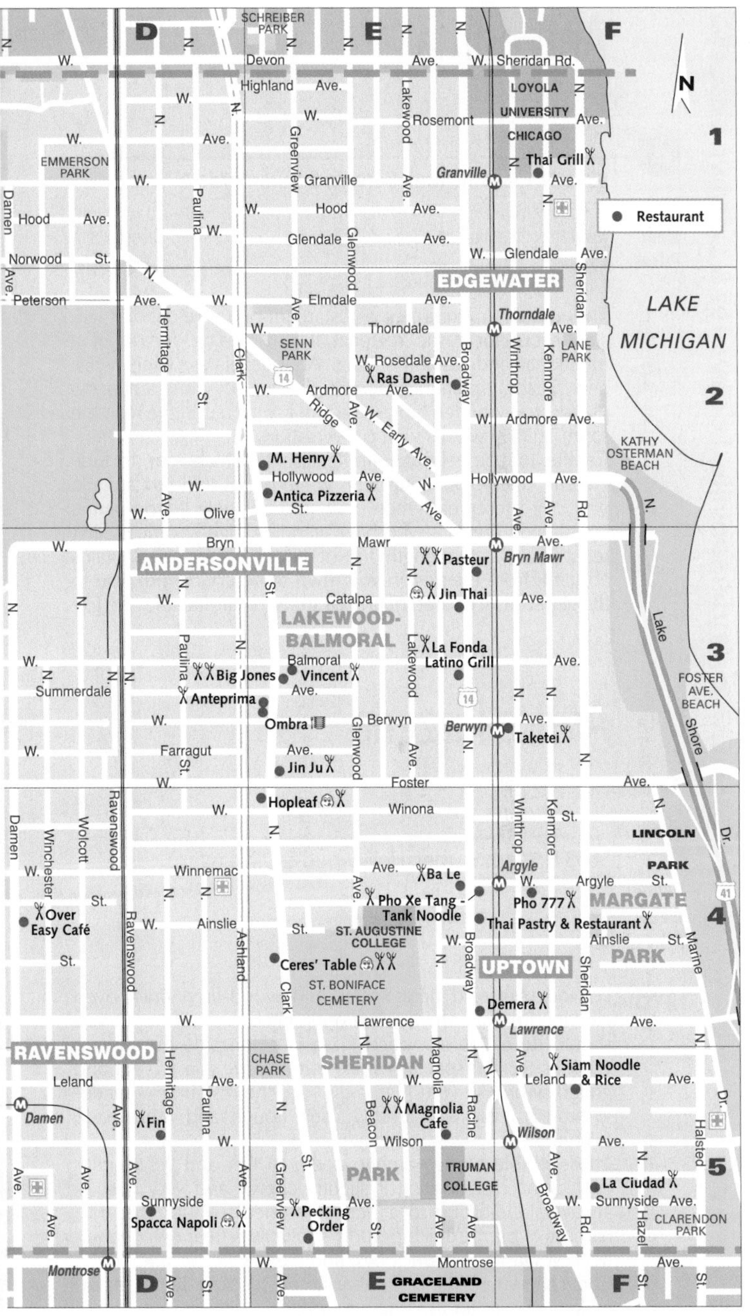
Restaurant
Thai Grill
Ras Dashen
M. Henry
Antica Pizzeria
Pasteur
Jin Thai
La Fonda Latino Grill
Big Jones
Vincent
Anteprima
Ombra
Taketei
Jin Ju
Hopleaf
Ba Le
Pho Xe Tang - Tank Noodle
Pho 777
Thai Pastry & Restaurant
Over Easy Café
Ceres' Table
Demera
Siam Noodle & Rice
Magnolia Cafe
Fin
La Ciudad
Spacca Napoli
Pecking Order
EDGEWATER
ANDERSONVILLE
LAKEWOOD-BALMORAL
UPTOWN
RAVENSWOOD
SHERIDAN PARK
MARGATE PARK
LAKE MICHIGAN

Anteprima

5316 N. Clark St. (bet. Berwyn & Summerdale Aves.)

Phone: 773-506-9990 — Lunch Sun
Web: www.anteprimachicago.net — Dinner nightly
Prices: $$ — Berwyn

This casual trattoria on a restaurant-rich stretch of Clark stands out for rustic regional Italian cuisine served in a traditional and tasteful setting. Antique plates, wine racks, and pastoral paintings accent the walls, while antipasto platters top wooden tables. Near the small bar in the rear, the room quickly warms with conversation.

Careful touches elevate simple dishes, which may include creamy celery root soup with white beans and tart arugula pesto, or preserved lemon peel atop a wiggly lemon panna cotta. Even regulars who have standing nightly orders can't resist peeks at the lengthy list of seasonal specials. Bargains abound, from the design-your-own three-course prix-fixe to the generously poured *quartinos* from the all-Italian wine list.

Antica Pizzeria

Italian

E2

5663 N. Clark St. (bet. Hollywood & Olive Aves.)

Phone: 773-944-1492 — Dinner Wed – Mon
Web: www.anticapizzeriachicago.com
Prices: ⊖⊖

BYO

Let the oversized flour scales and wood-fired brick oven glowing from a corner of the open kitchen signify what you should be eating at Antica Pizzeria. Alongside the menu's copious Sicilian specialties, like *orecchiette alla Norma* and grilled swordfish with *salmoriglio*, are the restaurant's made-to-order pizzas with freshly risen dough and homemade everything.

Those visible orange embers seem to lick and gently char each thin crust, leaving it slightly chewy and very crisp—always standing up to a rich assortment of toppings. The namesake pizza Antica proudly showcases their own fennel-flecked sausage, salami, peas, and creamy *fior di latte*.

Chef/co-owner Mario Rapisarda hosts occasional pizza-making classes for aspiring *pizzaiolos*.

Ba Le

Vietnamese X

5014 N. Broadway (at Argyle St.)

Phone: 773-561-4424 — Lunch & dinner daily
Web: www.balesandwich.com
Prices: ⊜ — Argyle

BYO

Though the French influence in Vietnamese cuisine has been well-documented, Ba Le makes sure it's front and center, literally, with a mouthwatering display of baguettes, macarons, and chocolates at its clean, modern storefront in Little Saigon.

Take a seat at a table or the L-shaped bar overlooking Broadway before digging in to a thrilling (and filling) *bánh mì* overflowing with lemongrass-seasoned sausage, homemade pickled daikon, and jalapeño on a crusty baguette. Get the most bang for your buck with crispy pork egg rolls which hit the spot perfectly, as do *pâté chaud* and *chao tom* from the grab-and-go coolers. Be warned, though: many a hungry patron stopping by to pick up a lunch sandwich has been swayed by the pastry case of impulse treats.

Big Jones

5347 N. Clark St. (bet. Balmoral & Summerdale Aves.)

Phone: 773-275-5725 — Lunch & dinner daily
Web: www.bigjoneschicago.com
Prices: $$ — Berwyn

Bistro tables, genteel brocade wallpaper, and iron chandeliers set the scene, but you know you're getting a real Southern experience when your meal starts with a pitcher of sweet tea and basket of honey butter-slathered cornbread. From start to finish, Big Jones showcases the best of the South from classic dishes like gumbo *ya-ya* in a dark, smoky roux; shrimp and grits with tasso gravy; and a can't-miss version of red velvet cake.

Aficionados of Lowcountry cooking keep coming back for Big Jones' frequent period dinners including the Boarding House Lunch ca. 1933 prix-fixe starring fried chicken, hoppin' John, and voodoo greens. Meanwhile, Bourbon lovers can't help but work their way down the vast whiskey and artisanal spirits list.

Bistro Campagne

French

4518 N. Lincoln Ave. (bet. Sunnyside & Wilson Aves.)

Phone: 773-271-6100 — Lunch Sat – Sun
Web: www.bistrocampagne.com — Dinner nightly
Prices: $$ — Western (Brown)

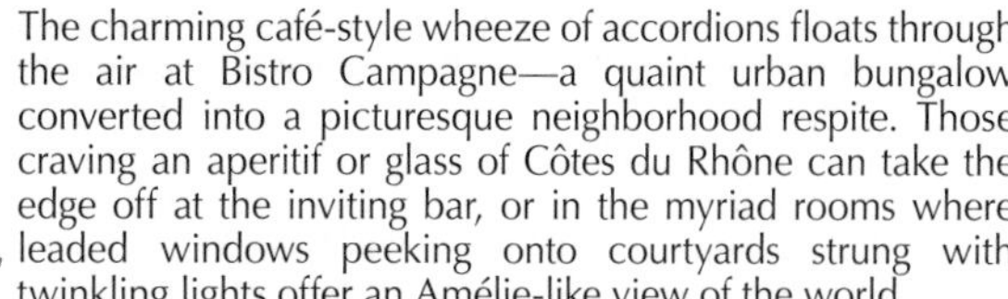

The charming café-style wheeze of accordions floats through the air at Bistro Campagne—a quaint urban bungalow converted into a picturesque neighborhood respite. Those craving an aperitif or glass of Côtes du Rhône can take the edge off at the inviting bar, or in the myriad rooms where leaded windows peeking onto courtyards strung with twinkling lights offer an Amélie-like view of the world.

A warm, crusty mini baguette served in a paper ascot offers an appropriate entry point for dinner. The country French menu may features classics like *escargot au beurre d'ail* and plump *côte de porc* spotlighting a Berkshire chop, roast heirloom carrots, and balsamic-*cipollini* jam. Finish the feast with an Armagnac and a simple *tarte au citron* with crème chantilly.

Ceres' Table

Mediterranean

4882 N. Clark St. (bet. Ainslie St. & Lawrence Ave.)

Phone: 773-878-4882 — Dinner Mon – Sat
Web: www.cerestable.com
Prices: $$ — Lawrence

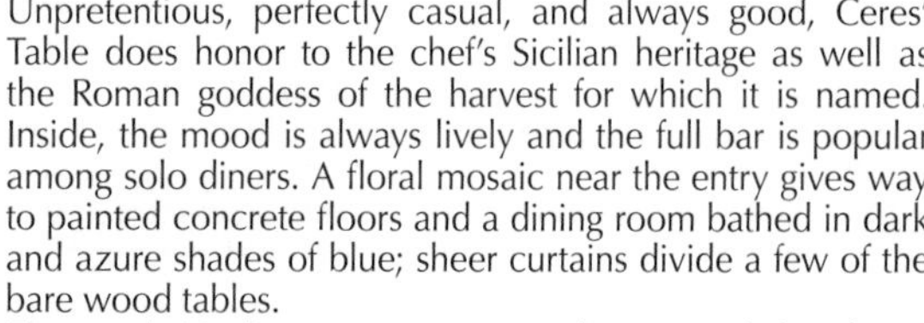

Unpretentious, perfectly casual, and always good, Ceres' Table does honor to the chef's Sicilian heritage as well as the Roman goddess of the harvest for which it is named. Inside, the mood is always lively and the full bar is popular among solo diners. A floral mosaic near the entry gives way to painted concrete floors and a dining room bathed in dark and azure shades of blue; sheer curtains divide a few of the bare wood tables.

The mostly Mediterranean menu may focus on Italy but shows American flair. Expect freshly chopped lamb tartare with cornichons, capers, and garnishes of mint and horseradish; or pan-roasted duck breast and sausage with vinegar-braised black kale. Wednesdays offer a $40 prix-fixe for three courses and a glass of wine.

Demera

E4 Ethiopian

4801 N. Broadway (at Lawrence St.)

Phone: 773-334-8787 Lunch & dinner daily
Web: www.demeraethiopianrestaurant.com
Prices: $$ Lawrence

A short skip off the red line at Lawrence, this bright corner location is as welcoming for a quick bite or drink and good people-watching as it is for an authentic Ethiopian feast. On the weekends Demera also welcomes musicians for live performances, promising that this spot goes beyond other ethnic eateries.

As is tradition, Demera serves *injera,* the spongy, pancake-like bread used as a utensil on a communal plate. Its tangy flavors pair wonderfully with the *yebeg alicha* dish of tender lamb in a rich and creamy aromatic ginger sauce; as well as the *ye-kwanta firfir,* featuring beef tips stewed in a spicy *berbere* sauce. Don't skip the Ethiopian tea, which is an oregano tea infused with anise, clover, and cinnamon. Sweeten with honey and savor.

Due Lire

4520 N. Lincoln Ave. (bet. Sunnyside & Wilson Aves.)

Phone: 773-275-7878 Dinner Tue – Sun
Web: www.due-lire.com
Prices: $$ Western (Brown)

Naples native and gentleman's gentleman Massimo Di Vuolo welcomes guests from near and far to charming Due Lire. Smartly situated near the Old Town School of Folk Music, the dining room is often dotted with locals taking in dinner and a show. Understated khaki-colored walls, dark woods, and rustic ceiling beams keep the spotlight on the plate.

Comforting but refined modern Italian dishes warm up Lincoln Square residents on those cold Chicago nights. Sample braised chicken thighs and roasted fennel with a root vegetable ragù; saffron-hued *arancini* stuffed with asparagus and fontina; or fresh, made-to-order short rib ravioli nestled with porcini and *Parmigiano.* Pair the simple, seasonal fare with a selection from the Italian-dominated wine list.

Elizabeth 

C4

Contemporary XX

4835 N. Western, Unit D (bet. Ainslie St. & Lawrence Ave.)

Phone: 773-681-0651 — Dinner Tue – Sat

Web: www.elizabeth-restaurant.com

Prices: $$$$ — Western (Brown)

Elizabeth Restaurant

Elizabeth is a distinctly real and modern American restaurant that puts on no airs—if not for the logo outside, one might confuse it for a hardware store. The inside is warm with low lighting, folk-art hens, and flea market-chic accents including tables (for both couples and quartets) lined with mismatched chairs.

There is a pervasive focus on professionalism and quality over conventionality, so the excellent servers probably have more tattoos than you. The unique reservation system requires guests to pay for meals (and gratuity) in advance, resulting in a vibe that is more casual than highfalutin.

Chef Iliana Regan has a commendable dedication to Midwestern foods, which she combines with her own ingenuity and skill into a 20-course meal. Each dish is a surprise, but may include fantastically rich, slow-cooked salmon with raw beet, white potato, parsley gel, and Meyer lemon purée. This can lead to shaved orange vegetables over cashew flan with smears of goat butter. Desserts are mod and deliciously intense as in clumps of mirepoix-like carrot cake with shaved celery, cream cheese sauce, and blue cheese ice cream; or porcini-infused caramel topped with sea salt and an edible flower.

Fin

D5

1742 W. Wilson Ave. (at Hermitage Ave.)

Phone: 773-961-7452 — Lunch & dinner daily
Web: www.finsushibar.com
Prices: ₫₫ — Montrose (Brown)

This mod-industrial sushi spot just off the Ravenswood El stop brightens an awning-lined street with its sleek presence. Angled plate glass windows play up the corner location, and though there are only a few spots at the sushi counter, a flotilla of mod blonde wood tables fills the airy room. Scalloped pendant lights add to the clean feel.

BYO

Along with Thai and Japanese standards, Pan-Asian dishes such as roast duck and asparagus spring rolls join the wide-ranging menu. Plenty of familiar maki like spicy tuna and California appease the traditionalists. More adventurous eaters go for special rolls like the "Chillis" with hamachi, *masago*, and crispy bell pepper tempura wrapped in chili-flecked soy paper and topped with fluorescent wasabi *tobiko*.

gather

American

C5

4539 N. Lincoln Ave. (bet. Sunnyside & Wilson Aves.)

Phone: 773-506-9300 — Lunch Sun
Web: www.gatherchicago.com — Dinner nightly
Prices: $$ — Western (Brown)

Communal tables and intimate two-tops help gather live up to its name in a cozy spot across the street from the Old Town School of Folk Music. Small but sophisticated, the space shines with vibrant blue and silver tones, bare wood, and polished granite counters that separate the open kitchen from the dining room.

Sharing is encouraged, so grab a fork as boards piled with creamy brandade and lemon confit, or house-made ricotta with honeycomb arrive at the table. Larger entrées may include seared diver scallops with moist shredded oxtail and candied pumpkin seeds; while desserts like chocolate-and peanut butter-semifreddo with Amarena cherries satisfy. Sunday night family-style dinners bring in the locals, especially since kids under 10 eat for free.

Goosefoot ✿

B4 Contemporary XX

2656 W. Lawrence Ave. (bet. Talman & Washtenaw Aves.)

Phone: 773-942-7547 Dinner Wed – Sun
Web: www.goosefoot.net
Prices: $$$ Rockwell

BYO

Anthony Tahlier

A place this upscale may be unusual for Lincoln Square, but Goosefoot blends in seamlessly offering nothing flashier than a white-lettered black awning on an unassuming one-story brick building. Inside, a similarly minimal décor carries the simple dining room, using caramel-toned bentwood chairs and tangerine-padded banquettes as colorful contrast to bare dark wood tables, abstract paintings, and sculptures.

Personable service and a welcoming informality from Chef/owner Chris Nugent and his wife Nina keeps the complicated cuisine from becoming too serious. The conversation level rises from a hum to a dull roar as guests make good use of their booze.

A single nine-course prix-fixe is available nightly, leaving diners completely in thrall of Nugent's vision. Edible flowers and fresh herbs garnish many dishes like beef tenderloin slow-poached in consommé, then finished on the grill and paired with the namesake Goosefoot spinach and truffled Bordeaux-shallot jus; or seared *loup de mer* resting on diced leek confit with tapioca pearls in a yuzu-infused beurre blanc. Save your menu for a lasting memory of the meal—it is printed on biodegradable paper embedded with wildflower seeds.

Hopleaf

Gastropub

5148 N. Clark St. (bet. Foster Ave. & Winona St.)

Phone: 773-334-9851 — Lunch & dinner daily
Web: www.hopleaf.com
Prices: $$ — Berwyn

For over two decades, Hopleaf (or Michael & Louise's Hopleaf Bar, if you want to call it by its given name) has been bringing beer lovers from all corners of the city up to Andersonville to sip from its series of American and European drafts. While a recent renovation doubled the size of the bar's dining areas, it included a glassed-in kitchen to boot.

Steamed mussels are a house specialty here, though the gastropub menu has a little something for all appetites—picture savory arugula, pesto, and tomato tartlets, hearty Niçoise-style lunch salads, and wood-grilled *porchetta* with preserved lemon and goat cheese polenta at dinnertime.

This is a true-blue tavern, so leave under-aged abettors at home until they can sample all Hopleaf has to offer.

Isla

2501 W. Lawrence Ave. (bet. Campbell & Maplewood Aves.)

Phone: 773-271-2988 — Lunch & dinner Tue – Sun
Web: www.islapilipina.com
Prices: — Western (Brown)

BYO

The two signs reading "Tuloy Po Kayo!" and "Salamat Po!" (*welcome* and *thank you* in Tagalog) say it all at this family-run favorite in Lincoln Square. The parking lot outside its small strip-mall exterior is always filled to capacity with locals ready for huge plates of authentic Filipino cuisine.

Regulars go with a side of garlic fried rice to pair with the kitchen's carnivorous specialties. Plan on indulging in hearty portions of pork and chicken *adobo* in traditional garlic-vinegar sauce; deep-fried slabs of pork belly, *lechon kawali*, with Filipino-style gravy; or onion- and tomato-stuffed whole squid. Come dessert, the vibrant purple *ube* ice cream, made from violet sweet potatoes and coconut, might be even more fun to look at than eat.

Jibek Jolu

B4 — Central Asian

5047 N. Lincoln Ave. (bet. Carmen & Winnemac Aves.)

Phone: 773-878-8494 — Lunch & dinner daily
Web: www.jibekjolu.us
Prices:

BYO

Jibek Jolu translates to "silk road," so think of this as a Lincoln Square stop along that historical trade route, where Eastern Europe meets Central Asia. Though it focuses on the cuisine of Kyrgystan, the kitchen weaves influences from surrounding regions (time to break out the map). The décor is comprised of multi-colored silk panels, a disco ball, and Russian music videos.

The Zabiha Halal menu doesn't serve pork or alcohol, but it offers a veritable U.N. of dumplings like blini stuffed with flavorful ground beef; or delicate *vareniki* with mashed potatoes, sour cream, and dill. The Chinese-influenced *lagman* stew of daikon, peppers, and tender beef with hand-pulled noodles is a local favorite. To drink, try the fruity *kompot* or yogurt-based *ayran*.

Jin Ju

E3 — Korean

5203 N. Clark St. (at Foster Ave.)

Phone: 773-334-6377 — Dinner Tue – Sun
Web: www.jinjurestaurant.com
Prices: $$

A sexy spot on a stretch of bustling Clark Street, Jin Ju spins out luscious Korean classics with aplomb. Inside, dim lighting, dark wood furnishings, and lush red walls create a sophisticated coziness, while servers are gracious and attentive.

The menu showcases a range of specialties to start, like plump *mandoo*, batter-fried spicy chicken wings, or *pajun*, a savory Korean-style pancake filled with the likes of kimchi, served sliced in wedges with a tangy soy and rice vinegar dipping sauce. The *dak dori tang* could warm the coldest day in the Windy City—its fiery red pepper broth is brought to the table bubbling and brimming with braised chicken, potato, carrots, and leafy herbs served with sticky rice, along with a tasty assortment of *banchan*.

Jin Thai

Thai

E3

5458 N. Broadway (at Catalpa Ave.)

Phone: 773-681-0555 Lunch & dinner daily
Web: www.jinthaicuisine.com
Prices:  Bryn Mawr

As if Jin Thai's location in the shadow of Edgewater's Saint Ita bell tower weren't holy enough, Buddhist monks blessed this small restaurant before it opened in 2011. Owners Chai and Jin Roongseang keep the front and back of the house in harmony, while Buddha statues perched around the black-and-gray room maintain watch over the spicy, crispy, and tangy dishes cooked to order.

Guests looking to expand their repertoire beyond satay and pad Thai will find new favorites among such vibrant dishes as tempura chicken pieces with house-made lime sauce; and boneless catfish fillets floating in a spicy curry studded with Thai eggplant and green beans. Chicken noodle soup bobbing with rice vermicelli and chopped scallions does more than soothe—it transcends.

Katsu

Japanese

B2

2651 W. Peterson Ave. (bet. Talman & Washtenaw Aves.)

Phone: 773-784-3383 Dinner Wed – Sun
Web: N/A
Prices: $$

Since 1988, this family-run Japanese spot has charmed West Rogers Park with its convivial atmosphere. Chef Katsu Immamura and his wife mingle with the regulars in the two tastefully arranged dining rooms and provide welcoming touches like warm hand towels at the beginning of the meal. It's minimal, but with a sense of humor: check out the Ultraman figures on the sushi counter.

The menu focuses on fish with simple flair: sushi, *chirashi*, sashimi, and a few rolls, though none of them fat and overdone. Omakase may include sashimi that is expertly cut and garnished with precision featuring the likes of salmon topped with *ikura*, julienned squid with spicy cod roe, or mackerel, all creatively embellished with shiso and flecks of edible gold leaf.

La Ciudad

Mexican

4515 N. Sheridan Rd. (bet. Sunnyside & Windsor Aves.)

Phone: 773-728-2887 — Lunch & dinner daily
Web: www.laciudadgrill.com
Prices: — Wilson

La Ciudad is a family-owned favorite that seems to smile upon this rather gritty strip-mall neighborhood. Inside is a contemporary space featuring cherry red walls hung with black-and-white prints of bustling Mexico City and lined with contemporary white chairs. Upbeat Latin music brightens the mood.

Be sure to start by reviewing the white board for specials like guava empanadas or *pozole Sinaloan,* brimming with chunks of avocado, chicken, and hominy. Burrito fans will relish the grilled version here, stuffed, plump, and perfectly wrapped. The menu is teeming with different *sopes,* while beef ribs and pork chops supplement classic enchiladas and tacos.

It is BYOB, but they offer all the fruit-flavored mixers to complete a margarita.

La Fonda Latino Grill

Latin American

E3

5350 N. Broadway (bet. Balmoral & Berwyn Aves.)

Phone: 773-271-3935 — Lunch & dinner Tue – Sun
Web: www.lafondalatinogrill.com
Prices: $$ — Berwyn

This family-run spot offers a host of Latin American cuisines, but has a heartfelt dedication to Colombian food. The long bi-level space is modestly decorated in shades of tan, mocha, and roasted corn, with folk-art figurines decorating the walls. A recent face-lift inside and out has refreshed the look, but it is still warm and homey.

While the lunch buffet is popular, the regular menu is offered at any time. The two-dollar empanadas are not only a bargain, but are deliciously stuffed with beef and raisins or spinach and mushroom. Potent potables like the *mangorita* or sangria pair festively with grilled steaks or *cazuela de mariscos* full of seafood in a creamy tomato broth. Beans, rice, and tostones are staples of any Colombian feast here.

Los Nopales

Mexican 

4544 N. Western Ave. (bet. Sunnyside & Wilson Aves.)

Phone: 773-334-3149 — Lunch & dinner Tue – Sun
Web: www.losnopalesrestaurant.com
Prices: ⊜ — Western (Brown)

BYO

Beyond the deceptively small green awning, find a true fiesta that is as pleasing to the eyes as it is to the stomach. The tidy space is not large but feels big and bright with decorative cacti, holiday lights, and avocado walls trimming the two dining areas. The little thatch-roofed cabana bar sees a flood of festivity.

The house-made chips and creamy puréed salsas (one with avocados and tomatillos, the other *chile de arbol*) are worth a visit on their own, as are the delicious *picaditas*. *Nopales*—crisp green cactus paddles—appear throughout the menu, perhaps sliced and grilled in a salad to accompany that delicious char-grilled skirt steak special with *frijoles borrachos* (drunken beans) and tortillas nestled in an embroidered kerchief.

Magnolia Cafe

American

E5

1224 W. Wilson Ave. (at Magnolia Ave.)

Phone: 773-728-8785 — Lunch Sun
Web: www.magnoliacafeuptown.com — Dinner Tue – Sun
Prices: $$ — Wilson

French sophistication meets casual American allure at this refined local bistro. A garden of tasseled lampshades hang from exposed wood beams, framed prints of the namesake flower blossom from rustic brick walls, and soft jazz soothes frayed edges after a rough day. Note: half-price bottles of wine on Tuesday nights can also help in that department.

Fresh fish specials like a shrimp and tuna tartare timbale held together by a soy-based vinaigrette and laced with golden *tobiko* change daily; but regulars heave a sigh of relief knowing that signature crab cakes are a staple. Not feeling the fish? Tuck into a hanger steak with frites, or a grilled double-cut pork chop fit for Fred Flintstone before taking a forkful of flourless chocolate-banana cake.

M. Henry

American

E2

5707 N. Clark St. (bet. Edgewater & Hollywood Aves.)

Phone: 773-561-1600 — Lunch Tue – Sun
Web: www.mhenry.net
Prices: Bryn Mawr

Before settling into the sunny dining room teeming with happy hippies and trendy hipsters, take a good hard look at the shelves of pastries and cakes. These flaky, sugary confections are possibly the crown jewels of this farmhouse-esque sanctum, so plan on leaving room at the end for at least one of the sweets.

After deciding on dessert—maybe the likes of Belgian chocolate cookies, apple cake, or brioche cinnamon rolls—it's probably wise to move on to savory fare like "Fannie's killer fried egg sandwich" with Gorgonzola and bacon; apple-maple chicken sausage; or even a roster of other globally inspired sandwiches. If you're going sweet all the way, pancake and French toast variations abound, and bottomless cups of coffee wash it all down.

Ombra

Italian

E3

5310 N. Clark St. (bet. Berwyn & Summerdale Aves.)

Phone: 773-506-8600 — Dinner nightly
Web: www.barombra.com
   Berwyn

A spinoff of nearby cousin Acre, Ombra shares a main entry with the flagship but not the seasonal menu, instead focusing on Italian small plates. Raised booths upholstered with old leather jackets, orbital lights papier-mâchéd with weathered strips of newsprint, and wooden plank dividers telegraph a casual-cool mood.

Peruse the *salumi*, cheese, wine, and daily specials listed on the chalkboard, or pick from the dozens of *cicchetti* displayed behind glass at the dining counter. Panko-crusted pork trotter terrine set over an acidic arugula salad is at once rich and crunchy; while cold composed salads with grilled chicken, olives, and raisins are antipasti on steroids. Negronis, Bellinis, and pours of house-made grappa or limoncello keep the bar hopping.

Opart Thai House 

Thai

C5

4658 N. Western Ave. (bet. Eastwood & Leland Aves.)

Phone: 773-989-8517 Lunch & dinner daily
Web: www.opartthai.com
Prices: 🅢 Western (Brown)

While it may be mixed in and among other local Thai eateries, this well-kept spot sets itself apart with its highly spiced and hearty cooking. The trio of rooms combines a mix of natural wood and dark stone tile floors, with intricate teak carvings accenting the exposed brick.

BYO

The large menu features an expansive selection of noodles, stir-fries, and soups. Be forewarned: they aren't playing games with the little spicy indicators, so if it says it's hot, it really is. Slices of char-broiled beef (*neau sa-ded*) are tasty and tender, with a sweet-sour sauce that brings a creeping heat. Curries are a popular highlight, as in the spicy, yellow *gaeng musaman* with coconut milk, chicken, and potatoes. Quench your fire-ridden palate with a Thai iced tea.

Over Easy Café

American

D4

4943 N. Damen Ave. (bet. Ainslie & Argyle Sts.)

Phone: 773-506-2605 Lunch Tue – Sun
Web: www.overeasycafechicago.com
Prices: 🅢 Damen (Brown)

This place takes the life's work of the hen seriously—from the menu to the décor. Exposed brick and red-tin ceilings hug the cozy room, where tables are snug, the vibe is friendly and communal, and a painting of Humpty Dumpty stands sentinel over the dining counter.

Breakfast sandwiches like the "carbonara" with Parmesan and provolone, are a highlight; and many of the dishes have a Latino flair, like sassy eggs with chorizo, guacamole, cheddar, and ancho ketchup. Sweeter starts are offered with the likes of an upside-down apple pancake with cinnamon-butter and whipped cream, or pumpkin pie French toast. Lunches may reveal a red chili chicken torta.

Complimentary coffee is offered in the tiny foyer if there is a line, and this alone is worth the wait.

Paprika

Indian

B4

2547 W. Lawrence Ave. (bet. Maplewood Ave. & Rockwell St.)

Phone: 773-338-4906 Dinner Tue – Sun
Web: www.paprikachicago.com
Prices: $$ Rockwell

Chef Shah Kabir and his family know hospitality. Prepare to be swept up in their warmth and care (with maybe a splash of kitsch) the minute you enter this richly colored space, adorned with artifacts—and even the chef himself is at the door welcoming guests to sit and sip a cool, refreshing *lassi*.
From aromatic, homemade curries to tasty twists on *dahls* (*turka dahl ki shabzi* is a revelation), everything is fresh and fragrant. Bengali fish curry is a notable attraction—its flavors mild yet lively with mustard seeds, firm and fresh green beans, and silky-sweet onions. A very nice selection of vegetarian dishes might include the veggie samosa, its soft, light shell stuffed with spiced potatoes, peas, and cauliflower, served with a trio of tangy chutneys.

Pasteur

Vietnamese

E3

5525 N. Broadway (bet. Bryn Mawr & Catalpa Aves.)

Phone: 773-728-4800 Lunch & dinner Tue – Sun
Web: www.pasteurrestaurantchicago.com
Prices: ©© Bryn Mawr

The newest incarnation of the Vietnamese restaurant that originally opened in 1995 is named after Saigon's Avenue Pasteur. The inside features an attractive layout that is fresh looking yet heavily influenced by colonial design with its bright white façade topped by ornate black lacquered roof work. Tablecloths dress the tables in the airy room where beveled mirrors and painted scenes adorn the walls.
Items to be enjoyed include *nem*, skewers of ground chicken and pork seasoned with lemongrass, wrapped around sugarcane and grilled; or *ga kho gung*, claypot ginger chicken. *Tom xao sa-te*, wok-tossed shrimp with dried red peppers and a bright assortment of vegetables, is nestled in a flavorful and aromatic sauce with subtly sweet-funky undertones.

Pecking Order

Filipino

4416 N. Clark St. (bet. Montrose & Sunnyside Aves.)

Phone: 773-907-9900 — Lunch & dinner Tue – Sun
Web: www.peckingorderchicago.com
Prices: ⓈⓈ — Montrose (Brown)

Chef/owner Kristine Subido isn't chicken to showcase poultry as the star of her menu at this cluck-centric Ravenswood spot, where her mother, Melinda, lends a hand with the preparation of family recipes loaded with Filipino essence. Framed pictures of hens and roosters grace the walls, no doubt approving of the hormone- and antibiotic-free birds in the kitchen.

The signature banana ketchup makes a stellar dipping sauce for crispy marinated wings available by the pound; and whether grilled, fried, or roasted, whole or half chickens are consistently juicy with flavor from a tamari-garlic-bay leaf marinade. Sides like coconut milk-braised collards or *sriracha*-tinged slaw finish the plate, and a carafe of sweet and boozy Ladybird punch washes it all down.

Pho 777

Vietnamese

1063-65 W. Argyle St. (bet. Kenmore & Winthrop Aves.)

Phone: 773-561-9909 — Lunch & dinner Tue – Sun
Web: N/A
Prices: ⓈⓈ — Argyle

A market's worth of fresh ingredients make Pho 777 stand out in a neighborhood where Vietnamese restaurants—and their signature soup—seem to populate every storefront. Bottles of hot sauce, jars of fiery condiments, and canisters of spoons and chopsticks clustered on each table make it easy for regulars to sit down and start slurping.

Add choices like meatballs, tendon, flank steak, and even tofu to the cardamom, ginger, and clove-spiced beef broth, which fills a bowl the size of a bathroom sink, then throw in jalapeños, Thai basil, and mint to your liking. If you're not feeling like *pho* this time around, snack on spring rolls with house-made roasted peanut sauce; or a plate of lacy *banh xeo* stuffed with shrimp, sprouts, and herbs.

Pho Xe Tang - Tank Noodle

Vietnamese 

E4

4953 N. Broadway (at Argyle St.)

Phone: 773-878-2253 Lunch & dinner Thu – Tue
Web: www.tank-noodle.com
Prices: ⊜ Argyle

A stone's throw from the Little Saigon El stop, this humming corner spot keeps *pho*-enthusiasts slurping and satisfied. Join the crowds during prime meal times at the highly communal, cafeteria-style tables displaying caddies stocked with soup spoons, chopsticks, and deeply spiced, umami-rich sauces. Service is basic and the simple room lacks charm, but no one seems to notice.

The massive, hardcover menu offers all manner of goodies, like noodle plates, *báhn mì*, DIY wraps, and *congee*, along with an impressive array of bubble teas and fruity drinks. However, nearly every place is set with small plates brimming with heaps of fresh herbs, sprouts, and lime wedges to garnish the myriad *pho* options, all made with an alluring, sweetly spiced broth.

Ras Dashen

Ethiopian 

E2

5846 N. Broadway (bet. Ardmore & Thorndale Aves.)

Phone: 773-506-9601 Lunch & dinner daily
Web: www.rasdashenchicago.com
Prices: $$ Thorndale

Take the hostess up on her offer to sit at a traditional table and enjoy Ras Dashen's Ethiopian fare in a truly authentic environment. Cushioned rattan chairs surrounding low *mossab* tables with conical domed lids await communal trays arriving from the kitchen. The bar serves Ethiopian honey wine, African beers, and cocktails like the rosy champagne *qay arafa* for those who want to fully immerse themselves in the culinary culture.

Delicately crisp lentil-stuffed *sambusas* whet the appetite for *doro wat*, the national dish of Ethopia, which does its country proud with aromatic and tender braised chicken in a sumptuous *berbere* sauce. Sides of warm *ib* cheese, freshly made from buttermilk, and spongy *injera* cool the palate from the creeping heat.

Siam Noodle & Rice

Thai

F5

4654 N. Sheridan Rd. (at Leland Ave.)

Phone: 773-769-6694 Lunch & dinner Tue – Sun
Web: www.siamnoodleandrice.com
Prices: Wilson

BYO

On the first floor of a brick building in a still rough and scruffy neighborhood, Siam Noodle & Rice has nonetheless offered a cozy (and spicy!) respite for hungry locals since 1987. The sherbet-toned walls, lined with landscape paintings in the narrow dining room, complement the beautifully designed Thai postage stamps displayed under the glass-topped tables. The menu offers a homey take on classic cuisine with numerous noodle and rice dishes, as the name implies, and a few intriguing items like fried dried beef. Even the spring rolls have a twist, filled with tofu, Chinese sausage, and cucumber, and topped with jalapeño slices. Tender braised beef, simmered in lime leaf-scented coconut *panang* curry, gets slurped down without a second thought.

Spacca Napoli

Pizza

D5

1769 W. Sunnyside Ave. (bet. Hermitage & Ravenswood Aves.)

Phone: 773-878-2420 Lunch Wed – Sun
Web: www.spaccanapolipizzeria.com Dinner nightly
Prices:  Montrose (Brown)

A warm greeting awaits, just bypass the door at the corner and enter on Sunnyside, under the *Vera Pizza Napoletana* sign—you are in the right place for authentic Neapolitan pizza. Named for the historic street that bisects Naples, Spacca Napoli is the Chicago home to the thin-crusted and truly authentic Neopolitan pie. This should be no surprise, as it is equipped with an extraordinary Bisazza glass-tiled pizza oven and Naples-trained Chef/owner Jon Goldsmith.

The menu is built around a dozen or so perfectly blistered pizzas; they arrive uncut to your table to stay hot and simply topped with myriad mozzarella options or as more lavish specials decked with egg, truffles, and *guanciale*. Couple this with chilled antipasti and wine in juice glasses.

Taketei

F3 Japanese

1111 W. Berwyn Ave. (bet. Broadway & Winthrop Ave.)

Phone: 773-769-9292 Dinner Mon – Sat
Web: N/A
Prices: $$ Berwyn

BYO

Though it's a mere sliver of a space, Taketei's Japanese temple of fresh piscine makes a bold statement in this neighborhood, noted for its Vietnamese joints. The wee room, so small there's not even a true sushi counter, remains serenely bright but minimal, filled with a handful of white tables and chairs.

A limited menu makes the most of shiny pieces of fish. With the majority of nigiri available for less than $3 each, regulars know to load up or go all out with a sashimi platter featuring a wide selection of generously sliced seafood like mackerel, octopus, and *maguro* with a bowl of rice. Manageably sized, non-gimmicky rolls along with appetizers like pert, crunchy *hyashi wakame* salad or spinach with sweet sesame sauce supplement this appealing array.

Thai Grill

F1 Thai

1040 W. Granville Ave. (bet. Kenmore & Winthrop Aves.)

Phone: 773-274-7510 Lunch & dinner Tue – Sun
Web: www.thaigrillchicago.com
Prices: $$ Granville

BYO

Neighborhood Thai food gets chic at this streamlined spot just south of the Loyola campus, where zebrawood tables and gray stone floors set the modern but casual tone. A selection of Thai art and artifacts adorning charcoal walls provide warmth to the contemporary feel of the space, which frequently fills with young locals and families.

Bubbles and noodles are the restaurant's specialties, with an entire drinks menu devoted to smoothies and teas spiked with tapioca; and made-to-order rice, bean thread, and egg noodle dishes. Traditional dishes like crisp crab rolls and spicy curry chicken with Kaffir lime and Thai basil are on the money. Lunch specials keep budget-conscious bellies satisfied, and free parking across the street doesn't hurt either.

Thai Pastry & Restaurant

Thai

4925 N. Broadway (bet. Ainslie & Argyle Sts.)

Phone: 773-784-5399 — Lunch & dinner daily
Web: www.thaipastry.com
Prices: $$ — Argyle

Thriving since 2000 in the stretch of North Broadway known as Little Saigon, this unassuming restaurant and bakery showcases authentic Thai cooking from Chef/owner Aumphai Kusub. Traditional artifacts on the walls and ceramic serving vessels brought to each table echo the delicate and colorful handiwork of the individual cakes and pastries on display.

Savory dishes favor classic preparations and flavors that balance spice, creaminess, and acidity. These might feature chicken *massaman* curry; lightly fried crab Rangoon; or *nam tok* with tender sliced beef, chilies, and mint. But it's the pastry and ice cream parade loaded with treats like *klong klang,* taro custard, and curry puffs that's truly eye-catching. Take some home to assuage a late-night craving.

Vincent

Belgian

1475 W. Balmoral Ave. (bet. Clark St. & Glenwood Ave.)

Phone: 773-334-7168 — Lunch Sun
Web: www.vincentchicago.com — Dinner Tue – Sun
Prices: $$ — Berwyn

Go Dutch at Vincent, where traditional cuisine from the Netherlands meets a tried and true bistro menu. Tall votive candles, high-top marble tables, and gilded frames lining brocade-papered walls warm the dual rooms. While the interior is comfortably informal, a dog-friendly patio offers a warm-weather option for pooch-loving customers.

The juicy grilled lamb burger is a menu mainstay, though its toppings—perhaps Montchevre goat cheese, violet mustard, and arugula—change regularly. Five variations of *moules frites* range from the customary beer, garlic, and parsley to tangy tamarind, *sambal,* and lime leaf. Other standouts include a thick slice of crisped pork belly topped with tomato jam and drizzled with a warm bacon-garlic vinaigrette.

Bucktown & Wicker Park

Ukranian Village · West Town

Finesse and Flair

Like many of the Windy City's neighborhoods, Bucktown and Wicker Park has seen its fair share of transition. Ranging from Polish immigrants to wealthy businessmen (who have built stately mansions on Hoyne and Pierce avenues), it has been home to people from all walks of life. But, don't let the hushed residential streets and bewitching brownstones fool you—this neighborhood still knows how to mix it up. While you're more likely to run into bankers than Basquiats these days, Bucktown and Wicker Park remains an international hotbed of creative energy and trendsetting style.

Shopping Sanctum

Shake out the remains of your piggy bank before arriving. After all, this neighborhood has some of the most stylish shopping in the Midwest. It is worlds away from the international chains of the Magnificent Mile. Instead, think über-cool indie shops. Don't have time to travel the world for funky home accessories, or love the flea market look but don't want to get out of bed on the weekends? Get the rare and one-of-a-kind look by visiting Penguin Foot Pottery, where you can pick up original and innovative ceramics. To experience a taste of Wicker Park's vast and vivid music scene, be sure you make the time to stop by Reckless Records and get schooled on the latest underground band. You can even get creative and design your own T-shirt at the appropriately named T-shirt Deli—and rest assured that this is only the beginning of a wonderful journey.

Gathering of the Arts

The neighborhood also shows off its artistic roots by hosting two of the city's largest and most loved festivals. Wicker Park Fest is an annual two-day music festival held each July that features no less than 28 bands. The annual Green Music Fest is distinctive in its blending of talented bands with eco-minded production and events. Additionally, Wicker Park is home to a number of art galleries, including the unique 4Art Inc., where artists create their works during the opening night show. Even starving artists can find something to eat in foodie-friendly Bucktown and Wicker Park. Hot dog fanatics simply must take a tour of the famed **Vienna Beef Factory**—visitors will be blown away by the assembly lines of products made here. After a view of the manufacturing line, indulge your appetite by dining in the large employee cafeteria. Parched after all this meat eating? Quench your thirst by heading straight to **Black Dog Gelato**, where you can savor outstanding whisky gelato bars dipped in milk chocolate and candied bacon; or taste unusual flavors like goat cheese- cashew- and caramel.

Fascinating Foods

Bucktown and Wicker Park locals also love and savor the flavors and tastes of the **Butcher & Larder**. Husband & wife, Rob & Allie Levitt are the meat and potato behind this Noble Square butcher shop. Since leaving Mado in 2010, the couple has focused on the dwindling profession of artisan butchery and supporting local farmers in the process. Whole animal butchery isn't seen much these days, but the Levitts even offer classes on how to break down whole animals and produce wonderful sausages, terrines, and cured bacon, also available in their shop. Go whole hog and bone up on your cooking skills at **Cooking Fools**, and discover that you will never be teased about your tiramisu again. If you're planning to entertain friends with an elaborate meal at home, be sure to swing by the **Wicker Park & Bucktown Farmer's Market** for a full range of fresh produce, glorious cheeses, and other specialty items. And while basking in cheese paradise, don't forget to grab a pie at **Piece**—hugely frequented by natives due to its repute as Chicagoland's most favored pizza place. However, Piece has garnered a following that come by not only for their crunchy pizzas, but also for their hand-crafted beers and delicious spectrum of appetizers, sandwiches, and desserts. Sweet tooths worth their salt certainly know all about **Red Hen Bread**. Atkins would turn over in his grave if he ever got a taste of the bread and pastries from this terrific bake shop. Lauded as an exceptional carrier of high quality, artisan breads and pastries, Red Hen satiates scores with the likes of croissants, muffins, scones, cookies, tarts, quiches, and Red Hen Signature treats. Think your mama makes a good pie? Grab a fork and taste a lip-smacking piece from **Hoosier Mama Pie Company**. Run by Paula Haney, the former pastry chef at Trio, this is a little slice of paradise. And of course, no bakeshop is complete without cake, and **Alliance Bakery**'s window display of cakes is quite stupendous.

Crowning Cocktails

Speaking of stupendous, lull on the late night at **Violet Hour**, the speakeasy that serves some of the most tantalizing cocktails in town. Slurp up these concoctions while chowing on toasted Pullman bread spread with goat cheese and tomato jam, or smoked prosciutto and melon skewers. The **Map Room** with its bevy of beers from around the world is a voyager's dream come true. While we all may know a bit about beer, a class at their noted beer school does much to augment one's appreciation. Similarly, perennially-packed **Moonshine Brewing Company** showcases a solid and serious beer collection, with packs brewed on-site; while **Silver Cloud** is foolproof for sidewalk boozing, chicken pot pie, or a

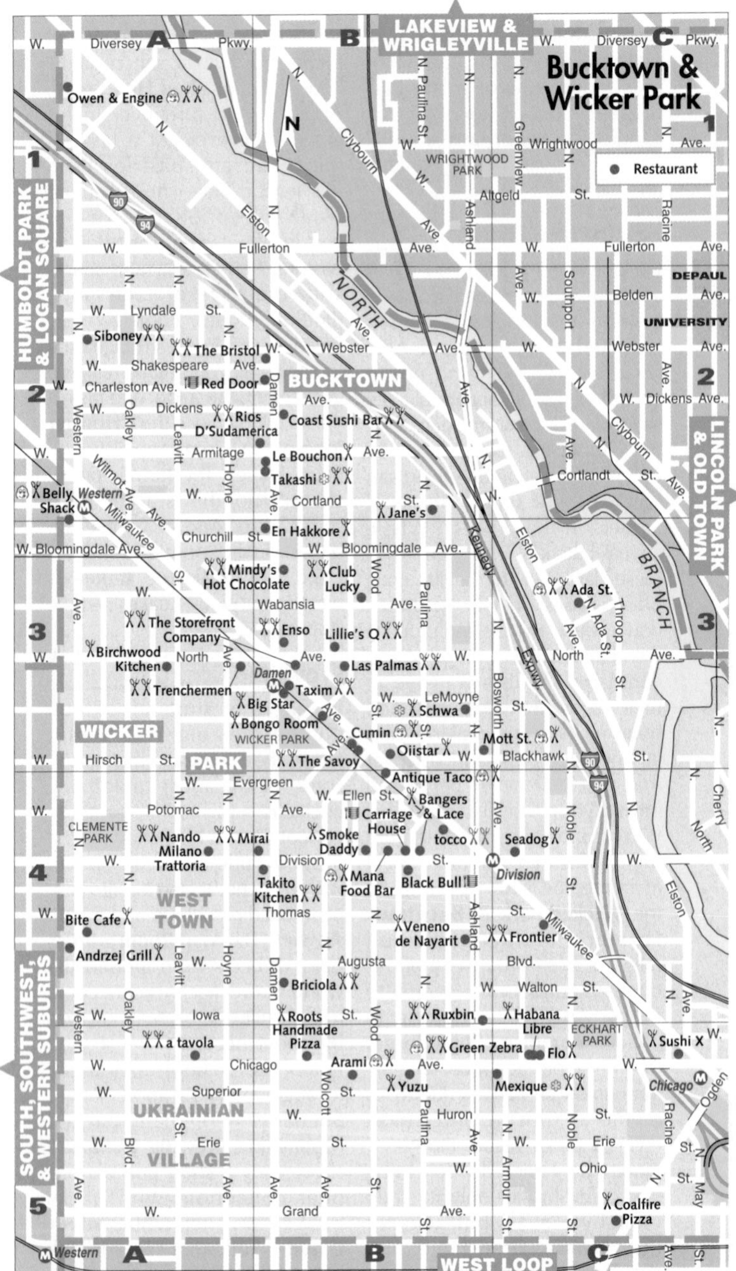
Bucktown & Wicker Park
Restaurant
LAKEVIEW & WRIGLEYVILLE
HUMBOLDT PARK & LOGAN SQUARE
LINCOLN PARK & OLD TOWN
SOUTH, SOUTHWEST, & WESTERN SUBURBS
WEST LOOP
BUCKTOWN
WICKER
PARK
WEST TOWN
UKRAINIAN
VILLAGE
WRIGHTWOOD PARK
DEPAUL
UNIVERSITY
CLEMENTE PARK
ECKHART PARK
WICKER PARK
NORTH BRANCH
N
Owen & Engine
Siboney
The Bristol
Red Door
Rios D'Sudamerica
Coast Sushi Bar
Le Bouchon
Takashi
Belly Shack
Jane's
En Hakkore
Mindy's Hot Chocolate
Club Lucky
Ada St.
The Storefront Company
Enso
Lillie's Q
Birchwood Kitchen
Las Palmas
Trenchermen
Taxim
Big Star
Schwa
Bongo Room
Cumin
Mott St.
Oiistar
The Savoy
Antique Taco
Bangers & Lace
Carriage House
Smoke Daddy
tocco
Seadog
Nando Milano Trattoria
Mirai
Mana Food Bar
Black Bull
Takito Kitchen
Bite Cafe
Veneno de Nayarit
Frontier
Andrzej Grill
Briciola
Roots Handmade Pizza
Ruxbin
Habana Libre
a tavola
Green Zebra
Flo
Sushi X
Arami
Yuzu
Mexique
Coalfire Pizza
Western
Damen
Division
Chicago
W. Diversey Pkwy.
W. Fullerton Ave.
W. Webster Ave.
W. Armitage Ave.
W. North Ave.
W. Division St.
W. Chicago Ave.
W. Grand Ave.
N. Elston Ave.
N. Milwaukee Ave.
N. Clybourn Ave.
Kennedy Expwy.
N. Damen Ave.
N. Ashland Ave.
N. Western Ave.
A
B
C
1
2
3
4
5

grilled cheese sandwich. This comfort food haven makes one feel completely at home by virtue of its casual vibe and interior that is flooded with warmth. Whether you're here for "small bites," "big bowls," or a crowning cocktail, Silver Cloud is sure to be a crowd-pleaser and oozes all that is Bucktown.

Late Night Fun

Defining the 'tude of the 'hood is **Drumbar**. Elevating the concept of a classic speakeasy, this sleek and welcoming lounge, complete with an outdoor terrace, delivers warmth and style to its patrons thanks to an exceptional roster of wines and spirits. Displaying a splendid array, this neighborhood delight never fails to satisfy, no matter the day or time. Speaking of "spirit," carry on your Saturday night fever at **Taco Burrito Express #3**. This retreat is not only a fast, family-run, and cash-only late-night favorite, but folks who flock here also love their *pastor*, offered into the wee hours of the morning. Straight from the horse's mouth, eat well but drink better at **Emporium Arcade Bar**. Feed your inner playboy by indulging in an old-school arcade game alongside a serious sip of beer, whiskey, vodka, or gin.

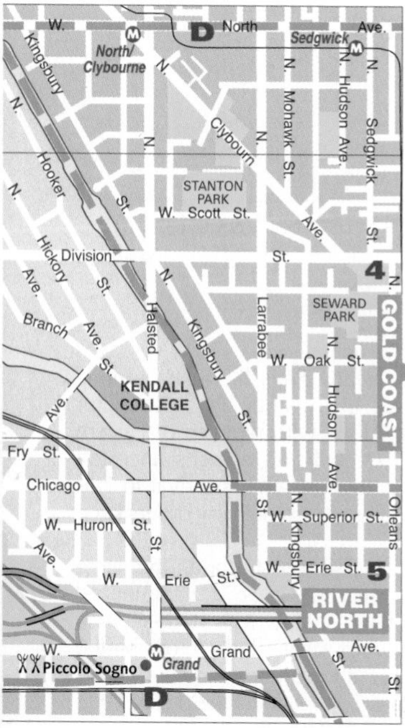

Wholesome Ways

Local Folks Food is a family-run enterprise whose chief charge is to develop delicious, natural, and gourmet condiments (mustard and hot sauce anyone?) perfect for slathering upon burgers. Find these tangy treats at the lauded **Green Grocer** and know that they will elevate your burger to ethereal. And finally, much to every foodie's delight, Bucktown and Wicker Park also features **Olivia's**, an exquisitely unique marketplace. This paragon is rife with the finest quality products, including hard-to-find specialty items displayed beside a selection of organic, locally made items, as well as everyday brands. Choose your favorite foods, a precious collection of artisan cheeses, then your best beverage (from an incredible collection of wine and beer), and end the affair with a dramatic ensemble of flowers before heading home to execute an elegant and enticing dinner party.

Ada St.

C3 — Contemporary XX

1664 N. Ada St. (bet. Concord Pl. & Wabansia Ave.)

Phone: 773-697-7069 — Dinner Wed – Sun
Web: www.adastreetchicago.com
Prices: $$ — North/Clybourn

Give your eyes a minute to adjust to the lobby's twinkling candelabras before strolling down a dim corridor to arrive at this hip and happy dining room. Guests congregate around picnic and ping-pong tables on the Astroturf patio, or lounge inside on banquettes covered in repurposed wool Army blankets.

The vinyl collection is as impressive as the cocktail list. Enjoy a deep cut from Marvin Gaye while soothing your soul with an applejack julep. The small plates menu builds from simple *salumi* and cheese, to salmon tartare tossed with bacon lardons, trout roe, and smoky, crispy salmon skin; or grass-fed beef tenderloin cooked rare with a horseradish vinaigrette. It's first come, first served for the bar and patio; otherwise, opt for a table reservation.

Andrzej Grill

A4 — Polish X

1022 N. Western Ave. (bet. Augusta Blvd. & Cortez St.)

Phone: 773-489-3566 — Lunch & dinner Mon – Sat
Web: www.andrzejgrillrestaurant.com
Prices: ⊕

BYO

There are no frills and barely any English spoken among the regulars at Andrzej Grill, but neither are needed for a dose of true Polish flavor. Along with pictures of Eastern European dishes, some of the chef and owner's ancestral papers grace the walls indicating his family's arrival to Ellis Island on the Königin Luise. Takeout and delivery orders keep the kitchen hopping.

For a hearty introduction to real Polish food, the large combination platter covers all the bases: a caramelized potato pancake, tender cabbage stuffed with herb-scented rice, smoky kielbasa, and plump meat-filled pierogi paired up with a cool, refreshing dish of cucumber and sour cream salad for good measure. Classic specialties like pickle soup tantalize native palates.

Antique Taco

Mexican

1360 N. Milwaukee Ave. (at Wood St.)

Phone: 773-687-8697 — Lunch & dinner Tue – Sun
Web: www.antiquetaco.com
Prices: ⇔ — Damen (Blue)

Antique doesn't mean staid or out of touch when it comes to the food at Antique Taco. In fact, the flavor combinations here are nothing short of modern. Order at the walk-up counter and take a numbered wooden spool to one of the boxy varnished plank tables. The composed Mexican dishes may take a few minutes to cook and plate, but that's how you know they're coming out fresh.

Bold dishes like a tender masa biscuit ladled with luxurious lobster gravy; chorizo chili topped with beer-battered cheese curds and scallion *crema*; or habanero-tinged popcorn arrive on old-school china plates. Desserts like *abuelita's* pop tart with Mexican chocolate and marshmallow are too good to pass up, but get them with your meal so you won't have to wait in line a second time.

Arami

Japanese

1829 W. Chicago Ave. (bet. Wolcott Ave & Wood St.)

Phone: 312-243-1535 — Dinner Tue – Sun
Web: www.aramichicago.com
Prices: $$ — Division

On a stretch of gated doors, window displays of dangling bamboo, moss, and river stones offer an inviting, serene retreat at Arami. Inside, a long sushi bar and skylights cut into cathedral-like ceilings enhance the minimalist space framed with soft green walls. Specialty cocktails with Japanese spirits complement an ample inventory of sake, Scotch, *sochu*, and beers.

Arami is not the destination for fat, gimmicky maki. Instead, fresh seafood spiked with garlic, truffle, and pickled items let flavors sparkle in a more subtle way. Toro tartare comes in a single bite of minced tuna with bonito-soy sauce, Asian pear, and black *tobiko*; while hamachi sashimi draped over black river rocks shine with pickled mushroom, truffle oil, and sprouts.

a tavola

Italian

A5

2148 W. Chicago Ave. (bet. Hoyne Ave. & Leavitt St.)

Phone: 773-276-7567 Dinner Mon – Sat
Web: www.atavolachicago.com
Prices: $$

Don't bother looking for a sign: a tavola takes up residence in a stately brick house on an otherwise storefront-lined block in the Ukrainian Village—an ivy-covered façade is a dead giveaway in the summer. Stepping inside is like arriving at Chef/owner Dan Bocik's home for a dinner party, where a convivial and gracious atmosphere reigns from the three-seat wine bar and gorgeous original wood floors, to the serene back patio.

A concise menu offers straightforward Italian food, though who needs frills when pillows of gnocchi with crispy sage and brown butter; or on-point beef tenderloin with roasted rosemary potato coins are so effective on their own? Dessert follows the same simple blueprint with a tangy lemon curd-filled shortbread tart.

Bangers & Lace

Gastropub

B4

1670 W. Division St. (at Paulina St.)

Phone: 773-252-6499 Lunch & dinner daily
Web: www.bangersandlacechicago.com
Prices: $$ Damen (Blue)

Despite the frilly connotations, this sausage-and-beer mecca's name refers not to doilies, but to the delicate layers of foam that remain in the glass after your craft brew has been quaffed. You'll also have lots of opportunity to study the lace curtains as you plow through the extensive draft beer menu, noted on blackboards in the comfortably worn-in front bar room.

Decadent foie gras corn dogs (actually French garlic sausage wrapped with soft-sweet brioche cornbread) and veal brats with melted Gouda elevate the humble sausage; while a slew of sandwiches suit simpler tastes. Grilled cheese gilds the lily with taleggio, raclette, and Irish cheddar; and dreamy house-made chips drizzled with truffle oil and malt vinegar are more than a bar snack.

Belly Shack

Fusion

1912 N. Western Ave. (at Milwaukee Ave.)

Phone: 773-252-1414 — Lunch & dinner Tue – Sun
Web: www.bellyshack.com
Prices: $$ — Western (Blue)

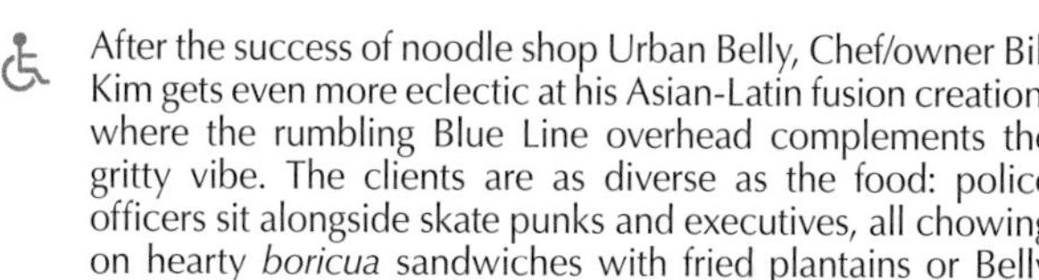

After the success of noodle shop Urban Belly, Chef/owner Bill Kim gets even more eclectic at his Asian-Latin fusion creation, where the rumbling Blue Line overhead complements the gritty vibe. The clients are as diverse as the food: police officers sit alongside skate punks and executives, all chowing on hearty *boricua* sandwiches with fried plantains or Belly Dogs topped with egg noodles.

Place your order, take a number, and wait for the dishes to arrive...in no particular order. The menu is small but inventive with items like shaved barbecue beef with *ssäm* paste and kimchi; or the ever-popular pork meatball sandwich stuffed with sprouts, *somen* noodles, and the signature Belly Fire hot sauce. Cool down over vanilla soft serve with myriad toppings.

Big Star

Mexican

1531 N. Damen Ave. (bet. Milwaukee & Wicker Park Aves.)

Phone: 773-235-4039 — Lunch & dinner daily
Web: www.bigstarchicago.com
Prices: $$ — Damen (Blue)

Whiskey, rock and roll, and Mexican food—what else is there in life? Not much, apparently, at this jam-packed Wicker Park hipster haven where all are in affordable abundance. The crowd keeps the room pumping every night as they throw back shots, PBRs, and *micheladas*.

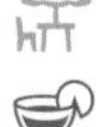

Despite the grungy décor, the food is as well-crafted as you'd expect from a Paul Kahan operation. Crispy braised pork belly drizzled with tomato-*guajillo* sauce and shredded spit-roasted pork shoulder in pineapple marinade make for delicious tacos; while *salsa de frijole con queso* (a crock of pinto bean dip with lime salt-sprinkled chips) is a dish far better than a simple bar snack is ever expected to be. Need a taco fix stat? Hit up the cash-only taqueria window and walk away happy.

Birchwood Kitchen

American

2211 W. North Ave. (bet. Bell Ave. & Leavitt St.)

Phone: 773-276-2100 — Lunch Tue – Sun
Web: www.birchwoodkitchen.com — Dinner Tue – Fri
Prices: — Damen (Blue)

On a stretch of brick storefronts, Birchwood Kitchen's periwinkle façade stands out like a gem. Inside, the earthy café has a country feel, with old church pews lining exposed brick walls and daily specials cleverly written on aluminum baking pans. Peruse the offerings in the dessert case, since items like shortbread lemon bars and chocolate chip banana bread may affect how much you want to order from the walk-up counter.

Along with daily brunch offerings like Belgian waffles, lunch standards like sandwiches, soups, and salads are forever in demand. If the tuna melt on toasted multi-grain bread with roasted tomato slices and Gruyère isn't enough, try a side of satisfying chickpea salad tossed with creamy mayonnaise dressing spiked pink with chipotles.

Bite Cafe

1039 N. Western Ave. (bet. Cortez & Thomas Sts.)

Phone: 773-395-2483 — Lunch & dinner daily
Web: www.bitecafechicago.com
Prices: $$

This charming, slightly bohemian café looks unassuming, but its homey food and friendly service leave an indelible impression. Hipster locals grab the latest issue of *The Onion* and wait for their coffee at the small back counter, while others take the comfy banquettes or powder-blue metal chairs. An eclectic selection of artwork rotates gallery-style on the walls.

Simple diner fare gets a homestyle upgrade across the board, with a menu that puts new twists on familiar breakfast bites like blueberry bread with lemon butter; or poutine with smoked bacon gravy. Careful homemade details add oomph to savory lunch and dinner items like an open-faced fried chicken sandwich on a fresh and fluffy biscuit with green tomato jam and melted cheddar.

Black Bull

B4

1721 W. Division St. (bet. Hermitage Ave. & Paulina St.)

Phone: 773-227-8600 Dinner nightly
Web: www.blackbullchicago.com
Prices: $$ Division

Like a matador brandishing his cape, the red neon silhouette of a bull draws hungry diners to this tiny, no-reservations tapas bar on Division. Inside, stacks of earthenware plates on glossy black communal tables and Andalusian ceramic wall tiles give the sultry interior the feel of an authentic but modern Spanish pintxos bar. Glasses of red and rosé sangria abound, though the Iberian Peninsula gets fair play on the wine list as well.

Snack on marinated olives while perusing the menu, where traditional tapas get a bit of finesse. *Pulpo a la Gallega* is braised, grilled, and dusted with paprika for a double punch of smokiness. The classic combination of *jamón Serrano*, manchego cheese, and fresh tomato on sliced baguette is a sexy, salty mess.

Bongo Room

B3

1470 N. Milwaukee Ave. (bet. Evergreen Ave. & Honore St.)

Phone: 773-489-0690 Lunch daily
Web: www.thebongoroom.com
Prices: $$ Damen (Blue)

Start the day with a smile at the original Wicker Park location of this Chicago mini-chain, where mimosas, Bloody Marys, and coffee go down easy whether you're ensconced in a comfy sunny yellow booth or in an oversized stool at the dining counter. It's a family favorite, so you might need to dodge a few strollers on the way to your seat.

Though pancakes are the Bongo Room's specialty, those without a sweet tooth will go for oversized omelets stuffed with chorizo, avocado, and *queso fresco*; Thai chicken sausage; or candied bacon. For others who want sugar, pumpkin carrot cake flapjacks or red velvet hotcakes with warm vanilla cream hit the spot and then some. Come lunchtime, the menu adds sandwiches and salads—never mind that they don't serve dinner.

Briciola

Italian XX

B4

937 N. Damen Ave. (bet. Augusta Blvd. & Iowa St.)

Phone: 773-772-0889 Dinner Tue – Sun
Web: www.briciolachicago.com
Prices: $$ Division

BYO

After decades of cooking and traveling, Chef/owner Mario Maggi was ready to open a small place—just a crumb, or "una briciola," of a restaurant. This tiny trattoria nestled between Ukrainian Village's brick buildings is indeed a speck of warmth and charm, festooned with party lights on the patio and mustard-toned walls inside.

Traditional Italian cuisine gets personalized tweaks from the chef. *Carpacci* may include paper-thin octopus, beets, or beef; *macaroncini alla Briciola* folds diced Tuscan sausage into a spicy garlic-sage sauce; and a hefty bone-in pork chop, pounded thin, breaded, and pan-fried until golden, is a house classic dressed with arugula and shaved Parmesan.

A bottle from the wine shop down the block makes the meal even more convivial.

The Bristol

American XX

B2

2152 N. Damen Ave. (bet. Shakespeare & Webster Aves.)

Phone: 773-862-5555 Lunch Sat – Sun
Web: www.thebristolchicago.com Dinner nightly
Prices: $$

Get to know your neighbors a little better at this dim, bustling haunt boasting a lineup of seasonal American fare with a Mediterranean twist. Regulars sit shoulder-to-shoulder at thick butcher block communal tables or at the concrete bar, squinting under filament bulbs to see the constantly changing menu's latest additions on chalkboards throughout the room. After sharing a Moscow Mule in a frosty copper mug, duck fat fries, or monkey bread with dill butter, it might be time for messy *elotes* tossed with sweet chili jam to be licked off each finger; or an heirloom tomato tart with a SarVecchio cheese crust and shaved onions. Do the right thing and save room for homemade Nutter Butter cookies with dark chocolate sabayon for dipping.

Carriage House

Southern

1700 W. Division St. (at Paulina St.)

Phone: 773-384-9700
Web: www.carriagehousechicago.com
Prices: $$

Lunch & dinner Tue – Sun
Division

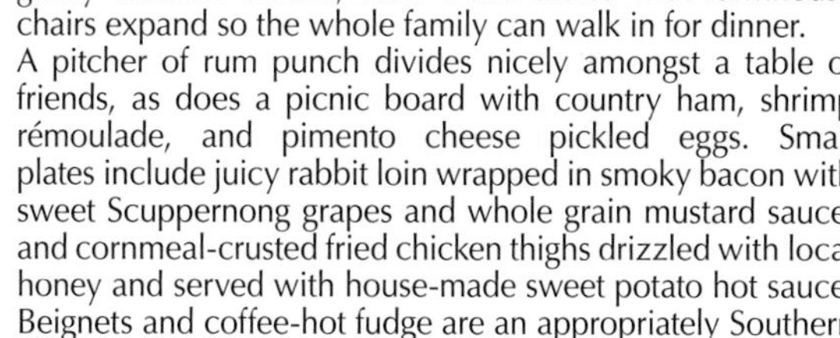

Wicker Park isn't exactly the Lowcountry, but Chef and South Carolina native Mark Steuer is intent on bringing Southern living to the neighborhood. In a softly lit room framed by gauzy window shades, bare wood tables with farmhouse chairs expand so the whole family can walk in for dinner.

A pitcher of rum punch divides nicely amongst a table of friends, as does a picnic board with country ham, shrimp rémoulade, and pimento cheese pickled eggs. Small plates include juicy rabbit loin wrapped in smoky bacon with sweet Scuppernong grapes and whole grain mustard sauce; and cornmeal-crusted fried chicken thighs drizzled with local honey and served with house-made sweet potato hot sauce. Beignets and coffee-hot fudge are an appropriately Southern finish.

Club Lucky

Italian

1824 W. Wabansia Ave. (at Honore St.)

Phone: 773-227-2300
Web: www.clubluckychicago.com
Prices: $$

Lunch Mon – Fri
Dinner nightly
Damen (Blue)

An Italian-American supper club for the ages, Club Lucky has played the part since 1990 and yet its glass block windows, red vinyl booths, and linoleum tiled-floor look no worse for the wear. Grab a signature "killer martini" and come to rest upon a round red cushioned stool in the front cocktail lounge. Alternatively, settle in for a big traditional spread at any of the black Formica tables.

All the classics are represented proudly from minestrone with chewy pasta shells among cannellini beans, greens, and potatoes; and golden brown chicken Parmesan with homemade marinara; to baked meaty littleneck clams. Should you need a little red sauce for the road, Club Lucky sells its packaged version along with salad dressing and freshly baked bread.

Coalfire Pizza

C5

1321 W. Grand Ave. (bet. Ada & Elizabeth Sts.)

Phone: 312-226-2625 — Lunch Wed – Sun
Web: www.coalfirechicago.com — Dinner Tue – Sun
Prices: 🪙 — Chicago (Blue)

Sure, you could come for a salad, but at Coalfire, the focus is rightly on pizza and yours should be too. Rust red walls put diners in the mood, and in a playful bit of recycling, empty tomato sauce cans on each table become the perfect stand for sizzling pizzas churned straight from the 800-degree coal oven.

Coalfire has its ratio down to a fine art and knows not to burden its thin crust with too many toppings. Simple combinations like mortadella and garlic; Calabrese salami, Italian sausage and pepperoni; or a few top-quality anchovies pair sublimely with tangy tomato sauce and a chewy crust that's blackened and blistered in all the right spots. Not feeling the combos? Build your own pizza and pick your own trappings from Gorgonzola to goat cheese.

Coast Sushi Bar

Japanese

B2

2045 N. Damen Ave. (bet. Dickens & McLean Aves.)

Phone: 773-235-5775 — Lunch Sat – Sun
Web: www.coastsushibar.com — Dinner nightly
Prices: $$

BYO

Dimly lit but not sedate in the least, Coast Sushi Bar is high volume—both in the amount of fish it sends out to its animated guests and the mix of chatter and thumping music that nearly overpowers the food. Japanese chefs donned in matching T-shirts and baseball caps crank out rolls at a dizzying pace behind the slender Formica counter, crowned by a glass case loaded with pristine seafood.

Spring for real wasabi root alongside sushi like hamachi and madai, neatly sliced and draped elegantly over rice; or signature maki like the White Dragon with shrimp tempura. A litany of appetizers like jalapeño-spiked miso soup, or tropical ceviche sporting fresh seafood in a cilantro-lime marinade make for divine accompaniments to every item on offer.

Cumin 

Indian

B3

1414 N. Milwaukee Ave. (bet. Evergreen & Wolcott Aves.)

Phone: 773-342-1414 — Lunch Tue – Sun
Web: www.cumin-chicago.com — Dinner nightly
Prices: $$ — Damen (Blue)

From the top of the Himalayas to the tropical sub-continent, Cumin offers an expansive look at neighboring Nepalese and Indian cuisines. Polished wood plank floors and steel-and-leather bar stools set a modern tone. Small butcher paper-topped tables can barely contain the many plates that pile up from the popular lunch buffet or diners exploring the extensive à la carte menu.

After crunching through wispy chips of fennel-flecked *pappadam* with tamarind chutney, move on to braised lamb masala with green chilies in a deeply complex curry; or Nepalese-spiced chicken *chhoela* cooked in a tandoor and served with *chewra,* Cumin's signature flattened rice. Vegetarians fill up on much more than the baked-to-order naan with a host of meat-free offerings.

En Hakkore

Korean

B3

1840 N Damen Ave. (bet. Churchill & Moffat Sts.)

Phone: 773-772-9880 — Lunch & dinner Mon – Sat
Web: N/A
Prices: $$ — Damen (Blue)

If Martha Stewart shifted her design skills from department stores to Korean restaurant interiors, one could almost be certain that she'd be the artist of En Hakkore. No tabletop grills or gruff servers here: instead, tall ceilings, mod painted walls, metal and rattan bistro chairs, and wine bottle chandeliers make it a distinctly upscale venue.

With only a handful of items to choose from, it's easy to sample everything if you go with a group and sit at the communal table. Sixteen kinds of vegetables in the *bibimbap,* including kimchi and pickled radish, combine traditional *banchan* into the overstuffed yet tasty entrée. Spicy pork or barbecue beef tacos also packed with tart vegetables and spicy homemade sauce, come wrapped in *parathas*—tortillas what?

Enso

Japanese XX

B3

1613 N. Damen Ave. (bet. North & Wabansia Aves.)

Phone: 773-878-8998 Lunch & dinner daily
Web: www.ensochicago.com
Prices: $$ Damen (Blue)

Round maki and cylindrical house-made noodles served in earthenware bowls echo the elliptical theme at Enso, whose name means "circle" in Japanese. Conversations do have a way of bouncing around the cavernous space, sleek with black nailhead chairs and bare wood tables set with flower-filled fishbowls. A contemporary hip hop and rock-heavy soundtrack keeps the mood lively.

If menu options like crispy pork belly ramen with a gently poached egg; steamed buns stuffed with grilled duck breast or soft shell crab; and grilled beef skewers with wasabi béarnaise don't strike your fancy, you can create your own maki. It might just end up as a permanent menu item, like the crunchy "Akuma's Head" tuna roll with yuzu *tobiko, togarashi*, and cilantro.

Flo

Southwestern X

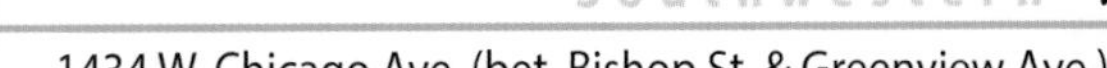

C5

1434 W. Chicago Ave. (bet. Bishop St. & Greenview Ave.)

Phone: 312-243-0477 Lunch Tue – Sun
Web: www.flochicago.com Dinner Tue – Sat
Prices: ◎ Chicago (Blue)

The name says "cozy down home diner" and the décor might straddle the line between modern and quaint, but Flo's café and bar is straight outta New Mexico, letting diners saddle up for a taste of the Wild West in Noble Square. The bar is small but quick to stir up a mimosa or Bloody Maria to start brunch on the right note.

An always-cranking kitchen serves breakfast through mid-afternoon featuring seriously flavorful dishes like the signature breakfast burrito with roasted poblanos and pickled jalapeños that will tide you over till dinner. Heaps of zucchini and corn lighten up turkey chili; while *carnitas* tacos come with all the bells and whistles. No matter what's on the plate, a drizzle of the kitchen's homemade red and green chile sauces are a must.

Frontier

American

1072 N. Milwaukee Ave. (bet. Division & Noble Sts.)

Phone: 773-772-4322 Lunch Tue – Sun
Web: www.thefrontierchicago.com Dinner nightly
Prices: $$ Chicago (Blue)

Vegans, you might want to make other dinner reservations. Frontier specializes in snout to tail dining, and though the plates are small, the game is big and diverse. This might be the only place in Chicago where talking about "the bears" actually means discussing a plate of braised black bear with tasso and pickled carrots.

While your vegetarian friends are bound to savor thinly sliced red and golden beet carpaccio, Chef Brian Jupiter gets truly excited about comfort food featuring esoteric meats like llama meatballs with smoked tomato sauce and sage *chimichurri*; or kangaroo chili with marrow beans. Give Frontier advance notice for Whole Animal Service, where the kitchen prepares an entire goat, pig, or boar with sides for up to 12 famished friends.

Green Zebra

Vegetarian

1460 W. Chicago Ave. (at Greenview Ave.)

Phone: 312-243-7100 Dinner nightly
Web: www.greenzebrachicago.com
Prices: $$ Chicago (Blue)

Chef/owner Shawn McClain stays true to his roots at this perennial Noble Square pearl, which has kept its minimalist, organic, and sustainable sensibility well intact over the years. Green Zebra telegraphs its intentions through recycled wood frames of living lichen and moss reliefs adorning the walls, and a number of organic and biodynamic wines among their international listings. If that doesn't' scream "green," the rooftop garden supplies the kitchen with its bounty whenever possible.

Graze freely with friends on the all-vegetarian menu which might include standouts like crispy sweet potato dumplings sopping up walnut-sage *pistou* and crab-apple ketchup; or mustard and caraway spaetzle punctuated by hon shimeji mushrooms and smoked cipollini onions.

Habana Libre

Cuban

C5

1440 W. Chicago Ave. (bet. Bishop & Noble Sts.)

Phone: 312-243-3303 — Lunch & dinner daily
Web: www.habanalibrerestaurant.com
Prices: $$ — Chicago (Blue)

BYO

The celebration of Cuban cuisine never ends at Habana Libre, where the potted palms and faux banana tree seem to sway to the festive music, and vibrant orange walls almost pulsate with the beat. If you're curious about the owners' passion for Havana, the Fidel Castro-embossed toilet paper set near the restrooms pretty much sums it up.

Plantains pop up in nearly every form on the comprehensive menu: smashed and fried into *tostones*, stuffed with *ropa vieja*, or even used as "bread" for a *jibarito* sandwich. More traditionally bound sandwiches like the Cubano, featuring the requisite double dose of ham and pork on a pressed baguette, hit the spot. Don't settle for the bottled red sauce on the table; ask for the fresh jalapeño-spiked salsa verde.

Jane's

American

B2

1655 W. Cortland St. (bet. Marshfield Ave. & Paulina St.)

Phone: 773-862-5263 — Lunch Fri – Sun
Web: www.janesrestaurant.com — Dinner Tue – Sun
Prices:

Jane's is nearly as much of an historic fixture as the well-kept 19th century building in which it resides, having made its name as a neighborhood favorite since 1994. Vaulted ceilings with chunky wood beams hover over claw-foot tables, thereby complementing exposed brick walls hung with artwork while emphasizing a rustic and homey vibe.

Global accents and vegetarian specialties on the menu showcase the kitchen's wide-ranging definition of comfort food. If the freshly ground half-pound sirloin burger topped with pancetta, grilled pineapple, mozzarella, and chipotle aïoli isn't enough, mashed potatoes and salad on the side should leave you fulfilled. Lighter fare like an Asian chicken salad, or a bowl of Jane's corn chowder are ideal taste bud teasers.

Las Palmas

Mexican

1835 W. North Ave. (at Honore St.)

Phone: 773-289-4991
Web: www.laspalmaschicago.com
Prices: $$

Lunch Sat – Sun
Dinner nightly
Damen (Blue)

Vivid décor complements the spirited flavors on the menu at Las Palmas, from the colorful Mexican artwork on adobe-style walls to exposed ductwork welded to resemble a scaly dragon winding through the deceptively large space. If the weather suits, the outdoor garden or glassed-in atrium beckon; if not, a cozy fireplace in the front room keeps things intimate.

The cocktail menu draws inspiration from both South and Central America, featuring myriad capirinhas and mojitos alongside inventive cucumber-lime and pineapple margaritas. Vibrant and modern Mexican dishes like crispy *taquitos* with chicken *barbacoa*, pickled red onion, and tangy salsa *cruda*; and seafood-filled cornmeal empanadas with peanut-jalapeño salsa showcase the kitchen's flair.

Le Bouchon

French

1958 N. Damen Ave. (at Armitage Ave.)

Phone: 773-862-6600
Web: www.lebouchonofchicago.com
Prices: $$

Lunch & dinner Mon – Sat
Damen (Blue)

Pressed-tin ceiling? Check. Brick-and-dijon color scheme? Check. Close-knit tables in a snug space? Check. A warm welcome from an actual Frenchman? Check. Owner Jean-Claude Poilevey has fashioned the quintessential bistro experience at Le Bouchon, where straightforward French fare never goes out of style. The informal atmosphere gets convivially raucous as the night goes on with regulars lining the bar and petite dining room.

Familiar, approachable favorites rule the menu: *soupe à l'oignon*, wearing its traditional topper of broiled Gruyère on a moist crouton, oozes and bubbles over the sides of a ramekin; and an ample fillet of *saumon poche* napped in beurre blanc is the essence of simplicity. A lunch prix-fixe keeps the wallet light but belly full.

Lillie's Q

Barbecue XX

B3

1856 W. North Ave. (at Wolcott Ave.)

Phone: 773-772-5500 Lunch & dinner daily
Web: www.lilliesq.com
Prices: $$ Damen (Blue)

This self-described "urban barbeque" is a honky-tonk celebration of smoked meats rubbed in "Carolina dirt" (their own recipe) and down-home sides in a rustic setting. Leather belts hold cushions on the banquettes in a room filled with iron light fixtures, exposed brick, and white subway tiles. Servers in modern mechanic's shirts hoist metal trays and carry Mason jars filled with "moonshine" whiskey cocktails. The bar is big on beer.

Tri-tip is tender and pink-tinged after its time in the smoker with the joint's signature dry rub, improved only by a squirt of one of Lillie's five sauces, like mustardy Carolina Gold or Hot Smoky. Smoked-fried chicken gets a drizzle of Tupelo honey over its peppery breading from a tableside ceramic honey pot.

Mana Food Bar

Vegetarian X

B4

1742 W. Division St. (bet. Paulina & Wood Sts.)

Phone: 773-342-1742 Lunch & dinner daily
Web: www.manafoodbar.com
Prices: Division

Feeling like your body needs a jump-start? Mana, whose name translates to "the life force coursing through nature," is a good place to get your mojo back. Though welcoming to vegans, vegetarians, gluten-free diners, and anyone who's looking for a nutrient boost, it's not just a health bar: the small space also offers a full bar with sake cocktails, smoothies, and freshly squeezed juices.

Mana may be a tiny spot, but its diverse menu of vegetarian dishes is big on taste—and spice. Korean *bibimbap* mixes a roster of vegetables like pea pods, roasted carrots, and pickled daikon with a fresh sunny side-up egg; while horseradish and cracked black pepper sneak into macaroni and cheese. House-made hot sauce with serranos and jalapeños adds extra pep to any dish.

Mexique ✿

Mexican XX

C5

1529 W. Chicago Ave. (bet. Armour St. & Ashland Ave.)

Phone: 312-850-0288 Lunch & dinner Tue – Sun
Web: www.mexiquechicago.com
Prices: $$ Chicago (Blue)

Mexique

Bucking the trend of serving south-of-the-border food in colorful and almost raucous surrounds, Mexique presents its blend of upscale Mexican cooking and French technique in an elegant, subdued space. In fact, you could say it's a little square: the shape is repeated throughout the décor, from square tables along banquette-lined walls, to the minimalist hanging fabric panels interspersed with exposed brick cutouts.

Peek through a window into the kitchen at the rear of the dining room to watch Chef Carlos Gaytan and team at work. Then continue down the back hallway to read congratulatory and complimentary graffiti from visiting chefs scrawled across the wall.

The marriage of Mexican and French elements is truly a love match through the menu. A zesty interpretation of the French classic *blanquette de veau* incorporates braised and shredded veal, ghost pepper *gastrique*, and hominy with a generous pour of creamy parsnip sauce added tableside. A trio of contemporary miniature *sopes* bridge the two culinary worlds with finesse: one topped with tender escargots and *chimichurri* butter; another with shrimp Provençal and avocado mousse; and a third with pan-fried plantains and dark *xico mole*.

Mindy's Hot Chocolate

Contemporary

1747 N. Damen Ave. (bet. St. Paul Ave. & Willow St.)

Phone: 773-489-1747 — Lunch Wed – Sun
Web: www.hotchocolatechicago.com — Dinner Tue – Sun
Prices: $$ — Damen (Blue)

After a brief closure for remodeling and some tweaking, owner Mindy Segal has flung open the floor-to-ceiling glass doors once more—re-opening as Mindy's Hot Chocolate Craft Food & Drink. Now that's a mouthful, but the lofty, industrial-chic space allures with rich brown hues on leather banquettes, a long wooden bar, and painted concrete floors. As the handle indicates, sweets are only part of the temptations on offer. A full lineup of savory fare like house-ground lamb sausage with creamy cheese on flatbread, shares menu space with Segal's renowned desserts. Six varieties of hot chocolate are served with homemade marshmallows; and the cookie cart is an instant favorite, stocked with a dozen choices like gingersnap and snickerdoodle for a buck each.

Mirai

Japanese

2020 W. Division St. (bet. Damen & Hoyne Aves.)

Phone: 773-862-8500 — Dinner nightly
Web: www.miraisushi.com
Prices: $$ — Damen (Blue)

Mirai is a bit like Disney World. You know it's not real, but who cares? The Japanese food is westernized and by no means traditional, but unless you're dining out with Mr. Miyagi, rest assured that nobody will cry foul.

Bold and appetizing flavors beg to take center stage. It's really all about the sushi at this spot—just look around and you'll find most devotees feasting on sashimi, *unagi*, and maki. If raw fish doesn't float your boat, take a shot at one of the house specialties like *kani nigiri*, a baked king crab concoction. There is also a surfeit of hot dishes, think chicken *togarashi* with spicy, sweet, and tangy flavors. Affable and alert service and a relaxed atmosphere, especially on the front patio, make this a hit among area residents.

Mott St.

Fusion

B3

1401 N. Ashland Ave. (at Blackhawk St.)

Phone: 773-687-9977 — Dinner Tue – Sat
Web: www.mottstreetchicago.com
Prices: $$ — Division

New Yorkers know Mott Street as the bustling artery in the heart of Chinatown, but to Chicagoans the name connotes something off the beaten path. Inspired by the night stalls of Asia, this funky joint set in a red building incorporates a chicken wire-caged pantry stocked with jars of red pepper, black vinegar, and other pungent edibles—all of which appear again in the food on your plate.

Offerings crisscross the globe from Korea, Latin America, and all the way back to India, melding diverse ingredients in spring rolls stuffed with minced kimchi and melted Oaxaca cheese; or layers of spicy fermented Napa cabbage, tender shredded pork, and seared sticky rice with kimchi broth. A frozen, chocolate-covered and peanut-coated baby banana cools things down.

Nando Milano Trattoria

Italian

A4

2114 W. Division St. (bet. Hoyne Ave. & Leavitt St.)

Phone: 773-486-2636 — Dinner nightly
Web: www.nandomilano.com
Prices: $$ — Division

A corner bar television constantly tuned to (European) football, vintage *aperitivo* posters, and a welcoming patio tailor-made for afternoon glasses of prosecco: charismatic host Dario Vullo has installed his own little slice of Milan in Wicker Park. The chic trattoria offers an intensely Italian menu and wine list to match the authentic accents of Vullo and family.

A trio of *arancini* are playfully prepared, with each rice ball sporting a unique shape—sphere, triangle, and cube—to denote a unique filling like Bolognese ragù and smoked mozzarella; or mascarpone and spinach. House-made pastas like beet gnocchi in saffron sauce steal the show from equally flavorful and fresh focaccia sandwiches layered with creamy burrata and *Prosciutto di Parma*.

Oiistar

Asian

1385 N. Milwaukee Ave. (bet. Paulina & Wood Sts.)

Phone: 773-360-8791 — Lunch & Dinner Tue – Sun
Web: www.oiistar.com
Prices: — Damen (Blue)

When college grads are ready to move up from supermarket ramen to grown-up noodles, Oiistar is there for them. Crowds of young noodleheads sit elbow-to-elbow at the blonde birch counters, bobbing their heads to the bouncing old-school hip hop beats as the kitchen crew slaps, stretches, and pulls fresh noodles daily.

While the giant bowls of ramen with ingredients like tree ear mushrooms, mussels, and bonito miso receive the bulk of attention, the menu showcases innovative Asian fusion. French kimchi soup combines melted Provolone with *togarashi*, pork belly, and chunks of andouille for a cross-cultural spin on traditional onion soup; just as Korean and Chinese-influenced duck buns are stuffed with juicy breast meat and golden raisin-jalapeño chutney.

Owen & Engine

Gastropub

A1

2700 N. Western Ave. (at Schubert Ave.)

Phone: 773-235-2930 — Lunch Sat – Sun
Web: www.owenengine.com — Dinner nightly
Prices: $$

This Victorian pub's glossy black façade hints at what awaits—think Pippa and Kate look-alikes chatting with bearded guys in skinny jeans. The constants are polished woods, a long inviting bar, studded black leather, and beer. Lots and lots of beer...Belgians, Brits, Germans, and a few Americans get along swimmingly over good food without pretense.

Mole pork rinds, pork rillettes, and oysters are spot-on snacks. Roasted bone marrow is deliciously hefty, while fish and chips get highbrow with malt vinegar aïoli and pea purée. Fun and simple, the Tuesday burger special includes a beer and shot for an additional buck.

Parking is a bit dodgy but once inside, the Clash and a Pimm's Cup will have you springing for that "five-dollar six-pack for the kitchen."

Piccolo Sogno

Italian

464 N. Halsted St. (at Milwaukee Ave.)

Phone: 312-421-0077
Web: www.piccolosognorestaurant.com
Prices: $$

Lunch Mon – Fri
Dinner nightly
Grand (Blue)

Power lunchers and socially minded dinner parties descend on this stately building, which stands out at its gritty intersection, for equal parts glad-handing and hearty eating. A labor of love for co-owners Tony Priolo and Ciro Longobardo, the swank space exudes conviviality and charm with brick archways and terrazzo floors. The fraternal camaraderie of the all-male staff keeps things running efficiently.

Like the décor, the menu brings refinement to rustic Italian cuisine: *ribolitta*, traditionally a peasant's stale bread-and-vegetable soup, becomes a richly flavored pan-fried appetizer in Chef Priolo's hands. *Maiale ripeno* pairs pork tenderloin and fennel-stippled sausage with soft lentils and polenta. An all-Italian wine list is the perfect match.

Red Door

International

2118 N. Damen Ave. (at Charleston St.)

Phone: 773-697-7221
Web: www.reddoorchicago.com
Prices: $$

Lunch Sat – Sun
Dinner nightly

Don't look for a sign—an imposing red door near a red fire hydrant is the only indication that imaginative (read: eclectic) gastropub eats can be found inside. Servers behind the gracefully curving wooden bar shake and stir funky concoctions, also pouring a respectable list of American and European microbrews. Long red aprons on the staffers and red cotton napkins on chunky wooden tables play off the name.

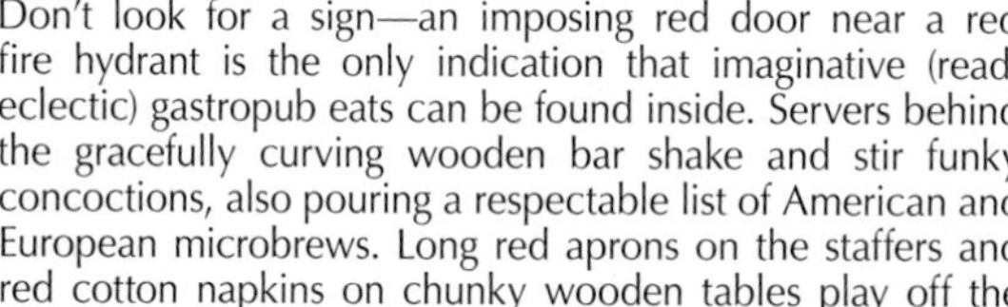

In the summer, the back patio is the place for sharing small plates like fried oyster *ssäm* with crunchy kimchi and tasso ham; snacks like bacon-wrapped artichokes with chicken liver; or boozy snow cones at long candlelit communal tables. It's like a global neighborhood barbecue and you don't have to bother cleaning up at the end of the evening.

Rios D'Sudamerica

B2 — Peruvian XX

2010 W. Armitage Ave. (bet. Damen & Hoyne Sts.)

Phone: 773-276-0170 — Lunch Sun
Web: www.riosdesudamerica.com — Dinner nightly
Prices: $$ — Damen (Blue)

It's simply called "Rios" by its regulars, all of whom seem to adore drinking and dining in this two-story space flanked by cream walls and murals of icons like Macchu Picchu and the Christ the Redeemer statue towering over Rio de Janeiro. Posh lounge seating for pre-dinner caipirinhas gives way to white tablecloths throughout this cavernous dining room.

Peruvian food takes center stage, but the menu spans South and Central American traditions. A standout *tamal Peruano* stuffed with tender slices of pork loin and hard-boiled egg, pairs seamlessly with sautéed *lomo saltado al pisco* and *camarones enrollado en cangrejo* that pay tribute to the miles of Pacific coastline. A $13 Sunday *criollo* buffet lets Peruvian cuisine fans sample to their hearts' content.

Roots Handmade Pizza

B5 — Pizza X

1924 W. Chicago Ave. (bet. Winchester & Wolcott Aves.)

Phone: 773-645-4949 — Lunch & dinner daily
Web: www.rootspizza.com
Prices: $$ — Division

In a town synonymous with deep-dish, it takes a certain amount of chutzpah to bring a new pizza style to Chicago. Roots does just that and succeeds winningly with Quad Cities-style pizza from the Iowa-Illinois border: a round, hand-tossed pie scissor-cut into rectangular strips with a key ingredient—malt in the crust—that adds a bronzed edge and subtle sweetness.

Quality ingredients abound: finely ground sausage is liberally sprinkled across the signature Quad Cities pie, and fresh mozzarella, hand-pulled each day, arrives in breaded planks for a take on the ubiquitous appetizer. Little touches, like the exclusively Midwestern brews on tap and the plate of warm washcloths that come with the check, make the spot an endearing neighborhood player.

Ruxbin

American XX

B4

851 N. Ashland Ave. (at Pearson St.)

Phone: 312-624-8509 Dinner Tue – Sun
Web: www.ruxbinchicago.com
Prices: $$ Division

Refurbished, repurposed, and reclaimed: that's Ruxbin. Its décor is á la mode and mixes decoupage cookbook pages, salvaged apple juice shipping crates with vintage Herman Miller chairs and even a darkroom door as the restroom entry. The atmosphere resonates with the international flavors that make their way onto the quirky menu, envisaged by Chef/owner Ed Kim's Korean-American upbringing.

Instead of bar snacks, try dessert first. "Pretzels and beer" are really beignets dusted in ground pretzels with beer-milk sorbet and pair nicely with a homemade lemongrass-passion fruit soda. After dessert, tuck into "chicken and dumplings" or buttermilk-battered quail and amaretto-pumpkin agnolotti, both deep-fried and doused with whiskey-brown butter vinaigrette.

The Savoy

Seafood XX

B3

1408 N. Milwaukee Ave. (bet. Evergreen & Wolcott Aves.)

Phone: 773-698-6925 Lunch Fri – Sun
Web: www.savoychicago.com Dinner nightly
Prices: $$ Damen (Blue)

A sumptuously reserved atmosphere gives hints of luxury at this absinthe- and seafood-focused Wicker Park haven. Subtle nautical elements like thick, rough ropes and filament bulbs encased in fish trap lighting fixtures nod to the menu's oceanic theme, while elegant glass drippers for diluting the more-than-40 absinthes on offer highlight the bar's specialty. Beyond raw bar selections such as slurpable oysters with smoked tomato cocktail sauce and rhubarb mignonette; or starters like house-cured gravlax, the kitchen fires up a variety of seafood dishes. These have included sweet scallops atop buttery escarole and peas; pan-seared swordfish with creamy basil and corn; as well as a few meat-based options off the "From the Prairie" menu section.

Schwa ✿

B3 — Contemporary

1466 N. Ashland Ave. (at Le Moyne St.)

Phone: 773-252-1466 — Dinner Tue – Sat
Web: www.schwarestaurant.com
Prices: $$$ — Division

BYO

nickb@hystk

First, the bad news: securing a table at Schwa is a frustrating exercise to put it mildly. And don't plan on arriving early lest you be asked to wait on the sidewalk since the setting lacks a bar for pre-meal mingling. Yes, Schwa is deficient in the expected comforts. But now the good, make that great, news—Super Chef Michael Carlson and his renegade brigade dole out a tasting menu that shines a spotlight on this curious spot.

A menu isn't presented prior to the meal (or after for that matter); but each course even if they don't all score, leaves a lasting impression. Movie snacks inspired a recent array of oh-so-Schwa canapés like pizza cotton candy washed down by buttered popcorn soda, followed by a clever merger between tagliatelle and rabbit liver sauce with Taleggio and charred gooseberries. Butter-poached lobster is fetchingly trimmed with sour orange purée, candied olive crumble, and savory cake; while honey ice cream strewn with honeycomb candy makes for a harmonious close.

Besides performing culinary alchemy, the cooks also serve each composition, delivering a speedy yet fervent rundown that keeps beat with the eclectic playlist reverberating through this stark little room.

Seadog

Japanese

1500 W. Division St. (at Greenview Ave.)

Phone: 773-235-8100 — Dinner nightly
Web: www.seadogsushibar.com
Prices: Division

BYO

Dim lighting, deep wood tones, and warm bronze hues set the stage for romance at this sexy little sushi bar just off the Division St. El stop. Not in the mood for love? Do not let that stop you from stopping in for a bite. Glazed brick walls and mosaic floors tiled with granite shards are as texturally interesting as the dishes turned out of the sushi counter.

Creative, contemporary appetizers and maki take center stage here, with a number of spicy options for the heat-seekers. Miso soup gets fresh jalapeños for a zesty kick; chopped scallop and wasabi *tobiko* tops crisp, light, and greaseless asparagus tempura; and dots of spicy *sriracha* and fried garlic adorn hamachi carpaccio.

Got cash in your wallet? Seadog will take 10 percent off your bill.

Siboney

2165 N. Western Ave. (at Palmer Ave.)

Phone: 773-276-8776 — Lunch & dinner daily
Web: www.siboneychicago.com
Prices: Western (Blue)

Though legend has it that the seaside Cuban village of Siboney played a role in the 1953 Cuban revolution, its Chicago namesake is much more serene. Outside its Western Avenue corner façade, the bustling Latin American groceries of the area do brisk business; inside, the setting evokes the beach with ceramic floors and touches of cerulean blue. Live music peps things up on weekends.

Cuban staples populate the menu with meats and seafood from chorizo to *gambas al ajillo* represented, and a lineup of carbs like *plátanos*, malanga, and yucca to complement them. *Ropa vieja* is authentically tasty with tender shredded flank steak and caramelized plantains. Though expats won't be able to snag a Cohiba, a can of Materva yerba maté soda provides that taste of home.

Smoke Daddy

American

B4

1804 W. Division St. (at Wood St.)

Phone: 773-772-6656 — Lunch & dinner daily
Web: www.thesmokedaddy.com
Prices: — Division

After a recent renovation doubled the size of this barbecue joint and live music venue, it's easier to grab a bite of burnt ends and a touch of the blues. The original room still oozes soul and smoke from its brick walls and vinyl floor, while the new space is bright and airy with a retractable glass door leading to an umbrella-shaded patio.

No matter which barbecue style you pledge allegiance to—Kansas City, Memphis, or Carolina—you'll find something worth gnawing on, from moist pulled pork and chicken to spare and baby back ribs. Order any sandwich "Daddy Style" to get a few slices of brisket slapped on top, or fill up on jalapeño cornbread. Fans of the in-house Bloody Mary mix grab a bottle to-go, along with smoked pig ears in a true doggy bag.

The Storefront Company

Contemporary

B3

1941 W. North Ave. (bet. Damen Ave & Honore St.)

Phone: 773-661-2609 — Dinner Tue – Sat
Web: www.thestorefrontcompany.com
Prices: **$$$** — Damen (Blue)

While this "storefront's" glossy white boxy exterior and modular cubic window box herb planters seem square, the inside is anything but. A stylized pastoral mural reigns supreme and the fashionable farmhouse décor starring leather-padded benches and caged-back chairs are a clear sign this isn't any run-of-the-mill farm-to-table spot.

Chef Bryan Moscatello puts an avant-garde spin on contemporary seasonal cuisine. His prix-fixe and tastings are as delicious as they are adventurous: think of scallops with prosciutto air and pickled watermelon rind; surf and turf by way of razor clams and pork cheek pastrami; composed cheese courses and savory elements incorporated into desserts. Artisanal libations like FEW Spirits are put to good use in cocktails.

Sushi X

1136 W. Chicago Ave. (bet. May St. & Racine Ave.)

Phone: 312-491-9232 — Lunch Mon – Fri
Web: www.rollingatsushix.com — Dinner Mon – Sat
Prices: $$ — Chicago (Blue)

X doesn't mean anonymous in this instance; it's the Roman numeral ten, and now that this hip sushi joint has been around for a decade, the X seems almost prophetic. There's nothing demure about this spot to begin with—inside the industrial chunk of a building, animé projected on dark walls, thumping background music, and low candle-lit lounge tables make Sushi X more of a club than an eatery.

Don't bother with plain nigiri here; instead go for signature "neo" and "mega" rolls. The Godzilla roll lives up to its name, filled with shrimp tempura, scallion, roe, avocado, and at least four other sauces and components. Non-sushi choices unveil hot and cold fusion dishes like Chinese-style red chicken in a red pepper-bean marinade with avocado.

Takito Kitchen

2013 W Division St. (bet. Damen & Hoyne Aves.)

Phone: 773-687-9620 — Lunch Sat – Sun
Web: www.takitokitchen.com — Dinner Tue – Sun
Prices: $$ — Division

Chicago's upscale taco circuit gets a new contender with Takito, where fresh ingredients make Latin-inspired food sing. Tequilas take pride of place in the front dining room, waiting for their moment in a chile-salted margarita, while skylights and mirrors make the narrow, modern-industrial space seem even brighter and larger.

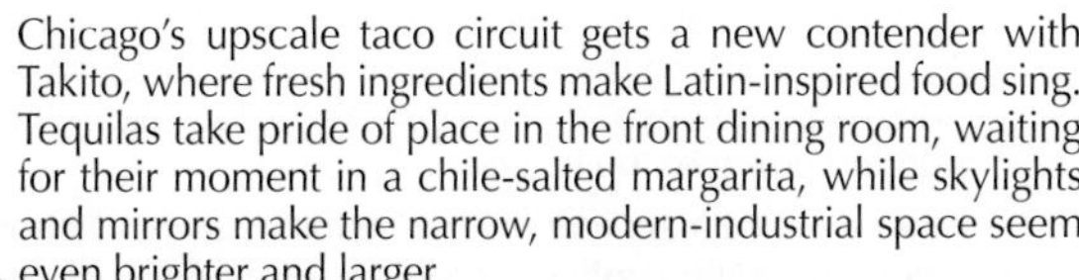

Sure, you can get a corn tortilla here, but sesame and hibiscus options let the kitchen get creative as evident in tacos filled with cornmeal-crusted redfish, beef *barbacoa*, or tamarind-chayote *pequin*. Shared plates like *sope de carne asada* blur culinary boundaries with the addition of Brunkow cheddar and green onion kimchi. It's an across-the-board mishmash of colorful flavors, but it's a good way to go over the top.

Takashi ✿

Contemporary XX

B2

1952 N. Damen Ave. (at Armitage Ave.)

Phone: 773-772-6170 — Dinner Tue – Sun
Web: www.takashichicago.com
Prices: $$$ — Damen (Blue)

Tyllie Barbosa Photography

Nestled within a small brick townhouse that's shyly and discreetly set back from other façades on the block, Takashi takes up residence in a modestly decorated artist's studio. Inside this food-focused space, charcoal gray, pure white, and warm wood provide a soothing palette, watched over by a red Daruma statue for good luck.

You can't help but get a little intimate with neighboring tables in the small room. Eavesdroppers will have a field day, while those looking for private dinner theater can sit back and watch Chef Takashi Yagihashi in his element through a large window into the kitchen. Though detail is evident in each dish and the dramatic dinnerware they're delivered on, disposable wooden chopsticks give a nod to the casual undercurrent of the place.

European culinary influences find their way into almost every element of the contemporary Japanese menu. Airy gnocchi made with soba noodle dough are served alongside equally tender sea scallops topped with celery root-Parmesan foam; and delicate corn flan complements creamy Brussels sprouts fricassee with Arctic char. Glazed peach wedges, crème fraîche ice cream, and yuzu gelée cubes harmoniously balance sweet and tart for dessert.

Taxim

Greek XX

B3

1558 N. Milwaukee Ave. (bet. Damen & North Aves.)

Phone: 773-252-1558 Dinner nightly
Web: www.taximchicago.com
Prices: $$ Damen (Blue)

Though Taxim channels the spirit of Greece in its food, its Moroccan-esque décor takes inspiration from Turkey and other Mediterranean coastal neighbors. The large room glints with light from hanging Moorish lanterns and copper-topped tables. Share small plates on the sidewalk patio to take full advantage of Wicker Park people-watching.

Many of Taxim's dishes get a modern twist while remaining respectful to the islands' traditional cuisine. Wild Greek oregano and ouzo-preserved lemon offer a perfect balance to roasted Amish Miller Farms chicken; while *loukoumades* prove that no one can resist fried dough, especially when tossed in wildflower honey and topped with rosewater-infused pastry cream. The all-Greek wine list is an adventure for oenophiles.

tocco

Italian XX

B4

1266 N. Milwaukee Ave. (bet. Ashland Ave. & Paulina St.)

Phone: 773-687-8895 Dinner Tue – Sun
Web: www.toccochicago.com
Prices: $$ Division

Are we in Milan or Wicker Park? Tocco brings haute design and fashion to the table with such upscale textural touches as polished resin, faux ostrich skin, and bubblegum pink accents in this sleek black-and-white space. Don your catwalk best before visiting: a fashion-centric display near a long communal table hints at the chichi theme present throughout. The décor is cutting-edge, but the menu respects and returns to Italian standbys. *Gnocco fritto,* a pillow served with charcuterie is irresistible to even the most willowy fashion plates; while cracker-crisp artisan pizzas from wood-burning ovens are equally pleasing. Traditional *involtini di pollo,* pounded thin and rolled around prosciutto, gets a hit of brightness from lemon and white wine sauce.

Trenchermen

Contemporary

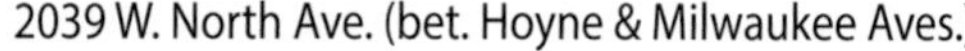

2039 W. North Ave. (bet. Hoyne & Milwaukee Aves.)

Phone: 773-661-1540 — Lunch Sat – Sun
Web: www.trenchermen.com — Dinner Mon – Sat
Prices: $$ — Damen (Blue)

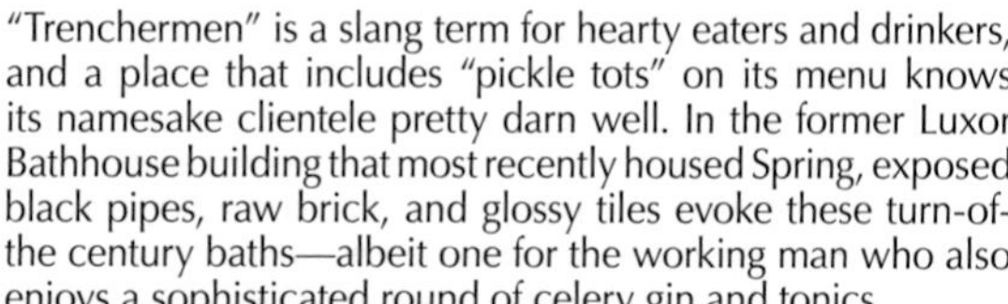

"Trenchermen" is a slang term for hearty eaters and drinkers, and a place that includes "pickle tots" on its menu knows its namesake clientele pretty darn well. In the former Luxor Bathhouse building that most recently housed Spring, exposed black pipes, raw brick, and glossy tiles evoke these turn-of-the century baths—albeit one for the working man who also enjoys a sophisticated round of celery gin and tonics.

Chicken breast *bresaola* takes on focused flavors and textures after air-drying when paired with the aforementioned fried pickle-and-potato tots; beet-tinged yogurt steps in to balance the plate. Octopus pozole with masa balls and green beans is enlightening; while fried chicken and grits with *togarashi* and hot sauce adds spicy comfort.

Veneno de Nayarit

Seafood

B4

1024 N. Ashland Ave. (at Cortez St.)

Phone: 773-252-7200 — Lunch & dinner daily
Web: N/A
Prices: $$ — Division

BYO

Roll up your sleeves, or even better, BYOB (bring your own bib) to this small but shining spot that sizzles with activity and intoxicating aromas. A sink in the corner of the vividly painted dining room lets diners wash up after cracking into crab legs and sucking down ceviches, while buckets in the corner hint at the shells-on affair.

After the complimentary crab-and-shrimp tostada that's a vehicle for testing your taste buds against the house-made habanero salsa, it's time to dig into a seafood stuffed pineapple or oysters on the half shell. Langoustines split down their middle are broiled with garlic- and butter-soaked breadcrumbs, piled on a platter with salad, rice, seasoned fries, and garlic bread. It's meant for one, but cowards can share.

Yuzu

B5 Japanese

1715 W. Chicago Ave. (bet. Hermitage & Paulina Sts.)

Phone: 312-666-4100 — Lunch Mon – Sat
Web: www.yuzuchicago.com — Dinner nightly
Prices: $$ — Chicago (Blue)

Yuzu isn't that old, but its sushi bar and *robata* grill come with a few features that are truly broken-in: reclaimed weathered planks line the walls, and the crave-worthy counter is a slab of wood that's over a 100 years old. Décor elements like hand-painted manga murals, metal drafting stools, and Ball Jars provide rustic-retro contrast.

The menu's mix of cool sushi and hot *robata* items proves to be equally complementary. Each item off the grill is matched with simple sauces—perhaps beef short ribs glazed in *kalbi* marinade; or ahi brushed with white miso and Japanese mustard. Those in need of smaller bites should opt for creative and quirky maki which come as jumbo or small. Juicy, sweet watermelon slices for dessert are on the house.

Look for BYO symbol and bring your own beverage to completment the meal.

Chinatown & South Loop

Chinatown and the South Loop were two neighborhoods that for years didn't have much linking them, besides of course that north-south running Red Line El. Geographically, they may be close, but are in fact worlds apart in terms of population, architecture, gentrification, and a gastronomic vibe.

Recent development has slowly but surely allowed for these two neighborhoods to meet in the middle. While they are still very distinct, both expanses have managed to combine their old and new in ways that should appeal to any true gastronome residing in the Windy City.

Strolling Through South Loop

Revered as one of Chicago's oldest neighborhoods, the South Loop houses a number of buildings that were fortunately spared the Great Chicago Fire. In particular, Prairie Avenue is a concentration of magnificent homes that were built by some of the wealthiest in the city. Similarly, Glessner House and Clarke House are distinctive gems. Glimpses of all sorts of history can be toured through time-tested churches; Willie Dixon's Blues Heaven Foundation, whose main mission is to preserve the blues legacy; National Vietnam Veterans Art Museum; and other impressive landmarks. In previous incarnations, the South Loop (which begins south of Roosevelt Road) housed famed mob man Al Capone, Chess Records, and other buzzing industrial spaces. However, over the last 15 years, this neighborhood has undergone a serious transformation and it now includes new condos and shopping, which have helped fuel a rash of fresh restaurants. Also home to former mayor, Richard M. Daley, Columbia College, Museum Campus, and Soldier Field, it seems as if almost anything can be found in the South Loop.

Magnificent Munching

Nurse that Chinese addiction at the well-maintained **Go 4 Food**, where the likes of a Sichuan beef lunch combo or wok-fried, hundred-spiced chicken amid bright red walls and contemporary high-backed chairs are bound to sate your pungent palate. Want a glimpse of the way real natives eat? Nearby **Manny's Coffee Shop and Deli** is ground zero for local politicians. Pastrami, corned beef, and crispy potato pancakes are solid here, and the speedy staff keeps the line moving. So follow suit, make your pick, and grab it! Come to watch the wheeling and dealing, or just eat a giant pastrami on rye. Either way, you will be satisfied. Admired and applauded as one of Chicago's most authentic Italian markets, **Panozzo's** creative produce and talent brings a host of foodies, locals, and tourists alike. A welcoming landmark in the Windy City's vibrant South Loop, this glorified Italian deli's well-stocked shelves are arranged with carefully prepared foods. From cold and hot sandwiches and traditional entrées, to salads and freshly-baked breads, they personify the art behind Italian home-style cooking.

Printers Row

These massive historical printing lofts were converted into a hotel, condos, and related retail spaces (such as browse-worthy used bookstores) before the rest of the area was gentrified. Now this multi-block strip is chockablock with restaurants, offices, stores, as well as a Saturday farmer's market from June through October. Just north of the district is the looming Harold Washington Library Center, which serves as a city resource and showcases a beautiful glass-top garden on the ninth floor. On the south end is the landmark Dearborn Station, the oldest remaining train depot in all of Chicago. It is now a multi-use space for retail stores, both small and large corporate offices, and the like.

Chinatown

Chicago is home to the country's fourth largest Chinatown, with a population of about 15,000 ethnic Chinese. Chicago's Chi-town also boasts a good combination of original Chinese-American history and contemporary Chinese-American life. At Wentworth Avenue and Cermak Road, you'll find the Chinatown Gate, an old yet elaborate and ornate icon for this neighborhood. Outdoor mall **Chinatown Square** is *the* hub for much of the commercial activity. This two-story extravaganza cradles restaurants, retail spaces, boutiques, and banks. While strolling through this locale, don't miss St. Therese Chinese Catholic Church, an edifice that points to the area's pre-Chinatown Italian roots. Much of the food served in restaurants here is classic Chinese-American fare, which is usually an amalgam of Sichuan, Cantonese, and Chinese-American delights, mostly from the Midwest. Crab Rangoon anyone?

Stellar Sweets and Spicy Eats

Locals come here, not just to eat out, but to stock up on good eats in order to dine in. **Hong Kong Noodle Company** is a factory and the place to go for wonton wrappers. **Mayflower Food** has one of the largest selections of fresh noodles; and **Ten Ren Tea** is lauded for its extensive tea selection and unique tea-making gadgets. To top off a day of feasting and adventure, try a freshly baked treat from **Golden Dragon Fortune Cookies**, or sweets from **Chiu Quon Bakery**. This precious pearl struts a range of baked goods, dim sum, and desserts. Those who need more guidance can pick up a cookbook from the Chinese Cultural Bookstore and all the necessary gear at **Woks 'n' Things**. After these ethnic delights, saunter over to the U.S. Cellular Field and home of the Chicago White Sox—the rare baseball park that serves veggie dogs alongside crispy house-made potato chips.

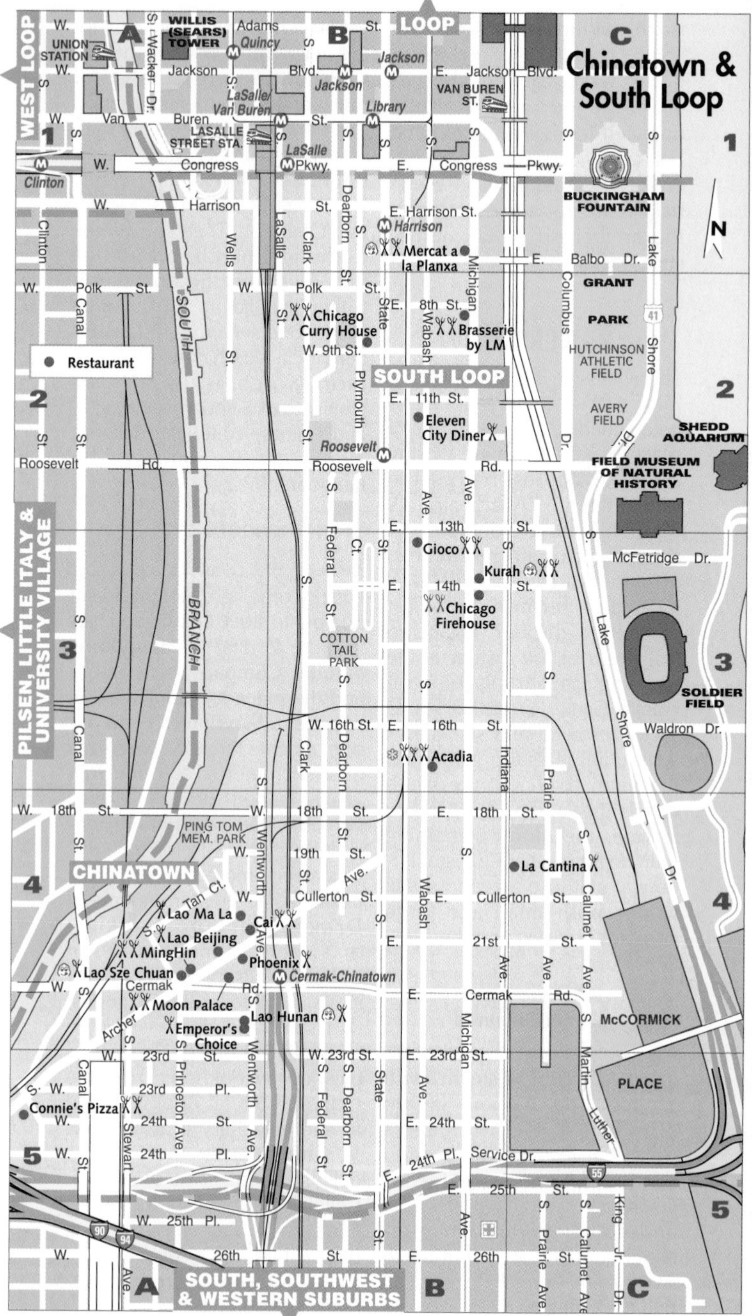
Chinatown & South Loop
WILLIS (SEARS) TOWER
UNION STATION
LOOP
WEST LOOP
LASALLE STREET STA.
VAN BUREN ST.
BUCKINGHAM FOUNTAIN
GRANT PARK
HUTCHINSON ATHLETIC FIELD
AVERY FIELD
SHEDD AQUARIUM
FIELD MUSEUM OF NATURAL HISTORY
SOLDIER FIELD
SOUTH LOOP
COTTON TAIL PARK
PING TOM MEM. PARK
CHINATOWN
McCORMICK PLACE
PILSEN, LITTLE ITALY & UNIVERSITY VILLAGE
SOUTH, SOUTHWEST & WESTERN SUBURBS
Restaurant
Mercat a la Planxa
Chicago Curry House
Brasserie by LM
Eleven City Diner
Gioco
Kurah
Chicago Firehouse
Acadia
La Cantina
Lao Ma La
Cai
Lao Beijing
MingHin
Phoenix
Lao Sze Chuan
Moon Palace
Lao Hunan
Emperor's Choice
Connie's Pizza

Acadia ✿

Contemporary XXX

B3

1639 S. Wabash Ave., Ste. 2F (bet. 16th & 18th Sts.)

Phone: 312-360-9500 — Dinner Wed – Sun
Web: www.acadiachicago.com
Prices: $$$

Anthony Tahlier

Though most of the South Loop is gentrified, there are still pockets that are in the throes of change. Acadia, in a low-slung building on a still-to-be-tamed stretch of Wabash, cleverly keeps its façade unobtrusive while waiting for its environs to evolve. Inside, this comfortable and inviting multi-room space done in warm birch, stone, and slate tones, evokes a pastoral idyll accented by hints of wood and moss throughout. Contrasting chandeliers made from egg-like beakers wink to Chef Ryan McCaskey's focused menu of modern gastronomic cuisine.

Whether diners choose from a three-course prix-fixe or immerse themselves in the tasting, many of the seasonal, contemporary dishes feature ingredients sourced from the chef's own home state of Maine. That knowledge isn't necessary however to enjoy creative, well-crafted chicken noodle soup dancing with homemade "noodles" of chicken mousse surrounded by creamy velouté; or silky potato and Granny Smith apple "risotto" under a blanket of herbs and truffle shavings.

Stonington lobster with roe-infused sabayon is a study in delicate textures just as a single whoopie pie *mignardise*, the unofficial dessert of Maine, tips its hat to the Pine State.

Brasserie by LM

French XX

B2

800 S. Michigan Ave. (bet. 8th & 9th Sts.)

Phone: 312-431-1788 Lunch & dinner daily
Web: www.brasseriebylm.com
Prices: $$ Harrison

Elegant but unpretentious, Brasserie by LM—the casual sibling of LM, the long-loved and relocated Lincoln Square darling—aims to comfort and please. Traditional bistro décor goes modern here with persimmon walls, stylized chalkboard wall menus, and curvaceous Cherner chairs that echo mid-century and art deco lineage. The bistro sport of people-watching is A+ with windows facing Michigan Avenue and Grant Park.

Brasserie classics populate the all-day menu: hanger steak frites, *salade Lyonnaise*, mussels, breakfast crêpes, and quiches. Duck rillettes get the full brasserie presentation in a lidded glass jar served with cornichons and baguette croutons; while moist roast chicken arrives golden and crispy thanks to its time cooked under a brick.

Cai

Chinese XX

A4

2100 S. Archer Ave. (at Wentworth Ave.)

Phone: 312-326-6888 Lunch & dinner daily
Web: www.caichicago.com
Prices: Cermak-Chinatown

Cai rolls out the red carpet for a lavish dim sum banquet on the second floor of Chinatown Square. Under crystal chandeliers, tuxedoed servers navigate carts through a sea of silk-covered chairs and round banquet tables. With almost 100 choices of rolled, steamed, fried, crimped, and folded dim sum illustrated neatly on a single menu page, simply pointing to an order makes perfect sense.

Bamboo steamers may contain a bevy of buns and dumplings including *xiao long bao*; crisply baked green chive puffs; tender shrimp-filled *har gow*; or fluffy dessert parcels with creamy, sweet egg yolks inside. When the dim sum parade ends at 4:00 P.M., the menu shifts to Cantonese specialties and entrée choices nearly as numerous as the earlier menu options.

Chicago Curry House

B2 Indian XX

899 S. Plymouth Ct. (at 9th St.)

Phone: 312-362-9999 Lunch & dinner daily
Web: www.curryhouseonline.com
Prices: ⊜ Harrison

Maybe you sniff the wafting aromas of ginger, garlic, and cumin first; maybe you hear the sitar music tinkling its welcoming notes as you enter. Either way, you know immediately that Chicago Curry House is a worthy showcase of Indian and Nepalese cuisine.

The lunch buffet lets you eat your fill for under $12, with crispy *pappadum*, baskets of fresh naan, and must-have curries like the Nepalese *khasi ko maasu* with chunks of bone-in stewed goat in a velvety cardamom- and black pepper-sauce. Indian butter chicken, creamy and rich in a tomato- and *garam masala*-spiced stew, is equally sumptuous. À la carte offerings are even more extensive.

The staff has helpful suggestions for dealing with the area's draconian parking restrictions, so call ahead for tips.

Chicago Firehouse

B3 American XX

1401 S. Michigan Ave. (at 14th St.)

Phone: 312-786-1401 Lunch & dinner daily
Web: www.chicagofirehouse.com
Prices: $$ Roosevelt

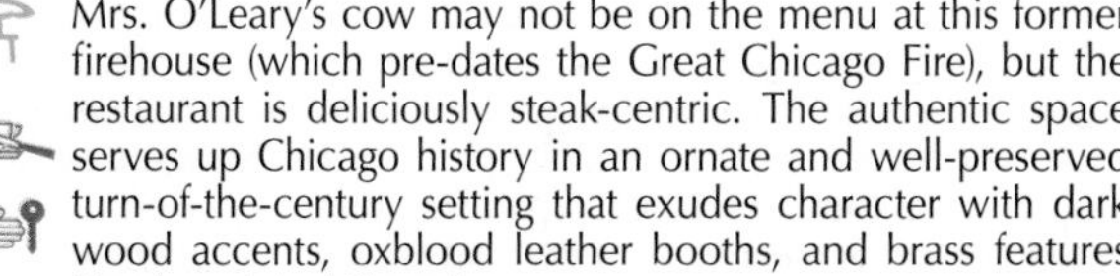

Mrs. O'Leary's cow may not be on the menu at this former firehouse (which pre-dates the Great Chicago Fire), but the restaurant is deliciously steak-centric. The authentic space serves up Chicago history in an ornate and well-preserved turn-of-the-century setting that exudes character with dark wood accents, oxblood leather booths, and brass features like the original firepoles.

American classics like a boneless ribeye, garlicky mashed potatoes, oysters Rockefeller, and iceberg wedge salad don't veer from the standard bistro playbook. The creamed spinach, however, is delish. "Three-alarm" soup and sandwich specials at lunch offer a fantastic opportunity for rushed diners and local history buffs to experience the noteworthy space.

Connie's Pizza

Pizza XX

A5

2373 S. Archer Ave. (at Normal Ave.)

Phone: 312-326-3443 Lunch & dinner daily
Web: www.conniespizza.com
Prices: $$ Halsted

No one knows who Connie was, but the name happened to be on the building bought by Jim Stolfe back in 1963, and it stuck. Even Chicagoans who've never set foot in the spacious Archer Avenue location know its near-monopoly at (and shuttle to) White Sox games and constant presence at citywide festivals. Those who do step inside the flagship come for the family-friendly atmosphere and, of course, the pizza.

Of the many options, the deep-dish is Miss Popularity, but it's fun to go one further with a stuffed pizza topped with a buttery crust. The garlic- and oregano-laced sauce is pleasantly tangy, and carnivores sing the praises of Connie's plump fennel sausage. Call ahead to forego the 45-minute cooking time and pick your pie up at the drive-thru.

Eleven City Diner

Deli 

B2

1112 S. Wabash Ave. (bet. 11th St. & Roosevelt Rd.)

Phone: 312-212-1112 Lunch & dinner daily
Web: www.elevencitydiner.com
Prices: ⊜ Roosevelt

Nosh on a mile-high sandwich or chocolate malt at Eleven City Diner, a modern revival of the classic Jewish deli. Gleaming subway tiles play off retro leather booths and swiveling barstools, while jazz in the background keeps things moving with chutzpah and finesse.

Diner standards include patty melts, sandwiches piled with corned beef or pastrami, knishes, and latkes. Bubbie's chicken soup comes bobbing with a fluffy matzo ball the size of a baseball; while Junior's cheesecake from Brooklyn or a triple-decker wedge of red velvet cake sates all the sweet-loving guests. A full-service deli counter offers salamis and smoked fish to-go. For a true blast from the past, stop by the candy stand near the entry stocked with Bazooka Joe and other favorites.

Emperor's Choice

Chinese

2238 Wentworth Ave. (bet. Alexander St. & 22nd Pl.)

Phone: 312-225-8800 — Lunch & dinner daily
Web: N/A
Prices: — Cermak-Chinatown

This striking Quasi-Chinese building—rife with decorative columns alongside ornamental lions—dates back to 1928 and often draws a crowd for being one of the most haunted areas in Chicago (a funeral parlor resides next door). The inside pales in comparison to the façade.

The menu leans Cantonese, but has a few westernized items like egg *foo yung*, chicken fried rice, and a pleasant rendition of hot and sour soup. The spicy dry-fried lamb is a delicious surprise, with thin slices of meat lightly coated and fried until tender-crisp and finished with jalapeños lending an addictively sweet heat. With a day's notice they'll prepare Peking duck the right way. Some may suggest that it's too western, so there is also a separate village menu for the Chinese purist.

Gioco

Italian

1312 S. Wabash Ave. (bet. 13th & 14th Sts.)

Phone: 312-939-3870 — Lunch Mon – Fri
Web: www.gioco-chicago.com — Dinner nightly
Prices: $$ — Roosevelt

Gioco offers a new definition of Italian-American. Within, original brick and plaster walls crafted in the 19th century, a wood-fired pizza oven, and crimson Berkel meat slicer share space with a walk-in cooler and wall safe used by infamous city gangster Al Capone. Warmly lit cubbies and tasseled golden pendant lamps infuse contemporary elements to this historic room.

A brief but hearty menu of traditional Tuscan and Umbrian food stars in this incongruously charming arena, and is deliciously supplemented by daily specials like grilled Kurobuta pork chops and a three-course lunch prix-fixe. *Bistecca alla Fiorentina, saltimbocca di vitello*, and ricotta gnocchi are pleasant standbys. Also classic yet delightfully charming is tiramisu served in a teacup.

Kurah

B3 — Middle Eastern — XX

1355S. Michigan Ave. (at 14th St.)

Phone: 312-624-8611 — Dinner nightly
Web: www.kurahchicago.com
Prices: $$ — Roosevelt

A glossy corner space on Michigan Avenue's South Loop stretch is now an inviting destination for Kurah's eclectic spread, also billed here as "Mediterranean tapas." Diners nibble flavorful bites near the stunning Moorish-mirrored bar, accompanied by other delightful touches like floor-to-ceiling windows and Edison bulbs dangling from soaring ceilings which add a romantic glow at dusk.

The menu, proudly stocked with organic meats and produce, skews Middle Eastern with small plates like rosemary-infused baba ghanoush served over roasted eggplant; or pine nut-stuffed beef *kubbeh* in a tart yogurt-dill dressing. Lamb abounds in racks and shanks as well as in shawarma and kebab platters; rose-infused flan with candied figs and pistachios is a refined finish.

La Cantina

C4 — Mexican — X

1911 S. Michigan Ave. (bet. Cullerton & 18th Sts.)

Phone: 312-842-1911 — Lunch & dinner daily
Web: www.lacantinagrill.com
Prices: — Cermak-Chinatown

With a chalkboard menu of margaritas at the front bar, a lengthy list of tequilas, and over a dozen types of martinis, La Cantina certainly lives up to its moniker. Meanwhile its slender dining room lends itself to hours of relaxation, dimly decked in soft pendant lights and warm terra-cotta walls.

Appetizers like mini *chimichangas* stuffed with steak and dolloped with zesty *pico de gallo* are enough for a meal. Pair them with fragile freshly fried chips, addictively spicy salsa, and an icy, citrusy margarita and you're good to go. But, for a truly filling fiesta, pick from a large selection of tacos, fajitas, burritos, Mexican, and Tex-Mex specialties like steak *tinga*, pork carnitas, Michoacan *pollo mole*, and Veracruz seafood specials.

Lao Beijing

Chinese

2138 S. Archer Ave. (in Chinatown Sq.)

Phone: 312-881-0168 — Lunch & dinner daily
Web: www.tonygourmetgroup.com
Prices: — Cermak-Chinatown

Bringing bold flavors and pungent spices to the ginkgo tree-lined Chinatown Square, Lao Beijing offers great deals and enormous variety to groups large and small. The room may seem no frills, with little more than a colorful quintet of *fuwa* (Beijing Olympic mascot dolls) to perk up the space, and the tuxedoed waitstaff are often untucked and rough around the edges. However, let the room's deep-red hues remind you of the aromatic chili oil sure to enhance the many good things to come.

The menu is thick with over 100 choices and colorful photos of dishes from China's spicier southern regions: Hunan, Yunnan, and Sichuan (home to these wonderfully fiery dumplings). Cheap lunch specials with a soup, main course, and rice can be had for around six dollars.

Lao Hunan

Chinese

2230 S. Wentworth Ave. (bet. Alexander St. & 22nd Pl.)

Phone: 312-842-7888 — Lunch & dinner daily
Web: www.tonygourmetgroup.com
Prices:  — Cermak-Chinatown

The Communist propaganda blanketing Lao Hunan ain't just a clever design scheme. Owner Tony Hu is an unapologetic fan of the Chairman and Maoism, and no matter what locals think of his politics, one thing is for certain—he takes the tenet of "serving the people" to heart with this homage to Hunan cuisine.

Hot, spicy, and aromatic dishes are cardinal here and reveal an authentic creeping heat that gets more addictive with each bite. There are numerous items across the menu to suit just about every palate like roasted green chilies in black bean sauce; Sichuan pepper-laced chicken tossed with ginger and garlic; or lamb sautéed with cilantro. If the heat overwhelms, a smoothie-ologist offering several semi-frozen concoctions is more than happy to soothe.

Lao Ma La

A4 — Chinese

2017 S. Wells St. (at S. Wentworth Ave.)

Phone: 312-225-8989 — Lunch & dinner daily
Web: www.tonygourmetgroup.com
Prices: $$ — Cermak-Chinatown

"Ma la" is the Chinese expression for that fantastic, tingling sensation from eating spicy Sichuan peppercorns. Prepare to exclaim it often at this hot spot, where Tony Hu lends his signature fiery touch to a menu that gets hotter with every mouthful. Styled in hardwood benches and black tables, the interior gets a dash of disco from floor lights and splashes of color overhead.

A recent addition to Chinatown Square's ever-growing Lao empire, Lao Ma La is a mostly small plates affair. Blazing offerings include quivering pork belly punched with raw garlic in a pool of scarlet chili oil, spicy hot pots, and tender morsels of stir-fried beef with ginger and massive amounts of dry red chilies. Note: soda refills aren't complimentary, so pay up to cool down.

Lao Sze Chuan

A4 — Chinese

2172 S. Archer Ave. (at Princeton Ave.)

Phone: 312-326-5040 — Lunch & dinner daily
Web: www.tonygourmetgroup.com
Prices: $$ — Cermak-Chinatown

One of the most adored spots in Chicago for tongue-tingling, lip-numbing, and belly-warming Sichuan dishes, Lao Sze Chuan is perpetually jammed with chili fiends craving that fiery, tingling sensation of *"ma la."* Even the décor screams "hot, hot, hot" with crimson tablecloths, waiters donning red aprons, and plastic chairs emblazoned with a bright curvy chili.

Mongolian beef tenderloin in a brown sauce with mushrooms is sweetened by onions and beloved by those who can't handle the heat. But, spice devotees should try the chef's special dry chili chicken, flash-fried with garlic, scallions, and heaps of dried red chilies. Even simple vegetables like crunchy cabbage get a piping dose of Sichuan heat when massaged with chili paste and chili oil.

Mercat a la Planxa

Spanish XX

638 S. Michigan Ave. (at Balbo Ave.)

Phone: 312-765-0524 — Lunch & dinner daily
Web: www.mercatchicago.com
Prices: $$ — Harrison

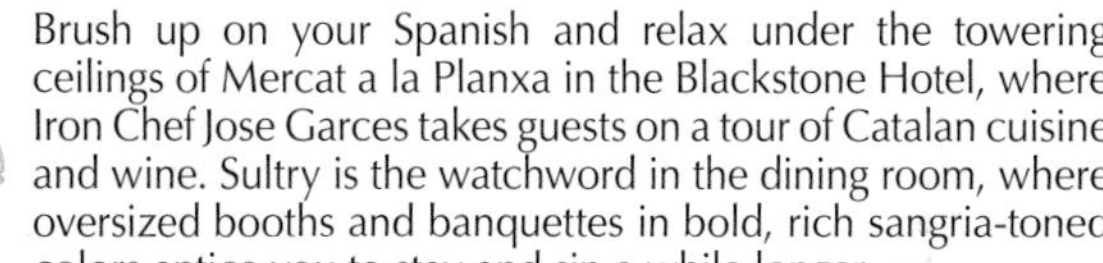

Brush up on your Spanish and relax under the towering ceilings of Mercat a la Planxa in the Blackstone Hotel, where Iron Chef Jose Garces takes guests on a tour of Catalan cuisine and wine. Sultry is the watchword in the dining room, where oversized booths and banquettes in bold, rich sangria-toned colors entice you to stay and sip a while longer.

Meats and seafood are seared on the namesake *planxa*, as servers deliver plates of whisper-thin *jamón Ibérico* and cheeses for sharing. Fresh takes on vegetables include the likes of spinach with golden raisins, pine nuts, and julienned apple. Inventive desserts always stand out, such as *croquetas de xocolata*, filled with chocolate and deep-fried with rosemary- caramel- and banana-marshmallow for dipping.

MingHin

Chinese XX

2168 S. Archer Ave. (at Princeton Ave.)

Phone: 312-808-1999 — Lunch & dinner daily
Web: www.minghincuisine.com
Prices: ◎◎ — Cermak-Chinatown

Do dim sum in style at this chic, bi-level restaurant on the edge of Chinatown Square. The swanky, bright, and high-ceilinged space attracts a younger crowd than most other eateries in the neighborhood—with guests filling elegantly set tables spaced across stone tile floors or in private rooms adorned with vibrant colors.

Drool over the kitchen's glistening slabs of ribs, pork belly, and roast duck hanging on hooks. Then, sip a cup of jasmine tea while checking off a multitude of dim sum choices on the menu board. Crispy-skinned braised pork belly Macau-style, served with a bowl of sugar for sprinkling and dipping, is a must. That said no trip here is complete without seafood selections like glossy shrimp dumplings filled with sweet green pea pod tips.

Moon Palace

A4

216 W. Cermak Rd. (bet. Princeton & Wentworth Aves.)

Phone: 312-225-4081 — Lunch & dinner daily
Web: www.moonpalacerestaurant.com
Prices: $$ — Cermak-Chinatown

Chef/owner Jones Wang has kept this lovely, friendly, and family-run Chinatown favorite packed for nearly 20 years. There is no doubt that their repeat business is thanks to the authentically prepared (yet Western-friendly) Mandarin and Shanghai specialties. Sparkly clean and stylish, the contemporary space is outfitted in dark woods and buttery yellows, with a fully stocked modern bar.

Steamy bowls of noodle soups share the menu with the likes of crispy salt and pepper squid; spicy *kung pao* chicken in a soy-chilli pepper glaze with peppers and onions; and Sichuan eggplant tossed with red chilies and hot garlic sauce. *Xiao long bao* (soup dumplings) have a zealous following. Business folk lead the lunchtime charge, while families crowd in at dinner.

Phoenix

Chinese

A4

2131 S. Archer Ave. (bet. Princeton & Wentworth Aves.)

Phone: 312-328-0848 — Lunch & dinner daily
Web: N/A
Prices: $$ — Cermak-Chinatown

Grab a group and ready your pencils. Phoenix specializes in made-to-order dim sum that brings family-friendly crowds to this simply decorated, banquet-style, big-box restaurant in Chinatown. "X" off your choices on the extensive and colorful menu or choose from the carts of additional dim sum items that circulate on busier weekends.

A boneless, red-stained slab of moist and tender barbecue pork gets even better when dipped into hot Chinese mustard. *Har gao* and *siu mai* are delicately steamed and filled with whole rock shrimp, fragrant ginger, and garlic. Potstickers are expertly fried and won't leave you greasy.

À la carte menu items also offered for dinner include the chef's special crispy beef tenderloin, Peking duck, and traditional Sichuan dishes.

大華
食品公司
TAI WAH
GROCERY STORE
達
ONE
WAY

Gold Coast

Glitz and Glamour

What's in a name? When it comes to the Gold Coast, the name says it all. After all, this posh neighborhood is Chicago's wealthiest and most affluent. From the numerous swanky high-rises dotting Lake Shore Drive, to the glittering boutiques of Michigan Avenue, the Gold Coast is luxury defined.

Whoever said money can't buy happiness certainly hadn't strolled through the Magnificent Mile, because this strip presents a serious challenge to that adage. This "magnificent" stretch of shopping, where millionaires mingle over Manolos and heiresses rummage for handbags, is one of the world's best and most well-known. Oak Street, with boutiques from Barneys to Yves Saint Laurent, runs a close second. If in the market for new wheels, take your pick from billionaire boy toys like Bentleys and Bugattis—both of which have dealerships here.

Historical Homes

It's not just about the glitz and glamour though. This neighborhood, listed on the National Register of Historic Places, is also the perfect canvas for architecture buffs. The mansions and buildings crafted in regal Queen Anne, Georgian Revival, and Richardsonian Romanesque styles are just breathtaking. They're all glorious to simply see, even if you're not in the market for a new home.

Applauding the Arts

The stunning Gold Coast takes its history quite seriously, and following this philosophy, area residents host a series of annual events, including the block party extraordinaire—Evening on Astor. This immense event also helps raise money and awareness for preservation. It is home to the Museum of Contemporary Art and the Newberry Library, one of the world's leading research libraries. So it should be of no surprise that this neighborhood celebrates the arts in a big way. The annual Gold Coast River North Art Fair is a must-see celebration of art, music, culture, and food. Whether you're an artist or have constantly dreamed of being one, this is a don't-miss celebration of the visual arts. Culture vultures should rest assured as they are bound to find something edgy and unique at A Red Orchid Theater. Here, an ensemble of artists perform a variety of stunning shows throughout the year.

Boisterous Nights

Just because the Gold Coast is sophisticated doesn't mean this area doesn't know how to party. Visit any of the pubs, clubs, and restaurants along Rush and Division streets to get a sense of how the other half lives it up. Cold winter winds got you down? Find a perch at **Lawry's Prime Rib** for some soulful steakhouse fare. This second outpost (the original is in Los Angeles) features a rather opulent dining room with a few signs of wear and tear. Expensive steakhouse classics like shrimp cocktail, prime rib, and lobster tail are favorites among the regulars seated within this regal room dressed in old tapestries, framed portraits, and gilded chandeliers. For a more rootin'-tootin' good time, stop by the well-liked **Underground Wonder Bar**, where live jazz tunes have been played nightly until the wee hours of the morning for over two decades now. The bar takes up most of the front room at this intimate jazz lair. After sipping a stellar cocktail, make your way to the back where the stage is jammed with musicians of all genres including singers, bassists, guitarists, percussionists, and horn players.

Fast (and Fresh) Food

The stylish Gold Coast is a capital of white-glove restaurants, but don't think that means there isn't good junk food available here as well. **Mr. Kite's Chocolate** will have you flying on a sugar high with its tempting array of goodies including chocolate-covered smores and the like. Get your fill of classic American treats at **LuxBar**, a lounge that serves up good sliders and delicious truffled mac and cheese alongside a dynamic bar scene and some stellar people-watching.

Dog Delights

Up for a double dog dare or merely a hot dog fanatic? Stop by **Gold Coast Dogs** for one or several of its delicious char dogs. These are made even better and more decadent when topped with creamy cheddar cheese. Speaking of crowning hot dogs, famed **Downtown Dogs** carries an equally savory spectrum of traditional varieties. Regulars, tourists, and others gather here for char-grilled dogs, sumptuous street eats, and juicy hamburgers galore. Need to calm and come down from your hot dog high? Duck into **TeaGschwendner**, a lovely boutique where you can lose yourself in their world of exotic teas. And if you don't feel like steeping it on your own, snag a seat at **Argo Tea**. From hot tea drinks topped with whipped cream, to flavorful iced drinks, it's like Starbucks without the coffee.

Heaven on Earth

The idiom says that God is in the details, and this is most definitely apparent at the famed **Goddess & Grocer**, a neighborhood gourmet store where you can stock up on all foods like soups, salads, chillis, gourmet cupcakes, and other tantalizing desserts, just like Mom would make. Homemade but in an haute, upscale kind of way, this haven is all about cupcakes, cheeses, and chocolates galore. To add to this indulgence, they also cater, so you can pretend like you made those divine and delicate hors d'oevres at the baby's christening all on your own. For some quintessential old-world elegance, don your Grandmother's precious pearls for afternoon tea at the refined and resplendent **Drake's Palm Court**. Sip (not slurp!) your tea while listening to the gentle strains of a harp. Also on the agenda is a tasty selection of sandwiches, pastries, fruit breads, and scones. If it's good enough for Queen Elizabeth, it will certainly do.

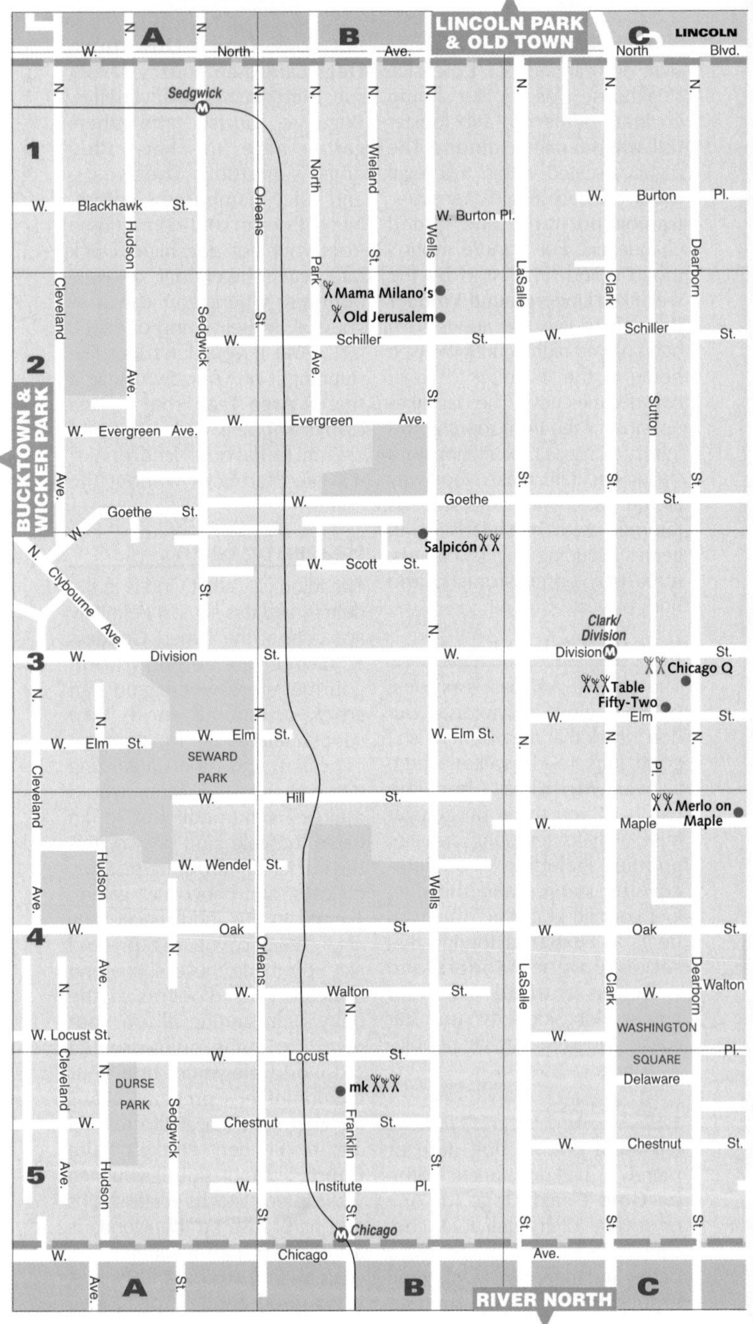
LINCOLN PARK & OLD TOWN
BUCKTOWN & WICKER PARK
RIVER NORTH
Sedgwick
Clark/ Division
Chicago
Mama Milano's
Old Jerusalem
Salpicón
Chicago Q
Table Fifty-Two
Merlo on Maple
mk
SEWARD PARK
DURSE PARK
WASHINGTON SQUARE
W. North Ave.
LINCOLN North Blvd.
W. Blackhawk St.
W. Burton Pl.
W. Schiller St.
W. Evergreen Ave.
W. Goethe St.
W. Scott St.
N. Clybourne Ave.
W. Division St.
W. Elm St.
W. Hill St.
W. Maple
W. Wendel St.
W. Oak St.
W. Walton St.
W. Walton Pl.
W. Locust St.
W. Delaware Pl.
W. Chestnut St.
W. Institute Pl.
W. Chicago Ave.
N. Cleveland Ave.
N. Hudson Ave.
N. Sedgwick St.
N. Orleans St.
N. North Park Ave.
N. Wieland St.
N. Wells St.
N. Franklin St.
N. LaSalle St.
N. Clark St.
N. Sutton Pl.
N. Dearborn St.
A
B
C
1
2
3
4
5

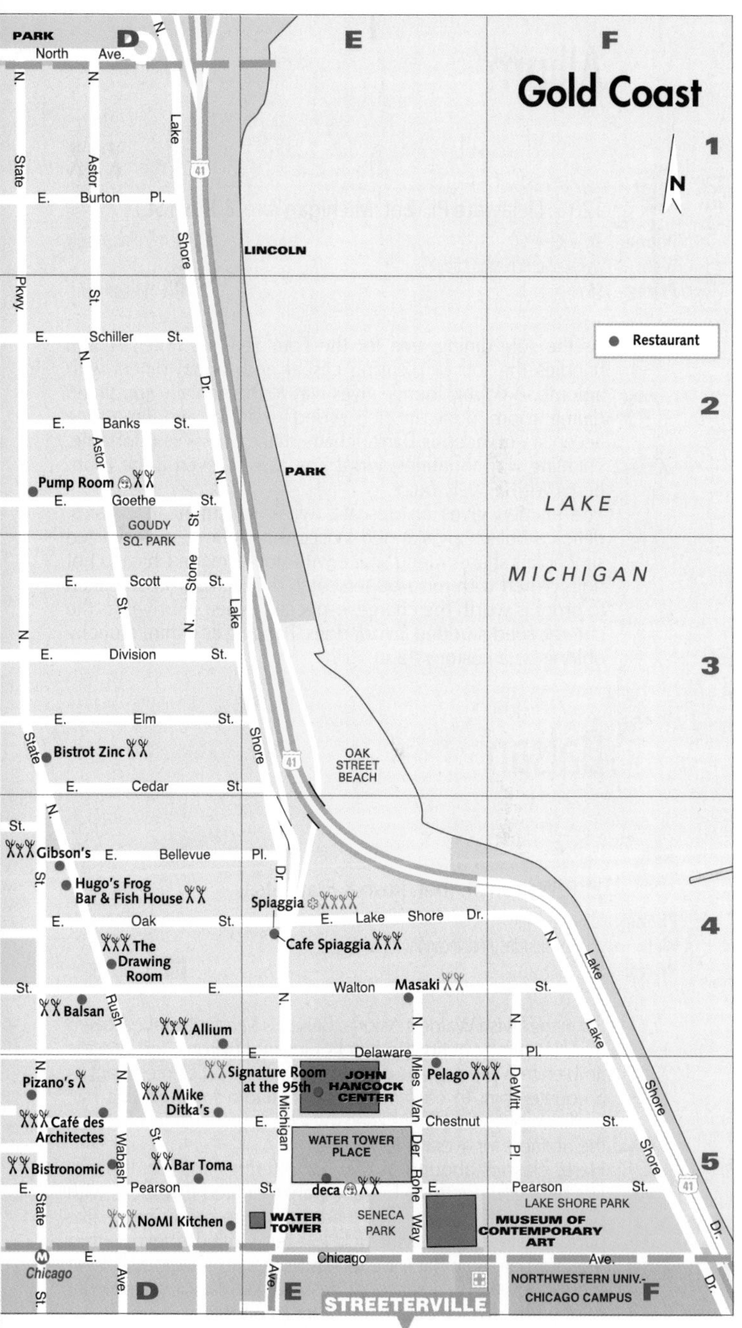
Gold Coast
Restaurant
LAKE
MICHIGAN
PARK
LINCOLN
PARK
North Ave.
E. Burton Pl.
E. Schiller St.
E. Banks St.
E. Goethe St.
E. Scott St.
E. Division St.
E. Elm St.
E. Cedar St.
E. Bellevue Pl.
E. Oak St.
E. Lake Shore Dr.
E. Walton St.
E. Delaware Pl.
E. Chestnut St.
E. Pearson St.
E. Chicago Ave.
N. State Pkwy.
N. Astor St.
N. Lake Shore Dr.
N. Stone St.
N. State St.
N. Rush St.
N. Wabash Ave.
N. Michigan Ave.
N. Mies Van Der Rohe Way
N. DeWitt Pl.
GOUDY SQ. PARK
OAK STREET BEACH
Pump Room
Bistrot Zinc
Gibson's
Hugo's Frog Bar & Fish House
Spiaggia
Cafe Spiaggia
The Drawing Room
Masaki
Balsan
Allium
Pizano's
Signature Room at the 95th
JOHN HANCOCK CENTER
Pelago
Mike Ditka's
Café des Architectes
WATER TOWER PLACE
Bistronomic
Bar Toma
deca
NoMI Kitchen
WATER TOWER
SENECA PARK
LAKE SHORE PARK
MUSEUM OF CONTEMPORARY ART
Chicago
NORTHWESTERN UNIV.-CHICAGO CAMPUS
STREETERVILLE
D E F
1 2 3 4 5
41

Allium

Contemporary XXX

D4

120 E. Delaware Pl. (bet. Michigan Ave. & Rush St.)

Phone: 312-799-4900 Lunch & dinner daily
Web: www.alliumchicago.com
Prices: $$  Chicago (Red)

As the sole dining area for the Four Seasons hotel, Allium handles the job of pleasing casual and formal diners with aplomb. A deluxe lounge gives way to this genially appointed dining room done in rich wood, marble, and limestone accents; curvaceous barrel chairs make guests comfortable. Trickling wall fountains add a Zen aspect, even if the room hums with a lively buzz.

The kitchen gives an upscale tweak to American classics: delicate but crispy skinned Wisconsin walleye with roasted sunchokes shares menu space with house-made Chicago hot dogs paired with miso-butterscotch milkshakes. Bread baked to order is worth the charge, especially when it arrives as the cheesy, seed-studded *lavosh* does, hanging as a thin, crunchy oblong on a custom stand.

Balsan

American XX

D4

11 E. Walton St. (bet. Rush & State Sts.)

Phone: 312-646-1400 Lunch & dinner daily
Web: www.waldorfastoriachicagohotel.com
Prices: $$  Chicago (Red)

Set in the lavish Waldorf Astoria, Balsan is a casually upbeat bistro that beautifully befits the hotel's elegant environs and upscale ambience. Warm, masculine leather and wood elements act as a counterpoint to cool marble floors and a long, inviting bar, while simple wood tables keep the vibe approachable, offsetting the ritziness for average Joes.

Here, classics abound in raw bar offerings and small plates like bass *goujonettes*—buttery, panko-coated fish sticks with parsley rémoulade—which lead the way to heftier meals like pappardelle swirled with rich lobster. Grilled ribeye with a melting pat of spinach butter and sea salt-flecked hand-cut fries; followed by a seasonal dessert like blackberry-polenta cake with corn ice cream are other standouts.

Bar Toma

Italian XX

110 E. Pearson St. (bet. Michigan Ave. & Rush St.)

Phone: 312-266-3110 — Lunch & dinner daily
Web: www.bartomachicago.com
Prices: $$ — Chicago (Red)

Bar Toma is an ambitious ode to Italian food as seen through the filter of hearty (read: heavy) Midwestern cooking. Enter this cool and urban respite featuring stations throughout the food hall-style room that showcase a revolving menu of *pizze, gelati,* Roman *fritti,* and more. But, it's best just to take a seat amid the bustling confusion and let the staff come to you. Family-style is the way to tackle their carte, especially when confronted with specials on tableside blackboards. Food arrives in stages, so be prepared to share the likes of mild Tuscan chicken liver spread; or the signature pizza Mantuano with *guanciale* and rapini. For a quick pit stop among the Mag Mile gawkers, breeze by for a glass off the smartly chosen wine list.

Bistronomic

French XX

840 N. Wabash Ave. (bet. Chestnut & Pearson Sts.)

Phone: 312-944-8400 — Lunch Wed – Sun
Web: www.bistronomic.net — Dinner nightly
Prices: $$ — Chicago (Red)

Red awnings, intoxicating smells, and the clink of glassware beckon diners to this casual, lived-in bistro. The patio gets packed when the weather cooperates. Revelry at the tiny bar often spills out into the buzzing dining room lined with charcoal banquettes, crown mouldings, and oxblood-red walls. No one gets tired of returning here.

Chef Martial Noguier serves French-American bistro food that's simply detailed and layered with flavor. Start by nibbling on a charcuterie plate or cheese flight before tucking into plump poached salmon paired with chunky mushrooms in a deep brown lobster emulsion, with roasted garlic purée. Brûléed meringue kisses and caramelized almonds blanket homemade vanilla bean ice cream for a fun take on Baked Alaska.

Bistrot Zinc

French XX

D3

1131 N. State St. (bet. Elm & Cedar Sts.)

Phone: 312-337-1131 Lunch & dinner daily
Web: www.bistrotzinc.com
Prices: $$ Clark/Division

If you couldn't tell from the bright red exterior and hand-painted windows, Bistrot Zinc is indeed a classic dressed in mosaic-tiled floors, lemon-tinted walls hung with mirrors, woven rattan chairs, and yes, that curvaceous zinc bar. Suits, locals, and Gold Coast power shoppers populate the tables from lunch through dinner, as white-aproned waiters happily uncork bottles of *rouge et blanc*.

Don't look for modern surprises on the menu; contentment here is attained through uncomplicated but expertly prepared French dishes from frites to frisée. Whole trout, pan-fried until golden and napped with butter sauce, hits all the right notes; while daily standards like croque monsieur or French onion soup are enhanced by more ambitious monthly specials.

Café des Architectes

Contemporary XXX

D5

20 E. Chestnut St. (at Wabash Ave.)

Phone: 312-324-4063 Lunch & dinner daily
Web: www.cafedesarchitectes.com
Prices: $$$ Chicago (Red)

With the word "architectes" in the name, you'd expect this mod spot in the Sofitel Water Tower to be nothing short of visually stunning, and it doesn't disappoint. Oversized striated light fixtures hang in between floor-to-ceiling windows punctuated by the building's striking steel beams; black-and-white photographs of Chicago landmarks throughout the space drive the point home.

Contemporary French-accented dishes are as invigorating as the surroundings with sparks of creativity, like a column of glossy red beef tartare, inventively augmented by cold whipped horseradish crème fraîche, a crispy parsnip *"chicharrón,"* and chervil plouche. Similarly, a green olive- and white anchovy-tapenade served with the bread basket makes for a pleasant surprise.

Cafe Spiaggia

980 N. Michigan Ave. (at Oak St.)

Phone: 312-280-2750 — Lunch & dinner daily
Web: www.spiaggiarestaurant.com/cafe
Prices: $$ — Chicago (Red)

A slightly more easygoing offshoot of perennial favorite Spiaggia, this chic café satisfies those seeking a taste of the Tony Mantuano experience without the commitment and price tag of the more formal destination next door. Natural light from deep-set windows floods the space, illuminating faux frescoes, should the slice of shimmering Lake Michigan not be stimulating enough.

As with its haute sibling, top-notch ingredients get their time to shine on the café's Italian-influenced menu. Vibrant salads like kale tossed with pomegranate seeds and apple-balsamic- and brown butter-vinaigrette steal the show; while Skuna Bay salmon tartare is perked up with Calabrian chilies and dilled ricotta. Classic desserts like cannoli or tiramisu are worth every bite.

Chicago Q

Barbecue 

C3

1160 N. Dearborn St. (bet. Division & Elm Sts.)

Phone: 312-642-1160 — Lunch & dinner daily
Web: www.chicagoqrestaurant.com
Prices: $$ — Clark/Division

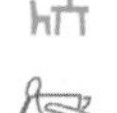

Banish all pre-conceived notions of rustic, honky-tonk shacks and smoky barbecue joints before you lay eyes on Chicago Q. Dolled-up in gleaming white subway tiles, glass enclosures, and shiny dark wood accents, this elegant bi-level row house nestled between buildings fits the prosperous atmosphere of nearby Rush Street to a T.

Chef/pitmaster Lee Ann Whippen, also the reigning queen of Chicago's barbecue scene, turns out lusciously tender Kobe brisket, pulled pork, and chicken that begs for a Bourbon flight or maybe a Q martini with smoked olives. Pony up for the competition-style ribs, rubbed with a secret concoction that puts other 'cue to shame. Watermelon salad with grapes and balsamic glaze is a fittingly refined side for such superb slabs.

deca 

Contemporary XX

E5

160 E. Pearson St. (at Water Tower Place)

Phone: 312-573-5160 — Lunch & dinner daily
Web: www.decarestaurant.com
Prices: $$ — Chicago (Red)

With deca, The Ritz-Carlton Chicago declares that luxury need not be stuffy. The hotel's product-driven brasserie is actually a come-as-you-are respite, sequestered off the 12th floor lobby. It's situated amid rich carpeting and grand artwork further beautified by a soaring skylight and the soothing sounds of a gently gurgling fountain.

This all-day café features a concise lunch offering that revolves around the bento box-inspired DLT (deca lunch trio) such as French onion soup, grilled tuna sandwich with avocado and black olive tapenade, and a slice of cake. Other treats include *plats du jour* like Wednesday night's rabbit *moutard*, or entrées such as plump seared scallops over corn bread gnocchi, sautéed with wild mushrooms and peppery watercress.

The Drawing Room

Contemporary XXX

D4

937 N. Rush St. (bet. Oak & Walton Sts.)

Phone: 312-266-2694 — Dinner Tue – Sat
Web: www.thedrchicago.com
Prices: $$$ — Clark/Division

Slide past the doorman guarding the narrow entry to this subterranean lair, only to discover new heights of culinary cocktail appreciation. Teardrop chandeliers cast a soft glow onto the pretty young things. Find them sitting atop low-slung velvet chairs and leaning across blonde wood tables, sipping from coupes and sharing punchbowls. A gadget-laden rack behind the bar is put to constant use by the mixologists.

Though drinks are the draw, a concise menu offers nibbles à la carte or a three-course prix-fixe selection that's just as carefully crafted. Hamachi crudo is drizzled with Arbequina olive oil; juicy *poussin* rests on fregola dressed with Wisconsin cheddar mornay; and plump scallops wrapped in ham play well with a pickled pineapple garnish.

Gibson's

Steakhouse XXX

D4

1028 N. Rush St. (at Bellevue Pl.)

Phone: 312-266-8999 — Lunch & dinner daily
Web: www.gibsonssteakhouse.com
Prices: $$$ — Clark/Division

Gibson's is the George Clooney of Chicago steakhouses: a little grey at the temples (it's been around since 1975), but still undeniably appealing to ladies and gents alike. Its sidewalk and atrium seating provide prime people-watching for the attractive locals gathered here, while a sultry, wood-paneled interior exudes timeless masculinity where white-jacketed waiters recite nightly specials.

The menu doesn't need to deviate from the classics—thick and juicy bone-in steaks charred expertly to medium-rare get a punch from creamy horseradish sauce; while raw bar grub like Alaskan king crab cocktail or lobster bisque are the real deal, served simply but flavorfully letting the seafood shine. Splurge on the valet to make your reservation on time.

Hugo's Frog Bar & Fish House

American XX

D4

1024 N. Rush St. (bet. Bellevue Pl. & Oak St.)

Phone: 312-640-0999 — Lunch & dinner daily
Web: www.hugosfrogbar.com
Prices: $$ — Clark/Division

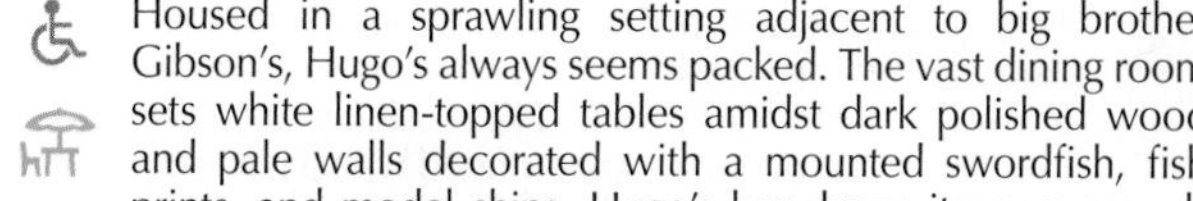

Housed in a sprawling setting adjacent to big brother Gibson's, Hugo's always seems packed. The vast dining room sets white linen-topped tables amidst dark polished wood and pale walls decorated with a mounted swordfish, fish prints, and model ships. Hugo's bar draws its own crowds with abundant counter seating.

The menu focuses on a selection of fish preparations as well as steaks and chops. These are supplemented by stone crab claws, oysters, crab cakes, chowders, and sautéed frog's legs. Speaking of frog's legs, the restaurant takes its name from the nickname of owner Hugo Ralli's grandfather, General Bruce Hay of Her Majesty's Imperial Forces.

Bring a football team to share a slice of the Muddy Bottom Pie, a decadent (and enormous) ice cream cake.

Mama Milano's

1419 N. Wells St. (bet. North Ave. & Schiller St.)

Phone: 312-787-3710 — Dinner Wed – Sun
Web: www.mamamilano.com
Prices: $$ — Sedgwick

Though the owners are great-grandsons of one of Chicago's early restaurateurs, Mama Milano's is a newcomer to Old Town. Outside, it feels like a Venetian hideaway—easy to miss and tucked off a stone-tiled courtyard. The smartly decorated interior offers zebra-print banquettes, vintage posters, and exposed bricks that lend a boutique feel to the casual but stylish pizza bar.

Neapolitan-like pizzas are wafer-thin with crisp, chewy crusts that hold up to the weight of tangy tomato sauce and hearty toppings like sausage, pancetta, ricotta, and eggs. Salads and sandwiches round out the menu, but a must for every table is an order of the family's signature spinach bread—an oozing, caramelized, and stromboli-esque combo of mozzarella, Romano, and spinach.

Masaki

Japanese

E4

990 N. Mies Van Der Rohe Way (at Walton St.)

Phone: 312-280-9100 — Lunch Mon – Fri
Web: www.masakichicago.com — Dinner nightly
Prices: $$$ — Chicago (Red)

Though connected to the Hilton Suites hotel, this intimate Asian jewel box stands on its own as an alluring Zen retreat from the Magnificent Mile. High ceilings add loftiness to this diminutive dining room, outfitted with a gleaming marble sushi counter, warm wood inlays, and rich purple accents.

Chef Jinwoo Han beautifully composes Japanese creations with pan-Asian influences for à la carte ordering, lunch prix-fixe, or nightly tasting menus. Colorful and dramatic dishes that showcase fresh ingredients have included Wagyu tartare with quail egg yolk and mushroom-miso rice; one-bite nigiri and sashimi with inventive garnishes like pickled ramps and beets; or seared scallops over green tea soba.

A broad sake selection offers plentiful pairing options.

Merlo on Maple

C4

Italian XX

16 W. Maple St. (bet. Dearborn & State Sts.)

Phone: 312-335-8200 Dinner nightly
Web: www.merlochicago.com
Prices: $$$ Clark/Division

This *ristorante* houses many floors, but no matter where you sit, the multi-level beauty boasts Victorian touches (hand-carved banisters and leather banquettes), and an informed waitstaff, who deliver the tastes of Emilia-Romagna. Of course, if you're here on a date, make sure to carve out a corner on their lower level, which—albeit a few feet below—is the most romantic space.

Red sauce isn't exactly their signature, but the amiable kitchen is happy to please a lady. So if you crave the typical tomato sauce, order away. The homemade pastas are lovely, but dishes like *stricchetti verdi* tossed with rabbit ragù; or the *imprigionata alla Petroniana* use top-notch ingredients from Italy's culinary epicenter and are definitely their more unique items.

Mike Ditka's

American 

100 E. Chestnut St. (at Rush St.)

Phone: 312-587-8989 Lunch & dinner daily
Web: www.mikeditkaschicago.com
Prices: $$ Chicago (Red)

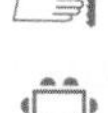

Chicago sports legends have a way of becoming restaurateurs at some point, and former Bears coach Mike Ditka is no exception. However, what is an exception is that locals come here not just because of his 1985 Super Bowl win, but because the food is actually quite good (though lighter appetites might be encouraged to man up). Come very hungry and start with Coach's pot roast nachos. Then, move on to the insurmountable meatloaf stack—layered with delicious jalapeño corn bread, meatloaf, creamy mashed potatoes, and fried onion straws. Doggy bags are de rigueur here, but try to save room for some banana cream pie.

The space is masculine, comfortable, and lined with sports memorabilia—souvenirs are available for purchase on your way out.

mk

American

B5

868 N. Franklin St. (bet. Chestnut & Locust Sts.)

Phone: 312-482-9179 — Dinner nightly
Web: www.mkchicago.com
Prices: $$$ — Chicago (Brown)

The larger than life "mk" emblazoned on the side of the former paint factory remains, but after 15 years on the western edge of River North, Chef Michael Kornick's eponymous flagship is celebrating with a face-lift. Rich, warm browns replace mustard tones within this lofty, skylit space, still a favorite for big nights and romantic evenings.

Fear not: mk's signature pommes frites with truffle cream have stuck around, but the new 40-seat bar features a revived lineup of bites as well as a hearty menu of mains like pan-roasted duck breast with anise-scented cherries and grilled Mission figs. Seasonal desserts such as the strawberry shorty are playfully named but gracefully constructed, pairing a lemon biscuit with pine nuts and white balsamic ice cream.

NoMI Kitchen

American

D5

800 N. Michigan Ave. (entrance on Chicago Ave.)

Phone: 312-239-4030 — Lunch & dinner daily
Web: www.nomirestaurant.com
Prices: $$$ — Chicago (Red)

Soak up the sun and skyline from the seventh floor of Michigan Avenue's Park Hyatt where spiraling windows offer views of the historic Water Tower and sparkling lake beyond. NoMi Kitchen's set boasts deep shades of leather and wood harmonized by white marble and polished chrome; attentive service amplifies the appealing aura.

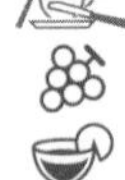

From an open kitchen, Chef Ryan LaRoche prepares seasonally skewed preparations bolstered by raw bar items. Local farms have been enlisted to provide an array of product for the highly enjoyable cooking that has focused upon the likes of artichoke purée studded by fried chickpeas and drizzles of truffle oil; or crisp-skinned, pan-roasted salmon resting atop toasted farro, sweet green peas, and sautéed maitake mushrooms.

Old Jerusalem

Middle Eastern 

B2

1411 N. Wells St. (bet. North Ave. & Schiller St.)

Phone: 312-944-0459 Lunch & dinner daily
Web: www.oldjerusalemchicago.com
Prices: ©© Sedgwick

Set on a charming and centrally located stretch of Old Town, this family-run Middle Eastern favorite has been eagerly accommodating its happy customers since 1976.

The menu focuses on Lebanese-style classics, such as tabbouleh with cracked wheat, scallions, and tomatoes, seasoned with lemon, olive oil, and plenty of crisp, green parsley. Hummus arrives rich with tahini, perhaps accompanying the likes of grilled chicken kebabs and traditional flatbreads. Finish with flaky-sweet baklava.

While the décor may not impress, Old Jerusalem manages to make its well-worn looks feel cozy and comfortable for everyone. Very reasonable prices, family-friendly service, and generous portions make this *the* neighborhood go-to spot, whether dining in or taking out.

Pelago

Italian XXX

E5

201 E. Delaware Pl. (at Seneca St.)

Phone: 312-280-0700 Lunch & dinner daily
Web: www.pelagorestaurant.com
Prices: $$$ Chicago (Red)

On those nights when you're dressed to impress but still want to keep things low-key, Pelago is the place to be. Adjacent to Hotel Raffaello's lobby, its inconspicuous entrance leads way to the serene, aquatic-themed, bi-level dining room done up in cream leather chairs and blue glass accents. An engaging mural of abundant food dominates the back wall.

Classical music and table votives set the mood for a menu of contemporary, upscale Italian food, that leans heavily toward pasta and seafood. Layered eggplant, sausage, and mushrooms form a tart garnished by a single fresh bay leaf; tomato *brodetto* spooned over grilled grouper and white polenta batons keep the dish light yet very hearty. Skip the tiramisu in favor of a fine array of imported cheeses.

Pizano's

D5 | Pizza

864 N. State St. (bet. Chestnut St. & Delaware Pl.)

Phone: 312-751-1766 | Lunch & dinner daily
Web: www.pizanoschicago.com
Prices:  | Chicago (Red)

While Chicago may be hailed as home of the deep-dish pizza, the thin-crust pies at Pizano's have justly earned their own devoted following. This refreshing and cozy local spot recalls Italo-American style without feeling like a chain-restaurant cliché; even the waitstaff's genuine warmth is palpable.

Of course, the crowds come for the crust—here it is flaky, buttery, thin (by local standards), and perfectly crisp. As unexpected as it sounds, their pizzas are some of the best in town. And yet, it should be no surprise as pizza has long been the family calling: owner Rudy Malnati's father founded Pizzeria Uno.

The "thinner" offspring at Pizano's sates its growing fan-base from three locations, and even ships to those who are only Chicagoan at heart.

Pump Room

D2 | Contemporary

1301 N. State Pkwy. (at Goethe St.)

Phone: 312-229-6740 | Lunch & dinner daily
Web: www.pumproom.com
Prices: $$ | Clark/Division

Pump Room is the Public hotel's main dining venue. This spacious and sunken room is awash in soothing pale browns and illuminated by planetarium-chic globe lights. Lofty columns, plush carpeting, and one wall covered in rich, floor-to-ceiling drapes impart a sense of grandeur; while grassy green velvet sofa cushions at the bar break up the monochromatic lull.

The menu's seasonal and locally sourced conceit mimics the approach Vongerichten has taken at his New York City hot spot, ABC Kitchen. Here, fresh flavors abound in inventive creations like roasted and paprika-dusted carrots with creamy avocado, pea shoots, and a bright lemon vinaigrette; or house-made tagliatelle studded with charred Brussels sprouts leaves and slicked with pistachio pesto.

Salpicón

Mexican XX

1252 N. Wells St. (bet. Division & Goethe Sts.)

Phone: 312-988-7811 — Lunch Sun
Web: www.salpicon.com — Dinner nightly
Prices: $$ — Clark/Division

Salpicón has serious pedigree but it's certainly not too solemn a place. Under the cerulean awning and past a striking glass façade, color reigns in the form of lime green chairs and Schiaparelli-pink tablecloths played against vibrant paintings on yellow walls. The tequila list is similarly eye-opening, boasting more than 100 choices available neat, over ice, or in a margarita.

As one of Chicago's pioneers of upscale Mexican food, Chef/owner Priscilla Satkoff turns out a sophisticated, dramatically flavored mix of classic techniques in modern presentations. Begin with pleasantly earthy *crêpes de huitlacoche* filled with serranos and a trickle of poblano crème; while a deep-red honey and ancho chile paste glazes smoky, garlicky butterflied quail.

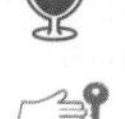

Signature Room at the 95th

American XX

875 N. Michigan Ave. (bet. Chestnut St. & Delaware Ave.)

Phone: 312-787-9596 — Lunch & dinner daily
Web: www.signatureroom.com
Prices: $$$ — Chicago (Red)

On a clear day, there are few views more dramatic than those from the 95th floor of the John Hancock building, so hope for good weather when you make your reservation. Tables abutting the windows offer bird's-eye views, though panoramic art nouveau murals lining much of the room are eye-catching on foggy evenings.

The crowd-pleasing American menu does justice to the classics, though international influences seep in, as with the papaya-cilantro relish siding up to seared tuna. The much-lauded burger doesn't disappoint, especially when loaded with cheese, bacon, and avocado; and colorful lobster Cobb salad is tossed in piquant, creamy tarragon dressing.

Have an aperitif or nightcap one floor up at the Signature Lounge for a true Chicago night out.

Spiaggia ✿

Italian XXXX

E4

980 N. Michigan Ave. (at Oak St.)

Phone: 312-280-2750 — Dinner nightly
Web: www.spiaggiarestaurant.com
Prices: $$$$ — Chicago (Red)

Jeff Kauck

Tony Mantuano's address "One Magnificent Mile" has long taken its standing at the head of Chicago's famed boulevard to heart, bringing serious sophistication to Italian cuisine. With soaring windows overlooking Michigan and Oak including a slice of the lake visible from deep horseshoe banquettes, Spiaggia is clearly upmarket and very special—celebratory couples return repeatedly to appreciate the high-backed intimacy of this hushed, sleek, and romantic space. Gentlemen, don those jackets; you'll need them here.

Under the careful eye of Executive Chef Sarah Grueneberg, imported ingredients and exotic touches rub shoulders with local produce to create a collage of contemporary, Italian-inspired plates. Lavish bites of perfect bay scallops, uni, and osetra caviar garnish smooth sunchoke custard served in a hollowed-out sea urchin shell; just as the essence of the woods is distilled into succulent, wood-roasted roulades of Axis venison loin and sausage, chestnuts, and Barolo Chinato-spiked foie gras sauce.

Oenophiles can take a sippable tour of Italy across the wine list, which also pairs exquisitely with orange blossom honey- and cardamom-panna cotta set in a pink moat of grapefruit sauce.

Table Fifty-Two

Southern XXX

C3

52 W. Elm St. (bet. Clark & Dearborn Sts.)

Phone: 312-573-4000 — Lunch Sun
Web: www.tablefifty-two.com — Dinner nightly
Prices: $$$ — Clark/Division

Chef Art Smith's drawl floats overhead like a warm breeze as he chats up guests inside Table Fifty-Two's cozy white row house, a stately survivor of the Great Chicago Fire. Southern charm permeates every inch of the room, from the pressed copper ceiling to the white sideboards to a wood-burning oven churning out the restaurant's signature biscuits.

The meal might get started with an amuse-bouche of deviled eggs topped with pickled mustard seeds, and if it's a Sunday or Monday, the famous fried chicken will be making an appearance on many plates. Plump fried green tomatoes and thick pork chops are on order, but for a true down-home taste, get a tall wedge of hummingbird cake, fragrant with banana and pineapple and slathered in cream cheese frosting.

The sun is out – let's eat alfresco! Look for [terrace symbol].

Humboldt Park & Logan Square

Albany Park · Irving Park

This alluring collection of vibrant north side neighborhoods is the heart and soul of where locals live and eat. While the area may live a few blocks off the beaten path, it is certainly great for anyone seeking that perfect dessert, ethnic grocer, hidden bodega, or quick falafel. Plus, any trip through these up-and-coming neighborhoods is sure to be divine with those tree-lined streets, quaint architecture, and affordable, trendy shops. First, begin your adventure in Chicago's prized Koreatown, a commercial thoroughfare spanning miles along Lawrence Avenue, from Cicero to California Avenue.

Humboldt Park

The core of the Chicago's Puerto Rican community is found here. If there's any confusion as to exactly where it begins, just look for the Paseo Boricua, the flag-shaped steel gateway demarcating the district along Division Street. These storefronts are as much a celebration of the diaspora as the homeland, with their impressive and enticing selection of traditional foods, hard-to-find ingredients, and authentic, slow-cooked *pernil*.

Logan Square

An eclectic mix of cuisines (from Cuban and Mexican, to Italian) combined with historic buildings and boulevards, attract a crowd of hipsters, working-class locals, artists, and students to this quarter. Within this community, locally minded at-home cooks and foodies flock to the **Dill Pickle Food Co-op** for bulk groceries. Visitors opt for Sunday's **Logan Square Farmer's Market** on Logan Boulevard, with stalls hawking everything from artisanal soaps and raw honey to organic zucchini. Adults and kids have been saving their allowances for a trip to **Margie's Candies**, for its homemade chocolates, toffees, and rich hot fudge sundaes. A melting pot of global foods, Albany Park offers every gastronomic delight at budget-friendly prices. Highlights include **Al Khyam Bakery**, a Middle Eastern grocery with cheeses, olive oils, and flatbreads. For dessert, lull at **Nazareth Sweets** and bite into brittles and pastries like walnut baklava. **Charcoal Delights** is a time-tested, unique burger joint with such treasures as chicken delight, cheesesteak, and hot dogs with "the works" rounding out the menu. You will be in good hands at **Wellfleet** whose dining counter is perfect for patrons in the mood for first-rate fish. This market also supplies restaurants and home cooks with primo seafood and service. The nearby **Independence Park Farmer's Market** is fast-growing and will sate with its produce, plants, and baked goods.

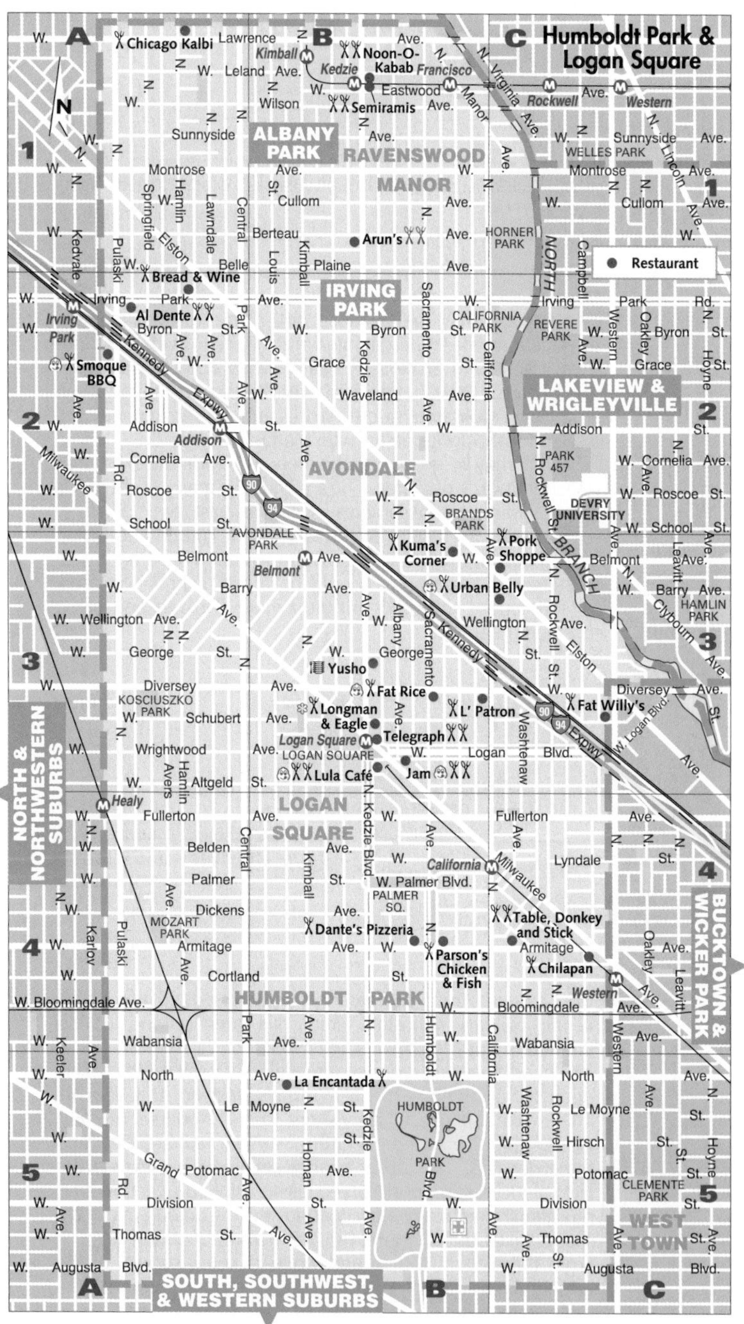
Humboldt Park &
Logan Square
Restaurant
Chicago Kalbi
Noon-O-Kabab
Semiramis
Arun's
Bread & Wine
Al Dente
Smoque BBQ
Kuma's Corner
Pork Shoppe
Urban Belly
Yusho
Fat Rice
Longman & Eagle
L' Patron
Fat Willy's
Telegraph
Lula Café
Jam
Table, Donkey and Stick
Dante's Pizzeria
Parson's Chicken & Fish
Chilapan
La Encantada
ALBANY PARK
RAVENSWOOD MANOR
IRVING PARK
AVONDALE
LOGAN SQUARE
HUMBOLDT PARK
LAKEVIEW & WRIGLEYVILLE
WEST TOWN
NORTH & NORTHWESTERN SUBURBS
BUCKTOWN & WICKER PARK
SOUTH, SOUTHWEST, & WESTERN SUBURBS
WELLES PARK
HORNER PARK
CALIFORNIA PARK
REVERE PARK
PARK 457
DEVRY UNIVERSITY
BRANDS PARK
AVONDALE PARK
HAMLIN PARK
KOSCIUSZKO PARK
LOGAN SQUARE
PALMER SQ.
MOZART PARK
HUMBOLDT PARK
CLEMENTE PARK
Kimball
Kedzie
Francisco
Rockwell
Western
Irving Park
Addison
Belmont
Logan Square
Healy
California
Kennedy Expwy
NORTH BRANCH
W. Lawrence Ave.
W. Leland Ave.
W. Wilson Ave.
W. Eastwood Ave.
W. Sunnyside Ave.
W. Montrose Ave.
W. Cullom Ave.
W. Berteau Ave.
W. Belle Plaine Ave.
W. Irving Park Rd.
W. Byron St.
W. Grace St.
W. Waveland Ave.
W. Addison St.
W. Cornelia Ave.
W. Roscoe St.
W. School St.
W. Belmont Ave.
W. Barry Ave.
W. Wellington Ave.
W. George St.
W. Diversey Ave.
W. Schubert Ave.
W. Wrightwood Ave.
W. Logan Blvd.
W. Altgeld St.
W. Fullerton Ave.
W. Belden Ave.
W. Lyndale St.
W. Palmer Blvd.
W. Dickens Ave.
W. Armitage Ave.
W. Cortland St.
W. Bloomingdale Ave.
W. Wabansia Ave.
W. North Ave.
W. Le Moyne St.
W. Hirsch St.
W. Potomac Ave.
W. Division St.
W. Thomas St.
W. Augusta Blvd.
N. Milwaukee Ave.
N. Elston Ave.
N. Lincoln Ave.
N. Clybourn Ave.
W. Grand Ave.
N. Pulaski Rd.
N. Kedzie Blvd.
N. Humboldt Blvd.
N. California Ave.
N. Western Ave.
A
B
C
1
2
3
4
5
N

Al Dente

Contemporary XX

A2

3939 W. Irving Park Rd. (bet. Pulaski Rd. & Springfield Ave.)

Phone: 773-942-7771 — Dinner Tue – Sun
Web: www.aldentechicago.com
Prices: $$ — North/Clybourn

"Al Verde" may be a more apt name for this spirited destination where the dining room is decked with avocado-rich greens and browns. A wall of leafy cutouts delineates the bar area, and Chef/owner Javier Perez sports a lime green coat as he welcomes guests, works in the open kitchen, and serves tables alongside his wife Maria.

The vibe may be green, but the menu is a veritable exhibition of Chef Perez's pedigree—he's worked in many of the city's finest dining establishments over the past two decades. Latin-American flavors do the tango with French and Italian influences in dishes like *guajillo*-marinated calamari with buttery wild mushrooms adeptly balanced by habanero aïoli; or fork-tender short ribs set atop *mole Poblano* and garlic mashed potatoes.

Arun's

Thai XX

B1

4156 N. Kedzie Ave. (at Berteau Ave.)

Phone: 773-539-1909 — Dinner Tue – Sun
Web: www.arunsthai.com
Prices: $$$$ — Kedzie (Brown)

Chef/owner Arun Sampanthavivat oversees every detail at this culinary mainstay, which has been serving a well-dressed, moneyed crowd since 1985.

No need to bring your reading glasses, since you won't need to fuss with a menu at Arun's. Instead, this upscale Thai restaurant treats its visitors to a 12-course prix-fixe of six appetizers, three entrées (served family-style), and three desserts. The dishes change regularly, but expect the likes of diced spicy pork served inside a grilled sweet pepper; or Panang beef curry with coconut milk. Carved vegetables shaped like butterflies and fish are memorable flourishes.

From the elegant setting and white-jacketed servers to the bountiful feast, it's no wonder people return so often for the princely experience.

Bread & Wine

International 

A2

3732 W. Irving Park Rd. (at Ridgeway Ave.)

Phone: 773-866-5266
Web: www.breadandwinechicago.com
Prices: $$

Lunch Sun
Dinner Tue – Sat
Irving Park (Blue)

What Irving Park lost in a neighborhood Laundromat, it more than makes up for with this modern, casual bistro—boasting its own parking lot, no less. The smooth white bar or kitchen counter is ideal for snacking on fries with malt aïoli, or homemade Cajun cashews. Alternatively, relax at a table crafted from reclaimed wood for more substantial food.

A salad of heirloom tomatoes and spicy watermelon dances with peppery arugula, fresh basil, feta, and a bright lemon vinaigrette; while the humble chicken breast gets a flavor lift from fava beans, fingerling potatoes, tasso ham, and salty Parmesan broth.

A shop near the exit offers take-home treats, including the kitchen's popular nut varieties, with 10 percent discounts for dinner guests.

Chicago Kalbi

Korean 

A1

3752 W. Lawrence Ave. (bet. Hamlin & Lawndale Aves.)

Phone: 773-604-8183
Web: www.chicago-kalbi.com
Prices: $$

Dinner Wed – Mon

Take me out to the ballgame—or the Korean barbecue joint where a ballplayer would feel right at home, as the case may be at this quirky spot. Autographed baseballs line walls and shelves, while photographs and posters of ballplayers paper the walls. But the cluttered décor doesn't deter locals from frequenting this modest yet welcoming space.

Gas grills at each table give off an intoxicatingly savory perfume as patrons take their time searing their choice of well-marbled marinated beef, including the always-popular *bulgogi* or *kalbi*, and cool their mouths with a traditional array of *banchan*. For those who prefer their meat off the grill, a beef tartare takes an interesting twist of flavor when folded with Asian pears, sesame seeds, and sesame oil.

Chilapan

Mexican

C4

2459 W. Armitage Ave. (at Campbell Ave.)

Phone: 773-697-4374 — Dinner nightly
Web: www.tenangrypitbulls.com/chilapan
Prices: $$ — Western (Blue)

A newer and even bluer Chilapan debuted in 2012, but this original neon-painted Mexican spot keeps on trucking under the rumble of the Blue Line. Its snug dining room has fewer seats than an El car, but Chef/owner Jorge Miranda's food brings a crowd that spills out onto the sidewalk tables. Salmon-colored walls and Aztec-inspired art keep the space lively.

The focused menu showcases brightly flavored Mexican dishes, including *taquitos conchita* filled with slow-roasted pork and topped with mango guacamole and *chiltomate*; or *rollito de espinaca* with *Chihuahua* cheese and spinach-stuffed grilled skirt steak. Desserts may include roasted pineapple upside-down cake with piña colada salsa and homemade sour cream ice cream with strawberry sauce.

Dante's Pizzeria

Pizza 

B4

3028 W. Armitage St. (at Whipple St.)

Phone: 773-342-0002 — Lunch & dinner daily
Web: N/A
Prices: $$ — California (Blue)

Brush up on your knowledge of classic literature before heading to Dante's, where the Divine Comedy serves as inspiration. The no-frills décor, basic counter service, and metal soundtrack may seem like purgatory, but stay awhile as the pricey pies are pure paradise.

Each of the 20-inch pizzas—floppy and foldable in the classic New York-style—reference characters from this famous Italian epic. Try the Beatrice with garlic sauce and mushrooms; or the signature Inferno pie with nine rings of toppings like giardiniera, jalapeños, and pepperoni. It would be sinful not to share a starter of deep-fried poblano poppers oozing with cream cheese, bacon, and red onion; or deliciously rich mozzarella sticks. Not ready for such gluttony? Simply order by the slice.

Fat Rice

Macanese 

2957 W. Diversey Ave. (at Sacramento Ave.)

Phone: 773-661-9170 — Dinner Tue – Sat
Web: www.eatfatrice.com
Prices: $$ — Logan Square

Every night, early birds wait under the wooden pergola before Fat Rice opens, hoping to beat the rush at this quirky respite, specializing in the cuisine of Macau. Although the peninsula is currently known as the Las Vegas of China, you won't find a buffet in sight. Instead, the cooking—focused on the region's longstanding Portuguese culinary influences—makes for a seafood-centric adventure.

"Crazy squid" with Thai bird chilies and green garlic in inky black sauce gets a squeeze of chili-dipped lime tableside; and chili clams are a duet of steamed and fried bivalves. Mains like *piri piri* chicken served with a curiously enticing mix of spiced peanuts, grilled potatoes, black olives, and a side of habañero-ghost pepper sauce are for the truly valiant.

Fat Willy's

Barbecue 

2416 W. Schubert St. (at Artesian Ave.)

Phone: 773-782-1800 — Lunch & dinner daily
Web: www.fatwillys.com
Prices: $$

Fat Willy's telegraphs an authentic and messy barbecue experience by luring all with its wafting scent of smoke, hickory, and applewood piles stacked at the entrance. This is only further teased by homemade sauces and paper towel rolls poised atop kraft paper-protected tables. With customers' doodles from the tables plastering the walls, it's a sign everyone comes and leaves happy here.

Crack through the charred surface on baby back and St. Louis-style rib slabs to devour the pink-tinged center, an indication of superior smoking. Brisket might verge on the dry side, but pulled pork sandwiches are juicy, while corn dogs are hand-dipped and fried. Root beer from Milwaukee's Sprecher Brewery adds a little Midwest taste to the bona fide Southern flavor.

Jam

American XX

B3

3057 W. Logan Blvd. (at Albany Ave.)

Phone: 773-292-6011 Lunch daily
Web: www.jamrestaurant.com
Prices: $$  Logan Square

Relocated from its old Ukrainian Village digs, Jam has made its way to Logan Square with more moxie than ever. Formerly a breakfast-and-lunch-only operation, this bohemian lime- and charcoal-accented spot has expanded its kitchen to proffer dinners and prix-fixe menus highlighting produce from the Logan Square farmer's market.
But regulars still return for breakfast favorites that are big on flavor but manageable in size—perhaps German chocolate pancakes, or malted custard French toast that's cooked sous-vide to make sure the malt-spiked vanilla cream infuses every inch of brioche? Savory dishes like *guisado verde* gild the lily by nestling braised beef in tender risotto before topping the pile with fresh corn, tangy tomato *crema*, and a sunny-side up egg.

Kuma's Corner

American X

B3

2900 W. Belmont Ave. (at Francisco Ave.)

Phone: 773-604-8769 Lunch & dinner daily
Web: www.kumascorner.com
Prices: $$

Dig out your old Metallica T-shirt and you'll fit right in at this heavy metal-themed burger joint and dive bar serving locally made beers. It's racy and raucous with head-banging music, so leave Grandma and the kids behind. Forget about any conversation, since Iron Maiden will be pounding in your ears, but in a place with burgers this good, your mouth will be otherwise engaged.
Keeping with the unconventional theme, each burger is named for a heavy metal band from Megadeth to Black Sabbath. Juicy and delicious, these patties are the clear draw, as in the Lair of the Minotaur served on a pretzel roll piled with caramelized onions, pancetta, Brie, and Bourbon-soaked pears. Paired with crisp waffle fries, it's no wonder this plate is such a standout.

La Encantada

Mexican

3437 W. North Ave. (bet. Homan & St. Louis Aves.)

Phone: 773-489-5026 Dinner Tue – Sun
Web: www.laencantadarestaurant.com
Prices: $$

Run by the gracious Enriquez family, this *encantada* (enchanted) spot lives up to its name. Inside, royal blue, golden yellow, and exposed brick walls are hung with bright, gallery-style artwork (much of it is for sale), while contemporary Latin tunes waft through the air, creating a quixotic vibe. Culinary inspiration begins in the family's hometown, Zacatecas, but pulls from all around the country, with seriously delectable results.

Dig into the rich and cheesy *quesadilla de huitlacoche*; or the divine *chile en Nogada*, poblano peppers stuffed with tender ground beef, squash, fruit, and crunchy walnuts, topped with a creamy walnut sauce and pomegranate seeds. Match these delicacies with such decadent sides as chipotle-whipped potatoes.

L' Patron

B3

Mexican

2815 W. Diversey Ave. (bet. California Ave. & Mozart St.)

Phone: 773-252-6335 Lunch & dinner daily
Web: N/A
Prices: $$

It is impossible to miss the fluorescent green-and-orange façade of this diminutive Logan Square space. Not to mention those familiar Mexican staples presented by former Topolobampo cook Raul Gonzalez and his brothers which make it impossible to forget. Locals breeze in and out of this fuss-free room, taking their tacos to-go, while others call dibs on counter seating as it becomes available.

Burritos, like the pineapple- and *guajillo*-marinated *al pastor*, compete for a menu seat along with tacos and tortas, all showcasing tortillas made from scratch. A seasonal carte of salsas and cranberry-studded guacamole beg to be scooped up by warm corn chips; and the quesadilla-style *El Gringo* with carne asada and *Chihuahua* cheese is a specialty not to be missed.

Longman & Eagle ✿

B3

Gastropub

2657 N. Kedzie Ave. (at Schubert Ave.)

Phone: 773-276-7110 Lunch & dinner daily
Web: www.longmanandeagle.com
Prices: $$ Logan Square

Clayton Hauck

The ampersand dangling over the door of this painted-brick corner building is a characteristically restrained way of introducing Longman & Eagle—a hip but relaxed eatery named after Evelyn Longman, the artist who sculpted the eagle statue perched atop the column in nearby Logan Square. Hipsters who swarmed the spot in its early years still populate its screw stools and dowel farmhouse chairs in the rough-and-tumble room, but the attitude has left the building. Some come just to clink glasses and sample the vast selection of whiskey and Bourbon at the bar, while other patrons wait in the dim light of wax-splattered votives for elegantly composed plates.

Loud beats bounce off the exposed brick, perhaps in tune with the menu's riff on gastropub fare as Chef Jared Wentworth takes an haute approach to American cuisine. Carnivores get the pick of the litter with juniper-laced venison sausage and braised lamb shoulder calzones with bacon-tomato jam. A separate insert draws attention to vegetarian eats like agnolotti filled with celeriac ricotta.

Deep-fried apple pie is a savory triumph: crusted with caramelized cheddar, it is also paired with smoked graham cracker ice cream and bacon powder.

Lula Café

American

2537 N. Kedzie Ave. (off Logan Blvd.)

Phone: 773-489-9554 Lunch & dinner Wed – Mon
Web: www.lulacafe.com
Prices: $$ Logan Square

Lacy curtains frame the flannelled hipster crowd inside lively Lula Café, a mod, eclectic Logan Square favorite. Though no one's buttoned up here, a décor theme emerges: gumball machines dispense round pins; art installations tack them to walls; and in lieu of mints, Lula-labeled buttons are a whimsical takeaway.

Though the Cafe's breakfast and brunch garners a cult following, the diverse menu with many vegetarian dishes, keeps the spot busy from dawn till dusk. Squid stuffed with country ham and chestnuts gets acidity and depth from an infusion of tamarind; a crock of tender chickpeas tossed with roasted maitake mushrooms balances richness and texture with crisp fennel; and sesame brittle on a chocolate roulade is an expert blend of savory with sweet.

Noon-O-Kabab

Persian

4661 N. Kedzie Ave. (at Leland Ave.)

Phone: 773-279-9309 Lunch & dinner daily
Web: www.noonokabab.com
Prices: Kedzie (Brown)

The uninitiated may read the name and envisage a fast-food kebab shop, but Noon-O-Kabab is a friendly neighborhood spot that takes their food seriously. The simple décor is nicely accented by walls painted with colorful murals, alcoves adorned with hand-painted tiles, and linen-topped tables conveying an authentic culinary experience.

Shakers of sumac set on each table in lieu of salt and pepper and plates of fresh pita with onion, radish, and herbs set the scene for a traditional Persian feast. Smoky, tender *koubideh* and *joujeh* skewers showcase marinated chicken and sirloin with heaping mounds of saffron-infused rice; while spicy pomegranate chicken wings do Chicago bar food one better. Close with creamy *bastani* crowned with crushed pistachios.

Parson's Chicken & Fish

American

B4

2952 Armitage Ave. (at Humboldt Blvd.)

Phone: 773-384-3333 — Lunch & dinner daily
Web: www.parsonschickenandfish.com
Prices: $$ — California (Blue)

If the cherry-red 1977 El Camino emblazoned with a crossed fish-bone-and-drumstick logo doesn't pique your curiosity, the young, cool kids waiting to stuff their faces with tricked-out junk food makes Parson's impossible to miss. It's no surprise that this throwback chicken shack is the brainchild of the Longman & Eagle team.

Slurp a neon Negroni slushy while waiting for an open booth or communal table and peruse the menu, which draws inspiration from coastal, comfort, soul, and street food. Cold chickpea salad with grilled octopus and *chermoula* or hush puppies with chopped scallion should be a new picnic standard; as should the expertly seasoned, crunchy fried chicken with hot sauces. For sweet? Funnel cake with green peppercorn brittle, of course.

Pork Shoppe

Barbecue

C3

2755 W. Belmont Ave. (bet. California & Washtenaw Aves.)

Phone: 773-961-7654 — Lunch & dinner Tue – Sun
Web: www.porkshoppechicago.com
Prices: — Belmont (Blue)

Step into this den of macho—boasting boutique barbecue—and thank your stars the men are brilliant behind the smokers, as they certainly make for dull decorators. The stoic dining room (imagine wood floors, a rusted communal bar, tables, and chairs) is barely enriched by framed mirrors and relics of old farming equipment.

But, pork is Prada here and shoppers have perfected the routine: place an order, take a number, a wad of brown towels, and sauce (sweet, tangy, and wicked) up! A sammy with smoked pork belly pastrami may steal the show, but window-shop your way through other items like Texas brisket tacos, crunchy and fragrant with onion and cilantro; and oversized chocolate chip cookies. Best with your barbecue is beer, wine, and...Bourbon.

Semiramis

Lebanese XX

B1

4639 N. Kedzie Ave. (bet. Eastwood & Leland Aves.)

Phone: 773-279-8900 — Lunch & dinner daily
Web: www.semiramisrestaurant.com
Prices: $$ — Kedzie (Brown)

BYO

Heed the advice advertised on the staff's T-shirts and "take it easy, Lebaneasy" at the pleasantly casual Semiramis. Set in the heart of Middle Eastern-mobbed Kedzie Ave., this Lebanese café sees a diverse crowd fill their simple tables set atop tiled floors and lit softly through stained glass window shades. A separate counter and lounge caters to the stream of takeout regulars grabbing the popular $10 rotisserie chicken for tonight's dinner.

Fresh, flavorful fixings make classics like tabbouleh, crispy falafel, and flaky baklava shine. *Ful* is a warm fava bean-and-garlic stew tinged with zingy lemon juice and mint; while steak fries dusted with piquant sumac and whipped garlic mousse for dipping are best paired with a chicken shawarma special.

Smoque BBQ

Barbecue X

A2

3800 N. Pulaski Rd. (at Grace St.)

Phone: 773-545-7427 — Lunch & dinner Tue – Sun
Web: www.smoquebbq.com
Prices: $$ — Irving Park (Blue)

At this unassuming barbecue joint set upon a dull corner in Irving Park, the focus is on food and not as much the ambience. This may be a take-a-number counter service, but one forkful of meltingly tender brisket, smoked for 15 hours, and find that you won't need to muse on anything else around.

Beyond brisket, the meats—by the pound, on platters, or in sandwiches—are the main draw. Pulled pork, smoked chicken, saucy-slick ribs, and peppery Texas sausage weigh down platters, accompanied by piles of sides like cider vinegar slaw, crispy fresh-cut fries, or creamy macaroni and cheese. There's only one dessert option and it's peach cobbler. But, place your trust with the geniuses in the kitchen, and it's all one needs to end a meal here.

Table, Donkey and Stick

C4 — Austrian XX

2728 W. Armitage Ave. (bet. California Ave. & North Point St.)

Phone: 773-486-8525 — Lunch & dinner Wed – Mon
Web: www.tabledonkeystick.com
Prices: $$ — California (Blue)

With a name inspired by a Brothers Grimm tale and Alpine-influenced cuisine to match, Table, Donkey and Stick offers an appropriately transporting experience on this residential block of Armitage Avenue. Woodland touches like axes on the walls and a fire pit on the patio (complete with cozy blankets for those cool nights) don't overwhelm the otherwise minimal and modest décor.

Wines from regions surrounding the Alps along with a medley of Austrian and Bavarian beers complement dishes served on rustic earthenware and stone slabs. Thick-cut smoked sturgeon set off with fennel jam, or roasted chicken atop pickled ramps brings together meaty, tart, and smoky flavors; while the *Wanderteller* or "hiker's plate" presents the homemade charcuterie with pride.

Telegraph

B3 — Contemporary XX

2601 N. Milwaukee Ave. (at Logan Blvd.)

Phone: 773-292-9463 — Dinner nightly
Web: www.telegraphwinebar.com
Prices: $$ — Logan Square

Equal parts rustic and modern, this wine bar does actually (ahem) telegraph a distinctly urban-chic vibe that meshes seamlessly with the hip, food-focused Logan Square crowd. It's the kind of place where vintage blown-glass wine jugs are repurposed as light fixtures dangling over the bar, and rough slabs of wood contrast with cushioned banquettes.

The focused wine list features by-the-glass selections from all corners of the globe. The menu abounds with daring choices: think open-faced tartines topped with chèvre and blueberries, or roasted wild mushrooms with a Rioja reduction. Hearty entrées are just as eclectic, from seared venison loin with cranberry demi-glace and pink peppercorns, to the fennel streusel and pepitas accompanying veal sweetbreads.

Urban Belly

Asian

3053 N. California Ave. (bet. Barry Ave. & Nelson St.)

Phone: 773-583-0500 Lunch & dinner Tue – Sun
Web: www.urbanbellychicago.com
Prices: Belmont (Blue)

Chef Bill Kim's fiery Asian cuisine is easily the liveliest thing on this otherwise dreary stretch of California Avenue. Speedy ordering from laminated menus at the counter and even more rapid delivery to your seat at one of four communal tables means you can dig into the fragrant food as quickly as possible.

Duck and *pho*-spiced dumplings perk up ravenous taste buds with cinnamon, star anise, and cardamom. Flavorful bowls of udon with tender shrimp in a sweet chili-lime broth; or rice piled with pork belly and sweet pineapple get even zestier with a few shakes of *nanami togarashi* and Belly Fire sauces placed upon every table. Can't snag a chunky wood stool? Rest easy—even though Urban Belly doesn't take reservations, they definitely do takeout.

Yusho

Japanese

2853 N. Kedzie Ave. (bet. Diversey Pkwy & George St.)

Phone: 773-904-8558 Lunch Sun
Web: www.yusho-chicago.com Dinner Mon – Sat
Prices: $$

Logan Square

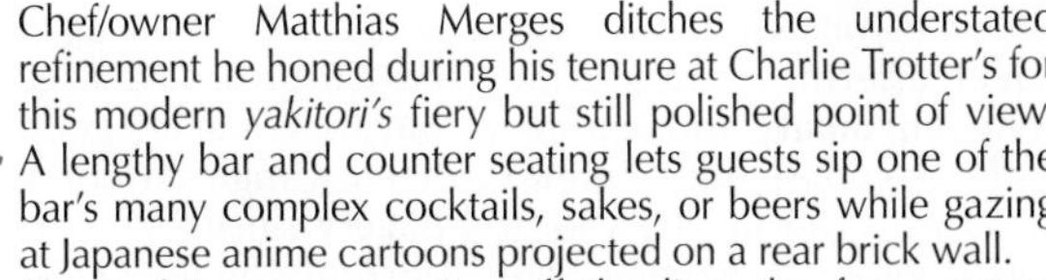

Chef/owner Matthias Merges ditches the understated refinement he honed during his tenure at Charlie Trotter's for this modern *yakitori's* fiery but still polished point of view. A lengthy bar and counter seating lets guests sip one of the bar's many complex cocktails, sakes, or beers while gazing at Japanese anime cartoons projected on a rear brick wall.

Once plates start popping off the line, the focus moves to grilled delicacies like tasty octopus with tiny enoki mushrooms, drizzled with rich egg-yolk vinaigrette; or diced ahi tuna tartare with fried taro strands, radish, and pine nuts. As with most *yakitori* items, the humble chicken gets tasty adornment and high billing, with all parts—wings, drumsticks, livers, skin, and more—offered up for gnawing.

Lakeview & Wrigleyville
Roscoe Village

"Peanuts! Get your peanuts!" When the Cubs are playing, expect to hear the call of salty ball-game snacks through the north side's best-known neighborhood, though locals may actually be stopping into **Nuts on Clark** for some pre-game caramel corn. Lakeview is the umbrella term for the area north of Lincoln Park, including Wrigleyville (named after its iconic ball field) and Roscoe Village.

Enter Eastern Europe

Even when the beloved Cubs finish their season at famed Wrigley Field (as sadly happens each October), American summertime classics continue to shape this area's cuisine, yet for historic reasons. Thanks to their large Eastern European immigrant population, an abundant variety of sausages and wursts can be found in casual eateries and markets located along a number of blocks. Showcasing these juicy and tender specialties is the reputed **Paulina Market**, where expected items like corned beef, lamb, veal, and turkey are offered beside more novel offerings like ground venison, meaty loin chops, and "baseball bat summer sausages." The local Swedish population knows to come here for tried and true favorites such as pickled Christmas hams and cardamom-infused sausages. Paulina's incredible growth and steadfast commitment to quality makes this not just a local institution, but also one of Chicago's biggest and most popular meat markets.

Classic Chicago

Equally important and comparably carnivorous is the Windy City's love for the humble hot dog. Here, chefs, foodies, and touristas stand in lines that may wraparound the block at **Hot Doug's**, the lunch-only purveyor of creatively encased meats in combinations named either to celebrate sultry starlets (like the spicy "Keira Knightly"), or maybe to immortalize their friends. Fridays and Saturdays are particularly crowded, because that's when Doug (the bespeckled gentleman at the counter) serves up duck fat fries. **Byron's Hot Dog Haus** isn't as gourmet, but both their hot dogs and burgers are classic Chicago and very tasty. Note that the location near Wrigley only has outdoor picnic tables and no inside seating.

Baking in Bavaria

Even Chicagoans can't live on hot dogs alone. When they hunger for something else, they have their choice in Lakeview. Bavarian baked goods have been a mainstay of **Dinkel's Bakery** since 1922 (and in its current locale since 1932). Originally opened by a master baker who hailed from Southern Bavaria, the business is still family-run and remains famous for its traditional renditions of strudels, butter kuchen, and, stollen (items can be purchased fresh, but are also available frozen for shipping). Also praiseworthy is Dinkel's Burglaur (a big breakfast sandwich), and their decadent donut selection is addictive and all the rage.

Sweet Indulgences

For a different type of sweet, stopover for the globally-influenced, Chicago-based **Mayana Chocolates** in flavors as accessible as cookies n' cream and raspberry-dark chocolate, to the more exotic Mayan Spice and hazelnut and coriander praline. At her **Bittersweet Pastry Shop**, Chef/owner Judy Contino is well-known for her wedding cakes, pastries, and other delights like breakfast breads, cheesecakes, brownies, and cupcakes. She's been sculpting these sweet treats for almost two decades now. Those seeking a more local, sustainable, and classic American experience should head to **Fritz Pastry** for tasty breakfast faithfuls or bakery offerings like banana bread, cinnamon rolls, hand pies, and macarons. Another laudation (even if they come in sinful buttery and sugary packages) to Chicago's neighborhoods is **City Caramels**. Walk in to this sanctum of sweet to be greeted by simple, lip-smacking treats. Eat your way through Bucktown (think coffee-inspired caramels with chocolate-covered espresso beans); Lincoln Square (toasted hazelnuts anybody?), and Pilsen (Mexican drinking chocolate with ancho chili, cinnamon, and *pepitas*) with their respective caramel and candy cuts. However, Chicagoans who prefer to end their meals with more of a bite should linger at **Pastoral**—hailed as one of the country's top spots for cheese. Their selection of classic and farmstead cheeses as well as fresh breads and olives is a local favorite, as are their weekend classes and tastings.

Fascinating Food Finds

An offbeat yet quirky vibe is part of what makes Lakeview thrive. Testament to this is **The Flower Flat**, which cooks up a comforting breakfast and brunch in an actual flower shop. Meanwhile, **Uncommon Ground** is as much a restaurant serving three meals a day, as it is a coffee shop known for its several musical acts. During the months between June through September, stop by on Friday evenings to tour America's first certified organic rooftop garden before tasting its bounty on your plate downstairs. Aspiring young chefs with big dreams proudly present a wholesome grab-n-go restaurant called **Real Kitchen** that features home-style dishes like baked Amish chicken paired alongside some unique, crusty sandwiches like a salty and heart-warming pork belly BLT.

Roscoe Village

The Guinness Oyster Festival is a street party attracting folks to Roscoe Village each September with diverse music, plenty of beer, and a certain mollusk believed to have aphrodisiac qualities. Homesick New Yorkers and transplants take note: this neighborhood is also home to **Apart Pizza**, Chicago's very own homage to the thin-crust pie, though you might be wise to refrain from admitting how much you enjoyed it. Remember, this is a true find and guilty pleasure in deep-dish land.

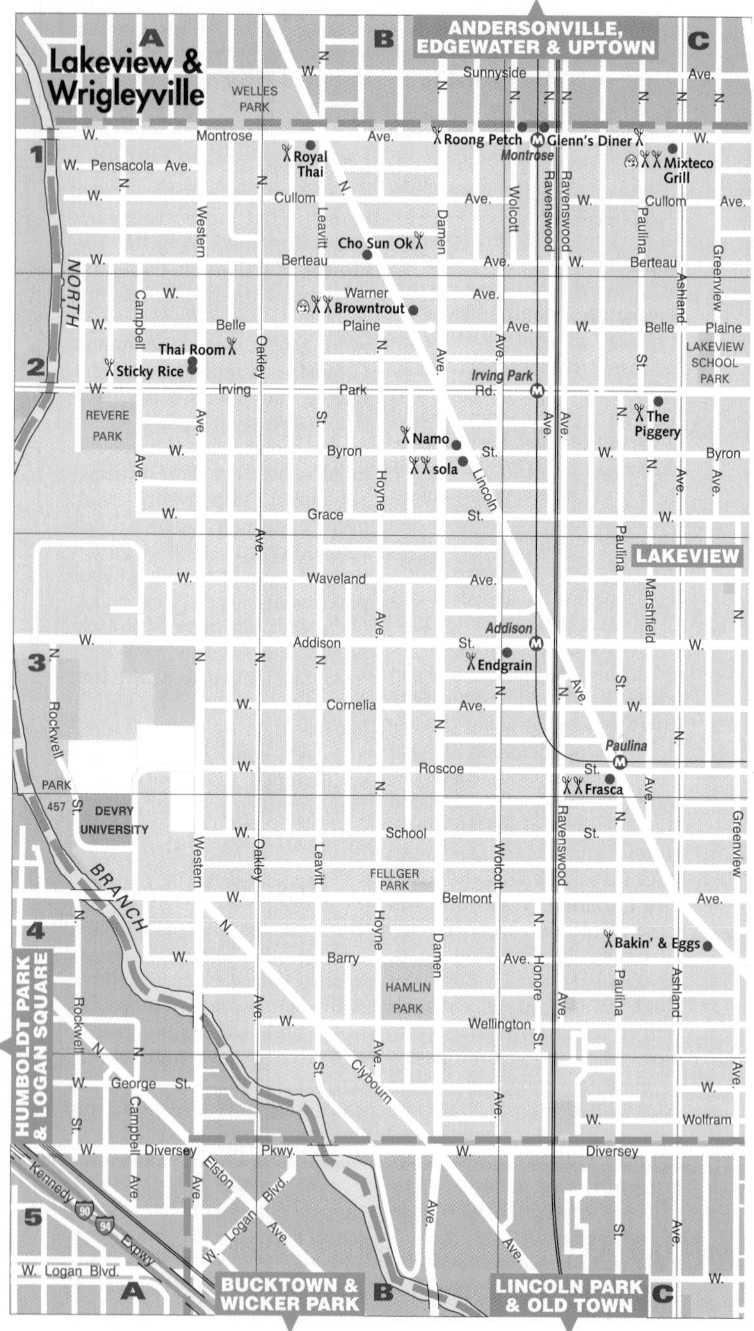

Lakeview & Wrigleyville
ANDERSONVILLE, EDGEWATER & UPTOWN
LAKEVIEW
HUMBOLDT PARK & LOGAN SQUARE
BUCKTOWN & WICKER PARK
LINCOLN PARK & OLD TOWN
A
B
C
1
2
3
4
5
WELLES PARK
REVERE PARK
LAKEVIEW SCHOOL PARK
FELLGER PARK
HAMLIN PARK
DEVRY UNIVERSITY
NORTH BRANCH
Roong Petch
Glenn's Diner
Mixteco Grill
Royal Thai
Cho Sun Ok
Browntrout
Thai Room
Sticky Rice
Namo
sola
The Piggery
Endgrain
Frasca
Bakin' & Eggs
Montrose
Irving Park
Addison
Paulina
W. Sunnyside Ave.
W. Montrose Ave.
W. Pensacola Ave.
W. Cullom Ave.
W. Berteau Ave.
W. Warner Ave.
W. Belle Plaine Ave.
W. Irving Park Rd.
W. Byron St.
W. Grace St.
W. Waveland Ave.
W. Addison St.
W. Cornelia Ave.
W. Roscoe St.
W. School St.
W. Belmont Ave.
W. Barry Ave.
W. Wellington Ave.
W. George St.
W. Wolfram
W. Diversey Pkwy.
W. Logan Blvd.
N. Western Ave.
N. Campbell Ave.
N. Rockwell St.
N. Oakley Ave.
N. Leavitt St.
N. Hoyne Ave.
N. Damen Ave.
N. Wolcott Ave.
N. Ravenswood Ave.
N. Honore St.
N. Paulina St.
N. Marshfield
N. Ashland Ave.
N. Greenview Ave.
N. Lincoln Ave.
N. Clybourn Ave.
N. Elston Ave.
Logan Blvd.
Kennedy Expwy
90
94
457

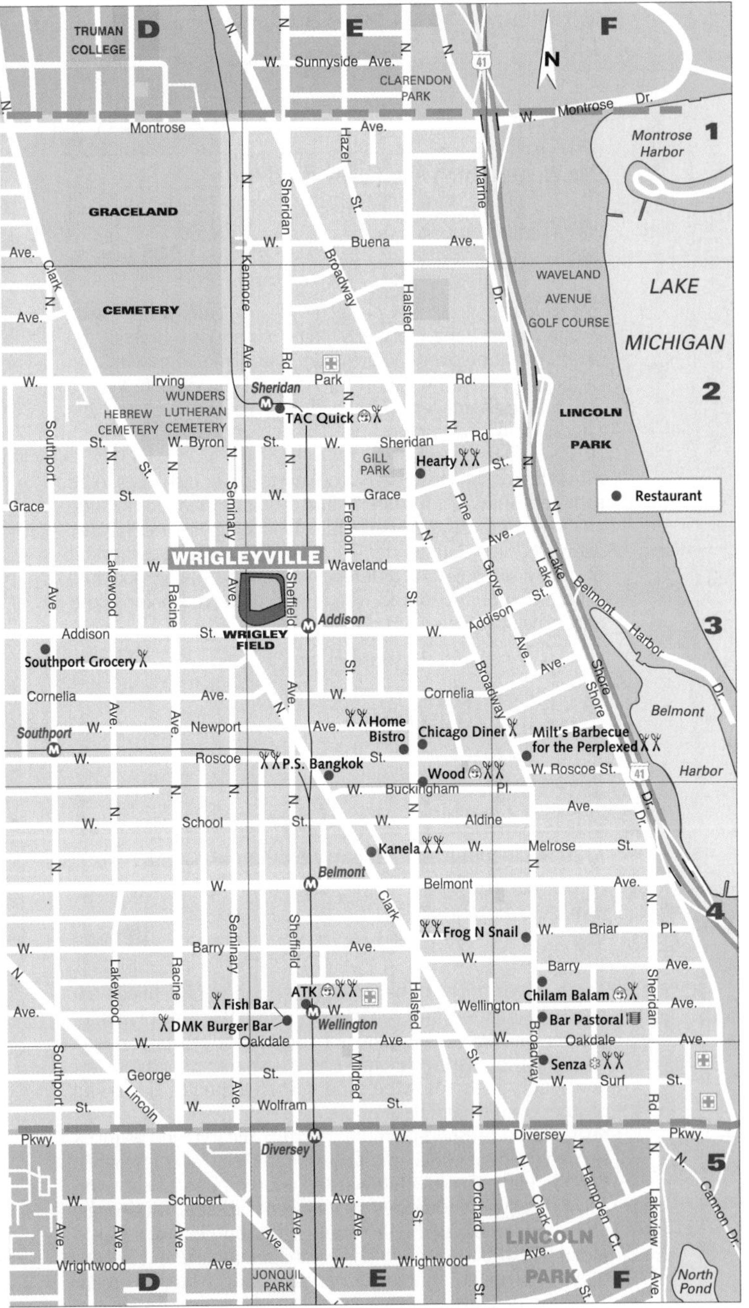

TRUMAN COLLEGE
GRACELAND CEMETERY
HEBREW CEMETERY
WUNDERS LUTHERAN CEMETERY
WRIGLEYVILLE
WRIGLEY FIELD
CLARENDON PARK
GILL PARK
WAVELAND AVENUE GOLF COURSE
LINCOLN PARK
LAKE MICHIGAN
Montrose Harbor
Belmont Harbor
North Pond
JONQUIL PARK
Restaurant
TAC Quick
Hearty
Southport Grocery
Home Bistro
Chicago Diner
Milt's Barbecue for the Perplexed
P.S. Bangkok
Wood
Kanela
Frog N Snail
Chilam Balam
Bar Pastoral
Senza
ATK
Fish Bar
DMK Burger Bar
Sheridan
Addison
Southport
Belmont
Wellington
Diversey
W. Sunnyside Ave.
W. Montrose Ave.
Montrose Dr.
W. Buena Ave.
W. Irving Park Rd.
W. Byron St.
W. Sheridan Rd.
W. Grace St.
W. Waveland Ave.
W. Addison St.
W. Cornelia Ave.
W. Newport Ave.
W. Roscoe St.
W. Buckingham Pl.
W. School St.
W. Aldine Ave.
W. Melrose St.
W. Belmont Ave.
W. Briar Pl.
W. Barry Ave.
W. Wellington Ave.
W. Oakdale Ave.
W. George St.
W. Surf St.
W. Wolfram St.
W. Diversey Pkwy.
W. Schubert Ave.
W. Wrightwood Ave.
N. Clark St.
N. Kenmore Ave.
N. Sheridan Rd.
N. Hazel St.
N. Broadway
N. Halsted St.
N. Marine Dr.
N. Southport Ave.
N. Lakewood Ave.
N. Racine Ave.
N. Seminary Ave.
N. Sheffield Ave.
N. Fremont St.
N. Pine Grove Ave.
N. Lake Shore Dr.
Belmont Harbor Dr.
N. Mildred Ave.
N. Lincoln Ave.
N. Orchard St.
N. Hampden Ct.
N. Lakeview Ave.
N. Cannon Dr.
41
D
E
F
N
1
2
3
4
5

ATK

E4 — Thai

946 W. Wellington Ave. (at Sheffield Ave.)

Phone: 773-549-7821 — Lunch & dinner daily
Web: www.andysthaikitchen.com
Prices: $$ — Wellington

BYO

TAC Quick's loss is Chicago's greater gain: Chef Andy Aroonrasameruang, formerly the mastermind behind the stove at that beloved Wrigleyville Thai place, is now master of the house at ATK—short for Andy's Thai Kitchen. Even if the polished spot weren't beneath the Wellington El stop, the chef's reputation for unusual Thai cuisine would ensure a steady rush of patrons.

Bring friends, because every cooked-to-order dish begs to be sampled. Spicy, sour, crunchy, and aromatic creations include chicken fried *kai tod*, each bite balancing the mahogany-lacquered skin with tender, juicy bone-in meat. Every forkful of crispy *onchoy* is a different adventure, mixing poached shrimp, tempura-battered watercress, sharp red onions, and minced chicken with tart dressing.

Bakin' & Eggs

C4 — American

3120 N. Lincoln Ave. (bet. Barry & Belmont Aves.)

Phone: 773-525-7005 — Lunch daily
Web: www.bakinandeggschicago.com
Prices: $$ — Paulina

Three words (flight of bacon) might be the only enticement needed for a meal at Bakin' & Eggs. But if the likes of maple- pepper- jalapeño- mesquite- or cherry-smoked bacon isn't enough, the easygoing café has a full menu of breakfast and lunch treats for sweet and savory appetites...including pastries from Lovely Bake Shop.

Seated atop brushed-aluminum chairs, bleary-eyed regulars sip Intelligentsia coffee and pots of Rare Tea Cellar tea; while families pile into old whitewashed church pews to chow on such creative sandwiches as chicken sausage, fried eggs, and cheddar drizzled with maple syrup on cinnamon-raisin bread. Fresh-baked muffins like vanilla cupcake and peanut butter brownie; or buttermilk pancakes with whipped cream smile for the kids.

Bar Pastoral

International 

2947 N Broadway (bet. Oakdale & Wellington Aves.)

Phone: 773-472-4781 Dinner nightly
Web: www.barpastoral.com
Prices: $$ Wellington

Wrigleyville wine and cheese store Pastoral offers instant gratification with its next-door bar and café, an intimate spot that lets artisan food lovers linger after they've trolled the shelves of the retail shop. Barrel-vaulted ceilings reminiscent of wine caves and tables assembled with planks from old wine crates remind guests of their purpose for visiting.

Choose from myriad cheeses and carefully selected charcuterie like a Widmer's Cheddar cheese ball with whipped salami and mustard, alongside a quenching list of wines available by the glass and half glass. Or try a composed dish like the simultaneously sweet, spicy, and savory merguez sausage-stuffed apricots with creamy *labne*; followed by duck rillette parfait with sweet potatoes and kale.

Browntrout

American 

4111 N. Lincoln Ave. (bet. Belle Plaine & Warner Aves.)

Phone: 773-472-4111 Lunch Sun
Web: www.browntroutchicago.com Dinner Wed – Sun
Prices: $$ Irving Park (Brown)

The natural beauty of a fish caught by Chef Sean Sanders during his New Zealand honeymoon inspired this pleasant neighborhood spot. Front windows swing wide open in warmer months and bring a breeze to the mocha-hued dining room. The neatly sketched chalkboard displays nightly specials and a list of their favorite (often organic) farmers—sources used in addition to their own rooftop garden.

The menu is broken down into "Smalls" like the whitefish brandade or smoked crappie and "Bigs" like Texas Bandera quail with almond, pineapple, and sage *pistou*. Brunch is a hit with the likes of blueberry beignets and cured salmon with a soft-cooked duck egg.

Kids eat free before 7:00 P.M. and Wednesdays allow you to create your own three-course bargain menu for $35.

Chicago Diner

Vegetarian

E3

3411 N. Halsted St. (at Roscoe St.)

Phone: 773-935-6696 — Lunch & dinner daily
Web: www.veggiediner.com
Prices: ⊜ — Addison (Red)

"Meat free since '83" is the slogan at Chicago Diner, where servers have been slinging creative, healthy fare to grateful vegetarians and vegans for decades. The ambience evokes a neighborhood diner with fire engine-red tables trimmed in chrome, shiny black vinyl chairs, and raised booths. And the food? It looks and tastes the part.

Convincingly crispy seitan buffalo wings cool down the spice factor with vegan ranch dressing; while *flautas* filled with mashed potato, faux cheese, and jalapeños are served with tons of flavorful fixings so that the meat is not missed at all. With a popular brunch menu, numerous gluten-free choices, and a stronghold on the local vegan scene, waits can be long. So, get there early or hope for good Karma—and a seat.

Chilam Balam

Mexican

F4

3023 N. Broadway (bet. Barry & Wellington Aves.)

Phone: 773-296-6901 — Dinner Tue – Sat
Web: www.chilambalamchicago.com
Prices: $$ — Wellington

$ BYO

The world may not have ended as the Mayans predicted, but you can still go out with a bang by ensuring that at least one of your last meals is at Chilam Balam. This clandestine no-reservations spot, named after the book foretelling the doomsday prophecy, quickly gets packed to the brick walls. A stool at the small four-seat bar offers a peek into the semi-open kitchen and a place to sample a lip-smacking virgin sangria while waiting for a table.

Though ostensibly a Mexican restaurant, the dishes are hardly predictable and may unveil crispy frog's legs with sour orange aïoli; or smoky chorizo meatloaf. Duck enchiladas with fried lemon and tomatillo sauce spotlight unorthodox flavor combinations and seasonal ingredients from local farms.

Cho Sun Ok

B1

4200 N. Lincoln Ave. (at Berteau Ave.)

Phone: 773-549-5555 — Lunch & dinner daily
Web: www.chosunokrestaurant.com
Prices: $$ — Irving Park (Brown)

BYO

Service with a smile may not be the motto here, but satisfaction with the food is a near-guarantee at this small but beloved Korean barbecue spot. Booths and tables with central cooktop grills crowd the cozy, wood-paneled room, ensuring that even if the staff is gruff, the atmosphere remains very warm.

Large portions are the norm, making it easy for groups to sample and share the flavorful entrées. Complimentary *banchan* including pickles and salads are copious enough to be a meal in itself, but don't fill up on the snacks. Save room to sample authentic Korean food like thin, tender *chadulgoi* and marinated *bulgogi* for grilling at the table; pork belly tossed with spicy kimchi; or eggy shrimp and octopus pancakes with a scallion-soy dipping sauce.

DMK Burger Bar

American 

E4

2954 N. Sheffield Ave. (at Wellington Ave.)

Phone: 773-360-8686 — Lunch & dinner daily
Web: www.dmkburgerbar.com
Prices: $$ — Wellington

Want a stellar burger? Hit DMK Burger Bar, brainchild of David Morton (of steakhouse fame) and Michael Kornick (mk). Grab a seat at the lengthy bar or cop a squat on an old church pew and admire concrete floors, exposed pale brick, and weathered wood borders contrasting the chocolaty-purple pressed-tin ceilings. What this place lacks in comfort, it makes up for in comfort food.

Follow the locals, and order by number. Perhaps #11: a dolled-up gyro featuring sheep's milk feta, olive tapenade, and *tzatziki* atop a grass-fed lamb patty; or go for #3: beef topped with pastrami, Gruyère, sauerkraut, and rémoulade. Cross over to the bad side and pair your sammie with hand-cut gourmet fries. And for a fine finale, slurp up a cold brew or homemade soda.

Endgrain

American

C3

1851 W. Addison St. (at Wolcott Ave.)

Phone: 773-687-8191 — Dinner Tue – Sun
Web: www.endgrainrestaurant.com
Prices: — Addison (Brown)

For those moments when you just want a bite of breakfast or snack on-the-go, Endgrain is happy to meet your needs. In an appropriately carpentry-themed room featuring a rustic wood counter lined with shop stools and cupboard shelved with stacks of planks, Roscoe Villagers stop here as part of their routine—for a cup of coffee with a blackberry-peppercorn or butterscotch-bacon donut. The treats arrive courtesy of pastry wunderkind and Chef/owner Enoch Simpson.
While the menu leans toward breakfast—with emphasis on baked and fried pastry items—savory dishes also abound. Gravy-smothered biscuits topped with *harissa*-tinged fried eggs and crispy onion rings are very hearty. A pulled pork hand pie balances rich meatiness with tangy soybean sprout kimchi.

Fish Bar

Seafood 

E4

2956 Sheffield Ave. (at Wellington Ave.)

Phone: 773-687-8177 — Lunch & dinner daily
Web: www.fishbarchicago.com
Prices: $$ — Wellington

Sidled up next to its sibling, DMK Burger Bar, this good-time seafood shack does it up right. The atmosphere is light and casual: old metal stools line a long wooden bar, strips of weathered wood panel the walls, and a table is set beneath the polished hull of a canoe.
Daily seafood dishes come raw (tartares, ceviches, and *carpacci*), grilled, and fried; while soups, bisques, and chowders warm the belly. Tasty sandwiches run the gamut from lobster roll and fried oysters to crab cake. Dive into a plate of crispy rock shrimp, lightly breaded and tossed in spicy *sriracha* mayo and fresh *tobiko*. Alternatively, a Ball jar loaded with a ceviche of corvina, pineapple, Serrano chiles, avocado, lime, and cilantro, served with crackers is super refreshing.

Frasca

Italian XX

C3

3358 N. Paulina St. (at Roscoe St.)

Phone: 773-248-5222 — Lunch Sat – Sun
Web: www.frascapizzeria.com — Dinner nightly
Prices: $$ — Paulina

Like stepping into a warm, aromatic wine barrel, Frasca embraces its name (Italian for "branch") with a wraparound wooden bar flanking the wood-fired pizza oven, tables fashioned from tree trunks, planked walls, and forest-motif wallpaper.

As denoted by the brick oven, Frasca's pizzas with fresh, flavorful toppings (perhaps the *rustica* with fennel sausage?) are the heart of the operation, though seasonal pastas and entrées are also available. An "Old World Farmer's Table" menu lets diners check off items from a list of *bruschette*, cheeses with homemade jams, and cured meats for a choose-your-own antipasto adventure. Sharing plates is encouraged, down to the list of wines by the glass that allows for mixing and matching with other menu components.

Frog N Snail

American XX

F4

3124 N. Broadway (bet. Barry Ave. & Briar Pl.)

Phone: 773-661-9166 — Lunch Sat – Sun
Web: www.frognsnail.com — Dinner Tue – Sun
Prices: $$ — Belmont (Brown/Red)

Dale Levitski, chef of Lincoln Park's Sprout, takes a more approachable and less conceptual—though not simplistic—tact at this playful venture that aims to please a variety of picky and eclectic palates. Tactile walls vary from wood and sparkling cork, to Formica and slate. A long wooden bar gives way to a coffee- and crêpe-station, while a mix of low booths, high tables and stools, and SRO counters keep it casual with earthy décor throughout.

Dishes like a hash of rabbit with asparagus, peas, and preserved lemon jus gravitate to kid-friendly inspiration. Whereas familiar items get sassy garnishes like pigs in a blanket wrapped in flaky croissants with piquillo piperade; or *croque madame* with rosemary ham and golden raisin mustard.

Glenn's Diner

American

C1

1820 W. Montrose Ave. (bet. Ravenswood & Wolcott Aves.)

Phone: 773-506-1720 — Lunch & dinner daily
Web: www.glennsdiner.com
Prices: $$ — Montrose (Brown)

A seafaring menu that would sate the likes of Captain Ahab meets an "anytime breakfast" including Cap'n Crunch in one of the area's quirkier spots. With over 16 varieties of fresh fish on any given day and a blackboard menu that makes Egyptian tombs look brief, there is surely something here for everyone.

This is food that strives to please, as in the cargo shrimp cooked in garlicky butter and blanketed in a bubbling veil of provolone and Parmesan cheese with a comparably cheesy toasted French roll. The country-fried Dover sole is a hearty treatment of delicate fish, alongside sautéed zucchini, red onions, and a potato cake.

And if none of this suits you, there are plenty of savory egg dishes and 30 types of cereal—yes, this is a Seinfeld kind of place.

Hearty

American

E2

3819 N. Broadway (bet. Grace St. & Sheridan Rd.)

Phone: 773-868-9866 — Lunch Sun
Web: www.heartyboys.com — Dinner Wed – Sun
Prices: $$ — Sheridan

Like the clever pun in their name, the playful food from Hearty Boys Dan Smith and Steve MacDonagh takes American comfort classics and gives them a spin. The whimsy begins in a mod room that mixes exposed brick with burnt orange and aquamarine accents at tables bedecked with "flower" bouquets made from soda cans.

Lavender-buttermilk fried chicken; *beefaroni* with braised short ribs; and state fair-worthy corndogs that may be filled with rabbit or bacon all transform childhood favorites into adult delicacies. More elegant dishes like a savory Parmesan cheesecake with black walnut shortbread and smoked beef brisket with carrot and fig tzimmes also might appear on a menu that changes quarterly, enhanced by herbs grown in the restaurant's rooftop garden.

Home Bistro

E3 — American XX

3404 N. Halsted St. (at Roscoe St.)

Phone: 773-661-0299 — Dinner Tue – Sun
Web: www.homebistrochicago.com
Prices: $$ — Belmont (Brown/Red)

BYO

Home Bistro dishes up loads of quirk and charm with a healthy dash of humor in the heart of Boystown. Its radiant yellow-hued walls, lined with quotes from Miss Piggy, Beethoven, and other luminaries, inspire contemplative chuckles from first-timers. As if that weren't enough, the friendly servers and cooks always put a smile on the face of locals and regulars alike.

Comfort food by way of France and the Netherlands translates to a roundup of satisfying plates like Amsterdam-style mussels with beer broth and truffle fries; or artichoke and Edam fritters with roasted garlic aïoli. Almond butter and raspberry-jalapeño *gastrique* perk up tender house-smoked chicken thighs; while homemade Belgian chocolate candy bars are almost too good to save for the end.

Kanela

E4 — American XX

3231 N. Clark St. (bet. Belmont Ave. & School St.)

Phone: 773-248-1622 — Lunch daily
Web: www.kanelachicago.com
Prices: ⓢ — Belmont (Brown/Red)

Since Kanela means "cinnamon" in Greek, there should be no hesitation in ordering one of the plump namesake rolls slathered with creamy glaze and whipped cream as soon as you slide into your chair. A mug of freshly brewed Julius Meinl coffee, as richly brown and inviting as the décor in this Lakeview breakfast standby, is the right accompaniment. Whether you prefer sweet or savory on your breakfast plate, Kanela covers all the bases with its local and seasonal menu. Banana split crêpes with strawberries and Nutella, or French toast with lemon crème fraîche are as equally satisfying as duck confit hash with sunny side-up eggs and herb-roasted red potatoes. Fresh juice blends and smoothies cater to those on-the-go, or just counting their calories.

Milt's Barbecue for the Perplexed

F3 — Barbecue XX

3411 N. Broadway (bet. Hawthorne Pl. & Roscoe St.)

Phone: 773-661-6384 — Lunch Sun – Fri
Web: www.miltsbbq.com — Dinner Sun – Thu
Prices: $$ — Addison (Red)

The full name of this kosher spot is Milt's Barbecue for the Perplexed, and those who wander in looking for baby back ribs or pulled pork may initially be confused. But even without these or dairy treats, the catalog of smoky barbecue and Jewish deli delights are bound to appease one and all. Additionally, 100% of their profits go to charity, so get in here and get your craving on.

Tender chopped brisket on a toasted hamburger bun arrives with a trio of barbecue sauces—mustardy Carolina, smoky Memphis, and sweet Kansas City—and fries in a wire fryer basket; while pulled smoked chicken makes its way into the homemade soup. Out of respect for the Sabbath, Milt's closes on Fridays at 2:30.P.M until Saturday at 7:30P.M.—so plan accordingly.

Mixteco Grill

C1 — Mexican XX

1601 W. Montrose Ave. (at Ashland Ave.)

Phone: 773-868-1601 — Dinner Tue – Sun
Web: www.mixtecogrill.com
Prices: $$ — Montrose (Brown)

BYO

Floor-to-ceiling windows that wraparound the corner of Montrose and Ashland are flanked by cheery orange curtains that reflect the fiery and flavorful Mexican cuisine inside Mixteco Grill. A large open kitchen splits the dining room, giving the front room's hungry patrons a first-hand look at the mesquite-fired grill action.

As Mixteco is a region in culinary diverse Oaxaca, Chef Raul Arreola has room to play with a variety of meats, seafood, *moles*, and salsas. Standouts in his menu include *chiles rellenos* stuffed with sweet bay shrimp, scallops, and crab in a creamy chipotle sauce; and crispy *taquitos* with an *escabeche*-spiked sauce that's only for the bold, not the bashful. *Flan de mamey* exudes a sweet potato-like accent to the traditional custard.

Namo

B2 Thai

3900 N Lincoln Ave. (at W Byron St.)

Phone: 773-327-8818 Lunch & dinner daily
Web: www.namothaicuisine.com
Prices: ⊜⊜ Irving Park (Brown)

BYO

Namo tweaks traditional Thai food with deliciously contemporary touches in a mod space that matches its culinary philosophy. Woven baskets and fish traps double as pop art-style ceiling installation and lighting fixtures in this restrained dining room; wooden banquettes and tables in dark tones counterbalance the whitewashed brick.

Authentic flavors come in novel packages throughout the menu. "Sea bags" are actually crispy, deep-fried dumplings filled with spicy scallops, shrimp, and glass noodles; and "mozza crab sticks" replace cream cheese with mozzarella for a chewier version of crab Rangoon. A neatly constructed egg net covers an entire lobster tail in a luxurious take on lobster pad Thai.

Lunch and dinner prix-fixe are a splendid steal.

The Piggery

C2 American

1625 W. Irving Park Rd. (at Marshfield Ave.)

Phone: 773-281-7447 Lunch & dinner daily
Web: www.thepiggerychicago.com
Prices: $$ Irving Park (Brown)

The bacon is back—and the ham, the shoulder, and the rest of the pig too. Newly re-opened after a 2012 fire, this Lakeview sports bar and shrine to all things porcine has returned to its whimsical ways, with kitschy pig paraphernalia sharing shelf and wall space with flat-screens tuned to Cubs and Sox games, naturally.

The menu may be hell for vegans, but it's a pork lover's paradise: cuts from every part of the animal find their way into nearly each dish, from ham-stuffed burgers to the signature bacon-wrapped jalapeño poppers. Gently charred slabs of ribs basted with the Piggery's own heady barbecue sauce are teeth-sinkingly tender. Even salads may give you the meat sweats, with pulled pork or buffalo chicken—and bacon, of course—offered as icings.

P.S. Bangkok

E3 — Thai XX

3345 N. Clark St. (bet. Buckingham Pl. & Roscoe St.)

Phone: 773-871-7777 — Lunch & dinner Tue – Sun
Web: www.psbangkok.com
Prices: $$ — Belmont (Brown/Red)

Carved wood artwork, a faint ring of wind chimes, and engaging service makes even first-time visitors feel like they're being graciously welcomed to a private home instead of ducking into a Thai respite on one of Lakeview's busiest drags. P.S. Bangkok's simple but polished setting sets the tone for the carefully prepared and sumptuous dishes served here. The menu runs the gamut through rolls, dumplings, noodles, and rice dishes. "Dreamy, creamy, crispy crab" lives up to its description as a luxurious take on the ubiquitous crab Rangoon. While other intriguing specialties like red curry with stir-fried corn and tomatoes; *rama* curry with peanuts, coconut, and tamarind; or duck marinated in Chinese spices and served on rice noodles are equally satisfying.

Roong Petch

C1 — Asian 

1828 W. Montrose Ave. (bet. Ravenswood & Wolcott Aves.)

Phone: 773-989-0818 — Lunch & dinner Mon – Sat
Web: www.roongpetch.com
Prices: $$ — Montrose (Brown)

The décor may not have changed since Roong Petch opened its doors over a decade ago, but that's not why Ravenswood regulars have been wearing down the carpet at this Thai standby. Beyond just delivery and takeout, sit-down customers are warmly welcomed by a medley of mellow tunes, even if they're just stopping by for the $5.95 lunch special.

Dishes might take a few extra minutes to arrive on your table, but rest assured each accompaniment is fresh and unique. Double 00 chicken gets its name from the "top-secret" chili sauce that blankets tender cubes of poultry with sweet heat; while cumin, turmeric, and coconut milk penetrate deeply to flavor chicken satay. Noodle staples like spicy basil and pad Thai are sprightly rather than rote.

Royal Thai

Thai

2209 W. Montrose Ave. (bet. Bell Ave. & Leavitt St.)

Phone: 773-509-0007 — Lunch & dinner Wed – Mon
Web: www.royalthaichicago.com
Prices: Western (Brown)

BYO

Stately elephants march down the silk runners on each linen-draped table at this age-old Lakeview Thai spot, adding a regal air to the already-polished dining room. Glossy bamboo floors, dark wood high-backed chairs, and ceiling fans atop light walls hung with mirrors make the space look larger than it is; orange koi add color.

What this minuscule spot lacks in size, it makes up for in big, bold flavors. Be mindful of your spice tolerance, as the kitchen is known to turn up the heat. They're not fooling around so don't plan on kissing anyone after sucking on plump Royal Thai prawns topped with a potent mix of minced fresh garlic, dried red chillies, and cilantro. Ask for a second bowl of rice to sop up the homemade peanut curry in spicy *rama* chicken.

sola

Contemporary

3868 N. Lincoln Ave. (at Byron St.)

Phone: 773-327-3868 — Lunch Sat – Sun
Web: www.sola-restaurant.com — Dinner nightly
Prices: $$ — Irving Park (Brown)

This is a place that feels alive and warm—even before you've started on one of their seasonal cocktails, like The Great Pumpkin. The bar is a nice stop for a solo meal, while high-backed striped banquettes, orange fabric panels, and a boxy motif lend a contemporary feel to the dining area.

The very eclectic, Asian-influenced menu offers a sense of border-crossing and island-hopping adventure. Expect a colorful rendition of wasabi-crusted scallops with plump peas, roasted carrots, ginger-carrot butter, and a dark soy-based sauce. Weekend brunch may offer *huevos benedictos* with chorizo, corn bread, and salsa hollandaise. Tropical desserts might feature juicy circles of warm, braised pineapple with creamy coconut sorbet and macadamia shortbread cookies.

Senza ✿

F5 Contemporary XX

2873 N. Broadway (bet. Oakdale Ave. & Surf St.)

Phone: 773-770-3527 Dinner Tue – Sat
Web: www.senzachicago.com
Prices: $$$ Wellington

Ryan R. Taylor/ Senza

Senza's youthful exuberance is at once endearing and serves as a delightful complement to the stellar work underway here. The staff is cool—don't be surprised if the sommelier rocks a fedora or expeditor calling the orders is dressed in a leather jacket—but they're also genuinely gracious and impressively versed. And talk about talented: Senza's dapper milieu is accoutered with tables crafted by the brigade themselves.

Chef Noah Sandoval has made the rounds among some of Chicago's most esteemed dining rooms, and now pilots this kitchen. When the bread arrives, prepare to be amazed. This warm mini loaf is crusty, moist, and gluten-free. What follows is also completely gluten-free and titillates palates by mingling sweet and savory notes as in plump sea scallops arranged with wilted wild leeks, caramelized onion soubise, and pickled blueberries; tailed by parsnip and apple whirled into a purée and gilded with poached lobster and soy sauce "caviar."

Pan-seared foie gras atop caramel corn crème brûlée may sound like a carnivore's dessert fantasy, but the feast is actually brought to a finish by sweets like airy white chocolate mousse edged with miso-butterscotch and rosemary gelée.

Southport Grocery

D3 — American

3552 N. Southport Ave. (bet. Addison St. & Cornelia Ave.)

Phone: 773-665-0100 — Lunch daily
Web: www.southportgrocery.com — Dinner Thu – Sat
Prices: $$ — Southport

Whether breakfast or lunch is your bag, you'll find a plate to suit your style at this hopping local hangout that's both a café and (of course) a grocery. Browse the racks of locally made specialty ingredients or peruse the counter stacked with made-from-scratch baked goods while you wait for a spot at the wooden communal table.

Bread pudding pancakes or a "grown-up" pop tart filled with local preserves, mascarpone, and roasted vanilla-walnuts send sweet lovers into seventh heaven. On the savory end of the spectrum, the Southport Cuban, layered with ham and house-smoked brisket, giardiniera, and Swiss on freshly grilled challah, gets even better with a side of creamy mashed Red Bliss potatoes. An ancho chile Bloody Mary is sure to end any hangover.

Sticky Rice

A2 — Thai

4018 N. Western Ave. (at Cuyler Ave.)

Phone: 773-588-0133 — Lunch & dinner daily
Web: www.stickyricethai.com
Prices: $$ — Irving Park (Blue)

BYO

Yes, there's no dearth of Thai joints in this neighborhood, but Sticky Rice stands out not only for its focus on Northern Thai specials, but for the quality and abundance of dishes made to order. Step in the sunny lemon- and tangerine-hued space with teak wood carvings, but step away from the satay and pad Thai. In fact, move outside your comfort zone and find a new favorite craving from their extensive menu.

Gang hung lay exemplifies the dark, chili-rich, and Northern-style curry with chunks of pork, garlic, and julienned ginger. Banana blossom salad, one among nearly thirty on the menu, mixes sour, floral, and spicy flavors in a vinegar-rich shrimp chili paste. Feeling truly bold? More exotic dishes include jellyfish salad and fried bamboo worms.

TAC Quick 

Thai

E2

3930 N. Sheridan Rd. (at Dakin St.)

Phone: 773-327-5253 — Lunch & dinner daily
Web: www.tacquick.net
Prices: $$ — Sheridan

Only a short jaunt from Wrigley Field, this modest, modern corner spot hides a secret behind its windowed façade: some of the most authentic Thai cooking in Chicagoland. Loyal followers fill every seat in the minimal dining room framed by tall windows. They are here to slurp up curries, chow down on mouthfuls of noodles, and snap up spicy stir-fries.

Though there is a so-called secret menu, TAC Quick happily posts it everywhere, much to the relief of diners looking for such genuine dishes as sour curry with *cha om*-flecked omelette. Even familiar plates like pork *prik king* or *yum woon sen*, a spicy, refreshing cold mélange of glass noodles, shrimp, and chicken tossed with lime, cilantro, and chilies, superbly mix crisp textures with aromatic flavors.

Thai Room

Thai

A2

4022 N. Western Ave. (at Cuyler Ave.)

Phone: 773-539-6150 — Lunch & dinner Tue – Sun
Web: www.thairoomchicago.com
Prices: $$ — Irving Park (Blue)

BYO

This longtime fixture has been fulfilling curry cravings for decades. Still looking good after all these years, it must be that Thai chillies and Botox have similar effects as you'd never guess the age of this popular place. Dressed in wood panels, teak carvings, and crisp white tablecloths which look as refined as they did on opening day in 1979, soft tunes in the background finish this elegant venue.

Beyond Asian favorites like pineapple fried rice or teriyaki, Thai Room's menu boasts such memorable items as beef meatballs in sweet chili sauce; crisp wide rice noodles in aromatic, basil-flecked Panang curry; or salmon *kang som* soup replete with a deliciously hot-sour red curry broth. Three-course lunch specials for well under $10 are a bargain.

Wood

Contemporary 

3335 N. Halstead St. (at Buckingham Pl.)

Phone: 773-935-9663 — Lunch Sat – Sun
Web: www.woodchicago.com — Dinner nightly
Prices: **$$** — Belmont (Brown/Red)

Lest you wonder if there might be a connection between a spot so named and its litany of treats, it's true there is a wood-fired oven in the kitchen. But the double entendre is very much intentional, played up with cheekily named cocktails like "a stiff one" and "rough rider" to be sipped in the warm wood plank-lined room decked with handsome furnishings.
Affordably priced small plates match the cocktails at this Boystown setting, focusing on contemporary American classics like a delicate soft shell crab atop summer vegetable succotash; or squares of wood-grilled flatbread topped with country ham, charred kale, and raclette. Belgian frites off the "Backwoods" late night menu, offered with a choice of 12 sauces, are near-legendary for local night owls.

Feast for under $25 at all restaurants with ☺.

Lincoln Park & Old Town

Lincoln Park

History, commerce, and nature come together in these iconic Chicago districts. The eponymous park, running along the Lake Michigan shore, offers winter-weary Chicagoans an excuse to get outside. And to add to the outdoor fun, famed Lincoln Park keeps its patrons happy and frolicking with a splendid spectrum of outdoor cafés, restaurants ranging from quick bites to the city's most exclusive reservations, and takeout spots perfect for assembling a picnic.

Populated by post-college roommates, young families, and affluent yuppies, Lincoln Park is a favorite amongst locals and visitors, no matter the time of the year. It includes more than a handful of designated historic districts, pre-Great Chicago Fire buildings, museums, shopping, music venues, and the famous (and free) Lincoln Park Zoo.

Delicious Dining

Well-heeled foodies make reservations to come here for some of the most exclusive restaurants in town including legendary **Charlie Trotter's** (though now sadly shuttered), **Alinea**, and **L2O** to name a few. During the weekend, the area is hopping, thanks to a combination of the theater, bar scene, and scores of apartment buildings that cater to the twenty- and thirty-somethings crowd. On summer Wednesdays and Saturdays, the south end of the park is transformed into hipster-chef-foodie central during the **Green City Market**. With the objective to elevate the availability of top-notch produce, and to improve the connect between farmers and local producers with restaurants and food organizations, this market aims to educate the masses about high-quality food sourcing. (In winter it is held inside the Peggy Notebaert Nature Museum). Additionally, the market draws long lines largely by dint of its fresh meats, cheeses, and fluffy crêpes.

Best of Bakeries

Fans of the sweets made from local ingredients at **Floriole Café & Bakery** have reason to rejoice—Floriole also has a Lincoln Park storefront that showcases a lunch menu alongside the daily specials. Also luring a pack of visitors are their perfect pastries, breakfast delights, sandwiches, salads, cookies, and sweet treats. Those with an affinity (or addiction) for all things baked can now get them even when Green City is closed. For other stomach-filling options outside of the market, try the heartwarming **Meatloaf Bakery**, where meatloaf and mashed potatoes are crafted into all manner of dishes, such as a cupcake-shaped "loaf" (with mashed potato icing). Other treats may include the "mother loaf," "a wing and a prayer loaf," "loaf-a-roma," and the "no buns about it burger loaf." Don't let the quirky titles fool you, because this may just be some of the best and most gratifying food in town. This expanse is also a great place in which to satisfy that Chicago hot dog craving. Like many foods (Juicy Fruit, Cracker Jack, and Shredded Wheat, for example), it is said that the Chicago-style dog may have originated at the Chicago World's Fair and Columbian Exhibition (in 1893), although that provenance is not definitive. Others credit the Great Depression for its birth. One newcomer is the chef-driven **Franks 'n' Dawgs**. Bustling at most hours, this Lincoln Park gem employs fresh and locally sourced ingredients featured in their fun bill of fare. Look forward to hand-crafted, juicy hot dogs, homey artisan breads, and gourmet sausages. Speaking of meat, **Butcher & the Burger** is doing its part to say at the helm of the burger chain. **The Wieners Circle** is as known for its late hours (as late as 5:00 A.M.) and purposefully rude service, as for its tasty repertoire of dogs and fries. Lincoln Park is one of the dog-friendliest areas around, but then what else would you expect from a neighborhood named after a park? Bold foodies and college grads are forever flocking to **Etno Village Grill** whose flavorful Balkan-style sandwiches are bound to sate Fido's appetite as well as your own. Chase this down with a stop at **Racine Plumbing** whose deep-fried Oreos and wings of myriad varieties have people raving. Wash down all that tasty grease at **Goose Island Brewery**, makers of the city's favorite local beers. Speaking of enticing brews, Goose Island also boasts numerous varieties like Matilda Belgian style ale, 312 Urban Wheat Ale, and Green Line pale ale. If you're still parched, visit the friendly and casual **Webster's Wine Bar**. Nab a seat on their streetfront patio, where you can enjoy a glass from their expansive wine selection. It is a whole different ballgame at **Karyn's Fresh Corner and Raw Café**, a restaurant with a full vegan and raw menu. The adjacent **Fresh Corner Market** sells meals to-go, plus fresh juices and supplements. "Meatballs" are made from lentils, and "sloppy Joes" from soy protein, and the raw food experience is unlike anything else you've seen.

Old Town

The Old Town quarter sports a few quaint cobblestoned streets that house the Second City comedy scene (now with a Zanies, too, for even more laughs); June's annual must-see (and must-shop) Old Town Art Fair; the Wells Street Art Fair; and places to rest with beers and a groovy jukebox like the **Old Town Ale House**. Wells Street is the neighborhood's main drag, and is where browsing should begin. Any epicurean shopping trip should also include the **Old Town Oil** for fab hostess gifts like infused oils and aged vinegars. Prefer a sweeter vice? **The Fudge Pot** tempts passersby with windows full of toffee, fudge, and other chocolaty goodness. Whether you smoke or not, the **Up Down Cigar** is worth a peek for its real cigar store Indian carving.

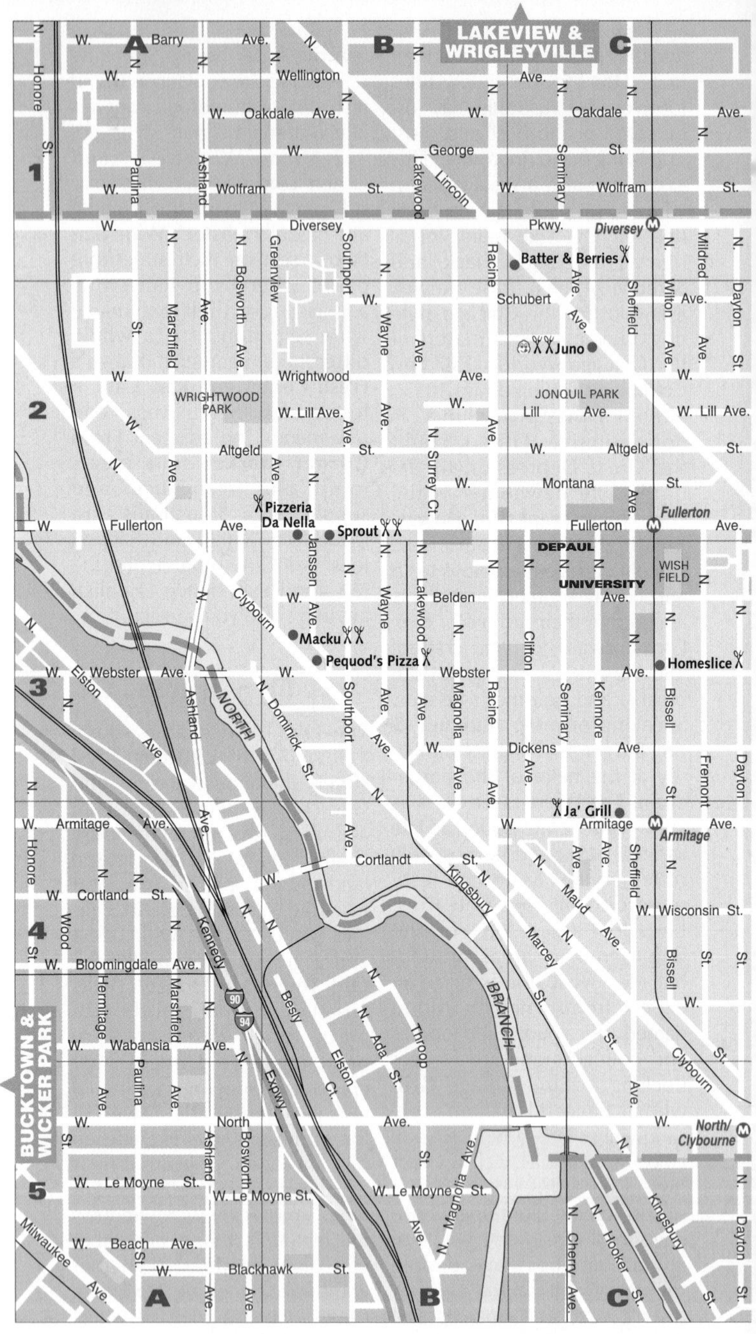

LAKEVIEW & WRIGLEYVILLE
BUCKTOWN & WICKER PARK
Batter & Berries
Juno
Pizzeria Da Nella
Sprout
Macku
Pequod's Pizza
Homeslice
Ja' Grill
Diversey
Fullerton
Armitage
North/ Clybourne
WRIGHTWOOD PARK
JONQUIL PARK
DEPAUL UNIVERSITY
WISH FIELD
NORTH BRANCH

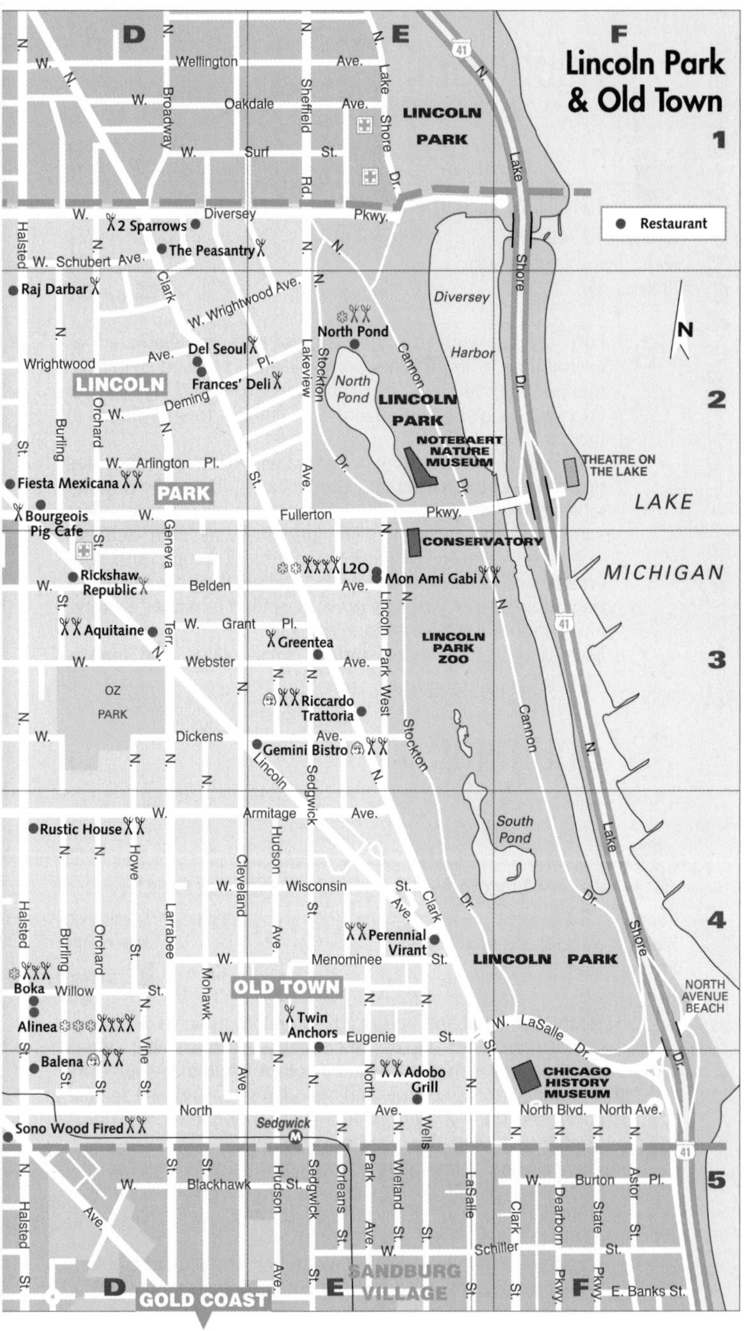
Lincoln Park & Old Town
Restaurant
LINCOLN PARK
LINCOLN
PARK
OLD TOWN
GOLD COAST
SANDBURG VILLAGE
LAKE MICHIGAN
2 Sparrows
The Peasantry
Raj Darbar
North Pond
Del Seoul
Frances' Deli
Fiesta Mexicana
Bourgeois Pig Cafe
Rickshaw Republic
L2O
Mon Ami Gabi
Aquitaine
Greentea
Riccardo Trattoria
Gemini Bistro
Rustic House
Perennial Virant
Boka
Alinea
Twin Anchors
Balena
Adobo Grill
Sono Wood Fired
NOTEBAERT NATURE MUSEUM
THEATRE ON THE LAKE
CONSERVATORY
LINCOLN PARK ZOO
CHICAGO HISTORY MUSEUM
NORTH AVENUE BEACH
Diversey Harbor
North Pond
South Pond
Sedgwick

Adobo Grill

E5 — Mexican XX

1610 N. Wells St. (bet. Eugenie St. & North Ave.)

Phone: 312-266-7999 — Lunch Sat – Sun
Web: www.adobogrill.com — Dinner nightly
Prices: $$ — Sedgwick

Fun, festive, and flavorful, Adobo Grill is celebrated as a longtime Old Town crowd-pleaser. Housed within a meandering building, it is at once cozy and lively with everyone from local denizens and families to solo diners at the bar.

First, order a lip-smacking margarita with fresh lime, then flag down one of the roving guacamole carts for a wildly popular tableside rendition. The solid Mexican bill of fare offers something for everyone, like little tostadas with achiote-marinated chicken, pickled onions, black beans, and sour cream; and *arrachera adobado*—grilled flank steak with a rich adobo, smoky *frijoles puercos*, grilled tomatoes, onions, and their unique house-made tortillas.

Brunch brings signature starters, small plates, and *huevos rancheros*.

Aquitaine

D3 — American XX

2221 N. Lincoln Ave. (bet. Belder & Webster Aves.)

Phone: 773-698-8456 — Lunch Sun
Web: www.aquitainerestaurant.com — Dinner nightly
Prices: $$ — Fullerton

Eleanor of Aquitaine wasn't a restaurateur as far as we know, but Chef/partner Holly Willoughby channels her regal, refined spirit at this romantic Lincoln Avenue mainstay. Dark brocade wallpaper, polished wood floors, and red leather banquettes face a long, welcoming bar, while French doors swing open when the weather cooperates.

The seasonally changing menu complements the casually elegant space. Duck finds its way into many of the French-influenced entrées such as juicy roasted duck breast with crushed celery root and Sauternes-apricot jam; or duck crêpes with maple-shallot brown butter. The signature amber cake, reminiscent of a French opera cake, pairs caramel *fleur de sel* cream, lemon madeleines, and crisp streusel for multi-layered bliss.

Alinea ✿✿✿

Contemporary

D4

1723 N. Halsted St. (bet. North Ave. & Willow St.)

Phone: 312-867-0110 Dinner Wed – Sun
Web: www.alinea-restaurant.com
Prices: **$$$$** North/Clybourn

Lara Kastner

Spotting Alinea isn't easy—look for nondescript black doors next to a valet easel. Enter to find a dark, Wonka-style tapering hallway of low-hanging glass vessels loaded with aromatics. Black tables and a single piece of modern artwork highlight a sense of minimalism that is upended by the cuisine. Peek into Chef Grant Achatz's immaculate workshop-cum-kitchen and let the funhouse begin.

The menu is sure to include plenty of bells and whistles, but there is a familiar brilliance behind this cooking. Plays on temperature and expectation include the cold wax cup of black truffled soup and hot skewer of potato and truffle-butter to be quickly submerged and drunk. Duck is a DIY dream, served as seared foie gras, poached mousse, sliced breast, rillettes, and leg confit with a show-stopping glass pane holding 60 condiments; if it isn't good, it's your own fault. The green apple taffy balloon is tart and fun, if also an accident waiting to happen (remove your glasses and tie back your hair). Servers are personable and ready to offer complex explanations of each dish, often specifying exactly how you should eat it.

Online bookings require perseverance and pre-payment (no refunds, no changes).

Balena

Italian XX

D5

1633 N Halstead St. (bet. North Ave. & Willow St.)

Phone: 312-867-3888 — Dinner nightly
Web: www.balenachicago.com
Prices: $$ — North/Clybourn

Since it's a mere stone's throw from the Steppenwolf and Royal George theaters, Balena is always popular among the pre-show crowds. Those who can linger and disregard the giant clock hanging from the back wall should go for lucky seats at the chef's counter for a little dinner theater of their own.

Italian techniques and flavors inspire the menu, but your *nonna* wouldn't recognize many of these dishes at first glance. Modern interpretations include house-made *orecchiette* tossed in a lemony cream sauce, hearty Tuscan kale salad dressed with a Caesar-like riff on classic *tonnato* sauce, or pizza with cauliflower, burrata, and *anchoïade*. Splurge on the bread basket for seasonal surprises like heirloom beet crostini or orange and anise *grissini*.

Batter & Berries

American X

C1

2748 N. Lincoln Ave. (bet. Diversey Pkwy & Schubert Ave.)

Phone: 773-248-7710 — Lunch daily
Web: N/A
Prices: — Diversey

BYO

It's hard not to adopt a disposition as sunny as the walls in this small brunch space when you see Chef/owner Derek Rylon's smiling face (and colorful chef's pants) cruising from table to table. Motown legends crooning from the stereo keep the mood buoyant, as does the tantalizing menu boasting a Southern bent. French toast, so moist that syrup seems overindulgent, comes in a variety of flavors that change by the week. Can't decide between brown sugar Bourbon, blueberry, or lemon? Get the flight. The signature "cluck-n-*gaufre*" is a mouthful to say as well as to eat: a sweet potato waffle is topped with fried chicken breast, then slathered with nutmeg-spiked hot sauce and maple butter.

BYO bubbly for a mimosa and they'll happily supply the OJ.

Boka ✿

Contemporary

D4

1729 N. Halsted St. (bet. North Ave. & Willow St.)

Phone: 312-337-6070 — Dinner nightly
Web: www.bokachicago.com
Prices: $$$ — North/Clybourn

Eric Kleinberg Photography

From your first steps through the painted brick courtyard with its gurgling fountain, Boka announces that this will be a special night. Leave attitude and stress at the door (next to the clever cell phone nook that modernizes the traditional phone booth) and let Chef Giuseppe Tentori and team anticipate your needs. Three dining areas scale up from casual night out to romantic showstopper. The polished wood bar with chic faux alligator stools leads to a front dining room with exposed brick and street views; the modern back room showcases white fabric sails billowing from the ceiling and cascading down a wall.

Chef Tentori works his wizardry on complex dishes with multitudes of deliciously harmonious ingredients. Mediterranean and Asian influences peek through tangerine-marinated snapper carpaccio dusted with seaweed salt, topped with tangerine ice, *hijiki,* and a mélange of pickled radishes. A variation on *pho* marries sliced Muscovy duck breast and shredded juniper-smoked duck leg with house-made *bigoli* and snappy finger lime garnish in a flavorful broth.

Sweet and savory combine beautifully in desserts like peanut butter semifreddo with miso-soy caramel and candied sesame crumble.

Bourgeois Pig Cafe

Deli

D2

738 W. Fullerton Pkwy. (at Burling St.)

Phone: 773-883-5282 Lunch & dinner daily
Web: www.bpigcafe.com
Prices: Fullerton

This old brownstone is a bookish coffee house and cozy, lived-in feeling café. Seats are available downstairs, but a trek upstairs brings added character with shabby-chic chandeliers, straw baskets, and a fireplace surrounded by young kids wearing vintage clothes. Despite the antiques and bookcases, this is a place for Kindles.

Excellent bread is paramount to every cleverly named sandwich and panini. *The Great Gatsby* is a riff on the club, *The Catcher in the Rye* means Reuben here, and *The Old Man and the Sea* is their tuna salad. *The Hobbit* is a triple-decker BLT *panino* on good sourdough with sun-dried tomato pesto, mayo, bacon crumbles, tomatoes, avocado, and alfalfa sprouts—a combination so outrageously good that you will be sad when it is gone.

Del Seoul

Korean

D2

2568-2570 N. Clark St. (bet. Deming Pl. & Wrightwood Ave.)

Phone: 773-248-4227 Lunch & dinner daily
Web: www.delseoul.com
Prices: Diversey

The Korean "street" food craze has hit the nation, but Del Seoul's moan-worthy delights are far beyond some passing fad. Thank the Jeon family for whipping up those intoxicating flavors into a menu of addictive fusion specialties, as well as *bulgogi* and *báhn mì*. Savory "Seoul style" dumplings are made from a 100-year old recipe, and *gamja* fries are smothered in kimchi, pork belly, and melted cheese.

And the tacos...oh, the tacos. Grilled white corn tortillas stuffed with chicken, spicy pork, braised beef *kalbi*, or sesame-chili shrimp, then crowned with cilantro-onion relish, chili-garlic salsa, and a secret slaw. Luckily, tacos are not too big, so try a variety. Order at the counter from the overhead video screen, take a number and grab a seat.

Fiesta Mexicana

Mexican

2423 N. Lincoln Ave. (bet. Fullerton Ave. & Halsted St.)

Phone: 773-348-4144 — Lunch & dinner daily
Web: www.fiestamexicanachicago.com
Prices: Fullerton

A longtime hangout for the twenty-somethings and young families living in Lincoln Park, Fiesta Mexicana lives up to the party-style atmosphere its moniker promises. The brick-lined space features a high ceiling, separate bar, and a number of dining rooms, with a large mural of a colorful mountain scene welcoming diners.

Guests are greeted with tasty chips and salsa and an expansive menu offering a cross-section of Tex-Mex, traditional Mexican, and Mexican-inspired fare. The combination platters are a solid way to sample these southwestern choices; while chile poblano-spinach-artichoke *fundido* shows off the kitchen's creative juices. Opt for a starter rather than a dessert, as these are the weakest link.

Good value specials are offered at lunch.

Frances' Deli

Deli

2552 N. Clark St. (bet. Deming Pl. & Wrightwood Ave.)

Phone: 773-248-4580 — Lunch daily
Web: www.francesdeli.com — Dinner Sat – Sun
Prices:

Frances' Deli is the type of quaint, lived-in diner everyone dreams of having just around the corner from home. Lucky Lincoln Park residents get that wish fulfilled at this authentic pre-war haunt packed with American antiques and memorabilia, where weekend waits are the norm as half the neighborhood vies for a place at one of the closely spaced tables.

As with any good diner, breakfast, lunch, and dinner all know how to hit the spot. The deli roasts its own meats and does Jewish-American staples right, from flavorful, crisp-tender potato pancakes to oversized pastrami and brisket sandwiches with all the fixings (slaw, fries, and potato salad). As long as you're going for the full nostalgia trip, slurp down a made-to-order milkshake or malt.

Gemini Bistro

2075 N. Lincoln Ave. (at Dickens Ave.)

Phone: 773-525-2522 — Dinner Tue – Sun
Web: www.geminibistrochicago.com
Prices: $$ — Armitage

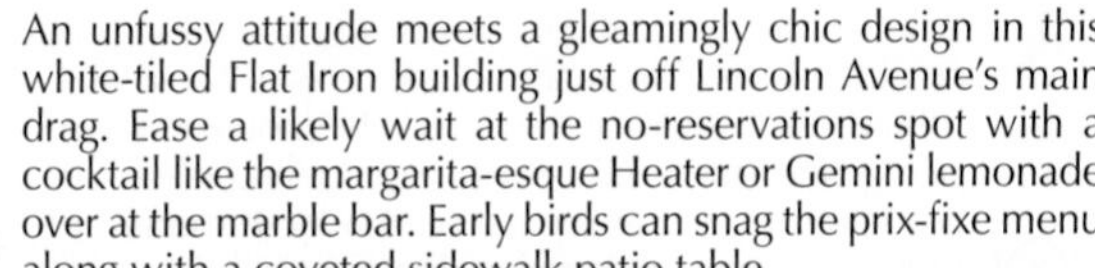

An unfussy attitude meets a gleamingly chic design in this white-tiled Flat Iron building just off Lincoln Avenue's main drag. Ease a likely wait at the no-reservations spot with a cocktail like the margarita-esque Heater or Gemini lemonade over at the marble bar. Early birds can snag the prix-fixe menu along with a coveted sidewalk patio table.

Loosely inspired by its Mediterranean neighbors, Gemini's menu might unveil a generous fillet of flaky pan-roasted halibut napped in lobster sauce alongside fava bean and corn succotash; or pea-studded risotto accented with mint, black pepper, and a healthy dose of *Parmigiano Reggiano*.

One tip: consider the reasonable valet instead of risking a parking ticket in this permit-heavy neighborhood.

Greentea

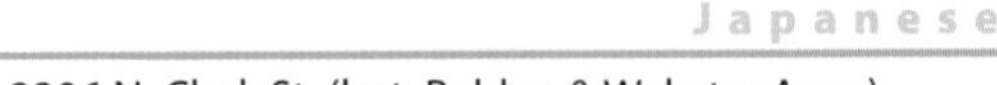

2206 N. Clark St. (bet. Belden & Webster Aves.)

Phone: 773-883-8812 — Lunch Tue – Sat
Web: N/A — Dinner Tue – Sun
Prices: $$

Regulars of this bento box-sized sushi spot are happy that its nondescript façade is easy to miss. They'd rather you walk on by as they keep this soothing space with pristine seafood their little secret. Restful seafoam-tinged walls and soft Japanese music keep the focus on the quiet but busy *itamae* sporting bright red shirts and ace slicing skills.

Those in-the-know flock here for fresh nigiri and sashimi like rich and dusky smoked salmon, creamy *otoro*, pure white hamachi, and silky *maguro*. Even the pickled ginger is perky and crisp. Fried baby crabs are an inventive starter—popcorn for the sushi set—and the maki are creatively prepared yet manageably sized. A lobster and jalapeño roll wrapped with tofu skin is tasty, simple, and without kitsch.

Homeslice

C3

Pizza

938 W Webster Ave. (at Bissell St.)

Phone: 312-789-4600 — Lunch & dinner daily
Web: www.getsomehomie.com
Prices: $$ — Fullerton

Only a pair of restaurateurs dedicated enough to ship, cut, and varnish timber from their native Oregon to build this glossy log cabin could succeed in serving "Northwest style" pizzas to deep-dish diehard Chicagoans. Shimmering icy copper mugs filled with Moscow Mules glint from the reflection of hanging lanterns among thick wooden beams; even the restrooms are lined with thousands of pennies.

The "wheels," as they call their beloved pizzas, begin with hand-tossed dough that bakes up fluffy and chewy with a slight crunch from the cornmeal-sprinkled crust. Quirky names make picking your pie a pleasure, as in the Special K, with spinach-ricotta sauce, sliced Italian sausage, and sun-dried tomatoes; or the Lew-Wow with Canadian bacon and pineapple.

Ja' Grill

C4

Jamaican

1008 W. Armitage Ave. (bet. Kenmore & Sheffield Aves.)

Phone: 773-929-5375 — Lunch Fri – Sun
Web: www.jagrill.com — Dinner nightly
Prices: ⊖⊖ — Armitage

Ja' Grill conveys the Jamaican spirit loud and clear. Patron saint Bob Marley (dreads aglow in red, yellow, and green) kicks out the jams from a large mural set off by a sunset orange back-lit bar. Reggae beats and a bottle of Red Stripe further heighten the mood. A downstairs lounge caters to the drinks-and-DJ crowd, where dancehall, dub, and ska spin live on weekends.

The menu schools the palate on Jamaican classics with rubs and sauces that build with a slow burn. Hearty mains like pork ribs, or jerk shrimp benefit from a healthy slathering of spices. The kitchen smartly offers veggie sides like fried sweet plantains and a warm cabbage salad to cool the heat.

Caveat emptor: ask for the prices of daily specials before ordering or risk sticker shock.

Juno

Japanese

C2

2638 N. Lincoln Ave. (bet. Seminary & Wrightwood Aves.)

Phone: 872-206-8662 Dinner Tue – Sun
Web: www.junosushi.com
Prices: $$ Diversey

Geishas just wanna have fun, according to the amusing murals in Juno's bar. One plays ping pong, another sidles up to a guitar amp, and all give the distinct impression that you're not entering some run-of-the-mill, serenely appointed sushi bar.

Since his days at Arami, followers of Chef B.K. Park have lined the onyx counter to experience his gorgeously presented seafood creations, inspired by extensive travel through Japan and Korea. Shooters in ice-filled orbs are layered with marigold-yellow uni, *tobiko*, cucumber, shiso, and house-made soy sauce. Smoked sashimi (your choice of fish) arrives under a glass dome fogged with aromatic applewood smoke. One end of the sushi counter is reserved for the chef's personal omakase—call in advance for a seat.

Macku

Japanese

B3

2239 N. Clybourn Ave. (bet. Greenview & Webster Aves.)

Phone: 773-880-8012 Dinner nightly
Web: www.mackusushi.com
Prices: $$

Sushi fans fall into two camps: east and west. There are those who love their westernized maki (spicy tuna anyone?) and those who go the traditional nigiri route. Whether you're a newbie or an aficionado, Macku has you covered.

This contemporary Japanese restaurant literally lays out every option; its neat display of fresh fish at the sushi bar is an enticing sign of what's to come. Start with straightforward favorites like salmon, tuna, and yellowtail; or choose from the nice selection of specialty rolls like the spicy spider roll with soft-shell crab, *kanikami*, chili oil, avocado, and cucumber.

The menu may have it all, but this modern and stylish favorite is small with just a sprinkling of tables and seats at the pristine counter.

L20 ✿✿

E3 — Seafood

2300 N. Lincoln Park West (bet. Belden Ave. & Fullerton Pkwy.)

Phone: 773-868-0002 — Dinner Thu – Mon
Web: www.l2orestaurant.com
Prices: **$$$$**

Katherine Bryant

L2O has an upscale personality that is never pretentious, yet expresses a sophisticated romance reserved for dates you'd like to impress. The dining room's white leather chairs, bare wood tables, and tall columns are focused on a stunning branch sculpture, painted gold and accented with live orchids.

The kitchen now displays its thriving fish tanks, organized by ocean and stocked with exotic fish awaiting their call of duty. Service is always on point, but those "oohs" and "aahs" are due to the focused and very talented cooking. Begin with a visit from the tableside cocktail cart while contemplating the two nightly prix-fixe; before savoring a crisp *feuille de brik* tartlet holding vibrant parsley-and-mussel mousse, a bacon chip, flower petal, and lemon zest. A Meyer Angus ribeye is beautifully cooked to pinkish-red, ladled with cider *gastrique*, and served with butternut squash gratin topped with melted Parmesan and feathered onions. A smart sense of whimsy continues through the end with desserts served as a highball of espresso mousse, mascarpone, and clove gelée, garnished with candied strips of lemon zest and coffee and vanilla meringues.

Choose the valet—street parking is at a premium.

Mon Ami Gabi

French

E3

2300 N. Lincoln Park West (at Belden Ave.)

Phone: 773-348-8886 Dinner nightly
Web: www.monamigabi.com
Prices: $$

Within the historic Belden-Stratford hotel, Mon Ami Gabi offers an instant trip to Lyon by way of Lincoln Park. This appealing brasserie stays lively with the cozy ambience of a French bistro straight from central casting. Leather banquettes, dusky yellow walls, and wooden wine racks set the scene, while old-world, tuxedo-clad servers play the part, perfectly.

Chef Gabino Soletino (the "ami" referenced in the restaurant's name) and team turn out faithful renditions of classic brasserie food such as an anchovy-rich Caesar salad with shards of baguette croutons, dusted with black pepper ground at the table; plump and on-point medium-rare filet mignon with a healthy dab of butter and béarnaise; or French onion soup capped with gooey Gruyère.

The Peasantry

Contemporary

D1

2723 N. Clark St. (bet. Diversey Pkwy & W. Drummond Pl.)

Phone: 773-868-4888 Lunch Fri – Sun
Web: www.thepeasantry.com Dinner Tue – Sun
Prices: $$ Diversey

The team behind critically acclaimed Franks 'N' Dawgs has expanded beyond hot dogs. They now run a roster of critters including eclectic street food in this cheeky modern-meets-rustic space. A mural running the length of the bare wood banquette features a playful black and white graffiti-ed animal menagerie ranging from cows to an octopus.

Though the food might have familiar names like pigs in a blanket, the ingredients surprise those who might expect standard comfort fare. These are chorizo wrapped in golden puff pastry and served on pancetta-studded white beans. Snacks like truffle fries with a triple hit of aromatic butter, salt, and oil; spicy kimchi popcorn; or a deconstructed *poutine* with duck confit make for unexpectedly tasty eating.

North Pond ✿

Contemporary XX

2610 N. Cannon Dr.

Phone: 773-477-5845 — Lunch Sun

Web: www.northpondrestaurant.com — Dinner Tue – Sun

Prices: $$$

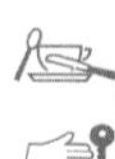

North Pond Restaurant

A pleasant stroll through the the neighborhood's namesake park leads you to North Pond. This former ice-skaters' warming house has been reincarnated as a cozy but elegant cottage with carefully considered Craftsman-era detail. With the Chicago skyline reflected in the rippling water and the verdant landscape framed by the windows, the scene is the very dictionary definition of "picturesque."

Inside, the gracious space is filled with sophisticated arts and crafts accents like patterned friezes and room dividers, as well as nature-inspired details and a recessed ceiling mural that echoes the view outside.

Chef Bruce Sherman presents surprisingly complex and modern seasonal dishes instead of straightforward farm-to-table fare, though his tremendous creativity can lead to competing flavors. Composed salads feature roasted Chioggia beets interspersed with cured Arctic char cubes as well as both smoked and fresh salmon caviars. Main courses can be decadently tender and rich as in pork medallions with cherry gelée, or rabbit served three ways: buttermilk-braised, bacon-wrapped saddle, and a "truffle" of nut-coated liver with rhubarb jam. Architecturally impressive desserts are an equal delight.

Pequod's Pizza

B3 — Pizza

2207 N. Clybourn Ave. (at Webster Ave.)

Phone: 773-327-1512 — Lunch & dinner daily
Web: www.pequodspizza.com
Prices: $$ — Armitage

Ditch your diet, grab your fellow Blackhawk fans, and head into this Lincoln Park stalwart for some of the best pies in town. Christened in 1970 for Captain Ahab's whaling ship, Pequod's sails a smooth menu of bar food apps, hearty sandwiches (try the tender Italian beef with melted cheese and hot peppers), and fantastic pizzas.

Crusts range from thin- to deep-dish, but the specialty is the pan pizza, with its cake-like crust and halo of caramelized cheese that sticks to the sides of the pan. Toppings like spicy sausage and pepperoni are heaped on with abandon, as if the pizza makers are whipping up a pie to take home for themselves. Pequod's stays open till 2:00 A.M. most nights, so stop by for a late-night nosh and ponder the great white whale.

Perennial Virant

E4 — American

1800 N. Lincoln Ave. (at Clark St.)

Phone: 312-981-7070 — Lunch Sat – Sun
Web: www.perennialchicago.com — Dinner nightly
Prices: $$

Chicago's king of pickling and preserving, Paul Virant, brings his farm-to-table philosophy to the edge of Lincoln Park at this country-chic restaurant. Empty Ball jars dangle from light fixtures, while jars filled with pickles and preserves line shelves until they're snatched away for kitchen use. Clearly, the restaurant's motto of "eat what you can, can what you can't" is very much on display.

Pickled vegetables pop up on just about every plate, such as a mound of vinegary green beans atop a grilled Skuna Bay salmon fillet; or summer beans and spring onion vinaigrette on the crispy Carnaroli rice cake, a Virant signature dish decadently oozing with fresh Wisconsin cheese curds. Puckery touches infuse the creative cocktail menu as well.

Pizzeria Da Nella

B2 Pizza

1443 W. Fullerton Ave. (bet. Greenview & Janssen Aves.)

Phone: 773-281-6600 Lunch & dinner daily
Web: www.pizzeriadanella.com
Prices: $$ Fullerton

The tradition, not the pizza, runs deep at this Neapolitan darling on West Fullerton. Naples-born *pizzaiola,* Nella Grassano takes center stage, stretching dough, then judiciously sprinkling toppings on her pies before sliding them into an oven burning with white oak for a mere two minutes. Her husband and brother pitch in to serve salads with fresh *mozzarella di bufala* and *Prosciutto di Parma,* homemade pastas, and crusty bread from the same oven.

Despite baking in temperatures that can seriously escalate, pizzas emerge crisp with the perfect char. Diavola pies are dotted with spicy salami rounds and red pepper flakes, washed down with an Italian or Midwest-brewed beer. An expansive brick-paved patio begs for a leisurely Italian lunch; why not indulge?

Raj Darbar

D2 Indian

2660 N. Halsted St. (bet. Schubert & Wrightwood Aves.)

Phone: 773-348-1010 Dinner nightly
Web: www.rajdarbar.com
Prices: $$ Diversey

Though discreetly set a few steps below street level, Raj Darbar feels roomy and bright, thanks to a warm color scheme, mirrored accents, and wide windows looking out onto Halsted Avenue. This large cavern is a favorite among Indians for family gatherings and celebrations, though locals and regulars pop in routinely for takeout and filling dinners.

The expansive menu covers all bases with a host of standards, pleasantly prepared with aromatic spices. Large half-moons of naan arrive fluffy and blistered from the tandoor, and are a perfect vessel for the spicy yogurt sauce in lamb *rogan josh* or richly balanced and velvety chicken *makhani.* Vegetable samosas, crispy on the outside and stuffed with spiced peas and potatoes, are impossible to put down.

Riccardo Trattoria 

Italian XX

E3

2119 N. Clark St. (bet. Dickens & Webster Aves.)

Phone: 773-549-0038 — Dinner nightly
Web: www.riccardotrattoria.com
Prices: $$

The understated wood-and-cream décor doesn't look anything like an Italian *nonna*'s kitchen. But, the soulful personality of Chef/owner Riccardo Michi and his cache of family recipes make his eponymous restaurant a second home to half the city, it seems—a go-to spot equally suited to flirty date-nights and big, boisterous dinners.

As intimated by the word "trattoria," authentic rustic Italian cooking presides over the menu. One baseball-sized *arancino* would suffice for a hearty appetizer, but in the spirit of *abbondanza*, you get two. Veal roulades, pounded thin, stuffed with sausage and pistachios, and paired with Tuscan fries are standouts among the *secondi*; while a light, fluffy version of tiramisu makes even those who beg off dessert take a second bite.

Rickshaw Republic

Indonesian X

D3

2312 N. Lincoln Ave. (bet. Belden Ave. & Childrens Plz.)

Phone: 773-697-4750 — Lunch Tue – Sun
Web: www.rickshawrepublic.com — Dinner Tue – Sat
Prices:  —  Fullerton

BYO

The fire engine-red façade of the Adler & Sullivan building grabs your attention, but the smells and tastes of the Southeast Asian street food at this fresh family-run spot keep you glued to your seat. The colorful handmade marionettes and inverted parasols hanging from the ceiling next to batik-patterned wood carvings and handcrafted Indonesian masks are eye-catching, too.

Specials are listed as "whatever mommy feels like making," and it's wise to trust Mom when it comes to dishes like crispy, sweet, and sticky chicken wings; *mie goreng* noodles with crunchy puffed shrimp chips; or fried *pastel* dumplings stuffed with ground chicken. The house-made *sambal*, red as the building's exterior with an equally fiery finish, goes with everything.

Rustic House

American

1967 N. Halsted St. (bet. Armitage Ave. & Willow St.)

Phone: 312-929-3227 Dinner Tue – Sun
Web: www.rustichousechicago.com
Prices: $$ Armitage

Lincoln Park denizens who aren't at Chef/partner Jason Paskewitz's Gemini Bistro are usually here at Rustic House, where wagon-wheel chandeliers and burlap walls add just the right touch of country. Cocktails and snacks like honey-peppered bacon or Marcona almonds fried in duck fat make the bar a destination in its own right.

At the rear of the dining room, the glass-front rotisserie displays juicy, organic chickens in constant rotation, often joined by Kurobata pork or whole ducks. Pair a rotisserie meat with sweet corn brûlée and garlicky, smooth mashed potatoes; or slice into a prime aged steak from the wood-burning grill. Arrive before 6:30 P.M. to take advantage of the $35 prix-fixe, with the option of Scotch whiskey or dessert as a third course.

Sono Wood Fired

D5

Pizza

1582 N. Clybourn Ave. (bet. Halsted St. & North Ave.)

Phone: 312-255-1122 Dinner Tue – Sun
Web: www.sonowoodfired.com
Prices: $$ North/Clybourn

The harlequin-tiled imported Italian pizza oven blazing away in the corner is not only the focal point of Sono's dining room—it's the reason for their lively crowd continually chowing down at the tightly packed tables and sleek oak bar. Everyone's here for the signature blistered, lightly charred but still chewy Neapolitan-style pizzas, made distinctively creative with fresh, local, and imported artisan ingredients like wild mushrooms, crispy sage, spicy *sopressata,* or *fior di latte* mozzarella.

Antipasti like mussels in a garlicky white wine broth spend some time in the oven for a touch of wood-fired flavor before hitting the table; while flash-fried artichoke hearts or Parmesan-dusted calamari served family-style ease the wait for those precious pies.

Sprout

Contemporary XX

B2

1417 W. Fullerton Ave. (bet. Janssen & Southport Aves.)

Phone: 773-348-0706 — Dinner Tue – Sat

Web: www.sproutrestaurant.com

Prices: $$$ — Fullerton

Polished marble floors, chunky flagstone walls surrounding a skylit-enclosed patio, and decorative twig accents lend an earthy, natural vibe to complement Chef Dale Levitski's ode to all things organic. In turn, tables and cubby booths provide an intimate and romantic feel to the space, though casually hip servers keep things from getting too precious. The approachable staff is pleased to answer questions about those abstractly described dishes outlined on the à la carte and three-course prix-fixe menus.

The oft-changing items include the chef's inventive take on *pho* with seared ono, sirloin carpaccio, and spicy seaweed broth; or the childhood favorite grilled cheese featuring a white cheddar *fritto* encasing slow-cooked onions and Granny Smith apples.

Twin Anchors

Barbecue X

E4

1655 N. Sedgwick St. (at Eugenie St.)

Phone: 312-266-1616 — Lunch Sat – Sun, Dinner nightly

Web: www.twinanchorsribs.com

Prices: $$ — Sedgwick

Within the brick walls that have housed Twin Anchors since 1932, generations have made their way across the checkerboard linoleum floor to throw a quarter in the jukebox and get saucy with a slab of their legendary ribs in one of the curved booths. Though the bar is wall-to-wall on weekends, most weekdays are low-key, with families and groups ready for a casual night out.

Fall-off-the-bone baby back ribs are the real deal, made with sweet and spicy rub, served with their own "zesty" sauce or the newer Prohibition version, with brown sugar and a hint of ghost-pepper heat. Classic sides like onion rings, baked beans, or hearty chili round out the meal. If there's a wait at the no-reservations spot, try the beer of the month while cooling your heels.

2 Sparrows

American 

D1

553 Diversey Pkwy. (Bet. Cambridge Ave. & Lehmann Ct.)

Phone: 773-234-2320 Lunch daily
Web: www.2sparrowschicago.com
Prices: $$ Diversey

Two veterans from Charlie Trotter's opened this daytime café—a spot as completely pleasing as it is busy. Fronted by plate glass, the lofty room is warm with sunshine, has a convivial buzz, and boasts a frenetic open kitchen.

The carte includes a breakfast-themed selection of sweets and savories that showcase the likes of "pop tarts." That mass-produced morning pastry of yore may elicit a stronger Proustian effect than madeleines, but the 2 Sparrows version is alike only in name and memorable in its own right. Flavors change daily and may feature caramelized apples tucked into a buttery shell drizzled with lemon and thyme glaze. The fresh-baked biscuit slathered with lamb sausage gravy is a heartier option; while the veggie burger is a healthier one.

Look for the symbol for a brilliant breakfast to start your day off right.

Loop

The constant hustle and bustle of Chicago's main business district is named after the El train tracks that make a loop around the area. Their clickety-clack noise is an intrinsic part of the soundtrack of the Windy City.

Today's Loop

This neighborhood has a culinary resonance as well—one that is perpetually evolving with the region. It wasn't that long ago that the Loop locked up at night. When offices, housed in the great iconic Chicago skyscrapers, closed at 5:00 P.M., so did the surrounding businesses, and thus, the area remained quiet and deserted. However, thanks to a revitalized Theater District, new residential living, hotels, and student dorms, there is now a renewed dining scene, wine boutiques, and gorgeous grocery stores open past dusk. Local foodies and visitors with queries can contact the Chicago Cultural Center's "culinary concierges" with any food tourism-related question.

Sensational Spreads

Start your voyage by exploring at Block 37, one of the city's original 58 blocks. It took decades of work, and several political dynasties, but the block is now home to a five-story atrium with shopping, restaurants, and entrances to public transportation lines. Here, you'll find New York City's sweet sensation **Magnolia Bakery**, where folks wait in line for such treasures as banana pudding, and of course, those enticing cupcake trees. Probiotic **Starfruit Cafe** with a spectrum of delicious frozen yogurts also has an outpost here, as does **Godiva Chocolatier**, an ideal choice for delectable chocolates or decorative gift collections. There are also several quick food options on the Pedway level that are popular for office lunches. (The Pedway system of tunnels links crucial downtown buildings underground, which is essential during those cruel Chicago winters.) In the same vein, for a quick grab and go lunch, **Hannah's Bretzel** is ideal. Lauded as "über sandwich makers," their version of the namesake is fashioned from freshly baked German bread and features ultra-divine fillings. While their menu may resemble that of an average diner, one bite into their sandwiches (perhaps the grass-fed sirloin special spread with showers of nutty Gruyére, vine tomatoes, field greens, onions, and spicy horseradish aïoli), and find yourself in sandwich nirvana.

Chicago Chocolate Tours gives two-plus hour tastes of downtown's candy and baked icons' sites on Thursdays and Fridays. These delicious walking tours leave from Macy's State Street location. Another popular preference is **Tastebud Tours**, which has a Loop option on its daily tour menu. Stops include hot dogs, pizza, and **The Berghoff**—the city's oldest restaurant. Check out the historic Berghoff bar for lunch, dinner, dessert, and of course, steins of beer. Also terrific is Berghoff's pre-theater, prix-fixe menu that reveals such juicy eats as *sauerbraten*, potato pierogies, and Thai codfish cakes. Their bevy of beers (think of the Berghoff Seasonal Special, Prairie Lager, and Sundown Dark) will keep you quenched; and if you're in the mood for something lighter, root for the root beer. When strolling these grounds, don't miss the range of public art that pops up in many of the government plazas and other open spaces across the Loop. Summer also brings a mélange of musical performances to Millennium Park, Grant Park, and the Petrillo Music Shell, that is just begging for a picnic *en plein air*.

Market Carousing

During warmer months, several farmers' markets cater to the downtown crowd, including the ones at Federal Plaza on Tuesdays and Daley Plaza on Thursdays. Concession carts freckle the streets of various locations in nearby Millennium Park, and are perfect for grabbing a snack whilst sauntering. Lake Street's **Pastoral Artisan Cheese** (a favorite of both *Saveur* Magazine and locals alike) is the go-to, made-to-order sandwich haven for the Loop's lunch crowd. For extraordinary sips, wine and beer connoisseurs flock here for their craft collection; while the catering division brings these artisan and specialty delights to your dining table. The city is filled with caffeine addicts as well as coffee connoisseurs; and since sightseeing can be quite tiring, make sure you get a pick-me-up at **Intelligentsia Coffee**, a local coffee chain with an emphasis on direct trade. Locations can be found all over town, but the **Millennium Park Coffeebar** is particularly convenient and delicious. Outfitted with an industrial-style decor, it reflects the architecture of nearby Millennium Park. Local foodies also appreciate the **Park Grill**, a full-service restaurant flanked by an ice rink in the winter. And of course, no trip to Chicago, much less the Loop, would be complete without munching on **Garrett Popcorn**. Head to one of their three Loop locations (follow the aroma for directions) for cheese, caramel, pecan, and other enticingly flavored popcorn.

Taste of Chicago

The Taste of Chicago is one of the city's biggest events. This five-day summer extravaganza in Grant Park draws hordes of hungry diners and food gourmands from all over the world. (The park itself was incorporated before the city was founded.) For the last 30 years, local restaurants have set up scores of food booths that feature delicacies from around the globe. The place is packed for this five-day duration, thanks to the great food and live music, but come mid-July, it's a bit of a madhouse! This ever-beloved festival is now the second largest attraction in the state; and the revered (local) **Eli's Cheesecake** is the sole remaining original Taste of Chicago exhibitor. In 2010, it celebrated its 30th anniversary with a giant, creamy cheesecake.

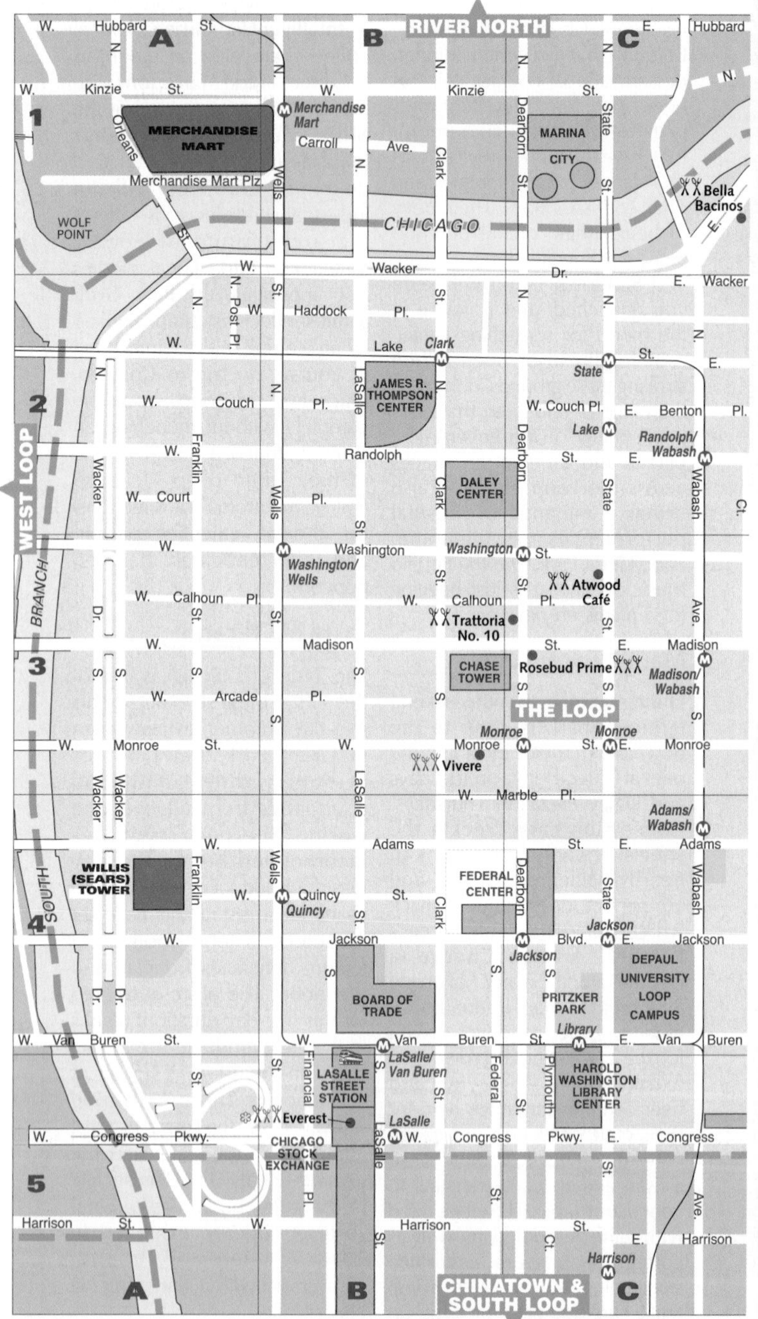
RIVER NORTH
WEST LOOP
THE LOOP
CHINATOWN & SOUTH LOOP
MERCHANDISE MART
Merchandise Mart
MARINA CITY
WOLF POINT
CHICAGO
BRANCH
SOUTH
JAMES R. THOMPSON CENTER
DALEY CENTER
CHASE TOWER
FEDERAL CENTER
WILLIS (SEARS) TOWER
BOARD OF TRADE
PRITZKER PARK
DEPAUL UNIVERSITY LOOP CAMPUS
HAROLD WASHINGTON LIBRARY CENTER
LASALLE STREET STATION
CHICAGO STOCK EXCHANGE
Bella Bacinos
Atwood Café
Trattoria No. 10
Rosebud Prime
Vivere
Everest
Clark
State
Lake
Randolph/ Wabash
Washington
Washington/ Wells
Madison/ Wabash
Monroe
Adams/ Wabash
Quincy
Jackson
Library
LaSalle/ Van Buren
LaSalle
Harrison
W. Hubbard St.
E. Hubbard
W. Kinzie St.
Carroll Ave.
Merchandise Mart Plz.
Orleans St.
Wacker Dr.
E. Wacker
W. Haddock Pl.
W. Lake St.
W. Couch Pl.
E. Benton Pl.
W. Randolph St.
W. Court Pl.
W. Washington St.
W. Calhoun Pl.
W. Madison St.
W. Arcade Pl.
W. Monroe St.
W. Marble Pl.
W. Adams St.
W. Quincy St.
W. Jackson Blvd.
W. Van Buren St.
W. Congress Pkwy.
W. Harrison St.
N. Post Pl.
N. Franklin St.
N. Wells St.
N. LaSalle St.
N. Clark St.
N. Dearborn St.
N. State St.
N. Wabash Ave.
Ct.
S. Financial Pl.
S. Federal St.
S. Plymouth Ct.
A
B
C
1
2
3
4
5

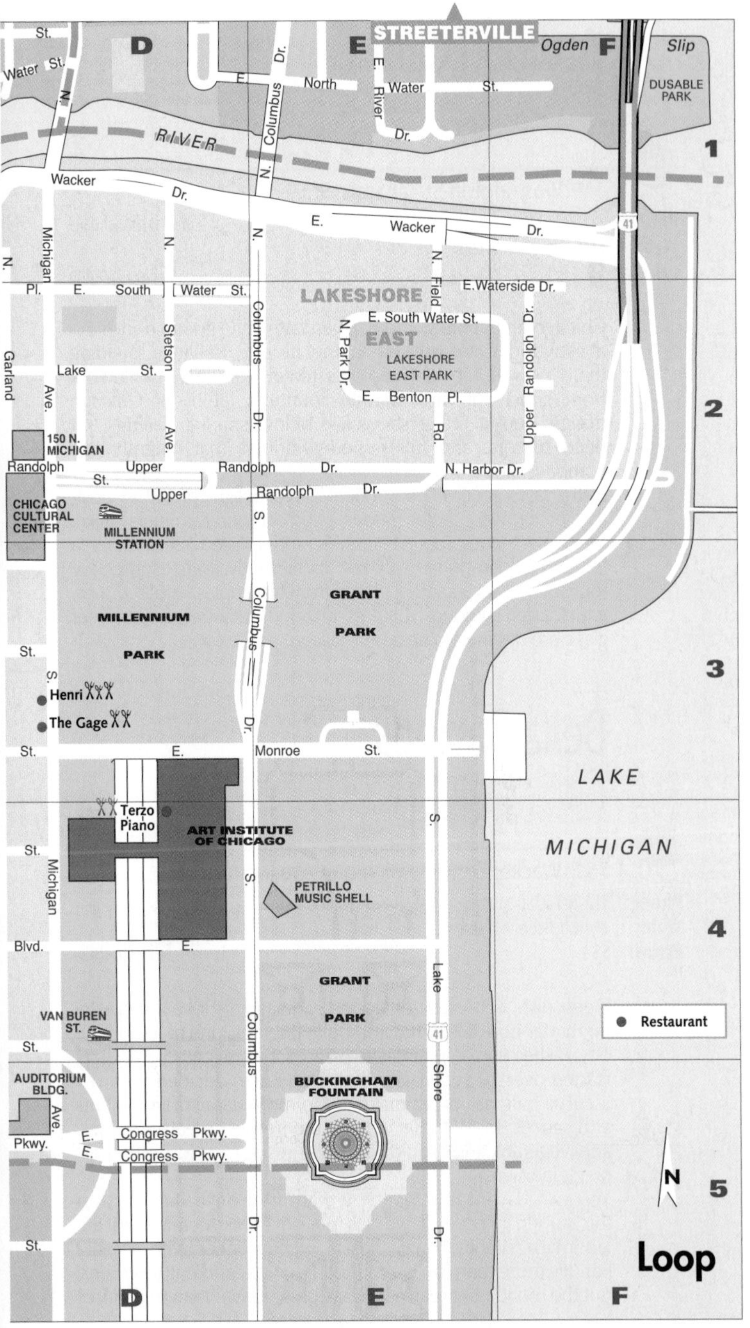
STREETERVILLE
D
E
F
Ogden Slip
DUSABLE PARK
North Water St.
E. River Dr.
N. Columbus Dr.
RIVER
Wacker Dr.
E. Wacker Dr.
N. Michigan Ave.
E. South Water St.
N. Stetson Ave.
LAKESHORE EAST
E. Waterside Dr.
E. South Water St.
N. Park Dr.
N. Field Rd.
LAKESHORE EAST PARK
E. Benton Pl.
Upper Randolph Dr.
Garland Pl.
Lake St.
150 N. MICHIGAN
Randolph St.
Upper Randolph Dr.
N. Harbor Dr.
CHICAGO CULTURAL CENTER
MILLENNIUM STATION
S. Columbus Dr.
GRANT PARK
MILLENNIUM PARK
Henri
The Gage
E. Monroe St.
LAKE MICHIGAN
Terzo Piano
ART INSTITUTE OF CHICAGO
S. Michigan Ave.
PETRILLO MUSIC SHELL
Blvd.
S. Lake Shore Dr.
41
VAN BUREN ST.
Restaurant
BUCKINGHAM FOUNTAIN
AUDITORIUM BLDG.
E. Congress Pkwy.
N
1
2
3
4
5
Loop

Atwood Café

Contemporary XX

C3

1 W. Washington St. (at State St.)

Phone: 312-368-1900 — Lunch & dinner daily
Web: www.atwoodcafe.com
Prices: $$ — Washington

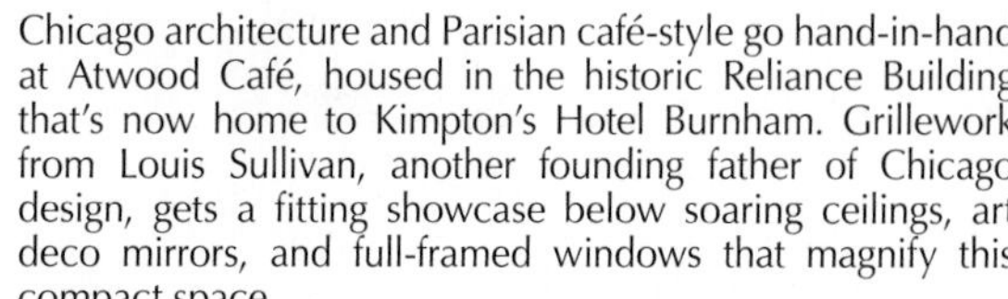

Chicago architecture and Parisian café-style go hand-in-hand at Atwood Café, housed in the historic Reliance Building that's now home to Kimpton's Hotel Burnham. Grillework from Louis Sullivan, another founding father of Chicago design, gets a fitting showcase below soaring ceilings, art deco mirrors, and full-framed windows that magnify this compact space.

Bistro faves receive luxe touches that delight pre- and post-theater crowds, hotel guests, and corporate diners alike. Meltingly tender root vegetables and roasted chicken fill a buttery, golden-domed pot pie; as elegantly composed celery root soup bears a textural punch from tart apples, cool radishes, and toasted almonds. Donuts drizzled with bacon-root beer glaze are destined to be a new classic.

Bella Bacinos

Italian XX

C1

75 E. Wacker Dr. (bet. Michigan Ave. & State St.)

Phone: 312-263-2350 — Lunch & dinner daily
Web: www.bellabacinos.com
Prices: $$ — State/Lake

Deep-dish, thin-crust, or stuffed, Chicagoans love their pizza no matter how it is sliced and Bella Bacinos, one of four in the city, dishes up some fantastic pizza with top ingredients. It all started over 30 years ago when Dan Bacin decided to throw a curve ball into pizza making. No more canned ingredients and sauces. Instead, Bacin used the freshest meats, cheeses, and vegetables he could find. The result? Some of the best pizza in town.

You can have it any way you want it at Bella Bacinos, but the stuffed pizza is always a pleaser. This location, in the landmark Mather Tower, has a swanky décor with a lively bar. It's more than just pizza (hearty pastas and entrées round out the menu), but really, why would you want anything else?

Everest ✿

French XXX

B5

440 S. LaSalle St. (bet. Congress Pkwy. & Van Buren St.)

Phone: 312-663-8920 Dinner Tue – Sat
Web: www.everestrestaurant.com
Prices: **$$$$** LaSalle/Van Buren

Lettuce Entertain You

Formerly a private club for the movers and shakers of the Chicago Stock Exchange, this swanky restaurant on the 40th floor of the Exchange building is worth the oft-confusing trek through security and high-altitude ascent—in an old-fashioned elevator cab that doubles as a time machine. The art deco room, gilded with mirrors, black-and-white lacquered accents, and abstract sculptures on each table, strikingly evokes Jazz Age glamour. As expected from a refined retreat this high in the sky, views from its bay windows stretch spectacularly across the western edge of the city.

Refined and contemporary French-Alsatian cuisine is the hallmark of Chef/owner Jean Joho, who pairs his culinary offerings with a wine list of more than 1000 bottles, including one of the most comprehensive Alsatian selections in the country.

Multiple menus, from pre-theater prix-fixe to long-form tasting tours, feature seasonally changing platters like house-smoked salmon with herbed *fleischnagga* noodle pinwheels and tangy caraway crème fraîche; or Everest signatures like creamy cabbage potage poured tableside onto a perfect landscape of caramelized onion cubes, chopped chives, and glistening black caviar.

The Gage

Gastropub XX

D3

24 S. Michigan Ave. (bet. Madison & Monroe Sts.)

Phone: 312-372-4243 Lunch & dinner daily
Web: www.thegagechicago.com
Prices: $$ Madison

In a sprawling set of historic buildings directly opposite Millennium Park, The Gage provides refuge from the teeming Michigan Avenue crowds—and has abundant room to hold them all. Clubby leather booths and celadon-tiled columns bring decorum to this bustling space. Sit at the long, curving counter flanked by old posters to get your sports fix, or stake your claim at one of the many tables for a more leisurely meal.

The broad menu covers British pub classics like Scotch eggs while appropriating international flavors with flair. Rich and satisfying fondue does rarebit one better with the addition of spinach and baguette slices; and piles of thinly sliced pork belly, pickles, grilled onions, and smoked Gouda comprise a fresh version of the Cubano.

Henri

French XXX

D3

18 S. Michigan Ave. (bet. Madison & Monroe Sts.)

Phone: 312-578-0763 Lunch Mon – Fri
Web: www.henrichicago.com Dinner nightly
Prices: $$$ Monroe

A restaurant with prime Michigan Avenue real estate likely doesn't need to fuss too much since foot traffic is guaranteed, but Henri has established itself as an elegant and charming hideaway on this otherwise tourist-clogged stretch. Charcoal walls offset breathtaking views of Millennium Park, while pendant chandeliers provide a romantic flush for couples settling into plush seats.

The modern French-inspired dishes are as polished as their surroundings. A quivering quail egg in its shell crowns gently smoked steak tartare; warm root vegetables and rich, lemon-infused caper-butter sauce offset pristine and pale Dover sole meunière. Finish in style with a decadent Manjari dark chocolate soufflé with Port-soaked cherries and caraway-vanilla ice cream.

Rosebud Prime

Steakhouse XXX

1 S. Dearborn St. (at Madison St.)

Phone: 312-384-1900 — Lunch Mon – Fri
Web: www.rosebudrestaurants.com — Dinner nightly
Prices: $$$ — Monroe

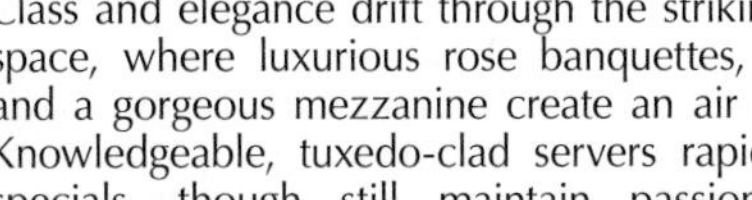

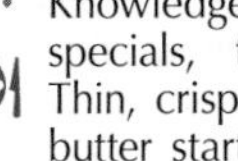

Class and elegance drift through the striking bi-level dining space, where luxurious rose banquettes, soaring ceilings, and a gorgeous mezzanine create an air of sophistication. Knowledgeable, tuxedo-clad servers rapidly fire off daily specials, though still maintain passion and sincerity. Thin, crispy, salted raisin bread and fresh rolls with honey butter start things off right, while scrumptious starters like peppercorn ahi tuna with ginger soy, coconut shrimp, and smoked salmon pastrami please the palate.

Slice into a juicy *petit* filet, seared just so and served with a side of jus. Complete the decadence with fresh blueberries, raspberries, and strawberries coupled with velvety sabayon—whipped with a touch of cream and spiked with Grand Marnier.

Terzo Piano

Italian 

D4

159 E. Monroe St. (bet. Columbus Dr. & Michigan Ave.)

Phone: 312-443-8650 — Lunch daily
Web: www.terzopianochicago.com — Dinner Thu
Prices: $$$ — Monroe

Setting a restaurant within the Art Institute of Chicago's Modern Wing leads to heightened aesthetic expectations, and Terzo Piano meets every one. A bright white room with clean lines befitting a Malevich composition is comfortably scattered with tables offering up Stieglitz-worthy skyline views. Stroll in from the museum or enter via the suspended bridge from Millennium Park.

The kitchen takes pride in making all menu elements from scratch, executing refined and delightful farm-to-table cuisine. Seasonal ingredients from local farms lead to a frequently changing menu, which may include eggy *fettuccini alla chitarra* tossed with spring garlic and almond pesto; or milk chocolate *crémeux* tucked between toasted brioche and placed atop raspberry jam.

Trattoria No. 10

10 N. Dearborn St. (bet. Madison & Washington Sts.)

Phone: 312-984-1718
Web: www.trattoriaten.com
Prices: $$

Lunch Mon – Fri
Dinner Mon – Sat
Washington

Don't be deceived by its small entrance next to Sopraffina Market—Trattoria No. 10's cavernous subterranean rooms seem to spread out for miles under the Loop. Lunch reservations are necessary to secure a spot here among the legal and financial power lunchers scarfing up rustic Italian specialties, alongside a selection of beer lovers perusing the craft varietals.

Seasonality is the driving force behind many of their items including the justly famous ravioli, filled one day with squash blossoms and pancetta, and another day with the always in-demand spicy sausage. Other fresh pasta creations may include fluffy spinach *gnudi* with fennel pollen in a creamy heirloom tomato sauce; or miniature orecchiette tossed with chopped rapini and fontina.

Vivere

71 W. Monroe St. (bet. Clark & Dearborn Sts.)

Phone: 312-332-4040
Web: www.vivere-chicago.com
Prices: $$

Lunch Mon – Fri
Dinner Mon – Sat
Monroe

Within the venerable Italian Village restaurant family, Vivere is the relative spring chicken of the group, with only two decades on the job compared to its sibling's 85 years of tradition. The third generation owners keep this experience as sparkling as the copper and brass in the dining room, mixing formality with spirited charm in a vibrant and curvaceous wood-toned space.

Italian specialties abound here: tiered layers of smoked *scamorza*, spinach, and San Marzano tomato sauce in *pasticcio affumicato* warm with each forkful; while linguini Calabresi is redolent with jumbo lump crab, shaved garlic, and red chili rings. Exceptional pheasant *agnolottini* is justly lauded. Allow the well-informed staff to guide you through the vast wine selection.

MICHELIN

Pilsen, Little Italy & University Village

This cluster of neighborhoods packs a perfect punch, both in terms of food, spice, and sheer energy level. It lives up to every expectation and reputation, so get ready for a tour packed with literal, acoustic, and visual flavor. The Little Italy moniker applies to one stretch of Taylor Street. While it abuts the University (of Illinois at Chicago) Village neighborhood, Little Italy is bigger and more authentically Italian than it first appears. Make your way through these streets only to find that they are

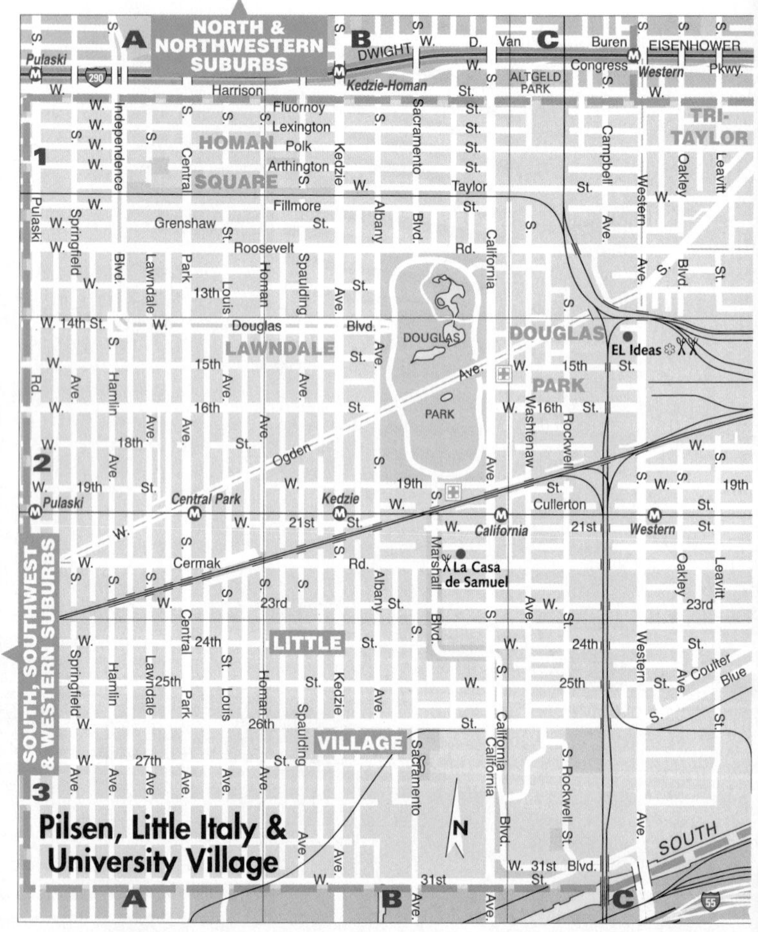

as stuffed with epicurean shops as an Italian beef sandwich is with meat. And, while on the topic, try a prime example of this iconic Chicago sandwich at the aptly named **Al's No. 1 Italian Beef**. When in Little Italy, one must start with **Conte Di Savoia**, an Italian grocery and popular takeout lunch counter. In June, folks flock here for the Oakley Festa Pasta Vino festival. Wash lunch down with a frozen fruit slush from **Mario's Italian Lemonade**. Lemon is the most popular flavor from the cash-only stand, but offbeat varieties like chocolate and banana are equally refreshing. On further strolling along these vibrant grounds, make sure you glimpse the famous Christopher Columbus statue, which was originally commissioned for the 1893 World's Columbian Exposition.

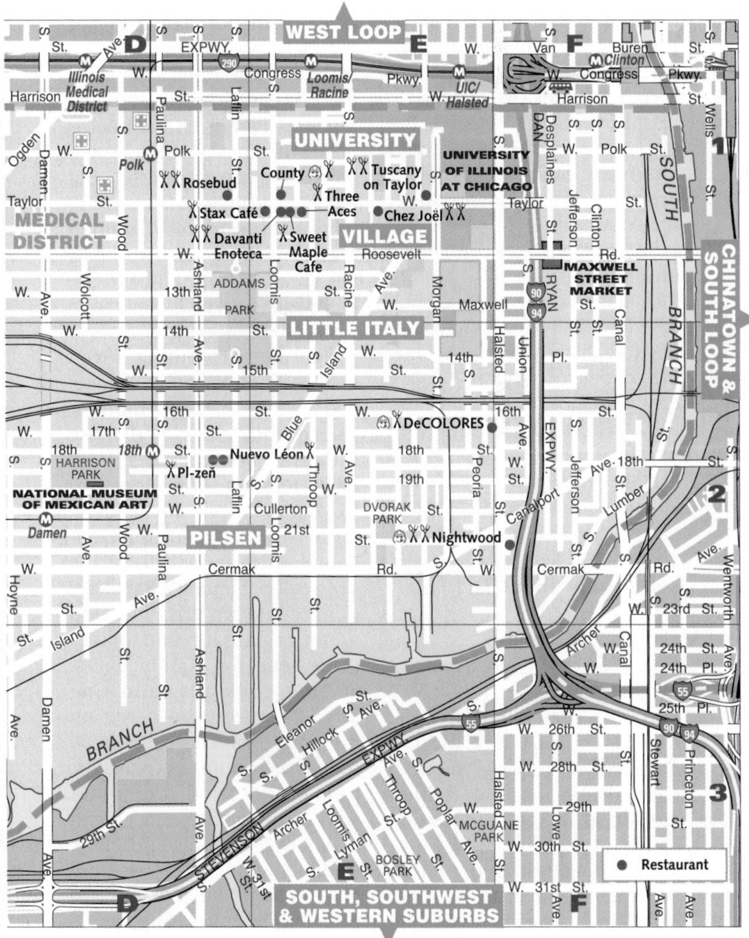

University Village

Like any self-respecting college "town," University Village houses a deluge of toasty coffee shops and cafés. A population of doctors, medical students, nurses, and others working in the neighborhood hospital contributes to an always-on-the-move vibe. **Lush Wine & Spirits** sells the expected, plus local obsession **Salted Caramel** is noted for its popcorn, especially the bacon-Bourbon variety. On Sundays, everybody seems destined for Chicago's legendary **Maxwell Street Market**. Relocated to Desplaines Street in 2008, this sprawling market welcomes more than 500 vendors selling produce and Mexican street food including tamales and tacos, as well as non-food miscellanea. Celebrity chef, Rick Bayless and the like shop here for locally grown tomatoes and tomatillos; while others buy ingredients for at-home culinary creations (not to mention tires, tube socks, and other flea market fare). Maxwell Street Market is also *the* choice for authentic Mexican delicacies.

Pilsen and Little Village

Chicago's massive Mexican population (more than 500,000 as per the last U.S. Census count) has built a patchwork of regional Mexican specialties, many of which are found in the south side's residential Pilsen and Little Village neighborhoods. Pilsen is home to the free National Museum of Mexican Art, the only Latino museum accredited by the American Association of Museums, as well as an abundance of authentic Mexican taquerias, bakeries, and other culturally relevant businesses. Everyone goes all out for Mexican Independence Day in September, including more than 25 participating area restaurants, while the Little Village Arts Festival packs 'em in every October. Stop by sumptuous **Sabinas Food Products** factory for freshly made tortillas and chips to take home, followed by a trip to the Sunday farmer's market at the Chicago Community Bank. Much of Pilsen's 26th Street is filled with auto chop shops and other workaday businesses. But the large-scale tortilla factories, where three or four women press and form corn tortillas, are an exception. Since 1950, **El Milagro** has offered a unique taste, with a cafeteria-style restaurant (presenting seven kinds of tamales on the menu) and a store that sells burritos, spiced corn chips, and those locally made tortillas. And while feasting, don't forget to fix your eyes upon the mural on the wall. Finally, environment-conscious fans can't resist the siren call of **Simone's Bar**. They congregate at this certified green restaurant and place-to-be-seen for quality beers, stirring cocktails, and fine food. Whether you perch on the patio, in "The Lab," or in their front room, empanadas, portobello fries (complete with a soy dipping sauce), and a black & blue grilled steak (topped with tomatoes, blue cheese, and fresh basil) are bound to have you smitten.

Chez Joël

French XX

E1

1119 W. Taylor St. (bet. Aberdeen & May Sts.)

Phone: 312-226-6479 — Lunch Fri – Sun
Web: www.chezjoelbistro.com — Dinner Tue – Sun
Prices: $$

A bit of Paris has landed in Little Italy with Chez Joël, the charming, red-brick corner bistro with its Francophile following and tasty fare. Gilded mirrors, pale yellow walls, a stunning crystal-beaded chandelier, and red velvet-draped windows weave an aura of timelessness, while French oldies piping through speakers add to the romance.

Owned and operated by brothers Joël and Ahmed Kazouini, the beloved spot spins out bistro favorites like crocks of French onion soup with a deliciously browned and bubbly lid of cheese; steamed mussels with white wine; crème brûlée; and profiteroles. Cocktails like the Bleu Margarita and the Calvados Royale also have a sexy accent. In warmer weather, snag a seat in the breezy courtyard and dine under the trees.

County

Barbecue X

E1

1352 W. Taylor St. (bet. Ada & Loomis Sts.)

Phone: 312-929-2528 — Lunch & dinner Tue – Sun
Web: www.dmkcountybarbeque.com
Prices: — Polk

Go ahead; guess which building on this block of Taylor belongs to County. If you chose the one done up in gingham, you're on the money. Chef Michael Kornick's barbecue-focused outpost exudes pure Americana, and is dressed in deep mahogany-tinted walls and the heavenly aroma of smoking meats.

The same cheeky 'tude that gave us County's technicolor façade appears in creative starters like the bacon-and-barbecue parfait: a shot glass layered with charred brisket and white cheddar grits, topped with a crisp bacon strip. Covering swaths of regional barbecue styles, other riches include St. Louis ribs smoked for five hours; moist, lacquered chicken; and spicy grilled hot links. Sides, like cheesy potato casserole with pickled jalapeños, are fun and fulfilling.

Davanti Enoteca

E1 — Italian XX

1359 W. Taylor St. (at Loomis St.)

Phone: 312-226-5550 — Lunch & dinner daily
Web: www.davantichicago.com
Prices: $$

Much more than a simple wine bar, Davanti warms both belly and soul with its wood-burning oven and welcoming atmosphere. The rustic interior, with pale brick archways and wood-plank ceilings and floors, is stacked to the gills with wine bottles and cases. Peek those humorous retro-style posters ("They're happy because they eat lard") which whet the appetite and spark smiles.

Classic Italian dishes are appetizing, plentiful, and may feature pizzas perched on commercial-size tomato cans; or warm wilted kale and *guanciale* salad. *Pollo "Sole Mio"* is slathered in spicy-sweet chili paste, then grilled, quartered, and partially deboned; while ricotta *gnudi* and grilled pork cheek in a chili oil-spiked broth tempts diners to pick up the dish and slurp it down.

DeCOLORES

E2 — Mexican X

1626 S. Halsted St. (bet. 16th & 17th Sts.)

Phone: 312-226-9886 — Lunch Thu – Sun
Web: www.decolor.us — Dinner Tue – Sun
Prices: $$

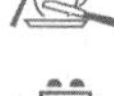

DeCOLORES isn't just a festive family-run Mexican restaurant; it's a *galeria y sabores*, a gallery that fits right into Pilsen's art district showcasing local artists. The often-changing artwork, illuminated by skylights and wide window panes throughout the stylish space, matches the creativity on each plate that comes from recipes passed down through generations.

After homemade corn chips with two salsas (green tomatillo or smoky roasted red pepper), choose from ceviches, grilled meats, shrimp-centric seafood dishes, and specialties like *taquitos de papa*—a vegetarian explosion of shredded beets, chayote, purple cabbage, mashed potatoes, and tart tomato-citrus sauce. The bar lures all via its generous offering of chilled beer glasses and mixers.

EL Ideas ✿

C2

Contemporary XX

2419 W. 14th St. (at Western Ave.)

Phone: 312-226-8144 Dinner Tue – Sat
Web: www.elideas.com
Prices: $$$$ Western (Pink)

BYO

Galdones Photography

EL Ideas is a complete original, right down to the setting. It is in the kind of neighborhood that doesn't shackle a deeply creative chef to high-maintenance crowds (read: desolate and edgy). The staff is hip, and their welcome is warm. Just a half-wall separates tables from the kitchen; also get to know the chefs as they personally present the dish they each created.

Much can be said to derail the pleasure of eating here. Some even think that this kitchen is full of itself. But yes, these cooks are really *that* talented and the point is that you need to eat here to fully understand its relaxed vibe and free-flowing format. El Ideas is a conceptual restaurant to be reckoned with. This is clear from the thrice-cooked potato, scrambled egg, and dill aïoli beneath osetra caviar through to the blackberry *pâté de fruits* and mini-oreo *mignardise*. Other courses might include a roasted garlic roll stuffed with oozing smoked raclette, strips of bacon-like sturgeon over thick soubise, topped with pickled onions and sunflower shoots; or neat peanut macarons filled with foie gras mousse.

Finish with a quenelle of applejack cider sorbet and a hot, sugar-dusted donut with caramelized yogurt sauce.

La Casa De Samuel

Mexican

B2

2834 W. Cermak Rd. (bet. California Ave. & Marshall Blvd.)

Phone: 773-376-7474 Lunch & dinner daily
Web: www.lacasadesamuel.com
Prices: ⊜ California (Pink)

Though the sign over the awning reads "Cocina Internacional," make no mistake: this Mexican restaurant has been bringing tacos and *queso fundido* to Pilsen since 1989. Exposed wood beams, brick walls, and bright oil paintings add a true-blue vibe; while a tortilla station where an *abuelita* works masa into thin discs gets the appetite going. Multi-generational families return time and again to share spicy *molcajete*-crushed salsa.

Along with the freshly made tortillas that arrive swaddled and warm from the grill, the bustling kitchen turns out solid standards like fajitas as well as unusual wild game options like grilled wild boar, rabbit, or alligator. Wash down baby eels sizzling with garlic and chile with an icy lime-infused margarita.

Nightwood

Contemporary

F2

2119 S. Halsted St. (at 21st St.)

Phone: 312-526-3385 Lunch Sun
Web: www.nightwoodrestaurant.com Dinner Mon – Sat
Prices: $$

An oasis of stylish simplicity on an otherwise bland stretch of Halsted, Nightwood gleams like a beacon with its enchanting courtyard and welcoming entrance. Solo diners love the chef's counter with its view into the bustling kitchen. Dark wood and brick accents throughout make the dining room casually romantic.

Speaking of which, get your palate going with a whiskey cocktail or seasonal non-alcoholic bevy like a concord fizz. Rustic inflections like spit-roasted chicken and hand-shaped pasta complement elegant touches that show the kitchen's finesse. A purse of soft scrambled eggs opens to reveal creamy quail egg yolks and steelhead roe; and caramelized pigs' ears take on the texture of peanut brittle when paired with maple-habanero butter.

Nuevo Léon

Mexican

D2

1515 W. 18th St. (bet. Ashland Ave. & Laflin St.)

Phone: 312-421-1517 — Lunch & dinner daily
Web: N/A
Prices: — 18th

From the minute your feet step on the clay tiles inside this Mexican eatery, you'll be transported into the cultural ambience for which Pilsen is known. Take in the artifacts like hand-painted plates and murals on the walls along with blasting Mexican music.

Like any good Mexican joint, this local darling has combination platters on the menu, and they're the finest way to get a cross-section of the kitchen's best. The *carne a la Tampiqueña* includes simply-seasoned tender grilled beef, tomato-scented rice, beans, and both a tomatillo-lime salsa verde and smoky red chile salsa, which elevate the taste to something extraordinary. The *horchata* is well-spiced and soups of the day vary by season. Large portions mean leftovers for lunch *mañana*.

Pl-zeň

Gastropub

D2

1519 W. 18th St. (bet. Ashland Ave & Laflin St.)

Phone: 312-733-0248 — Lunch Sat – Sun
Web: www.pl-zen.com — Dinner nightly
Prices: $$ — 18th

Look for the octopus mural crawling up the exterior of a three-story townhouse. Then, follow the ramp into the belly of the beast for the latest gastropub staking its claim in this rapidly gentrifying neighborhood. From the spartan concrete- and brick-donning dining room to the low lighting and obscure soundtrack (Beach Sluts, anyone?), Pl-zeň clearly isn't a place for the unadventurous.

Its menu brings elements of both the elegant and exotic to standard comfort food. *Guajillo*-marinated roasted chicken with porcini mustard; boar meatballs; and burgers made with lamb, bison, or scallops are scarfed down by the trendy crowd alongside pints from the lengthy beer selection. Weekend brunchers fork plates of short rib Benedict with their Bloody Marys.

Rosebud

Italian XX

D1

1500 W. Taylor St. (at Laflin St.)

Phone: 312-942-1117 — Lunch & dinner daily
Web: www.rosebudrestaurants.com
Prices: $$ — Polk

Handsomely appointed and sultry even at lunch, Rosebud evokes those Italian red-sauce joints where deals are brokered by wise guys in hushed voices over the likes of a fat pork chop Calabrese. This is the original location that launched a mini-chain of Rosebuds throughout Chicago, and its nostalgic charm still retains its character—as well as the characters who've been coming here for more than 30 years. Live out your Godfather fantasy in a seat by the leaded glass windows, watched over by a painting of the Chairman of the Board, while slurping down *pasta e fagioli*, sausage and peppers, or chicken Vesuvio. And since we're reliving this fantastical classic, leave the gun, as they say, and take the crispy cannoli garnished with pistachios and strawberries.

Stax Café

American 

E1

1401 W. Taylor St. (at Loomis St.)

Phone: 312-733-9871 — Lunch daily
Web: www.staxcafe.com
Prices: 

"We're Breakfast Geeks. We take this stuff way too seriously" reads one of the server's T-shirts at Stax Café, and UIC students and staff are grateful for their dedication to heart-warming wake-up fare. From the coffee and fresh juice bar for on-the-go types, to flat-screen TVs for those dying to catch up on sports, this corner restaurant aims to get everyone's day started right.

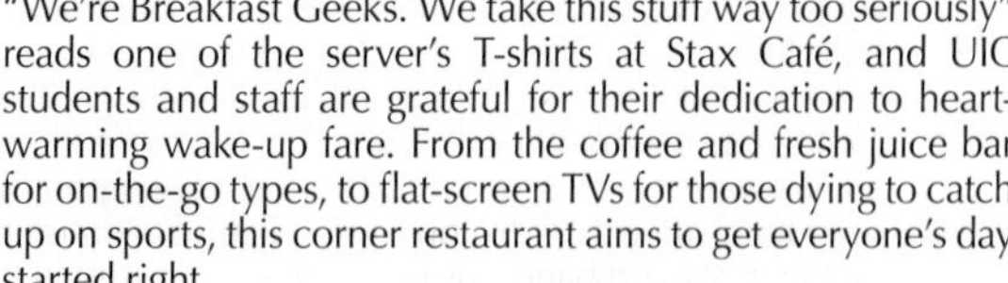

Breakfast items with tasty twists abound, like ricotta pancakes with strawberry-rhubarb compote; or the Spanish Harlem omelet served frittata-style with chorizo, roasted tomatoes, and poblano peppers. Can't choose? Get a side of mini waffles dusted with powdered sugar alongside your main dish, and don't forget to check out the chalkboards for specials—perhaps breakfast tacos?

Sweet Maple Cafe

American

1339 W. Taylor St. (bet. Loomis St. & Racine Ave.)

Phone: 312-243-8908 — Lunch daily
Web: www.sweetmaplecafe.com
Prices:

Sweet Maple piles on the country charm for the loyal crowd of regulars who know that its register of made-from-scratch breakfast plates (with a few lunch items too) is worth getting up for each morning. Checkered oilcloth tablecloths, scuffed wood floors, and rustic dowel furniture give this Taylor Street spot a lived-in look, while fresh flowers on each table brighten the mood.

Whatever your choice, make sure to include a homemade sweet milk or cornmeal biscuit with your order—whether as part of a sandwich with freshly scrambled eggs and cheese, or on the side of a rotating special like the *chorissimo* taco. Corned beef hash with expertly poached eggs and firm, flavorful bits of corned beef is an eye-opener for those who've avoided lesser versions.

Three Aces

Gastropub

1321 W. Taylor St. (bet. Loomis & Throop Sts.)

Phone: 312-243-1577 — Lunch & dinner daily
Web: www.threeaceschicago.com
Prices: $$

The trio of gleaming white aces makes this restaurant's façade hard to miss. But, it's the last shiny thing you'll see as you descend into the dark, rock n' roll-loving bar that, albeit oddly, offers classic American food with an Italian spin. Overhead cage lights reclaimed from the Joliet Prison (a site well-known to Blues Brothers fans) don't do much to illuminate tufted leather seats and band posters on the walls. But, in the glow of glass votives on each table, you'll see enough to dig into paprika-dusted roasted garlic soup; or *arancini* with arugula pesto and Parmesan.

A cracker-thin *pizzetta* with seasonal toppings like homemade merguez and crumbled *ricotta salata* is an all-time fave; whereas big appetites go for the famously towering Ace burger.

Tuscany on Taylor

E1 — Italian XX

1014 W. Taylor St. (bet. Miller & Morgan Sts.)

Phone: 312-829-1990 — Lunch Mon – Fri
Web: www.tuscanychicago.com — Dinner nightly
Prices: $$ — UIC-Halsted

Gazing down the parchment-lined walls in this airy dining room, hungry visitors can't help but notice (and smell) an open kitchen straight out of a Tuscan culinary brochure. Cooks in chef's toques bustle among polished copper pans and shelves stocked with pasta and cans of San Marzano tomatoes next to a wood-fired oven that sets the stage for a classic *festa Italiana*.

The menu boasts an array of pizzas, but also offers appetizing versions of traditional and modern items like sausage-stuffed agnolotti in a fennel- and tomato-cream sauce; trailed by decadent cocoa-dusted squares of tiramisu. If the values on the wine list don't excite, savants who like to store their own stash can take advantage of the brass nameplate-engraved wine lockers at the entrance.

Look for **red** symbols, indicating a particularly pleasant ambience.

River North

Art galleries, a hopping nightlife, well-known restaurants and chefs, swanky shopping, great views, even a head-turning fast-food chain: Almost everything that Chicago boasts is offered here. Perhaps because River North offers so much it also attracts so many. From ladies who lunch and office workers, to tour bus-style tourists, most folks who pass through the Windy City make a stop here.

Beyond the Ordinary

River North (which, it stands to reason, is located north of the Chicago River) has no shortage of food and drink attractions. True, as you pull up to Ontario and Clark streets, you might just think, "chain restaurant central," but even the chains in River North have a particular charm. Among them is the **Rock 'n' Roll McDonald's**, a block-long, music-themed outpost of the ubiquitous burger chain. One of the busiest **MickeyD's** in the world, this one has an expanded menu, music memorabilia, and bragging rights to the first two-lane drive-through. (Remember: McDonald's is a local chain, still headquartered in the suburbs.)

The Rainforest Café (with its wild range of flesh, fowl, and fish dishes); the forever hip and boisterous **Hard Rock Café**; and **M Burger** (a noted chain rolled out by the Lettuce Entertain You Enterprise) are all quite the hit, and popular tourist draws. One of *the* most beloved burger joints, **M Burger** is a Michigan Avenue marvel boasting an array of juicy burgers (try the no meat Nurse Betty) alongside fries and shakes. Speaking of drive-through chains, River North is the flagship location of **Portillo's**, a local, cherished hot dog, burger, and beer chain. Its giant exterior belies its efficient service and better-than-expected food. When it comes to size, few buildings can top the mammoth **Merchandise Mart** (so large it has its own ZIP code). Along with its history, retail stores, boutiques, and drool-worthy kitchen showrooms, it is also home to two great food shops. At **Artisan Cellar**, in addition to boutique wines, paninis, and specialty cheeses, you can also purchase Katherine Anne Confections' fresh cream caramels. Locals also love **The Chopping Block** for its expertly taught and themed cooking courses, well-edited wine selections, and their newly stocked shiny knife lines. (There's another location in Lincoln Square for north side courses.) Nearby, Le Cordon Bleu College of Culinary Arts cradles a student-run restaurant where diners can get a glimpse of the next big thing in Chicago kitchens. Well-tread by locals in-the-know, **Technique** displays a unique blend of elegance and comfort paired with gracious service and a daily-changing bill of fare. Open Books, a used bookstore that relies on its proceeds to fund literacy programs, has plenty of cookbooks on its shelves. Outfit any kitchen with finds from the Bloomingdale's Home store in the 1912 Medinah Temple. You'll smell the **Blommer Chocolate Outlet Store** before you see it. Late at night and early in the morning, the tempting chocolate aroma wafts down the river beckoning city dwellers to its Willy Wonka-esque confines. This is where to stock up on sweets from the 70-plus-year-old-brand. Blommer's also boasts a specialty cocoa collection ranging from such fabulously sinful flavors as black cocoa, cake-based cocoa powders, and Dutch specialty varieties.

Deep-Dish Delights

River North is as good a place as any to indulge in the local phenomenon of Chicago-style, deep-dish pizza. Also called stuffed pizza (referring to the pie, but it could also refer to the way you'll feel after you snarf it down), deep-dish pizza was created in the Windy City in the 1940s. Closer to a casserole (or, as they say in the Midwest, "hot dish,") than an Italian-style pizza, this is a thick, doughy crust, holding abundant cheese, sauce, and tasty toppings.

Some say it is Chicago water in the dough that makes that crust so distinctive. Deep-dish pies take a while to fashion, so be prepared to wait wherever you go. **Pizzeria Uno** (or its sister **Pizzeria Due**), and **Giordano's** are some of the best-known pie makers. If a little indigestion isn't a concern, chase down that priceless pizza with another Chicago-style specialty: the Italian beef sandwich. Very much like a messy, yet tasty French dip, an Italian beef isn't Italian, but all Chicago. Dating back to the 1930s, it featured thinly sliced, seasoned beef on a hoagie crowned with either hot or sweet peppers. If you order it "wet," both the meat and the bread will be dipped in pan juices. You could also add cheese, but this isn't Philly. Two of the biggest contenders in the Italian beef wars are in this 'hood: **Al's Italian Beef** and **Mr. Beef**. Both eateries have top-notch sausages and hot dogs on the menu as well.

Get Your Groove On

Nightlife in River North is a big deal with everything from authentic Irish pubs to cocktail lounges, for those who like to see-and-be-seen. Nestled in the landmark Chicago Historical Society Building, **Excalibur** is a multi-floor dance club and is all about velvet ropes, house music, and an epic drink list. **Blue Chicago** is a civilized place where you can sip on a drink and listen to that world-famous Chicago sound, the Blues. **English**, an aptly named British bar, is a popular watering hole for watching soccer and other sports, not usually broadcast at your typical sports bar. English is also home to some fantastic food like duck confit dumplings and lobster cake sliders. And finally, don't skip the **Green Door Tavern**, which gets its name from the fact that its colored front told Prohibition-era customers where to enter for a drink. Order their "famous sandwich" or "Green Door Burger" and you will understand what all the fuss is about.

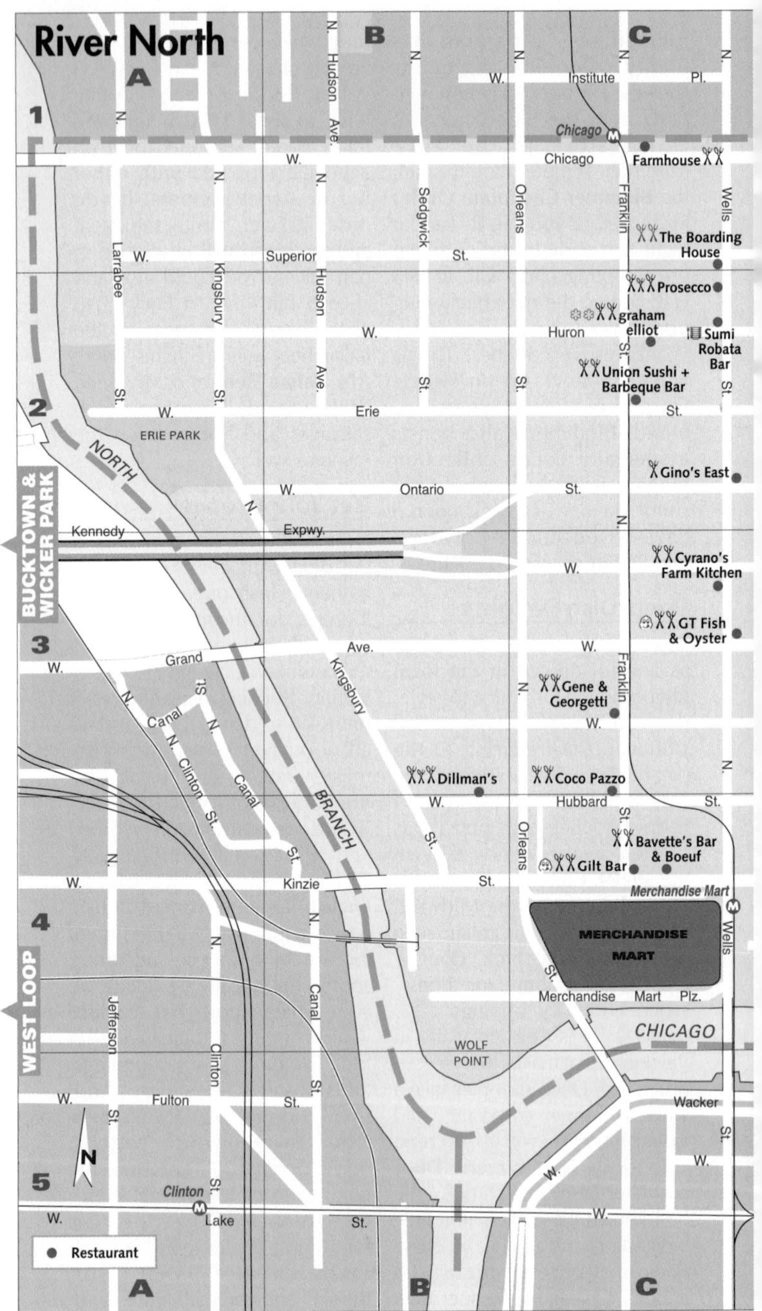
River North
Farmhouse
The Boarding House
Prosecco
graham elliot
Sumi Robata Bar
Union Sushi + Barbeque Bar
Gino's East
Cyrano's Farm Kitchen
GT Fish & Oyster
Gene & Georgetti
Dillman's
Coco Pazzo
Bavette's Bar & Boeuf
Gilt Bar
Merchandise Mart
MERCHANDISE MART
Chicago
Clinton
BUCKTOWN & WICKER PARK
WEST LOOP
ERIE PARK
NORTH BRANCH
CHICAGO
WOLF POINT
Kennedy Expwy.
W. Institute Pl.
W. Chicago
W. Superior St.
W. Huron
W. Erie St.
W. Ontario St.
W. Grand Ave.
W. Hubbard St.
W. Kinzie St.
Merchandise Mart Plz.
Wacker
W. Fulton St.
W. Lake St.
N. Larrabee St.
N. Kingsbury St.
N. Hudson Ave.
N. Sedgwick St.
N. Orleans St.
N. Franklin St.
N. Wells St.
N. Canal St.
N. Clinton St.
N. Jefferson St.
Restaurant

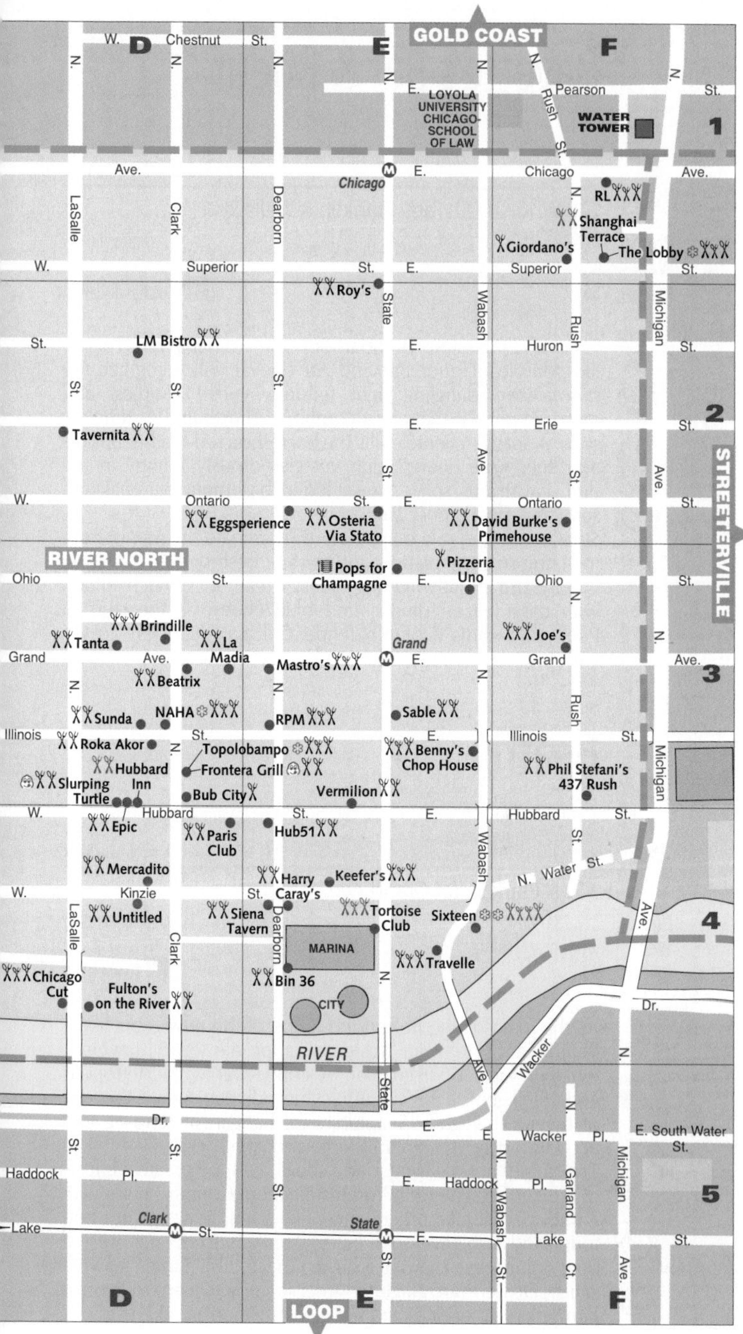
GOLD COAST
STREETERVILLE
RIVER NORTH
LOOP
LOYOLA UNIVERSITY CHICAGO-SCHOOL OF LAW
WATER TOWER
MARINA CITY
RIVER
RL
Shanghai Terrace
Giordano's
The Lobby
Roy's
LM Bistro
Tavernita
Eggsperience
Osteria Via Stato
David Burke's Primehouse
Pops for Champagne
Pizzeria Uno
Brindille
Tanta
La Madia
Joe's
Mastro's
Beatrix
Sunda
NAHA
RPM
Sable
Roka Akor
Topolobampo
Benny's Chop House
Hubbard Inn
Frontera Grill
Phil Stefani's 437 Rush
Slurping Turtle
Bub City
Vermilion
Epic
Paris Club
Hub51
Mercadito
Harry Caray's
Keefer's
Untitled
Siena Tavern
Tortoise Club
Sixteen
Travelle
Chicago Cut
Fulton's on the River
Bin 36
Chicago
Grand
Clark
State

Bavette's Bar & Boeuf

American 

218 W. Kinzie St. (bet. Franklin & Wells Sts.)

Phone: 312-624-8154 — Dinner nightly
Web: www.bavetteschicago.com
Prices: **$$$** — Merchandise Mart

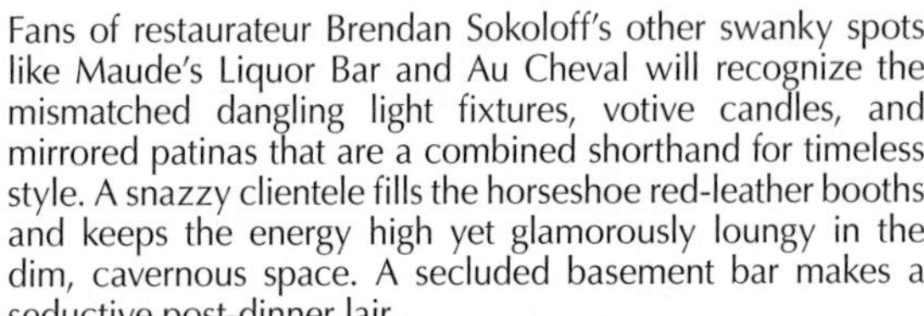

Fans of restaurateur Brendan Sokoloff's other swanky spots like Maude's Liquor Bar and Au Cheval will recognize the mismatched dangling light fixtures, votive candles, and mirrored patinas that are a combined shorthand for timeless style. A snazzy clientele fills the horseshoe red-leather booths and keeps the energy high yet glamorously loungy in the dim, cavernous space. A secluded basement bar makes a seductive post-dinner lair.

Steakhouse and raw bar standards dominate the menu, from towering seafood platters and trays of fresh oysters to steaks, chops, and mouthwatering sides. Creamed spinach folded with caramelized onions and blue cheese is the stuff of Popeye's dreams. A plump, tender Chicago-cut ribeye arrives with luscious tarragon béarnaise.

Beatrix

International 

519 N Clark St. (at Grand Ave.)

Phone: 312-284-1377 — Lunch & dinner daily
Web: www.beatrixchicago.com
Prices: **$$** — Grand (Red)

As the main dining hub in the lobby of the new Aloft hotel, Beatrix aims to offer sustenance for all weary travelers, whether local or from afar. A coffee bar with Metropolis and Intelligentsia brews offers fuel all day, while the rest of the mod, slightly Scandinavian, hangar-sized space can accommodate groups both large and small.

The quirky but pleasing menu showcases the creative efforts of the Lettuce Entertain You test kitchen. Comfort foods with a quirky twist take precedence, like a tender and warm pot-roast sandwich enveloped in a toasted white cheddar-crusted bun; or Japanese *tsukune* (chicken meatballs) in a spicy-sweet sauce. Desserts are all gluten-free, so no one needs to deprive him or herself of rich caramel pie with shortbread crust.

Benny's Chop House

E3 Steakhouse XXX

444 N. Wabash Ave. (bet. Hubbard & Illinois Sts.)

Phone: 312-626-2444 Lunch & dinner daily
Web: www.bennyschophouse.com
Prices: $$$ Grand (Red)

Old-school service meets modern elegance at Benny's Chop House. A far cry from the clubby, masculine steakhouses of yesteryear and just a stone's throw away from the Magnificent Mile, this expansive but welcoming space goes for understated glamour, with tasteful inlaid wood and burgundy columns offset by natural stone walls, white birch branches, and a marble bar.

Though Benny's steaks are the draw, those prime cuts of filet mignon and ribeye are matched by fresh seafood like simply roasted bone-in halibut fillet and classic raw bar towers, along with a variety of pastas and salads. A trio of sliders featuring mini portions of Benny's burger, crab cake, and sliced filet with horseradish cream elevate the idea of bar snacks to new heights.

Bin 36

E4 American XX

339 N. Dearborn St. (bet. Kinzie St. & the Chicago River)

Phone: 312-755-9463 Lunch & dinner daily
Web: www.bin36.com
Prices: $$$ Lake

From morning coffee at the marble bar to a dedicated evening of wine tasting, Bin 36 is a gourmet's paradise. Snack on wine and cheese at the tavern or restaurant, learn about your favorite fermented sips and bites with evening flights and classes, or simply grab a well-priced bottle of Bordeaux and wedge of blue to-go at the retail store.

Inside, dining bars are scattered throughout the eclectic, multi-level space and a communal table set before a cheese cave put signature products on tantalizing display. A tweak on classic *ribollita* "soup" arrives as a crock of toasted bread cubes topped with hot, beefy broth, poached farm egg, and grated cheese. Desserts like maple *pots de crème* with popcorn ice cream are offered with wine or Bourbon pairings.

The Boarding House

International XX

C1

720 N. Wells St. (at Superior St.)

Phone: 312-280-0720 — Dinner nightly
Web: www.boardinghousechicago.com
Prices: **$$** — Chicago (Red)

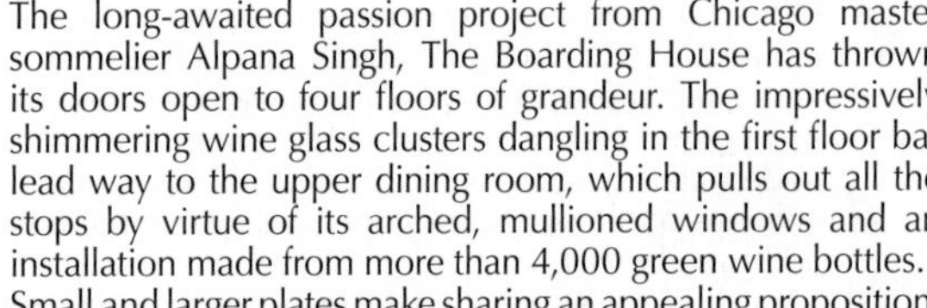

The long-awaited passion project from Chicago master sommelier Alpana Singh, The Boarding House has thrown its doors open to four floors of grandeur. The impressively shimmering wine glass clusters dangling in the first floor bar lead way to the upper dining room, which pulls out all the stops by virtue of its arched, mullioned windows and an installation made from more than 4,000 green wine bottles. Small and larger plates make sharing an appealing proposition. House-made *tagliolini* ribbons tossed with fresh peas, mint, and pickled ramps are bright and zesty. Garlic lovers use crispy chicken thighs to sop up every last bit of aromatic green-garlic pistou. Scoops of sour cherry gelée and merlot-chocolate chip ice cream crown rich brownies for dessert.

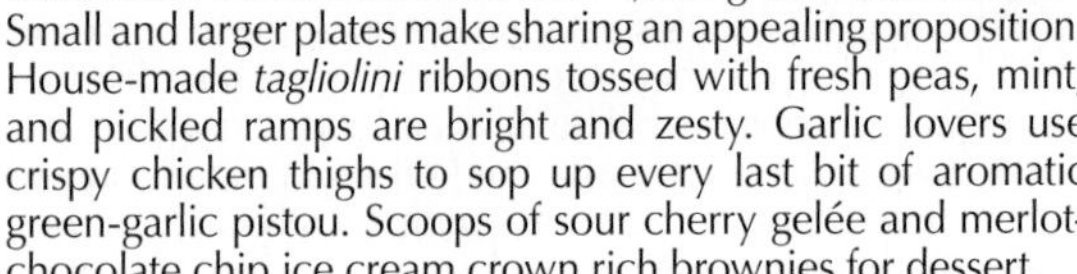

Brindille

French XXX

D3

534 N. Clark St. (bet. Grand Ave. & Ohio St.)

Phone: 312-595-1616 — Dinner nightly
Web: www.brindille-chicago.com
Prices: **$$$$** — Grand (Red)

River North habitués can double their pleasure now that cousins Carrie and Michael Nahabedian of the much-loved NAHA have opened a second, equally elegant restaurant not far from their flagship space. A jewel-box dining room accented in silver, amethyst, and cream conveys subtle luxury, with exquisitely presented dishes that are a feast for the eyes and palate.

French influences pervade the Mediterranean menu, like frog's legs and roasted ramps scattered with toasted hazelnuts and fresh pea shoots; or crispy monkfish tail paired with burgundy snails, flageolets, and wisps of micro-coriander. Bread with whipped honey butter starts the meal on a sweet note, while a dainty Paris-Brest atop macerated strawberries and rose ice cream ends it memorably.

Bub City

Barbecue

435 N. Clark St. (bet. Hubbard & Illinois Sts.)

Phone: 312-610-4200 Lunch & dinner daily
Web: www.bubcitychicago.com
Prices: $$ Grand (Red)

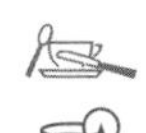

Bub City isn't as far south as Nashville or Memphis, but the country music vibe comes through just the same at this barbecue- and booze-focused hang. Two bars flank the main stage that hosts nightly live entertainment. One bar is a shrine to over 100 varieties of whiskey, and the other to beer—easily identified by the American flag made from empty cans stacked behind its counter.

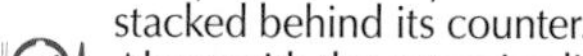

Along with the extensive lineup of traditional smoked brisket, ribs, and fried chicken, a raw bar brings chilled seafood refreshment before spicy cheese-stuffed Texas Torpedoes and loaded hot link sandwiches. A bowl of Smokie's chili arrives with a kick from sliced jalapeño, but the caddy of barbecue and hot sauces on each table lets heat fiends intensify the seasoning.

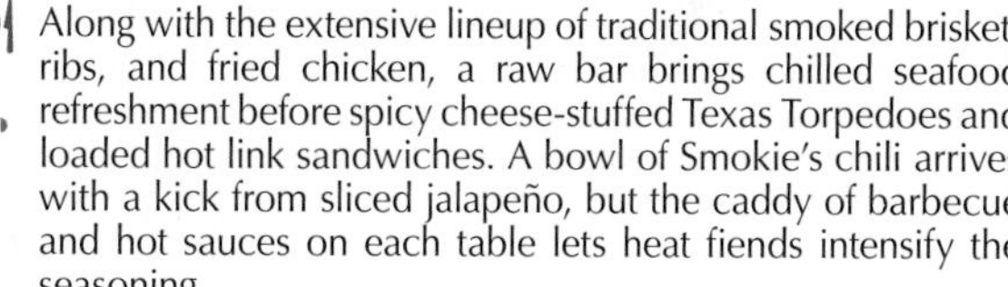

Chicago Cut

Steakhouse

300 N. LaSalle St. (at Wacker Dr.)

Phone: 312-329-1800 Lunch & dinner daily
Web: www.chicagocutsteakhouse.com
Prices: $$$ Merchandise Mart

Give the usual steakhouse trappings a face-lift, and Chicago Cut is what you'll get: a sleek, modern space for big spenders to play on the riverfront. Floor-to-ceiling windows cast light onto red velvet banquettes and rich mahogany wood accents. Umbrella-shaded riverwalk tables let you take your T-bone alfresco. As befits such a glossy place, the extensive wine list is presented tableside on iPads.

Classic American steakhouse options expand to include fish and poultry dishes at dinnertime, but beef is boss here. USDA Prime steaks, butchered and dry-aged in-house for 40 days, get just the right amount of time under the flame for medium-rare char. Sides like thick-cut, panko-crusted onion rings and buttery mashed potatoes make delicious accompaniments.

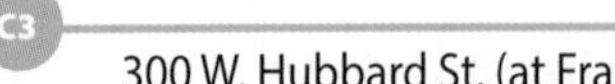

Coco Pazzo

Italian XX

C3

300 W. Hubbard St. (at Franklin St.)

Phone: 312-836-0900 Lunch Mon – Fri
Web: www.cocopazzochicago.com Dinner nightly
Prices: $$ Merchandise Mart

Windows framed with cheery blue and orange awnings are the first sign of welcome, but the real Italian greeting comes upon entering Coco Pazzo to see a prosciutto leg displayed prominently on a carving cradle. Add this to bowls of antipasti laid out on a serving stand, and a Bellini atop the dark wood bar or linen-topped table, and you know the type of conviviality that is in store here.

Tuscan cuisine, rustic by nature, gets a polished sheen in the open kitchen, where the line takes great care to turn out unfussy but flavorful preparations. Freshly sliced smoked beef carpaccio with goat cheese sauce and roasted hazelnuts balances taste and texture; and a dusting of grated *bottarga* on crispy sea bass and tender, garlicky lima beans adds a luxe touch.

Cyrano's Farm Kitchen

French XX

C3

546 N. Wells St. (bet. Grand Ave. & Ohio St.)

Phone: 312-467-0546 Lunch Tue – Sun
Web: N/A Dinner Mon – Sat
Prices: $$ Grand (Red)

Due to its façade which is just as vivid and colorful as the inside, Cyrano's transports diners to the South of France via cuisine and décor—now however, it's more country farm mouse than city bistro house. Quaintly rustic touches like walls covered in gray hay-hued plaster and ancient farm implements as well as a few rooster decorations for effect, set the charming stage.

As befits this homey concept, the menu emphasizes farm-to-table food by way of Provence, while still retaining bistro classics. *Salade Niçoise* is expertly composed and layered with crisp beans, poached egg, and brined red onions; whereas onion soup remains a French standard. End by dipping decadent foie gras-filled beignets into a trio of sweet dipping sauces—cherry compote anyone?

David Burke's Primehouse

Steakhouse XX

F2

616 N. Rush St. (bet. Ohio & Ontario Sts.)

Phone: 312-660-6000 Lunch & dinner daily
Web: www.davidburkesprimehouse.com
Prices: $$$ Grand (Red)

Though Prime, the bull that Chef David Burke bought years ago, has passed on to the pasture in the sky, his descendants provide all the USDA beef that sizzles its way onto the plates at this swanky steakhouse in The James hotel. A recent renovation brings the bar from the hotel lobby into the restaurant and adds Burke's Bacon Bar next door with "handwiches" for the grab-and-go set.

Pink Himalayan rock salt plays a major role in the décor while also starring in steaks dry-aged in a salt-tiled aging room and sided with homemade private label steak sauce. For an edgier plate, brunch's Little Bull bento box lets you sample steak two ways, barbecue duck dumplings, and green beans tempura.

Unleash your inner child with a grapefruit pound cake for dessert.

Dillman's

American XXX

B3

354 Hubbard St. (at Kingsbury St.)

Phone: 312-988-0078 Lunch & dinner Tue – Sat
Web: www.dillmanschicago.com
Prices: $$ Merchandise Mart

A trek to the far west reaches of Hubbard is rewarded with impressively tasty fare and a Dr. Brown's soda at the poshest delicatessen in town. And it should be no surprise that this beauty, with its pressed-tin ceilings, wingback chairs and chandeliers, is yet another creation of wunderkind Chicago restaurateur Brendan Sodikoff—also the master behind Au Cheval and Gilt Bar.

Those used to oversized sandwiches à la Carnegie and Katz's will do a double-take at smaller-sized treats like fried beef bologna with smoked provolone on a fresh egg bun; or mod mash-ups like a potato crisp Caesar salad with salt-and-vinegar chips subbing for croutons. Bagels and cream cheese are made daily, so grab some today for a great morning tomorrow—but don't call it a deli!

Eggsperience

American XX

E2

35 W. Ontario St. (at Dearborn St.)

Phone: 312-870-6773 — Lunch daily
Web: www.eggsperiencecafe.com — Dinner Thu – Sat
Prices: ◎◎ — Grand (Red)

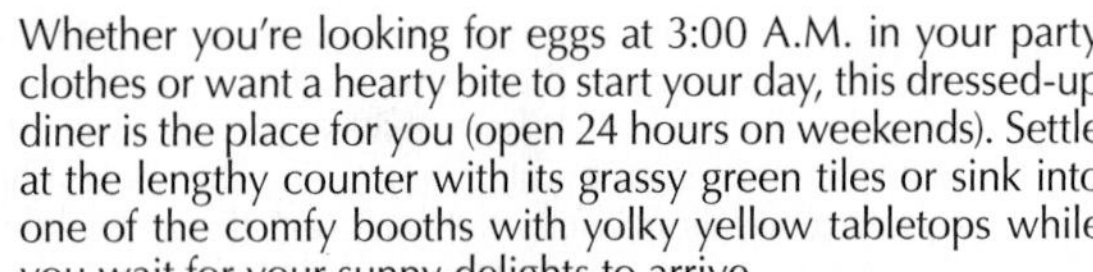

Whether you're looking for eggs at 3:00 A.M. in your party clothes or want a hearty bite to start your day, this dressed-up diner is the place for you (open 24 hours on weekends). Settle at the lengthy counter with its grassy green tiles or sink into one of the comfy booths with yolky yellow tabletops while you wait for your sunny delights to arrive.

Along with eggs every which way, all the breakfast standards are represented, from pancakes and waffles to corned beef hash and Benedicts of all kinds. Burgers and salads take care of the lunch end of the spectrum, and smoothies make sure the health-conscious aren't forgotten. Serve yourself from the pot of freshly brewed coffee at your table and leave fueled and fired up for a productive day.

Epic

Contemporary XX

D3

112 W. Hubbard St. (bet. Clark & LaSalle Sts.)

Phone: 312-222-4940 — Lunch Mon – Fri
Web: www.epicrestaurantchicago.com — Dinner Mon – Sat
Prices: $$$ — Grand (Red)

If M.C. Escher were still alive, he'd give a thumbs-up to the crisscrossing staircases winding seductively through each floor of Epic's three-story black brownstone. Ceilings that surpass the definition of "soaring" enhance the space's lofty layout, aided by walls of windows lining the warehouse-sized lounge and upper level dining room, capped by a sexy rooftop bar. Equally statuesque servers in minimal tanks seem unfazed by the Chicago cold.

Despite the clubby, funky feel, the kitchen turns out enjoyable contemporary American fare with broad appeal for diners ranging from suits and out-of-towners, to Ed Hardy-clad scenesters. Favorites may include Parmesan gnocchi with lamb sausage and herbs, or grilled salmon with ginger spinach and cucumber yogurt.

Farmhouse

Gastropub XX

228 W. Chicago Ave. (bet. Franklin & Wells Sts.)

Phone: 312-280-4960 Lunch & dinner daily
Web: www.farmhousechicago.com
Prices: $$ Chicago (Brown)

The pitchfork door handle might verge on silly, but the connection to regional farms is serious at Farmhouse. As is evident from blackboards scrawled with names of local purveyors and seasonal brews, the Midwest rules the menu, sourcing Illinois beef, Indiana chicken, Michigan wine, and soda syrup from Logan Square. Salvaged and industrial materials like steel and chunky wood mix with down-home inflections like faux sunflowers and a blues-meets-country soundtrack.

Split the Wisconsin cheese curds with alder-smoked catsup, or a bucket of mussels steamed in wildflower honey lager; before digging into short rib Sloppy Joes with blue cheese and sweet onion marmalade, or a chicken pot pie *pastie*. End with a slice of blueberry-lemon pie for true farm flavor.

Frontera Grill

D3

Mexican XX

445 N. Clark St. (bet. Hubbard & Illinois Sts.)

Phone: 312-661-1434 Lunch & dinner Tue – Sat
Web: www.fronterakitchens.com
Prices: $$ Grand (Red)

It may be the casual sibling to Topolobampo next door, but Frontera Grill is a cornerstone of Rick Bayless' empire. Tourists and locals alike line up for this famed dining room, as colorful as a kaleidoscope and peppered with Mexican masks, paintings, and artifacts. Those in-the-know hang at the bar with a margarita in hand until a table is ready, tapping their toes to peppy Latin music.

Despite Bayless' worldwide recognition, everyone is here for the food. The regularly changing menu focuses on regional dishes made with quality ingredients, such as smoky guacamole folded with crispy bacon, toasted chiles, and smoked tomato. Also sample grilled lamb in red peanut *mole* tucked with wintery squash and heirloom runner beans into fresh tortillas.

Fulton's on the River

Seafood XX

315 N. LaSalle St. (at the Chicago River)

Phone: 312-822-0100 — Lunch Mon – Fri
Web: www.fultonsontheriver.com — Dinner Mon – Sat
Prices: **$$$** — Merchandise Mart

The realtor's axiom on location might be tired, but it applies accurately to Fulton's on the River. This sizeable but warm space sports a warren of comfortable rooms, though the primo spot on a sunny day is an umbrella-shaded table outside. Salads, burgers, and bites like beer-battered fish and crispy calamari dominate the value-priced lunch menu.

A wood-paneled décor and glossy black-and-white photos keep company with steakhouse mains; while accompaniments like oysters or jumbo lump crab cakes are served at dinner as the crowd shifts to corporate and affluent regulars. Outdoor tables are first-come, first-serve, making early arrivals a must. The same killer scene makes Fulton's a prime wedding reception spot, so call ahead for weekend availability.

Gene & Georgetti

Steakhouse XX

C3

500 N. Franklin St. (at Illinois St.)

Phone: 312-527-3718 — Lunch & dinner Mon – Sat
Web: www.geneandgeorgetti.com
Prices: **$$$$** — Merchandise Mart

No, it's not a Hollywood set. This Italian-American steak joint is the real thing, and those wiseguys at the bar have been clinking their ice cubes in this wood-paneled room for decades. The historic spot, founded in 1941, is boisterous downstairs with the aforementioned regulars and guys grabbing a bite; upstairs is more refined for local politico lunches and a bit of old-school romance at dinner.

Gene & Georgetti is a steakhouse with an Italian bloodline, prominently displayed in the heaping helping of fried *peperoncini* and bell peppers with the signature "chicken alla Joe." The cottage fries (oversized potato planks that come with most entrées) might necessitate a doggie bag, but all the better to leave room for a slice of classic carrot cake.

Gilt Bar

Gastropub

230 W. Kinzie St. (at Franklin St.)

Phone: 312-464-9544 Dinner nightly
Web: www.giltbarchicago.com
Prices: $$ Merchandise Mart

This speakeasy-on-steroids covers all its bases—tufted leather banquettes for comfort and worn wooden chairs for a studied distressed style; an impressively gilded bar for casual noshers and serious cocktailers; and a semi-exposed kitchen serving up rustic cuisine with refined touches. High-spirited conversation from the packed-in, dressed-up revelers keeps sound levels at a dull roar.

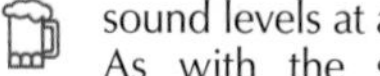

As with the space, there's a bite for every appetite. Mouthwatering nibbles like bone marrow and red onion jam, or steak tartare laced with shallots and capers populate the "On Toast" section of the menu. Hungrier guests will tear through exquisitely fuss-free entrées such as pan-roasted Gunthorp farm chicken with a rich jus; or bouillabaisse with red pepper rouille.

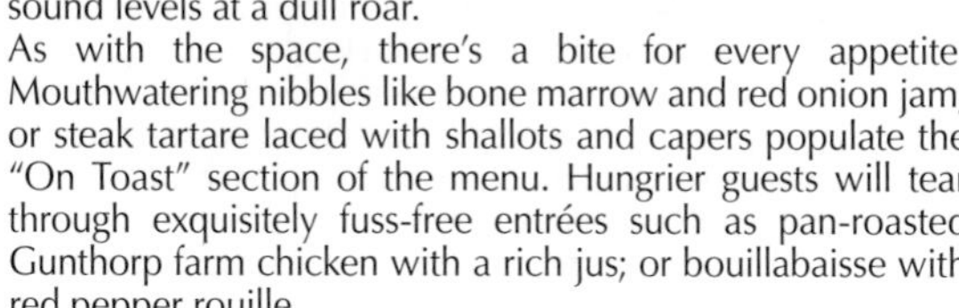

Gino's East

Pizza

633 N. Wells St. (at Ontario St.)

Phone: 312-943-1124 Lunch & dinner daily
Web: www.ginoseast.com
Prices:  Grand (Red)

When sated diners cover the walls of this massive, dark, and dizzyingly loud Chicago deep-dish pizza parlor with scratchy graffiti—a Gino's East tradition—they tell their stories, add to the legend, and speak to their longstanding loyalty for this divey yet venerable institution.

Be prepared for a wait, as families, tourists, couples, and regulars linger side-by-side for the famous deep-dish and thin-crust pizzas, all made to order. Both versions start with a round of sturdy golden dough before piling on tomato sauce, then layers of toppings, and finishing with copious handfuls of cheese. Though pepperoni and sausage are requisite offerings, a cheese-and-spinach pie isn't just a halfhearted concession to health but a true regional specialty.

Giordano's

Pizza 

F1

730 N. Rush St. (at Superior St.)

Phone: 312-951-0747 Lunch & dinner daily
Web: www.giordanos.com
Prices: Chicago (Red)

Value, friendly service, and delicious deep-dish pizza make Giordano's a crowd sweetheart. With several locations dotting the city and suburbs, this restaurant has been gratifying locals with comforting Italian-American fare for years. Come during the week—service picks up especially at dinner—to avoid the cacophony.

Giordano's menu includes your typical salads, pastas, et al., but you'd do well to save room for the real star: the deep-dish. Bring backup because this pie could feed a small country. The spinach pie arrives on a buttery pastry crust, filled with spreads of sautéed (or steamed) spinach and tomato sauce, and topped with mozzarella and Parmesan cheese. For those cold, windy nights, opt for delivery—their website sketches a detailed menu.

GT Fish & Oyster

Seafood

C3

531 N. Wells St. (at Grand Ave.)

Phone: 312-929-3501 Lunch & dinner daily
Web: www.gtoyster.com
Prices: $$ Grand (Red)

East or West Coast? There's no need to choose when there's so much to try from the depths of the Atlantic, Pacific, and beyond at Chef Giuseppe Tentori's ode to the maritime. Reserve in advance or expect to sit at the front oyster bar or a communal table in the rear dining room with its chic marlin mural. Plan on getting cozy with your tablemates over spiked iced teas, though you may have to shout to hear them over the music.

The menu offers limited options for vegetarians and landlubbers, but everyone's really here for the fish. Simple sandwiches might include an upscale poached tuna melt with oozing Gruyère and pear-pecan slaw. Also try glistening cubes of Hawaiian tuna poke with mango purée and nutty sesame oil, or scallop and short rib cannelloni.

graham elliot 

Contemporary XX

C2

217 W. Huron St. (bet. Franklin & Wells Sts.)

Phone: 312-624-9975 Dinner Tue – Sat
Web: www.grahamelliot.com
Prices: **$$$$** Chicago (Brown)

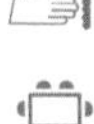

Graham Elliot

The eponymous dining room of Chicago's gallivanting chef and hometown superstar continues to evolve into a very serious venue. On the one hand, there is much here that is not for stuffy or sensitive types, like the infectious indie rock soundtrack and vibe that is slightly more romantic than a bar—but not by much. On the other, the knowledgeable service team is engaging and synchronized, the vibe is increasingly mature, and the food is downright memorable.

Graham Elliot's trademark humor and eccentricity guide the arrangement of the menus, which may begin with a skillfully made sweet-sour wine-vinegar lollipop to arouse the palate. This might lead to rice crackers cradling venison tartare hinting of juniper and dates. The flavors of butternut squash purée poured over an isomalt bridge infused with lime zest, chili, and caraway coalesce with lip-smacking result; while lamb loin is poached in olive oil, grilled rare, and then festooned with charred broccoli, pickled turnips, and lush lamb jus.

Desserts bring beautiful complexity, perhaps combining soft strawberry sorbet, strawberry-goat cheese macaron, pistachio cookie crumble, and a strawberry dipped in milky Tasmanian-peppercorn sauce.

Harry Caray's

E4 Steakhouse XX

33 W. Kinzie St. (at Dearborn St.)

Phone: 312-828-0966 Lunch & dinner daily
Web: www.harrycarays.com
Prices: $$$ Grand (Red)

The gone-but-never-forgotten Chicago sportscaster Harry Caray was known for his trademark "Holy Cow!" Guests might feel the need to utter it as they see this famous broadcaster's bronze bust complete with giant glasses. As Harry Caray is iconic to the Windy City, so too are steakhouses, so it makes perfect sense that the restaurant that sports his name is a classic steakhouse specializing in USDA Prime corn-fed beef. Make sure you show up hungry here: the 18oz dry-aged, bone-in ribeye or 23oz Porterhouse are on the hefty side of what is an ample selection on this massive, meat-centric menu. Like most steakhouses, all the sides—classics include rich garlic mashed potatoes, creamed spinach, and sautéed mushrooms—are served à la carte.

Hubbard Inn

D3 International XX

110 W. Hubbard St. (bet. Clark & LaSalle Sts.)

Phone: 312-222-1331 Lunch & dinner Mon – Sat
Web: www.hubbardinn.com
Prices: $$ Grand (Red)

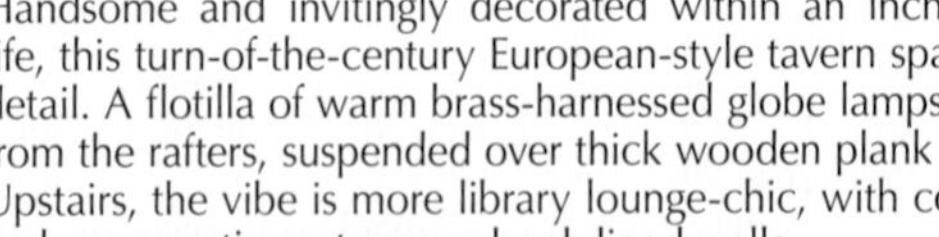

Handsome and invitingly decorated within an inch of its life, this turn-of-the-century European-style tavern spares no detail. A flotilla of warm brass-harnessed globe lamps hangs from the rafters, suspended over thick wooden plank tables. Upstairs, the vibe is more library lounge-chic, with couches and open seating set among book-lined walls.

Cocktails are the draw for mixology mavens, with an extensive list of classics and new favorites carefully etched on a wall-sized chalkboard behind the impressive marble bar. Pick your poison and embark on a relaxing lunch of globe-spanning plates like steak tartare, grilled duck bratwurst, or flatbread with merguez and pear chutney before the dinner crowd ambles in to fill each lounge chair and bar stool.

Hub51

International 

51 W. Hubbard St. (at Dearborn St.)

Phone: 312-828-0051 Lunch & dinner daily
Web: www.hub51chicago.com
Prices: **$$** Grand (Red)

If you've ever been unable to decide whether you want to eat sushi, hummus, cornbread, or Mexican food, Hub51 is the place for you and your peripatetic appetite. With a menu to sate almost any craving and a well-stocked bar with a multitude of craft beers on draft, the high-ceilinged space is constantly crowded.

Start with a sushi roll or heaping bowl of guacamole before shifting to a plate of nachos piled high with tender, organic pulled chicken and so many fixings you'll need a knife and fork. The menu balances lighter offerings like Brussels sprouts salad tossed with dates, cranberries, and mustard vinaigrette with heartier turkey meatloaf sandwiches and a first-rate cheeseburger.

Night owls roll downstairs to the swanky bar Sub51 after a bite.

Joe's

American 

60 E. Grand Ave. (at Rush St.)

Phone: 312-379-5637 Lunch & dinner daily
Web: www.joes.net
Prices: **$$$$** Grand (Red)

Despite the ample neighborhood competition, this outpost of the original Miami seafood, steak, and stone crab palace does just fine up north. Clubby, masculine décor fashions a classic scene, while business diners and lively martini-toasting groups keep the leather booths full from lunch through dinner.

Stone crab claws accompanied by signature mustard sauce are shared by nearly every table, followed by decadent dishes like a bone-in filet with their simple yet delicious coriander-spiked seasoning. Americana sides like Jennie's fontina and asiago mashed potatoes, or grilled tomatoes topped with cheesy spinach pesto, are ample enough to share. Joe's Key lime pie is rightly famous, but other retro sweets like coconut cream are worth a forkful.

Keefer's

E4 — Steakhouse XXX

20 W. Kinzie St. (bet. Dearborn & State Sts.)

Phone: 312-467-9525 — Lunch Mon – Fri
Web: www.keefersrestaurant.com — Dinner Mon – Sat
Prices: **$$$$** — Grand (Red)

A balance of old-school steakhouse and contemporary flair makes Keefer's the go-to spot for River North's business lunch and after-work crowds. Whether amid the sleek rotunda's towering wine racks, or in one of the many private rooms popular for deal-closing, diners eat up the welcoming, efficient service.

The kitchen adds modern touches to many familiar steakhouse offerings. While there are plenty of flavorful bone-in steaks, the slate of starters and sides highlight creativity, as in Chef Hogan's peas with pearl onions and ham folded into a light leek cream, or a panko-crusted plank of aged Irish Cheddar fried golden and plated with fresh bitter greens and cranberry compote.

The more casual Keefer's Kaffe eases the lunchtime rush.

La Madia

D3 — Pizza XX

59 W. Grand Ave. (bet. Clark & Dearborn Sts.)

Phone: 312-329-0400 — Lunch & dinner daily
Web: www.dinelamadia.com
Prices: **$$** — Grand (Red)

Those corner slice joints have nothing on this hip, contemporary Italian spot on Grand, where the see-and-be-seen crowd takes over the colorful striped booths and the marble dining counter surrounding the wood-fired pizza oven. A floor-to-ceiling wine wall telegraphs La Madia's upscale selection, but keeps it tasting-friendly with 4- or 7-oz. pours.

Pizza and salads are the draw for the club-happy crowd, though well-sourced ingredients like fresh butter lettuce and hearts of palm with a lemon-chili dressing ensures flavors are more "hey there!" than ho-hum. Neapolitan-style pies get sparing but flavorful toppings like homemade lamb sausage, pesto, and truffle oil. A pizza fondue featuring cheese-laced tomato sauce is perfect for the after-party.

LM Bistro

XX French

D2

111 W. Huron St. (bet. Clark & LaSalle Sts.)

Phone: 312-202-9900 Lunch & dinner daily
Web: www.lmrestaurant.com
Prices: $$ Chicago (Red)

This charming bistro is located at the Felix hotel and run by husband-wife team Nicole and Stephan Outrequin Quaisser. It boasts a low-key but distinctly French vibe, fashioned with walnut flooring, matte-black walls, sienna stucco columns and servers attired in orange shirts. Artfully scripted illustrations of Paris landmarks give diners an indication of the kitchen's direction.

The range of fare satisfies patrons throughout the day with breakfast, lunch, and tasty *croque monsieurs*, but the dinner menu is most expressive. Classic fare such as hearty *soupe à l'oignon* capped by melted Gruyère; *tarte Alsacienne* with bacon and caramelized onions; bouillabaisse; and duck leg confit sided by cassoulet and maple jus will please any Francophile.

Mastro's

Steakhouse

E3

520 N. Dearborn St. (at Grand Ave.)

Phone: 312-521-5100 Dinner nightly
Web: www.mastrosrestaurants.com
Prices: $$$$ Grand (Red)

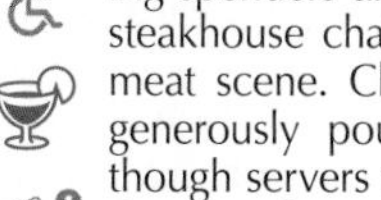

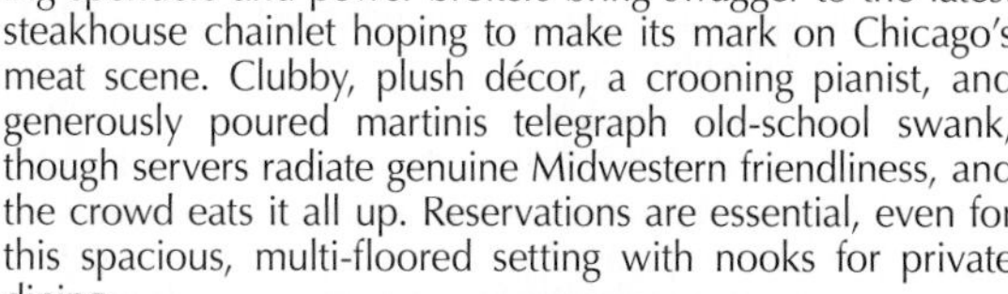

Big spenders and power brokers bring swagger to the latest steakhouse chainlet hoping to make its mark on Chicago's meat scene. Clubby, plush décor, a crooning pianist, and generously poured martinis telegraph old-school swank, though servers radiate genuine Midwestern friendliness, and the crowd eats it all up. Reservations are essential, even for this spacious, multi-floored setting with nooks for private dining.

Large and succulent portions of wet-aged Prime steak arrive simply broiled on screaming hot plates, with sauces and accompaniments upon request. Show restraint with the list of two dozen traditional sides like garlic mashed potatoes and creamed spinach in favor of a new classic: the rich, smooth, salty, sweet, and revelatory butter cake.

The Lobby ✿

Contemporary XXX

F1

108 E. Superior St. (at Michigan Ave.)

Phone: 312-573-6760 Lunch & dinner daily
Web: www.peninsula.com
Prices: $$$ Chicago (Red)

Mark Wieland Photography

Evidenced by the name, there is nothing cozy about the enormously airy space that comprises The Lobby—it *is* part of the grand entry to one of Chicago's most haute hotels, after all. Glimpse the valet parking a showroom's worth of pricey vehicles as you walk in.

As the main restaurant for The Peninsula, the showy room does double and triple duty as a venue for coffee breaks, brunch buffets, and afternoon tea, but manages to bring elegance, graciousness, and even a bit of romance to its guests. This multi-story arena flaunts towering ceilings and windows spanning the room; the feel is formal but very special as expertly trained servers nimbly flit about their suave clients.

Chef Lee Wolen, formerly of New York's iconic Eleven Madison Park, brings prowess and flavor to this contemporary menu that achieves epic status at dinner. He aims to please by way of soft ricotta gnocchi on a bed of sweet potato purée with juicy cranberries and baby sage leaves; or bass served bouillabaisse-style with tender Gulf shrimp and razor clams in an aromatic dashi-infused broth. Hearty plates like slow-braised lamb shank or crisp-skinned roast chicken bring high-class appeal to a medley of American classics.

Mercadito

D4 **Mexican** XX

108 W. Kinzie St. (bet. Clark & LaSalle Sts.)

Phone: 312-329-9555 Lunch & dinner daily
Web: www.mercaditorestaurants.com
Prices: $$ Merchandise Mart

After conquering New York with their fresh, spicy, and upscale tacos and ceviches, brothers Patricio, Alfredo, and Felipe Sandoval brought their winning formula to the Windy City. Mercadito's weathered metal façade hides a bold décor: custom graffiti art, Mayan murals, and pebbled glass plates are casually colorful and hip, evoking a beach club that invites you to stay just a little bit longer.

Sample or share a few ceviches like the smoky-sweet dorado with Asian pear and hints of tamarind; or spicy *mixto* with octopus, shrimp, and mahi mahi. Then dig into a stack of satisfying *tacos al pastor* studded with glistening ancho-rubbed pork and grilled pineapple, along with one or three tangy margaritas with just the right dip of salt on the rim.

Osteria Via Stato

E2 **Italian** XX

620 N. State St. (at Ontario St.)

Phone: 312-642-8450 Dinner nightly
Web: www.osteriaviastato.com
Prices: $$ Grand (Red)

Though it is adjacent to the Embassy Suites, this pitch-perfect cozy *enoteca* complete with stone walls and barrel-vaulted archways is a local standby for its across-the-board value in a neighborhood of pricey plates. The all-Italian wine list sparkles with well-priced gems, but those who can't decide can simply ask for the "just bring me wine" feature—a tasting flight of three different wines.

Order à la carte or bring a group for the *molto* popular "Italian dinner party" that lets diners choose their own entrée and share antipasti, pastas, and sides family-style. With hearty portions of mini meatballs in marinara sauce; braised lamb shank with cipollini onions and rosemary; or ravioli stuffed with tender short rib, no one leaves hungry.

NAHA ✿

D3 American XXX

500 N. Clark St. (at Illinois St.)

Phone: 312-321-6242 Lunch Mon – Fri
Web: www.naha-chicago.com Dinner Mon – Sat
Prices: $$$ Grand (Red)

Lara Kastner

One corner of this well-traveled intersection has belonged to the Rick Bayless empire for decades, but another has been held by Carrie Nahabedian for nearly as long. Here at NAHA, subtle sophistication stakes its claim in a welcoming, unpretentious environment. The window-wrapped façade is prime for people-watching yet lets light and air take a starring role in the décor.

Throughout the progression of dining rooms, soothing tones and textures of concrete and wood planks warm with touches of leather and vibrant greenery. The look is unfussy—those gentlemen in collared shirts might even feel loose enough to ditch the jacket, once seated.

Like its understated space, the menu doesn't shout to prove its worth. Instead, these American dishes rely on quality ingredient pairings to impart happy surprises with each course. Crustless peach tarte Tatin becomes a piquant appetizer when combined with caramelized fennel, lacquered Kurobuta pork, and shaved Pleasant Ridge Reserve cheddar. An ample Alaskan halibut fillet turns delicate when served over potato mousseline and shaved hearts of palm. Vanilla-spiked corn pudding, honey gelato, and popcorn garnish bring depth to a blueberry-almond tartlet.

Paris Club

French

59 W. Hubbard St. (bet. Clark & Dearborn Sts.)

Phone: 312-595-0800
Web: www.parisclubchicago.com
Prices: $$

Lunch Sat – Sun
Dinner nightly
Grand (Red)

Paris Club brings high-energy life to the standard French bistro, so if you're looking for calm white tablecloths and hushed conversation, this is not the place. The cavernous dining hall mixes industrial elements like steel I-beams with rustic tavern hallmarks like salvaged barn planks. Buzz from the club-ready crowd bounces off each surface, while those who really want to party head to the rooftop lounge Studio Paris.

The menu showcases casual yet refined French classics from chilled raw bar starters to velvety *pot de crème* desserts. Crispy-skinned, juicy duck breast pairs with a crunchy *pastille* filled with crushed almonds and tender braised duck. Escargots Bourguignon are appropriately herbaceous and garlicky beneath golden-brown pastry tops.

Phil Stefani's 437 Rush

Italian

F3

437 N. Rush St. (bet. Hubbard & Illinois Sts.)

Phone: 312-222-0101
Web: www.stefanirestaurants.com
Prices: $$$

Lunch Mon – Fri
Dinner Mon – Sat
Grand (Red)

Two classic styles of Chicago restaurant—steakhouse and Italian—converge at 437 Rush St. The tasteful room combines oversized black-and-white tile flooring, a massive bar with a jazzy backsplash, and linen tablecloths for just the right masculine, clubby look that make this a standout contender among the many stylish steakhouses throughout the city.

Elegant, unfussy Italian dishes complement the *primo* selection of well-prepared steaks, chops, and seafood platters. *Tonno con caponata Siciliana* arrives as seared slices of sashimi-grade tuna fanned over artichoke hearts, pine nuts, and eggplant caponata. Grilled Atlantic salmon with silky organic fava bean purée showcases the restaurant's commitment to sustainability without skimping on flavor.

Pizzeria Uno

Pizza

E3

29 E. Ohio St. (at Wabash Ave.)

Phone: 312-321-1000 Lunch & dinner daily
Web: www.unos.com
Prices: Grand (Red)

Since 1943, this establishment has been laying claim to the (somewhat disputed) title of creating the original Chicago-style pizza. Its tiny booths and wood tables wear their years of graffiti etchings like a badge of honor. Nonetheless, an intricate pressed-tin ceiling reflects the cheerful atmosphere as everyone counts down the 40 or so minutes it takes for these deep-dish delights to bake.

Of course, the main attraction here is, was, and always will be the flaky, buttery crust generously layered with mozzarella, other toppings, and tangy tomato sauce that comprise this belly-busting pizza. The menu also includes a selection of good basic bar food like Buffalo wings and a simple salad, but most just save the room for an extra slice.

Pops for Champagne

Contemporary

E3

601 N. State St. (at Ohio St.)

Phone: 312-266-7677 Dinner nightly
Web: www.popsforchampagne.com
Prices: $$ Grand (Red)

Who needs a celebration—or any excuse—to enjoy a glass of bubbly? With its prime State Street location, Pops for Champagne makes the idea irresistible. Tourists, shoppers from nearby Bloomie's and Nordstrom, and happy hour-ready clusters slouch into low sofas or crowd around crackled green glass tables with built-in champagne buckets to sip a flute or two.

Pops offers full and half pours of all things fizzy from champagne and cava to obscure sparkling wines and bubbling cocktails. A succinct menu of nibbles like oysters, charcuterie and desserts help offset the heady effervescence. Crispy black tiger shrimp with a sweet clementine glaze and "foie gras dust" are appropriately rich; whereas beef tartare is perked up by truffled edamame relish and chili oil.

Prosecco

Italian

710 N. Wells St. (bet. Huron & Superior Sts.)

Phone: 312-951-9500 — Lunch Mon – Fri
Web: www.prosecco.us.com — Dinner Mon – Sat
Prices: $$ — Chicago (Brown)

No matter the hour, it's always time for bubbly at Prosecco, where a complimentary flute of the namesake Italian sparkler starts each meal. This fizzy wine inspires the restaurant's elegant décor, from creamy pale walls and damask drapes to travertine floors. Sit at the long wooden bar or in one of the well-appointed dining rooms for a second glass chosen from the long list of *frizzante* and *spumante* wines.

Hearty dishes spanning the many regions of Italy cut through the heady bubbles. Carpaccio selections include the classic air-dried *bresaola* as well as whisper-thin seared rare duck breast. *Saltimbocca di vitello* marries tender veal medallions with crispy *Prosciutto di Parma* and creamy mozzarella, with hints of sage in the tomato-brandy sauce.

RL

American

115 E. Chicago Ave. (bet. Michigan Ave. & Rush St.)

Phone: 312-475-1100 — Lunch & dinner daily
Web: www.rlrestaurant.com
Prices: $$$ — Chicago (Red)

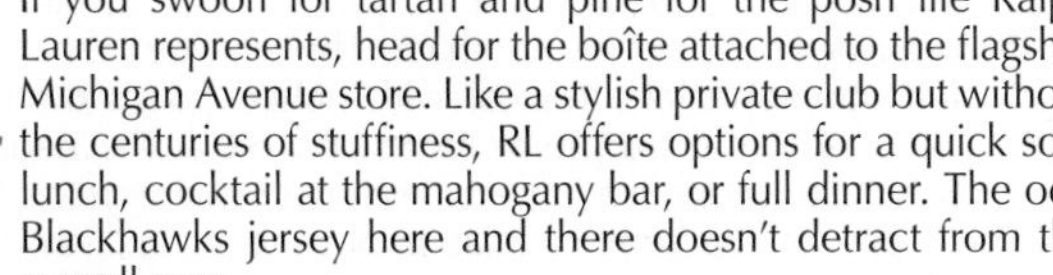

If you swoon for tartan and pine for the posh life Ralph Lauren represents, head for the boîte attached to the flagship Michigan Avenue store. Like a stylish private club but without the centuries of stuffiness, RL offers options for a quick solo lunch, cocktail at the mahogany bar, or full dinner. The odd Blackhawks jersey here and there doesn't detract from the overall aura.

The menu is as classically American as the name, featuring bistro favorites like Waldorf salad and raw bar offerings alongside well-prepared dishes like sweet and plump pan-seared scallops with white balsamic crème fraîche. The thin, flaky crust of a goat cheese- and caramelized onion-tart nearly steals the show from the rich atmosphere of the wood-paneled dining room.

Roka Akor

Japanese XX

D3

456 N. Clark St. (at Illinois St.)

Phone: 312-477-7652 — Lunch Mon – Fri
Web: www.rokaakor.com — Dinner nightly
Prices: $$$ — Grand (Red)

Chicagoans love their grilled meat, especially when it's Wagyu beef cooked over a charcoal-fueled *robata* grill. At palindromic Roka Akor ("roka" means fire), the grill may be the centerpiece, but the entire space is a sexy, sleek, and energetic hybrid lounge. Oversized wood accents are simple and artfully positioned—as if Frank Gehry had free reign of life-sized Lincoln Logs.

Expect very fresh and neatly cut sashimi plates, or large cubes of tender ribeye beef in *wafu* dressing. Other dishes include butterfish *tataki* with white asparagus and yuzu or shishito peppers with bonito. The omakase may range from "signature" to "decadent" which tend to speak for themselves. Fashionable foodies appreciate the wasabi grated tableside and house-brewed soy sauce.

Roy's

Hawaiian XX

E2

720 N. State St. (at Superior St.)

Phone: 312-787-7599 — Dinner nightly
Web: www.roysrestaurant.com
Prices: $$ — Chicago (Red)

Tourists and locals alike can't resist the elegant charm of this popular Hawaiian fusion chain. The spacious dining room feels appropriately tropical with potted palms dotting the landscape and ukelele-heavy music. Sit at the counter to watch the cooks in action at the exhibition kitchen, or lounge at one of the semi-circular booths or wide linen-topped tables.

The menu features all of Roy's classic items as well as dishes developed specifically for the Chicago location. Food arrives with flair on large platters, and may include comforting favorites like braised short ribs served with well-seasoned natural braising sauce and honey mustard-tinged mashed potatoes. More Hawaiian fare features blackened, seared ahi with spicy soy-mustard sauce.

RPM

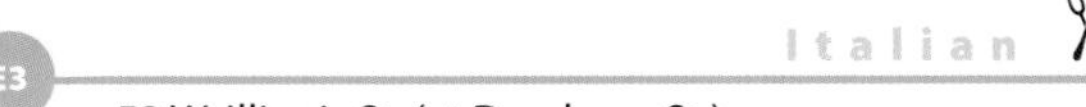

Italian XXX

E3

52 W. Illinois St. (at Dearborn St.)

Phone: 312-222-1888 Dinner nightly
Web: www.rpmitalian.com
Prices: $$ Grand (Red)

When powerhouse restaurant group Lettuce Entertain You partners with reality-TV couple Bill Rancic and his *E! News*-hosting wife, Giuliana, you get a high-wattage happening rather than family-style Italian. Carrara marble and black walls add modern glamour to the bar area, where a loud, see-and-be-seen crowd rubbernecks amid the first come, first served booths and tables. The stark white dining room suits anyone with a Milanese sense of fashion.

Snacks like antipasti, *salumi*, and (slightly) truffled garlic bread take precedence on the menu. Larger dishes include family recipes like Mama DePandi's *bucatini pomodoro* alongside urban rustic plates like wood-grilled and braised octopus tossed with celery and garbanzo beans, as well as gluten-free options.

Sable

American XX

E3

505 N. State St. (at Illinois St.)

Phone: 312-755-9704 Lunch & dinner daily
Web: www.sablechicago.com
Prices: $$ Grand (Red)

Like its lavish namesake, this cosmopolitan spot wraps itself in shades of pewter, bronze, and chocolate as it stretches the length of Palomar hotel's first floor. Sable labels itself a gastro-lounge with cocktails that get top billing in the ample bar, but patrons can also unwind in the garden patio that runs alongside the dining room.

Eclectic elements like hints of smoke and soy in homemade beef jerky elevate a carte of contemporary American food. Pickled mustard seeds dot the apricot chutney that dresses fennel sausage; while Bourbon-caramel sauce offers a heady finish to a banana cream tart. Almost every item is listed with two prices: one for a smaller portion and one for a full-size dish, letting guests decide if they'd rather share or hoard.

Shanghai Terrace

F1 — Chinese XX

108 E. Superior St. (bet. Michigan Ave. & Rush St.)

Phone: 312-573-6695 — Lunch & dinner daily
Web: www.peninsula.com
Prices: $$$ — Chicago (Red)

An upscale jewel box tucked into The Peninsula hotel, Shanghai Terrace is a business dining standby, but its outdoor element poses a true-blue urban oasis. Set with large plantings and trees, the social set comes out in force for cocktails and alfresco dining any time the Chicago temperatures zoom into the upper reaches.

A wide selection of à la carte dishes are complemented by three different lunch prix-fixe platters—land, sea, and garden—thereby offering unique samplings of menu options. Dim sum comes two to an order and includes crab wontons, pea shoot-and-prawn dumplings, or plum sauce-brushed roast pork and duck. Groups gathering for liquid refreshment appreciate the clever presentation of cocktails offered in bottles for sharing.

Siena Tavern

E4 — Italian XX

51 W. Kinzie St. (at Dearborn Pkwy)

Phone: 312-595-1322 — Lunch & dinner daily
Web: www.sienatavern.com
Prices: $$ — Merchandise Mart

Love or hate him, you can't deny Chef Fabio Viviani's authentic charisma (and accent), which packs 'em in at this gargantuan space. Wade through the hordes flocking for face-time with Viviani to one of the many bar stools, banquettes, and booths throughout this multi-level restaurant.

Along with multiple bars offering crudo, pizzas, and house-made mozzarella, the à la carte menu boasts a broad selection of modern Italian dishes. The Siena chop salad takes the "kitchen sink" approach to vegetables and pulls it off winningly, tossing boar salami, egg, *peperoncini* and a host of produce in a creamy, light dressing. Reward yourself with freshly fried, sugar-dusted *bombolini* with personal squeeze bottles of Bourbon-caramel and raspberry-Chianti sauce.

Sixteen ❀❀

Contemporary

E4

401 N. Wabash Ave. (bet. Hubbard St. & the Chicago River)

Phone: 312-588-8030 Lunch & dinner daily
Web: www.trumpchicagohotel.com
Prices: **$$$$** State/Lake

Steve Hall/Hedrich Blessing

The Trump International Hotel's dramatic formal dining room maximizes every angle of its setting with a stunning 35-foot slope of glass windows, ensuring that no table misses its view of the encircling cityscape. Outside, the terrace is ideal for soaking it all in with a cocktail. Inside, a gargantuan chandelier hangs like a 14-foot cascade of Swarovski crystals over white leather armchairs, plush fabrics, and a wall covered in polished West African kevazinga wood. It looks just as impressive as it sounds. This is not to mention the service, which is seamless, serious, and engaging.

Mind-boggling creativity is a hallmark of dining here. This is abundantly clear in a perforated dish of early spring vegetables, served raw but warmed when a minted pea jus is poured overtop tableside. The top plate is removed to divulge langoustine tartare, tasting of lemon and spices, gently heated by the broth. A whole roasted duck is carved to reveal rosy slices framed in crisped fat, set over rye pudding with red cabbage and potato dauphine stuffed with duck giblets.

Desserts can be *haute* playful, as in chunks of chestnut Mont Blanc set in Banyuls vinegar reduction, beneath a cloud of cream.

Slurping Turtle

Japanese

D3

116 W. Hubbard St. (bet. Clark & LaSalle Sts.)

Phone: 312-464-0466
Web: www.slurpingturtle.com
Prices: $$

Lunch Mon – Sat
Dinner nightly
Merchandise Mart

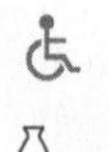

Chef Takashi Yagihashi takes a break from his eponymous Bucktown flagship at this casual spinoff dedicated to belly-warming noodles and other simple Japanese dishes. The restaurant's design seems bento box-inspired with booths, nooks, and communal tables—all of which are snatched up quickly at both lunch and dinner. Be quick like the hare to get a seat at the Turtle.

Graze on meaty skewers off the *bincho* charcoal grill or steamed buns with lacquered pork belly before diving into a deep ceramic bowl of rich, brothy noodles. Don't be shy, for slurping is a compliment to the chef. The über crispy duck fat-fried chicken is outrageously good. Finish up with a Yamazaki whiskey, bottle of Japanese craft beer, like Hitachino Nest, or a caramel-soy macaron.

Sumi Robata Bar

Japanese

C2

702 N. Wells St. (at Huron St.)

Phone: 312-988-7864
Web: www.sumirobatabar.com
Prices: $$

Lunch Mon – Fri
Dinner Mon – Sat
Chicago (Red)

From the carved ice cubes that chill freshly shaken cocktails to the height of the patio hedges blocking the outside world, every element is carefully considered at this temple to the art of Japanese grilling. A wide selection of hot and cold bites satisfy guests pulling boxy wood stools up to the main-level traditional *robata* bar, made from a varnished section of a tree trunk. Downstairs at the exclusive 11-seat charcoal bar, chicken hearts, thighs, and more reign supreme.

Minimal but impactful garnishes on each dish make the most of their inclusion: a skewer of grilled skirt steak comes dressed with *sansho* pepper; crispy-coated chicken *karaage* is topped by peppy shishito pepper paste; and soft tofu becomes luxurious beneath caviar and crispy ginger.

Sunda

D3

Fusion XX

110 W. Illinois St. (bet. Clark & LaSalle Sts.)

Phone: 312-644-0500 — Lunch & dinner daily
Web: www.sundachicago.com
Prices: $$ — Grand (Red)

The Sunda shelf, an underwater outcropping that stretches along the coastline of Southeast Asia, connects the countries that provide culinary inspiration for this enormous River North lounge and restaurant. The beautiful people are naturally attracted to the clubby vibe Sunda radiates, complete with thumping music and a wide range of cocktail and sake selections.

The seafood is as fresh as the vibe is sultry, with numerous raw and cooked options like tempura rock shrimp tossed with candied walnuts in a creamy honey aïoli; or maki like the "tail of two tunas" pairing yellowfin and super white tuna with pickled jalapeños and fried shallots. Meat-eaters won't go hungry with creative plates like lemongrass beef lollipops and oxtail potstickers.

Tanta

D3

Peruvian XX

118 W Grand Ave. (bet. Clark & LaSalle Sts.)

Phone: 312-222-9700 — Dinner nightly
Web: www.tantachicago.com
Prices: $$ — Grand (Red)

Globally acclaimed Chef Gaston Acurio brings his brand of colorful cuisine to the Windy City, blending contemporary Peruvian dishes with Asian touches. Start with a pisco tasting at the bar, situated under a 20-foot-long skylight, and drink in the beauty and bounty of Peru as you take a gander at the wall-length pop art mural in the dining room.

Creamy *aji amarillo* dip with crispy plantain chips get the palate revved up for substantial dishes like *niguiris pobre* draping ponzu-sprinkled skirt steak over sushi rice—the presentation is familiar to any sushi fan. Classic saffron-infused potato cakes are modernized with a shredded nori and ahi tuna tartare topping; while *leche de tigre cebiche* with habanero, lime, and cilantro is a tailor-made hangover cure.

Tavernita

Spanish XX

D2

151 W. Erie St. (at LaSalle St.)

Phone: 312-274-1111 — Lunch Sun – Fri
Web: www.tavernita.com — Dinner nightly
Prices: $$ — Chicago (Brown)

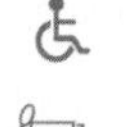

Don't bother complimenting any of the head-turners basking in the warm amber glow of Tavernita. They'll never be able to hear you over the high-decibel din in this sexy space. But fear not; they know they look damn good anyway. Everybody's here to indulge in food and drink, not deep conversations.

Dozens of wooden taps behind the bar pour homemade sodas, sangria, wine, beer, and ready-made cocktails to ensure the party keeps going and flowing. Take a seat if you can grab one and pass around modern tapas like corn pudding studded with rock shrimp and chile poblano; or baguettes artfully smeared with eggplant, pepper, and hazelnut romesco.

Late-night noshers will adore Barcito, the glass-enclosed *pinxtos* bar-within-a bar inside the restaurant.

Tortoise Club

American XXX

E4

350 N. State St. (bet. Kinzie St. & the Chicago River)

Phone: 312-755-1700 — Lunch Mon – Sat
Web: www.tortoiseclub.com — Dinner nightly
Prices: $$$ — State/Lake

The tortoise may be slow and steady, yet this very handsome supper club at the foot of the iconic Marina City complex is anything but stodgy. Nailhead-trimmed leather chairs, a flickering fireplace, and mahogany-paneled walls evoke thoughts of *Mad Men* or Chicago's own Hugh Hefner in his glory days as live jazz and piano alternates with Sinatra or Petula Clark tunes.

This level of class and decadence extends to the menu in wild pheasant pot pie with a peppered foie gras-Cognac sauce; or roasted quail with seared foie gras and red wine cherries. American favorites include steak tartare with sous-vide egg yolk; and lobster rolls boasting an entire pound of sweet meat. Save room for the Bourbon-pecan ice cream atop a spice-infused date-toffee cake.

Topolobampo ✿

Mexican XXX

D3

445 N. Clark St. (bet. Hubbard & Illinois Sts.)

Phone: 312-661-1434
Web: www.rickbayless.com
Prices: $$$

Lunch Tue – Fri
Dinner Tue – Sat
Grand (Red)

Jeff Maimon

Though it shares an entrance with casual sister restaurant Frontera Grill, make no mistake: Topolobampo is the fine-dining flagship of the Rick Bayless empire, still showing no signs of slowing after all these years. Beyond the boisterous bar, conversation in the main dining room remains lively, matching the colorful (never kitschy) Latin art, striped banquettes, and hammered copper chargers that evoke the free-spirited style of Mexico. Servers flaunt a little cocktail artistry by shaking margaritas tableside.

Authenticity has always been the watchword in the kitchen at Topolobampo, and its haute take on Mexican cuisine continues to blend creativity and tradition. Then again, if you're in the mood for guacamole, the creamy classic version here doesn't disappoint. A pool of "Jimmy's grandma's velvety Landero *mole*" surrounds garlic-infused Gunthorp rock hen and seared, braised red carrots and turnips. Chunks of Alaskan king crab add luxury to a corn and posole salad with a touch of lime mayonnaise.

Desayuno para postre brings the best flavors of breakfast to a dessert of amaranth granola sprinkled over guava purée, aromatic melon *gelatinas*, cereal-milk ice cream, and coconut *horchata*.

Travelle

Mediterranean

330 N. Wabash Ave. (bet. Kinzie St. & the Chicago River)

Phone: 312-923-7705 — Lunch & dinner daily
Web: www.travellechicago.com
Prices: $$$ — Grand (Red)

The newly minted Langham hotel showcases its fine dining chops with the swanky Travelle. In a Mies van der Rohe-designed building, the décor harkens back to the clean aesthetic of mid-century design, with stylized blonde wood nuances and spun brass light fixtures highlighting floor-to-ceiling windows. The view? Those iconic Marina Towers across the river, naturally.

Seafood dominates the Mediterranean-esque menu, with spicy-sweet Moroccan flavors seasoning pan-roasted halibut and roasted carrots; and fiery chilies and fresh mint complementing broiled head-on spot prawns. For dinner, caviar service or an opulent raw bar tower featuring "waves" of oysters and every crustacean under the sea seems appropriate when paired with the stunning Windy City skyline.

Union Sushi + Barbeque Bar

C2 — Japanese

230 W. Erie St. (at Franklin St.)

Phone: 312-662-4888 — Lunch Mon – Fri
Web: www.eatatunion.com — Dinner nightly
Prices: $$ — Chicago (Brown)

This colorful funhouse of Asian cuisine with a highly animated scene leaves the stereotype of whisper-quiet sushi bars in the dust. Energetic chefs and boisterous parties keep pace with the blaring music while a constant blur of plates passes from the counter and *robata* grill to the tables throughout this industrial space.

A slurp-inducing bowl of rich, spicy pig's tail ramen with chewy noodles and pork is enough to satisfy even the hungriest appetite, but those looking to fill their bellies further snap up saucy specialty rolls like the River North with eel, *gobo,* and pickled chili drizzled with black pepper sauce. Less adventurous palates will find classic maki like the crispy smoked salmon skin more entertaining than standard sushi options here.

Untitled

Contemporary XX

D4

111 W. Kinzie St. (bet. Clark & LaSalle Sts.)

Phone: 312-880-1511 Lunch Sun
Web: www.untitledchicago.com Dinner Tue – Sun
Prices: $$ Merchandise Mart

Yep, that is a doorman keeping watch over a pair of heavy wooden doors between a CVS and parking garage...and that's also the entrance to the warren of rooms comprising this surreptitious speakeasy. Servers decked in suspenders and fedoras navigate the cacophonous and cavernous club's four full bars, parlor, library, and private cabanas, making sure no guest ever runs dry.

The menu sports the de rigueur cheese and charcuterie choices along with inventive small plates that pair harmoniously with the vast whiskey and made-to-order cocktail list. Crispy wontons wrap up braised goat with a tangy blackberry sauce; boneless short ribs sit beside seared scallops atop herbed bread pudding; and a Key lime custard tartlet refreshes after such savory indulgences.

Vermilion

Indian XX

E3

10 W. Hubbard St. (bet. Dearborn & State Sts.)

Phone: 312-527-4060 Lunch Mon – Fri
Web: www.thevermilionrestaurant.com Dinner nightly
Prices: $$ Grand (Red)

Women rule at this modern Indian-inspired restaurant with a sexy, vibrant atmosphere. Sultry oversized black-and-white prints from Farrok Chothia, India's leading fashion photographer, punctuate the ground floor of the bi-level space, while Murano-esque chandeliers dangle under chrome shades.

The menu touches on an intercontinental marriage between Indian and Latin American cuisines with ingredients like tamarind, mangoes, coconut, and plaintains. In addition to the ambitious à la carte items, Vermilion offers prix-fixe meals with titles such as seared (meats), and the deep (seafood). Dishes may include a cumin-spiked grilled squid and octopus salad, served cold with tart tomatillo gazpacho, or duck *vindaloo arepas* brushed with pomegranate molasses.

Streeterville

If you simply had to pick a neighborhood that truly recapitulates Chicago, it would be Streeterville. Home to the Magnificent Mile, the iconic John Hancock Building, and the fun-loving Navy Pier, skyscraping and stirring Streeterville takes the cake.

Absorb the sights and smells of the stunning surroundings, especially upon arrival at Water Tower Place's **foodlife**—a simple food court elevated to an art form, located on the mezzanine floor of the shopping mall. Before going further, know that this isn't your average mall or airport food court. Instead, this United Nations of food courts satiates with 14 different kitchens whipping up everything from Chinese potstickers and deep-dish pizza to fried chicken. **Wow Bao** (also located within the

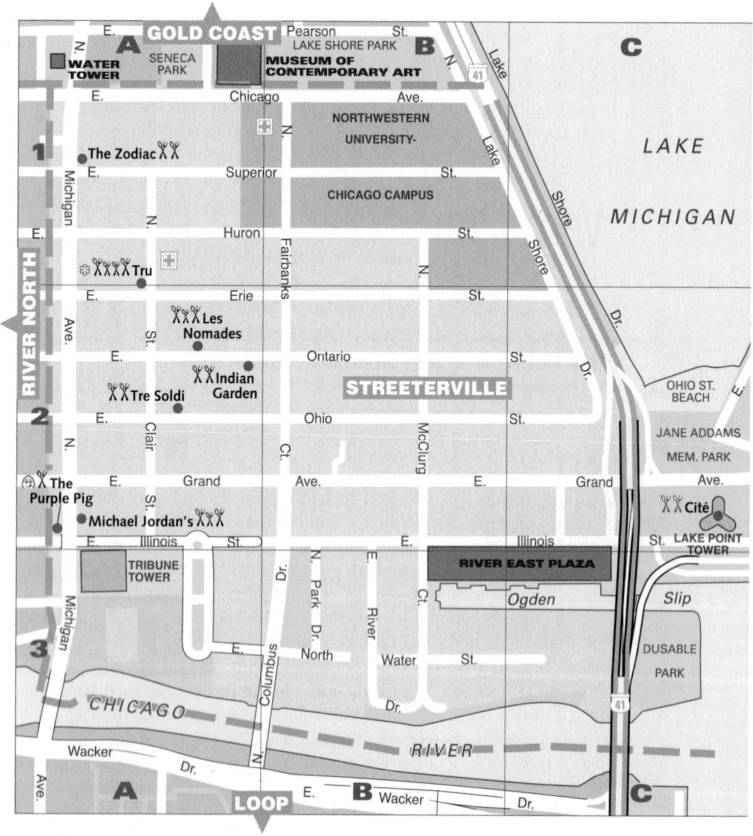

landmark building), doles out some of the best handheld treats in town (like steamed veggie- and meat-filled buns), and is so popular, they had to open a second spot in the Loop. The coolest part? Buy a card that gives you access to the many stands.

Food Court Fun

Prefer panini and pastry? Stop by the legendary **Hancock Building**, otherwise known as food lovers' paradise. The Italian deli **L'Appetito** is perfect for comforting breakfasts, Italian- and American-style sandwiches, baked goods, and other classic delights. Lucky locals and office types can shop for groceries with sky-high prices to match the staggering view at **Potash Brothers**, a supermarket stunningly set on the 44th floor of the Hancock Building.

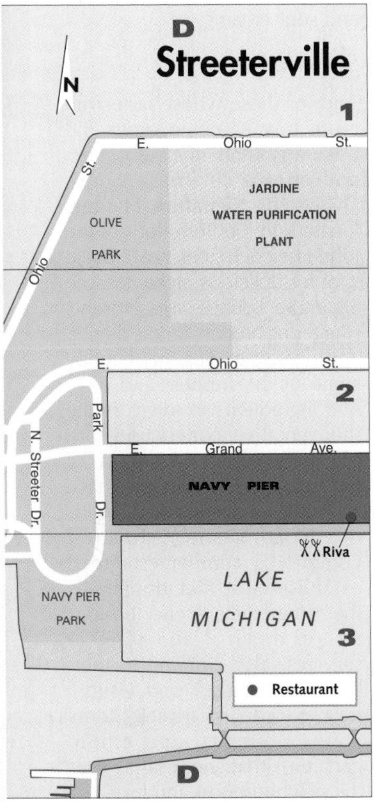

Museums and Markets

The Museum of Contemporary Art houses one of the world's leading collections of contemporary art, but it's also the peppers and potatoes that lure gaggles far and wide, to the farmer's market held here on Tuesdays from June through October. Those with fat wallets should hit up posh gourmet supermarket **Fox & Obel** for gorgeous groceries year-round. With a mission to showcase the love and creativity surrounding quality food, this European-style enterprise also houses a delightful café (or market bistro) whose menu struts a spectrum of spectacular treats for all-day dining. Such fine brunch, lunch, and dinner menus combined with boutique wines makes this place a huge highlight (especially among gourmands) in vibrant Streeterville. Carry on your darling adventure at **Teuscher** and **Godiva**—they both have boutiques here. But, it is Chicago's own **Vosges Haut-Chocolat** that has made a name for itself by thrilling taste buds with exotic ingredients—curry and chocolate anyone?

Tasty Treats

Where do all the savvy foodies and fashionistas in Chicago convene? Most likely at artisan food paradise, also known as **Dose Market**. This year-round bazaar features the finest in food and chefs (together with some of their secret ingredients) all under one roof. From acclaimed "dosers" (think **Indie Burger** and **Pear Tree Preserves**) to passionate "dosettes," Dose Market offers "a beautiful setting full of happy people." After such epicurean prowling, move on to more substantial chow like an all-natural Chicago-style dog (with mustard, onion, relish, sport peppers, tomato, pickle, and celery salt) from **America's Dog**. This dog heaven showcases a massive repertoire of city-style dogs from Houston, New York, and Philadelphia, to Detroit, Kansas City, and San Francisco. In the mood for some crunch? Venture towards world-famous Navy Pier and **Garrett Popcorn Shops** for some of the most addictive salty-sweet flavors including CheeseCorn and MacadamiaCaramelCrisp. The choices are plenty, so create your own tin here. These also make for great seasonal and corporate gifts.

Streeterville Faithfuls

The **Billy Goat Tavern** is a Streeterville institution. Now known more for its famous "cheezeborger, cheezeborger" Saturday Night Live skit, this is a "buy the tee-shirt" type of place with a spot in Navy Pier, and the original just off Michigan Avenue. The tavern's menu, which includes breakfast specials, an array of steaks, and sandwiches galore, is sure to please all who may enter its hallowed portals. Jonesing for a juicy burger? Hit up **M Burger** (another outpost thrives in River North), along with the hordes of business lunchers, tourists, and shoppers. It should be renamed "mmm" burger for its tasty, meaty gifts. Bacon, cheese, and secret sauce comprise the signature M burger, but if on a super strict diet, you can always order the all-veggie Nurse Betty. If you're the type who adores breakfast for dinner, linger at Michigan Avenue's **West Egg Cafe**. This comfortable coffee corridor may serve lunch and dinner as well, but crowds really flock here for their deliciously fluffy omelettes, pancakes, waffles, and other "eggcellent" dishes—maybe "The Swiss Account" featuring eggs, ham, mushrooms, and Swiss cheese baked to perfection, and crowned with olives, tomatoes, and sour cream?

Sip and Savor

And for those whose tastes run more toward champagne and cocktails than cheeseburgers and crinkle-cut fries, there's always the **Signature Lounge**, located on the 96th floor of the John Hancock Center. An idyllic spot for delicious nightcaps, the Signature Lounge also presents staggering brunch, lunch, dinner, and dessert menus that employ some of the freshest and most fine ingredients in town. While their creative concoctions are a touch pricey, one glimpse of the sparkling cityscape will have you lilting in delight. And finally, the Northwestern Hospital complex is another esteemed establishment that dominates the Streeterville scene. Besides its top medical and surgical services, also catering to their spectrum of staff and visitors is a parade of dining gems (cafés, lounges, and ethnic canteens) that loom large over the neighborhood and lake.

Cité

C2

Contemporary XX

505 N. Lake Shore Dr. (entrance on Grand Ave.)

Phone: 312-644-4050 Dinner nightly
Web: www.citechicago.com
Prices: $$$

Any restaurant with 360-degree views of a magnificent city skyline and the expanse of Lake Michigan has to know that what's outside is likely to detract from what's inside. That's true at this 70th-floor establishment atop Lake Point Tower, where the views of Navy Pier and the lake are particularly breathtaking.

In recent years, neither the décor nor the continental menu has been able to compete with the views, but that doesn't mean the kitchen isn't trying to keep the competition interesting. Start with escargot François, snails bathing in garlic-herb butter under golden hats of puff pastry; before moving on to a hearty bone marrow-crusted beef tenderloin. For dessert, bananas Foster flambéed tableside will challenge the Navy Pier for your attention.

Indian Garden

A2

Indian XX

247 E. Ontario St. (bet. Fairbanks Ct. & St. Clair St.)

Phone: 312-280-4910 Lunch & dinner daily
Web: www.indiangardenchicago.com
Prices: $$ Grand (Red)

Frequent diners know it as "The IG," but first-timers will appreciate the copious lunch buffet as much as the doctors, med students, and locals. These faithful droves routinely make the trip up a few flights of stairs to get their *pakora* and tandoori fix on, among kitschy but ornate touches like richly colored fabrics and wafting incense.

Though the à la carte menu offers Northern Indian dishes brought to the table in shiny copper vessels, the lunch buffet covers all bases with vegetarian, chicken, and lamb items. Staples like *saag*, *dal*, naan, and basmati rice are freshly made; *bhuna gosht* mixes succulent lamb with tomatoes, onions, and spices; while *lassi* or masala tea provide refreshment along with a decent selection of wine, beer, and cocktails.

Les Nomades

French XXX

A2

222 E. Ontario St. (bet. Fairbanks Ct. & St. Clair St.)

Phone: 312-649-9010 — Dinner Tue – Sat
Web: www.lesnomades.net
Prices: **$$$$** — Grand (Red)

The hush of old-world formality and restrained elegance fills this sliver of a two-story brownstone that houses Les Nomades. Whether greeted personally by Owner Mary Beth Liccioni or any of her besuited staff, courtesy and civility reigns among the dining room's voluminous floral arrangements, properly chilled martini glasses, and seated gentlemen in jackets.

With Executive Chef Roland Liccioni at the helm, contemporary touches enliven classic French cuisine available through four- and five-course prix-fixe menus. Lemongrass-infused tomato purée and black olive tapenade complement a firm piece of Arctic char. Whereas escargots in a yellow tomato coulis, or kabocha squash soup with caramelized fennel and truffle foam supplement sweet and savory flavors.

Michael Jordan's

Steakhouse XXX

A2

505 N. Michigan Ave. (bet. Grand Ave. & Illinois St.)

Phone: 312-321-8823 — Lunch & dinner daily
Web: www.mjshchicago.com
Prices: **$$$** — Grand (Red)

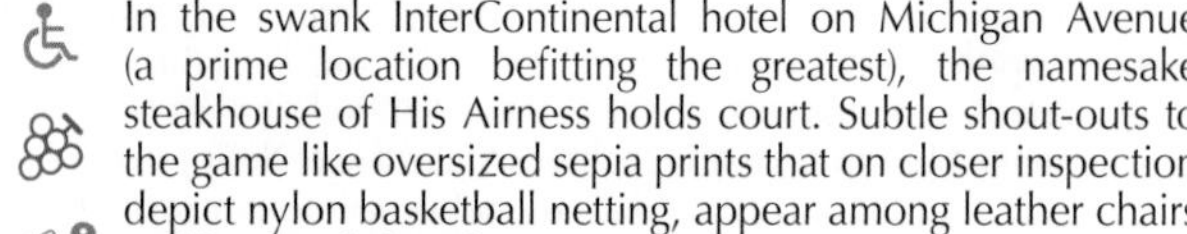

In the swank InterContinental hotel on Michigan Avenue (a prime location befitting the greatest), the namesake steakhouse of His Airness holds court. Subtle shout-outs to the game like oversized sepia prints that on closer inspection depict nylon basketball netting, appear among leather chairs and burgundy booths.

MJ is a Southern gent at heart, and the menu makes reference to his North Carolina upbringing by way of dishes like shrimp and grits; or fried chicken and waffles. Should you want to threepeat with your meal, slam-dunk menu items include dry-aged steaks with trophy-worthy char and minerality set beside mushrooms; toasted garlic ciabatta laden with Wisconsin Roth Käse buttermilk blue cheese fondue; and a 23-layer (get it?) chocolate cake.

The Purple Pig 

A2 Mediterranean 

500 N. Michigan Ave. (at Illinois St.)

Phone: 312-464-1744 Lunch & dinner daily
Web: www.thepurplepigchicago.com
Prices: $$ Grand (Red)

The aptly-named and buzzing Purple Pig bills itself as a place for "cheese, wine, and swine," and is a sight for sore eyes—even on over-stimulated Michigan Avenue. Arrive at this no-reservations spot in time to secure a table on the patio or inside at the Carrara marble bar with a full view of the kitchen. With wines available by the glass, quartino, half, or full bottle, you might be here...a while.

The extensive small plates menu is primed for pairing with wine list selections. Unusual cuts of meat take precedence, like pork jowl in an open-face "JLT," and more traditional dishes like chicken thigh kebabs in tzatziki don't disappoint. Departing with a full belly and wine-stained mouth, you may realize that The Purple Pig was in fact named after you.

Riva

D2 Seafood 

700 E. Grand Ave. (on Navy Pier)

Phone: 312-644-7482 Lunch & dinner daily
Web: www.rivanavypier.com
Prices: $$

Wind your way down Navy Pier's perennially crowded boardwalk and catch your breath just past the Ferris wheel. Yachts and tall ships are picture-perfect backdrops at this seafood-driven haven, which stays family-friendly without verging on touristy. Parents might want to cool their heels at the expansive bar area both in the upstairs dining room and downstairs café.

Cherished dishes have included horseradish-rich crab cocktail with jumbo lump chunks; a chopped seafood salad mingled with greens and tossed in a Dijon vinaigrette; or a crisp-skinned, pan-roasted salmon fillet drizzled with sweet barbecue sauce. Non-pescatarians will be happy to see prime steaks and other land-based entrées on offer, and everyone will steal a bite of the tasty tiramisu.

Tre Soldi

Italian XX

212 E. Ohio St. (bet. Fairbanks Ct. & St. Clair St.)

Phone: 312-664-0212 Lunch & dinner daily
Web: www.tresoldichicago.com
Prices: $$ Grand (Red)

Though it is set among Streeterville's fast-casual joints, Tre Soldi asks guests to adopt a "when in Rome" attitude here (read: take a more leisurely approach to their meal). The snazzy cranberry-red awning beckons, and a wall-sized black-and-white mural of "The Eternal City's" famous domed skyline dominates this easy space. An all-Italian wine list with various by-the-glass options helps diners get into a European state of mind.

Try not to fill up on crusty house-made bread and olive oil. Instead, hold out for crispy thin-crust pizzas topped with fennel sausage, spicy pepperoni, or fingerling potato rounds; followed by fluffy ricotta gnocchi in truffle-scented pea sauce.

Leave a few coins, as Trevi Fountain lore dictates, and you'll be sure to return.

The Zodiac

American XX

737 N. Michigan Ave. (at Superior St.)

Phone: 312-694-4050 Lunch Mon – Sat
Web: www.neimanmarcus.com
Prices: $$ Chicago (Red)

Even if you subscribe to the philosophy that nothing tastes as good as skinny feels—as many of the slender diners chatting and sipping flutes of Aperol-spiked arancia spritzes no doubt do—The Zodiac offers much to entice and satisfy beyond just salads. This hushed retreat on the fourth floor of Neiman Marcus is coolly elegant but genuinely welcoming.

A complimentary popover, served to all guests with a tiny amuse of consommé, should be set on a pedestal for its lasting pleasure: dense, chewy, and buttery, it's tempting to ask for a second one. While sandwiches like the turkey melt with applewood-smoked bacon and roasted Roma tomatoes, or freshly made soups like a filling cup of brothy lentils with a dollop of sour cream, are far more than deli faves.

Tru ✿

Contemporary

676 N. St. Clair St. (bet. Erie & Huron Sts.)

Phone: 312-202-0001 Dinner Mon – Sat
Web: www.trurestaurant.com
Prices: **$$$$** Chicago (Red)

Mark Ballogg

Comfort and pleasure are paramount at Tru, where the hush of elegance and polish of professional but genuine courtesy extends from its discreet entrance to the valets who warm up the cars of departing patrons on blustery Chicago evenings.

Double-height white walls in the lounge and dining room serve as gallery space for their exemplary art collection: a Warhol here, a Richter there. Lavish velvet banquettes make it easy to spend hours savoring the multi-course tasting. Gentlemen, you may feel out of place without a jacket, but rest assured as the moneyed atmosphere never verges into pretentious territory.

Dinner is offered as a seven- or thirteen-course prix-fixe, with luxurious add-ons like the famous Tru caviar staircase, a towering composition of up to ten varieties of osetra, sturgeon, *tobiko,* and roe served on abalone shells and coral. Contemporary plates elevate the freshest of ingredients and unexpected unions succeed wildly, like silky sunchoke mousse with tart sorrel oil and pert Arctic char roe. Day boat scallops dressed with ginger, lime, and Thai chili; or English peas and mint zapped into frozen "snow," then paired with ruby strawberry sorbet, hit all the right notes.

West Loop

Greektown · Market District

The New West Loop

What a difference a century (or two) makes—the West Loop was once home to smoke-spewing factories and warehouses, but walk through this natty neighborhood today, and you will discover young professionals instead of struggling immigrants. Transformed into luxurious lofts, cool nightclubs, art galleries, and cutting-edge restaurants, the warehouses and factories are a far cry from their former existence. Immigrants staked their claim to this neighborhood years ago, and traces of ethnic flavor are still found here. It's not as big as it once was, but nearby Taylor Street still buzzes and allures with its old-world, slightly kitschy feel. It is delis, groceries, and, restaurants galore.

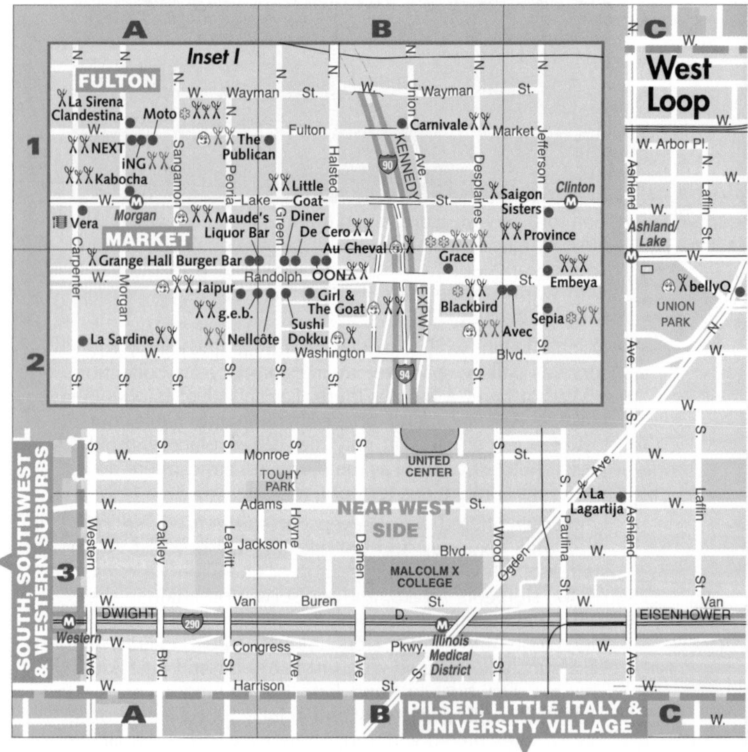

A Taste of Greece

Maintain this Mediterranean vibe by heading over to Greektown, where everybody's Greek, even if just for the day. Shout "oopa" at the Taste of Greece festival, held each August, or stop by **The Parthenon** for gyros and some serious showmanship—they even serve flaming *saganaki* cheese. If Greek and Italian foods don't fit the bill, there's definitely something to whet your appetite along Randolph Street, often referred to as "Restaurant Row." From sushi to subs, this street has it all. For those who enjoy binging at breakfast, head on over to **Ina's** on West Randolph Street. This local favorite satiates all and sundry with its daily breakfast menu proffering everthing from seasonal frittatas and pancakes, to scrapple followed by a sour cream coffee cake. Speaking of gratification, **Next** is an innovative and ever-changing restaurant from Chef Grant Achatz of Alinea (in Lincoln Park) fame. Next channels a different place in time each quarter (year). Its themes may vary from Escoffier-inspired dishes from Paris 1906 and childhood memories turned on their head, to chronicling

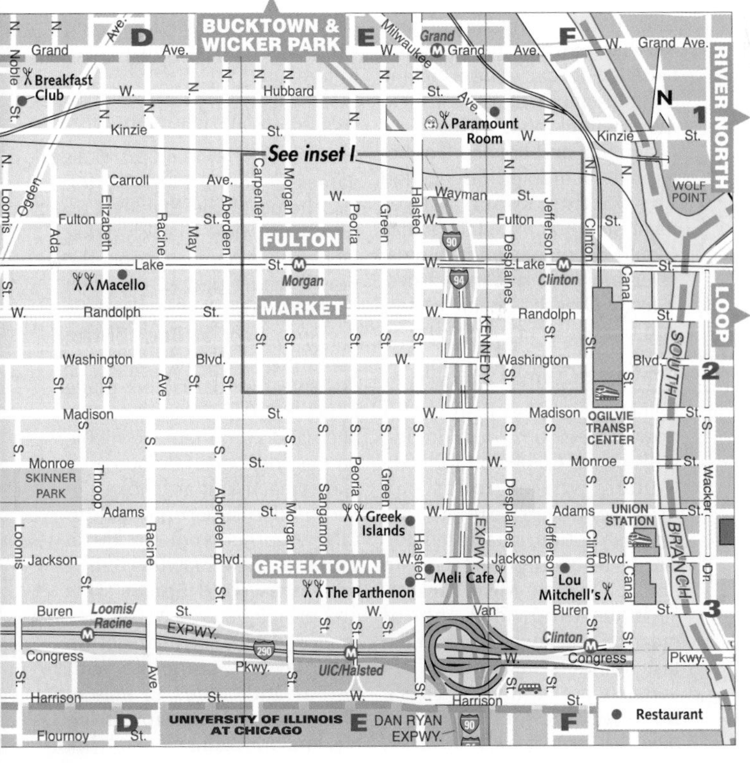

the evolution of El Bulli over the years. What also sets this hot spot apart is its unique online reservation system, where a countless number of fans refresh their computer screens every day in hopes of snagging a non-refundable ticket and coveted seat. Achatz's cocktails over ice at **The Aviary** next door also appreciate the buzz. Here, spherification and other playful techniques mix with booze to create such theatrical concoctions, where the ice is often a work of art in its own right. For a magnificent night about town, you can even round up say 1,000 of your closest friends and family to dine at one of the many Moroccan-Mediterranean restaurants flaunting delicacies from creamy hummus and baba ghanoush, to more faithful spreads like shrimp *charmoula* and *dolmeh*. Further west on Randolph Street, find **The Tasting Room**, a two-level stop for excellent wines usually accompanied by a great selection of à la carte dishes, artisan cheeses, small plates, and of course, rich desserts.

Crafting Culinary Skills

Rather whip it up than wolf it down? Beef up your kitchen skills at the Calphalon Culinary Center, where groups can arrange for private hands-on instruction. Mastered the bœuf Bourguignon? Get in line at **Olympic Meat Packers**. This leading, old-school meatpacking jewel is one of the last holdouts in the area. It's certainly not for the squeamish, but the butchers slice and dice the perfect meat to order. Speaking of carnivore central, gourmands love **Publican Quality Meats**, Paul Kahan's butcher/deli, for its mind-boggling eats amid a setting that is ideal for dinner parties as well as intimate cocktail groups. Switching gears, troll the stalls at the **Chicago French Market** for organic cheeses, roasted nuts, gourmet pickles, and other specialty items. If you don't have a ramekin or Dutch oven, Northwestern Cutlery Supply stocks everything a chef could need—even the requisite white coat. Treasure hunters mark the spot at the Chicago Antique Market. This massive indoor/outdoor market is held the last Saturday and Sunday of each month from May through September, and stocks everything from jewelry to furniture.

Beer and the Ballgame

Hoops fans whoop it up at Bulls games at the United Center, also home to the Stanley Cup winners—the Blackhawks. Depending on the score, the most exciting part of the night might be post game, especially if over a beer at **Beer Bistro**. You'll need to bring your most decisive friends as this place has over 120 varieties of bottled beer (and 20 on tap). To nibble on the side, bona fide pub grub like spinach-and-artichoke dip and fried calamari are sure to sate. Another spot for those who like a little brawl with their beer is **Twisted Spoke**. This proverbial biker bar (serving smut & eggs after midnight on Saturdays) is complete with tattoos and 'tudes to match. The music is loud, crowds are big, and drinks are plentiful, but it's all in good testosterone- and alcohol-fueled fun.

Au Cheval

American

B2

800 W. Randolph St. (at Halsted St.)

Phone: 312-929-4580 Lunch & dinner daily
Web: www.auchevalchicago.com
Prices: $$ Morgan

Another gem on West Randolph's ever-growing restaurant row, Au Cheval caters to the kind of go-with-the-flow crowd that doesn't mind waiting (and often eating) at the zinc-topped bar. They happily chatter above the hip tunes coming from the authentic reel-to-reel by the door, making a fun-loving ruckus.

Fitting the "diner for grownups" theme, the menu is packed with satisfying dishes that pair well with draft (or root) beer options. In-house butchers offer sausages like bratwurst (served with roasted garlic gravy); cured peppered bacon (sliced thick enough to be mini steaks); and accordion sliced 32-ounce pork Porterhouse stuffed with foie gras and roasted apples. Salmon rillettes with soft-cooked eggs and house-made pickles work for lighter appetites.

Avec

American

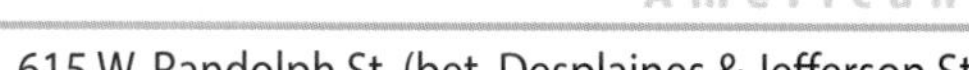

C2

615 W. Randolph St. (bet. Desplaines & Jefferson Sts.)

Phone: 312-377-2002 Lunch Sun
Web: www.avecrestaurant.com Dinner nightly
Prices: $$ Clinton (Green/Pink)

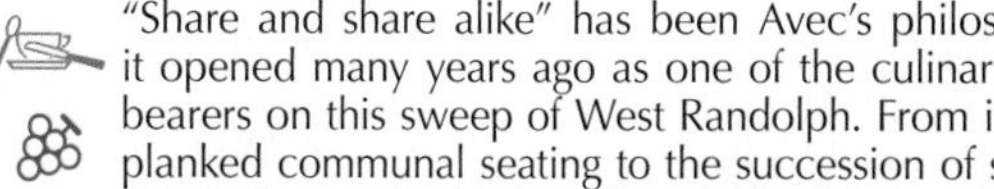

"Share and share alike" has been Avec's philosophy since it opened many years ago as one of the culinary standard-bearers on this sweep of West Randolph. From its wooden-planked communal seating to the succession of small plates that arrive as the kitchen fires them, this is a high-decibel hangout. A strict no-reservations policy can make prime-time waits brutal.

The town would riot if the bacon-wrapped, chorizo-stuffed dates; or "deluxe" focaccia sandwiching melted taleggio and truffle oil ever left the menu. But, other delights come and go with the seasons: crisp-skinned wild striped bass reaps flavor from green garlic *bagna cauda* and pickled fiddlehead ferns; just as *bottarga di muggine* brings a saline snap to English pea-and-ricotta crostini.

bellyQ

Asian

C2

1400 W. Randolph St. (at Ogden St.)

Phone: 312-563-1010
Web: www.bellyqchicago.com
Prices: $$

Lunch Sun – Fri
Dinner nightly
Ashland (Green/Pink)

The largest and most ambitious undertaking from Chicago Chef Bill Kim, BellyQ makes its home at the city's culinary epicenter on West Randolph, fully loaded and ready to play with the big boys. Gray wood and concrete dominate the urbane setting, though the full bar—a first for Chef Kim's otherwise BYO empire—boasts a comfortably lounge-worthy space.

For a full belly, come for dinner, when the fun and inventive menu pulls out all the stops. Since BellyQ's motto is "Tradition. Amplified," it's not surprising to see Asian elements turned up to 11. Savory Asian pancakes come from the wood-burning oven in intriguing flavor combinations like double-smoked bacon and kimchi. Grilled marinated beef gets a punch from pickled green papaya and crispy garlic.

Breakfast Club

American

D1

1381 W. Hubbard St. (at Noble St.)

Phone: 312-666-2372
Web: www.chicagobreakfastclub.com
Prices: ⊜

Lunch daily
Ashland (Green/Pink)

Brains, athletes, basket cases, princesses, and juvie thugs are all welcome at this Breakfast Club on the West Side. You can't miss the clapboard house with striped pink-and-brown awnings, though you might have to circle the block a few times for parking. Inside, it's quirky and quaint with light fixtures made of milk bottles and a marble counter for cocktails if the hair of the dog is what you need.

The menu covers all the breakfast, lunch, and even early dinner bases. House specialties include eggs Benedict, breakfast burritos packed with bacon and avocado, or stuffed French toast. Hungrier fiends may go for comfort food like a burger or grilled cheese sandwich. Open till 5:00 P.M., there's no reason not to make a visit to this club an all-day affair.

Blackbird ✿

Contemporary XX

B2

619 W. Randolph St. (bet. Des Plaines & Jefferson Sts.)

Phone: 312-715-0708 — Lunch Mon – Fri
Web: www.blackbirdrestaurant.com — Dinner nightly
Prices: $$$ — Clinton (Green/Pink)

Doug Fogelson Photography

Blackbird's white façade dazzles like a diamond on this industrial (read: rough) block, seemingly lit from within and still attracting bold palates years after pioneering restaurateur Paul Kahan introduced fine dining to the West Loop. The infectiously spirited vibe hasn't dimmed a bit in the intervening decade, as each table fills speedily at lunch and dinner.

This high-flying room exudes mod-minimalism, from clustered stools at the glossy bar-cum-counter, to the high-backed gray banquettes flanked by swivel chairs set on matte metal pedestals. Yellow daisies in bud vases at each table keep the mood sunny and the eyes happy—this isn't a hushed temple, but a joyous ride.

The seasonally fixated menu is equally jet-setting, gathering global flavors that work in harmony courtesy of Chef de Cuisine David Posey. Pristinely diced crimson lamb tartare lies on a bed of tangy cranberry yogurt, scattered with roasted maitake mushrooms and grated chestnuts; while creamy walnut *skordalia* balances juicy roasted chicken with tender escarot *barigoule*. A contemporary spin on Concorde cake, named after the retired jet, incorporates a Concord grape sherbet into the classic sticky dark chocolate dessert.

Carnivale

Latin American 

702 W. Fulton Market (at Union Ave.)

Phone: 312-850-5005
Web: www.carnivalechicago.com
Prices: $$

Lunch Mon – Fri
Dinner nightly
Clinton (Green/Pink)

As much a spectacle as it is a restaurant, Carnivale aims for a festive feel on all levels. In a lofty dining room that could double as a hangar for parade floats, the décor explodes in a Technicolor kaleidoscope that may over-stimulate even the color-blind. Coupled with pulsing Latin music, it's a riot for the senses that gets even wilder with a choice from the vast rum, tequila, and cocktail list.

The smaller lunch menu serves as the warm-up act with salads, sandwiches, and daily specials, but the real show begins at dinner. Dishes from Latin America, Spain, and the Caribbean mix and mingle in an all-embracing menu unveiling a Yucatán chicken soup with roasted chiles. Artisanal hams, cheeses, and *arrachera* with *chimichurri* also steal the spotlight.

De Cero

Mexican 

814 W. Randolph St. (at Halsted St.)

Phone: 312-455-8114
Web: www.decerotaqueria.com
Prices: $$

Lunch & dinner Tue – Sat
Morgan

This motto and name (meaning "from scratch") speaks for itself at De Cero, a contemporary taqueria where Mexican fare gets a fresh treatment. In a stylishly casual setting adorned with wooden skull masks to match the unfinished tables, diners sip pineapple-jalapeño margaritas while awaiting their plates.

With 16 taco varieties that can be ordered in any combination, along with creatively stuffed tamales like goat cheese with chile masa, a custom dining experience is almost guaranteed. The lunchtime motto is "Hello Tacos!" for good reason—think batter-fried shrimp nestled into a corn taco with avocado and *crema*. The *tacos al pastor* are a wondrous combination of pork marinated with *guajilla*, *morita*, and *chiles de arbol*, topped with pineapple and onions.

Embeya

Fusion XXX

1400 W. Randolph St. (at Jefferson St.)

Phone: 312-612-5640 — Dinner nightly
Web: www.bellyqchicago.com
Prices: $$ — Clinton (Green/Pink)

Hey, there's a new kid on the block and he's already making friends, judging from the buzzy crowd visible through floor-to-ceiling windows on Randolph. Tall cutout wooden screens and linen curtains do nothing to quell the reverberation from the enthusiastic diners lining the marble bar and pliant leather chairs; but, shareable plates from the French-influenced Asian menu justify the buzz and showcase Chef Thai Dang's creativity.

Garlic chicken prepared Peking duck-style, arrives with a glossy, mahogany-tinged skin stretched over incredibly juicy meat; and stuffed sea snails, a signature here, are chopped with ground pork, black garlic, and then skewered on lemongrass stalks. A pool of drinkable consommé serves as a chaser in the bottom of each shell.

g.e.b.

American XX

841 W. Randolph St. (bet. Green & Peoria Sts.)

Phone: 312-888-2258 — Lunch Sun
Web: www.gebistro.com — Dinner Tue – Sat
Prices: $$ — Morgan

Grab your earplugs and get ready to sing for your supper: Chicago über-chef Graham Elliot's casual bistro doubles as a shrine to rock n' roll. Those are Marshall amps stacked as a host stand, and the saints on the Mexican-style prayer votives lining the banquettes aren't from the Bible—they are food icons like Anthony Bourdain and Julia Child.

Where the décor is playful, the food is refined, playing up the best ingredients of the season. Dinner highlights may include chèvre agnolotti tossed with Swiss chard and pea tendrils; or local flaky whitefish with roasted sunchokes and citrus coulis. A full set of hearty brunch options like a tangy shredded beef barbecue sandwich topped with bubbly-broiled cheddar will keep you going until the nightly encore.

Girl & The Goat

Contemporary XX

B2

809 W. Randolph St. (bet. Green & Halsted Sts.)

Phone: 312-492-6262 — Dinner nightly
Web: www.girlandthegoat.com
Prices: $$ — Morgan

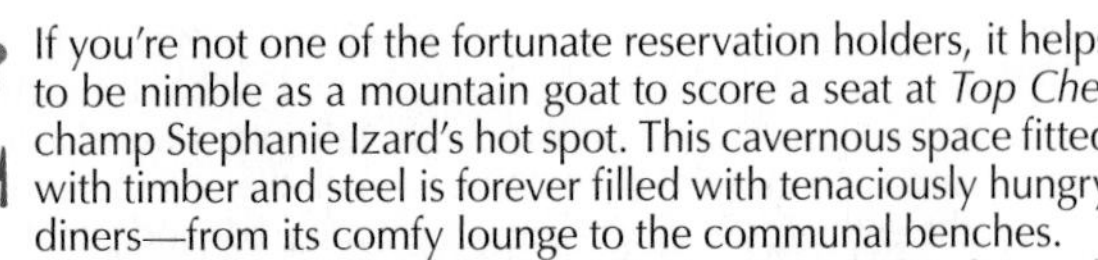

If you're not one of the fortunate reservation holders, it helps to be nimble as a mountain goat to score a seat at *Top Chef* champ Stephanie Izard's hot spot. This cavernous space fitted with timber and steel is forever filled with tenaciously hungry diners—from its comfy lounge to the communal benches.

Izard and team take their ingredients seriously by doing all butchering in-house and employing an artisan bread baker. Though the menu's simply sectioned into Vegetables, Fish, and Meat, the kitchen packs complex, bold flavors into each dish. Green beans tossed with a fish sauce vinaigrette and crushed cashews keep their al dente snap, but gain a caramelized char. Meanwhile, head-on smoked blue prawns mix it up with mushroom *gribiche* and creamy polenta.

Grange Hall Burger Bar

American 

A2

844 W. Randolph St. (bet. Green & Peoria Sts.)

Phone: 312-491-0844 — Lunch Tue – Sun
Web: www.grangehallburgerbar.com — Dinner Tue – Sat
Prices: — Morgan

American Gothic accents (think Grant Wood) invade the big city at Grange Hall, where a down-on-the-farm vibe is telegraphed loud and clear through swinging barn doors, quilted panels hanging above the lunch counter, and mismatched knit napkins set atop tables with wooden chairs and stools. The glassed-in pie kitchen in the back hints dessert won't be an afterthought.

Choose your own adventure when building a burger, starting with a six- or nine-ounce grass-fed beef patty and adding toppings like Midwestern cheeses, smoked bacon, jalapeños, or homemade pickles. If a wedge of strawberry rhubarb pie or Bourbon-spiked milkshake is calling your name (especially when freshly churned ice cream is involved), go easy on those hand-cut farmhouse chili fries.

Grace ✿✿

Contemporary XXXX

B2

652 W. Randolph St. (bet. Desplaines & Halsted Sts.)

Phone: 312-234-9494 Dinner Tue – Sat
Web: www.grace-restaurant.com
Prices: $$$$ Clinton (Green/Pink)

Michael Muser/Grace

Housed on primo West Randolph, Grace stands in good company. Its very modern design combines striated wood paneling, gray tabletops, and a kitchen visible behind a glass wall that is frosted at the bottom, clear at the top. Even service matches the flawless style, with a staff that is professional yet light and not entirely formal.

Chef Curtis Duffy's contemporary menu is refined, technically meticulous and, at times, ambitious to the point of genius. Begin with a humble "parsnip" interpreted here as parsnip purée topped with parsnip "water" and little green pearls of tarragon that remain frozen until eaten, then explode with flavor. Shatter a bit of frozen ginger water to reveal delectably fatty *nairagi* (striped marlin) sashimi twirled with golden trout roe, caramelized cashew, pomelo, and Thai basil over a bit of funky fish sauce and sweet coconut rice. Matsusaka beef is so perfectly marbled and beautifully cooked that it is nothing short of memorable, with umami-loaded king trumpet mushrooms, salsify crisps, and scattered sansho leaves.

Finish with an extraordinary composition featuring Asian citrus in caramelized *sudachi* custard with toasted cashews, Asian pears, and nasturtiums.

Greek Islands

Greek 

E3

200 S. Halsted St. (at Adams St.)

Phone: 312-782-9855 Lunch & dinner daily
Web: www.greekislands.net
Prices:  UIC-Halsted

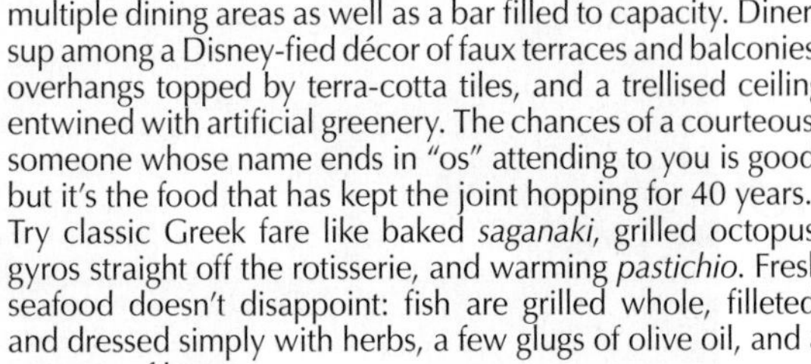

More crowded than the streets of Athens and just as busy—that's Greek Islands for you. This Chicago retreat sports multiple dining areas as well as a bar filled to capacity. Diners sup among a Disney-fied décor of faux terraces and balconies, overhangs topped by terra-cotta tiles, and a trellised ceiling entwined with artificial greenery. The chances of a courteous-someone whose name ends in "os" attending to you is good, but it's the food that has kept the joint hopping for 40 years. Try classic Greek fare like baked *saganaki*, grilled octopus, gyros straight off the rotisserie, and warming *pastichio*. Fresh seafood doesn't disappoint: fish are grilled whole, filleted, and dressed simply with herbs, a few glugs of olive oil, and a squeeze of lemon.

iNG

 Contemporary 

A1

951 W. Fulton Market (bet. Morgan & Sangamon Sts.)

Phone: 855-834-6464 Dinner Tue – Sat
Web: www.ingrestaurant.com
Prices: $$$  Morgan

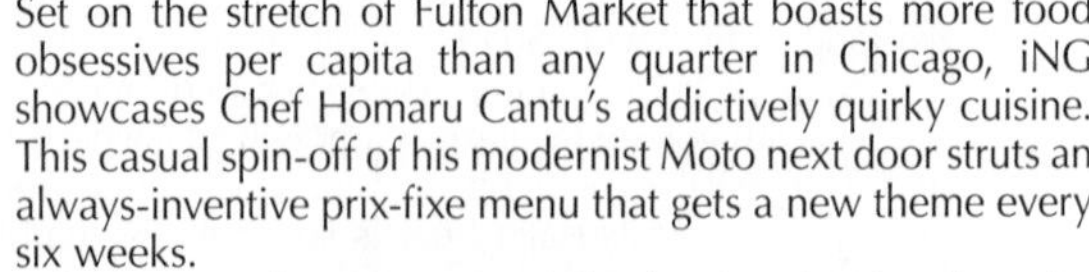

Set on the stretch of Fulton Market that boasts more food obsessives per capita than any quarter in Chicago, iNG showcases Chef Homaru Cantu's addictively quirky cuisine. This casual spin-off of his modernist Moto next door struts an always-inventive prix-fixe menu that gets a new theme every six weeks.

Whether an ode to Asian street food or '70s hard rock music, the menu—printed on a backstage pass—surprises and intrigues at every step. Deep Purple *poutine* boasts roast purple potatoes, cheddar, and short rib cubes with music notes drawn in white gravy; while oysters fried in corn chips and dusted in mignonette powder for a Blue Oyster Cult dish pair playfully with a chorizo-infused Bloody Mary. It sounds too crazy to work, but food nerds love it.

Jaipur

Indian XX

847 W. Randolph St. (bet. Green & Peoria Sts.)

Phone: 312-526-3655 — Lunch & dinner daily
Web: www.jaipurchicago.com
Prices: $$ — Morgan

Wait...a popular lunchtime Indian restaurant that doesn't do a buffet? And yet, these midday business diners digging into tandoor-charred and cheesy garlic naans don't seem to mind at all. They're coming for the equally affordable, full-service daily specials served in a parade of hammered copper bowls that are filled to the brim. With soft music and dusky pomegranate walls, it's an elegant way to spend lunch hour.

Tender morsels of chicken *kadahai* are boldly flavorful with galangal and curry, and the Jaipur platter is a golden-fried crunch fest of stuffed samosa and *pakoras* like banana peppers stuffed with spiced cheese. Dinner guests know to start with a martini before choosing from a vast selection of chicken, seafood, lamb, and vegetarian options.

Kabocha

Japanese XXX

952 W. Lake St. (at Morgan St.)

Phone: 312-666-6214 — Dinner Mon – Sat
Web: www.kabochachicago.com
Prices: $$ — Morgan

Bent balsa wood lanterns pay homage to the namesake squash inside this Morgan Avenue newcomer, where their striations meld with the natural tones of the spacious, airy dining room. Subtle embellishments like intertwining wooden staves and shuttered slat dividers play up the modern farmhouse connotations with a whisper.

Though billed as a Japanese brasserie, it's the seafood that shines brightest among the menu items here: opalescent hamachi and ahi mosaic need minimal garnish to showcase their clean flavor, though pickled shallot and house-smoked bacon play counterpoint. Groups craving all the raw bar has to offer can dig into the "Shellfish Aquarium," an impressively styled selection of king crab, prawns, oysters, and more in a mod acrylic bento box.

La Lagartija

Mexican

C3

132 S. Ashland Ave. (bet. Adams & Monroe Sts.)

Phone: 312-733-7772 — Lunch & dinner Mon – Sat
Web: www.lalagartijataqueria.com
Prices: ⊖⊖ — Ashland (Green/Pink)

From sunrise to sundown, La Lagartija serves up heart-warming *blanquillos*, platters of *alambres*, crocks of *cazuelitas* with melted *Chihuahua* cheese, and more in this contemporary-psychedelic space. Don't know what any of the food terms mean? Just check the tall walls, which illustrate the terminology in colorful fonts for an impromptu Spanish lesson your stomach will appreciate.

Pull up a brushed aluminium stool to one of the long counters and sink your teeth into a juicy *taco al pastor* made with pork spit-roasted with pineapple, then folded in one the taqueria's made-from-scratch tortillas. Cut through the spicy chile kick found in dishes and fresh salsas that accompany each platter with a refreshing pineapple or hibiscus *agua fresca*.

La Sardine

French

A2

111 N. Carpenter St. (bet. Randolph St. & Washington Blvd.)

Phone: 312-421-2800 — Lunch Mon – Fri
Web: www.lasardine.com — Dinner Mon – Sat
Prices: $$ — Morgan

In a neighborhood packed to the gills with gastronomic innovation, La Sardine may be the most daring option of all, flaunting hearty French bistro food in a warm, rustic set. The time-tested combination of wheezing accordion music, white linens, tile floors, and pastoral murals make it all the rage among diners craving the familiar—a $25 lunch prix-fixe doesn't hurt either.

Onion soup is straightforward yet sublime, with pungent cheese melting over a moist crouton and oozing down the side of a large ramekin; while fluffy gnocchi *Parisienne* with fresh peas and sweet corn purée help Chicagoans dream of summer and fields of gold. Other standards include a homemade sausage of the day, like the sprightly pheasant offering, served with warm potato salad.

La Sirena Clandestina

Latin American

954 W. Fulton Market (at Morgan St.)

Phone: 312-226-5300 Lunch Sun – Fri
Web: www.lasirenachicago.com Dinner nightly
Prices: $$ Morgan

La Sirena was made for summer nights, pulsing with a Cuban beat that spills onto the sidewalk patio as the temperature rises. Weathered metal chairs and steel-trimmed wood tables also serve as reflectors for any glinting light in the dim space. The younger crowd comes for the cocktails (and sometimes to cool their heels while hoping for a walk-in spot at Grant Achatz's Aviary across the street).

Gingham-clad mixologists pour standards like caipirinhas and daiquiris as well as more creative cocktails like the cusco cup, a Fernet-accented take on the pisco sour.

Flaky baked empanadas are forever in demand, though the filling changes daily; and small plates like charred octopus with red chiles and black olive vinaigrette prime the palate for more sips.

Little Goat Diner

American

820 W. Randolph St. (at Green St.)

Phone: 312-888-3455 Lunch & dinner daily
Web: www.littlegoatchicago.com
Prices: $$ Morgan

Not many diners in town offer valet service, but then, no other diner in Chicago is run by Chef Stephanie Izard, of the crushingly popular Girl & The Goat across the street. With an attached bakery and coffee bar next door, Izard-ites can get their fill on bustling Randolph from morning till night. Brocade wallpaper gives the diner a spiffy feel, while servers in retro purple dresses and horn-rims channel Flo and Alice.

All the usual suspects like tuna melts and short stacks get Izard's creative spin: a chicken *cordon bleu* sandwich adds sauerkraut and pickled peppers, while a mixed fry of tempura pickles and onion rings get a two-fer of ranch dressing and curry aïoli. Even diner standards like milkshakes are elevated with smoked pork and toffee crunch.

Lou Mitchell's

American

F3

565 W. Jackson Blvd. (bet. Clinton & Jefferson Sts.)

Phone: 312-939-3111 Lunch daily
Web: www.loumitchellsrestaurant.com
Prices: ⊜ Clinton (Blue)

At the top of Chicago's list of beloved names is Lou Mitchell. This eponymous diner is by no means an elegant affair, but thanks to its fluffy omelets and iconic crowd, it has been on the Windy City's must-eat list since 1923. Don't panic at the length of the lines: they are long but move fast, and free doughnut holes (one of the restaurant's signature baked goods) make the wait go faster.

Back to those omelets: they may be made with mere eggs, like everyone else's, but somehow these are lighter and fluffier, almost like a soufflé, stuffed with feta, spinach, onions, or any other ingredients of your choice. They arrive in skillets with an Idaho-sized helping of potatoes. Save room, because everyone gets a swirl of soft-serve at the meal's end.

Maude's Liquor Bar

Gastropub

B2

840 W. Randolph St. (bet. Green & Peoria Sts.)

Phone: 312-243-9712 Dinner nightly
Web: www.maudesliquorbar.com
Prices: $$ Morgan

Bring your vintage Miu Miu bag to the party at Maude's, where industrial and antique mix in a sea of candlelit tables, bistro-style mirrors, and aluminum chairs. It's trendy, sure, but who can fault the crowd for appreciating a bar that puts as much thought into its food as the cocktail program and whiskey flight? The first-floor dining room can get just as loud as the bar upstairs, which packs 'em in on the late night.

Helpful servers suss out how many plates you'll need based on your hunger levels. A range of ingredients change daily, but don't miss the excellent grilled sausage; or subtle chicken liver mousse with a shallot marmalade. Need a breather? A crunchy shaved vegetable salad balances out the indulgent richness of a dark chocolate mousse.

Moto ✿

Contemporary XXX

A1

945 W. Fulton Market (bet. Morgan & Sangamon Sts.)

Phone: 312-491-0058 Dinner Tue – Sat
Web: www.motorestaurant.com
Prices: $$$$

Morgan

Mike Silberman, A Sustainable Reality

Surrounded by loading docks, Moto is as unconventional as it is exceptional. Everything seems hip and utterly agreeable, from the mod lighting and gray-striped suede booths to the extraordinary care given to each plate. The staff is polite and knowledgeable enough to offer guests a complete explanation of each dish—no easy feat. Tables are filled with dedicated foodies and cool types celebrating a special occasion. The kitchen may seem to harp on dramatic presentations, but each is purposeful and fun. There are no gimmicks for gimmick's sake here.

Only one unique and highly inventive fixed menu is served, which probably makes possible the opening salvo: behold a miniaturized version of your entire meal.

Presentation is paramount in the glass terrarium filled with river stones and sashimi cubes, slowly picking up the rising applewood smoke as the thin film of plastic is peeled back. Paired with a mini everything bagel and chive macaron, this dreamy beach sequence may be tailed by a creative and delicious surprise when the "tree trunk" arrives as petite pancakes arranged with little slices of veal breast and sweetbreads, huckleberry compote, and a tiny birch trunk filled with maple syrup.

Nellcôte

Italian XX

833 W. Randolph St. (at Green St.)

Phone: 312-432-0500 — Dinner nightly
Web: www.nellcoterestaurant.com
Prices: **$$** — Morgan

Nellcôte is pervaded by a sexy, tactile presence: inspired by the French villa where the Rolling Stones recorded in the 1970s, it exudes a louche but luxe rocker vibe with a lacquered ivory counter, Italian marble staircase, and herringbone-patterned wood. Antique crystal chandeliers draw eyes up, as a showy bar runs down the room like a runway for those who want the spotlight.

Equally decadent is a creamy, chilled slice of foie gras torchon, poached in duck fat, rolled in crushed pistachios, and served with mini brioche and *marasca* cherries. Slightly more down-to-earth plates present fava bean- and spring onion-agnolotti mounded with shavings of *ricotta salata*; or halibut crowned with scrambled egg sabayon and black sturgeon caviar.

NEXT

Contemporary

953 W Fulton Market (at Morgan St.)

Phone: 312-226-0858 — Dinner Wed – Sun
Web: www.nextrestaurant.com
Prices: **$$$$** — Morgan

NEXT earns the right to broadcast that you're lucky to be here—you are! Landing a pricy pre-paid "reservation" for their highly conceptual dinners can be an arduous game of extreme Facebook.

Every four months, the menu is reinvented, perhaps as a feast from the Bocuse d'Or or an exploration of Childhood. Vegan featured curried cauliflower with harissa; its presentation involved glass straws and birch bark. Another course brought servers skimming tiny lilies from a pond-like centerpiece and gingerly depositing them onto sliced lily bulbs. The outrageously hyped "cuisine" has both creative hits and outlandish misses; whether one outweighs the other depends on if you like the theatrics. If you don't, the dining room overlords might explain why this is your fault.

OON

Asian XX

802 W. Randolph St. (bet. Green & Halstead Sts.)

Phone: 312-929-2555 — Dinner Mon – Sat
Web: www.oonrestaurant.com
Prices: $$ — Morgan

Staking its claim in the middle of one of the hottest restaurant rows in America, OON is a soothing oasis in the heart of West Randolph's hustle and bustle. Chef Matt Eversman's baby keeps things casually Zen, with a restrained décor—apart from the striking tamarack root chandelier welcoming guests for a pre-dinner cocktail or sip of sake at the bar.

Where the mood is polished and sober, the menu is broadly colorful, offering a fusion-tinged roundup of contemporary Southeast Asian eats. Grilled head-on prawns are dressed with spicy *togarashi* and preserved lemon butter; just as pork roulade is enhanced by pickled apricots and okra tempura. Yuzu panna cotta, as starkly pale as the walls themsleves, balances tart citrus with crunchy sesame granola garnish.

Paramount Room

Gastropub X

415 N. Milwaukee Ave. (bet. Hubbard & Kinzie Sts.)

Phone: 312-829-6300 — Lunch Thu – Sun
Web: www.paramountroom.com — Dinner nightly
Prices: $$ — Grand (Blue)

Though a few blocks north of the hot-and-heavy Fulton Market food scene, Paramount Room holds its own on this road less-traveled, thanks to elevated pub grub and a superior beer list. This soaring multi-level tavern lets you choose your style of hangout between a massive mirrored and patina-ed bar, cozy banquettes, high window perches, or a sultry semi-private lounge.

A plump burger made from 100 percent Wagyu beef on a toasted sweet brioche bun exemplifies the quality of ingredients across the menu; when crusted with salty bacon and coupled with crisp-tender green beans plus kicky *sriracha*, it makes for a very luscious meal. With "no crap on tap" as the beer motto, it's almost criminal not to wash down this hearty patty with a Belgian tripel.

The Parthenon

Greek XX

E3

314 S. Halsted St. (bet. Jackson Blvd. & Van Buren St.)

Phone: 312-726-2407 Lunch & dinner daily
Web: www.theparthenon.com
Prices: $$ UIC-Halsted

For a true taste of Greektown, get yourself to The Parthenon, where a kitschy but cheerful labyrinth of colorful dining rooms and bars has welcomed groups large and small since 1968. The bustle and blare of servers setting Metaxa-soaked *saganaki* aflame with a booming cry of "Opa!" never stops here. Yet, no one seems to mind—even the businessmen on lunch get into the spirit.

The large menu of traditional Greek dishes means you won't leave hungry, and a wide variety of ouzo by the carafe ensures that you'll likely be happy and flushed by the end of it all. Plump spinach-stuffed spanakopita is a crisp and filling teaser; followed by gyros which come piled with freshly sliced beef or lamb from the large spits roasting in The Parthenon's front windows.

Province

American XX

C1

161 N. Jefferson St. (bet. Lake & Randolph Sts.)

Phone: 312-669-9900 Lunch Mon – Fri
Web: www.provincerestaurant.com Dinner Mon – Sat
Prices: $$ Clinton (Green/Pink)

Natural and industrial elements complement one another at Province, where recycled cork tables and white tree branches "growing" from the ceiling mix with steel, glass, and walls splashed with magenta accents. The convenient Jefferson Street location makes it a hit with business types—an $18 lunch prix-fixe gets them in and out in a jiffy, and the bar sees its share of after-work revelers.

The carte is divided into categories like Bites, Raw, Small, Big, and Bigger and lets each diner dictate his or her level of hunger and propensity to share the American fare spiked with Central American flavors. Dishes have featured spice-rubbed ahi tuna tacos laced with a serrano chile-tartar sauce and julienned jicama; or pan-roasted salmon with parsnip gnocchi.

The Publican

Gastropub

837 W. Fulton Market (at Green St.)

Phone: 312-733-9555 — Lunch Sat – Sun
Web: www.thepublicanrestaurant.com — Dinner nightly
Prices: $$ — Morgan

The sceney Publican conjures the age-old tradition of a public house (offering a communal setting for animated conversations over a plate of food and pint of beer) to the modern gastropub age. Judging from its packed-to-the-rafters crowd emboldening themselves with beers from tasty on-tap options, it seems as if the new cohorts have no problem keeping this custom alive.

Though warned by the staff, courses come out willy-nilly. Entrées may arrive before appetizers, desserts before veggies. But who really cares if dry-aged duck breast with romesco and lentils share belly time with fried Lake Erie walleye, or caramelized blueberry *crostata*? The results are always dazzling.

Use the valet if trucks from the nearby meatpacking plants make parking scarce.

Saigon Sisters

Vietnamese

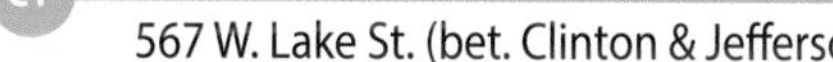

567 W. Lake St. (bet. Clinton & Jefferson Sts.)

Phone: 312-496-0090 — Lunch Mon – Fri
Web: www.saigonsisters.com — Dinner Mon – Sat
Prices:  — Clinton (Green/Pink)

Saigon Sisters is two restaurants in one: during lunch hours, Fulton River District workers line up for lively grab-and-go casual counter service; which transforms at dinner into a cozy, low-lit, sit-down restaurant with ambitious, westernized Vietnamese fare.

Stopping by at lunch, it's easy to fill up on the killer *bánh bao*: steamed buns filled with a choice of caramelized chicken, Wagyu beef in coconut milk, or to-die-for hoisin-glazed pork belly, all dressed with pickled carrot, daikon, cilantro, and jalapeño. Or try one of many modern variations on the classic *bánh mì*. Dinner is a more upscale affair: tasting menus and prix-fixe options—cleverly displayed on blackboards—offer great value, along with à la carte starters and entrées.

Sepia 

American XX

C2

123 N. Jefferson (bet. Randolph St. & Washington Blvd.)

Phone: 312-441-1920 Lunch Mon – Fri

Web: www.sepiachicago.com Dinner nightly

Prices: $$$ Clinton (Green/Pink)

Doug Snower

Like walking into an old-timey photograph (though you'll have to imagine the puff of smoke and popping flashbulb), Sepia does indeed bear that vintage patina. Housed in a 19th century building that was once home to a print shop (no surprise), original details like hulking freight elevator doors are still evident, and blend seamlessly with newer elements like attractive linoleum-tiled floors and crystal chandeliers encased in plastic cylinders. Coupes of retro cocktails are decanted at the bar in tune with the jazz wafting through the room.

The brick may be weathered and the serving boards distressed, but servers operate with casual polish and the menu betrays no rusticity. Chef Andrew Zimmerman tweaks American bistro cuisine, finessing and uplifting familiar dishes to a refined plane. A *puttanesca*-style sauce studded with tuna confit that enrobes toothsome, freshly made spaghetti is good enough to soak up with crusty bread that arrives on a cross-cut wood board.

Another trip down memory lane commences at dessert, where childhood favorites like malted milk and peanut butter meld in crispy-creamy layers of *feuilletine* and mousse, with shards of dark chocolate pretzel bark gilding the lily.

Sushi Dokku

Japanese

823 W. Randolph St. (at Green St.)

Phone: 312-455-8238
Web: www.sushidokku.com
Prices: $$

Lunch Fri
Dinner Tue – Sat
Morgan

Fans of the dearly departed Sushi Wabi can polish up their chopsticks and prepare to belly up to the bar once more: the same team has returned with this sleek spot just across the street. Thick wooden benches and tables line this dusky room, while the pristine counter shines like a beacon, reflecting light onto the mosaic of sushi boards hanging on the wall.

Artistry trumps classic Japanese minimalism on Sushi Dokku's frequently changing menu, where nearly every slice of fish comes with an embellishment or creative twist. Nigiri bites like sea bream are painted with smoked tomato vinaigrette and garnished with garlic chips and black lava salt; while feathery bonito flakes dance atop *takoyaki* with Kewpie mayonnaise and *unagi* sauce for dipping.

Vera

Spanish

1023 W. Lake St. (at Carpenter St.)

Phone: 312-243-9770
Web: www.verachicago.com
Prices: $$

Dinner nightly
Morgan

Cheese, ham, and wine are always enjoyable happy hour companions, especially when their names are Manchego, Iberico, and Oloroso. Ask the urban barflies—contentedly nibbling under Vera's bare filament Edison bulbs and over the ruckus of sherry-fueled chatter—and they'll agree wholeheartedly.

The range of *escabeche* and crudo change nightly, but sexified stalwarts like paella with rabbit, or grilled octopus with potatoes keep the menu purring. Adventurous types might go for rich *morcilla* rounds topped with a runny fried egg and spicy mizuna; while now-standard roasted Brussels sprouts perk up with crumbles of crispy Iberico ham. A traditional crème Catalan may be an established hit, but why not sip another sherry or share a selection of cheeses?

Photo by Robin Pendergrast courtesy of Northwestern University/Chicago's North Shore CVB

North & Northwestern Suburbs

North & Northwestern Suburbs

Evanston is the suburb that even city-dwellers love. As is the case in any metropolis, sometimes the suburbs fall victim to urban one-upmanship, but Chicago's first stop over the northern border lures a cluster of city folk with its lakefront charms and foodie finds. Additionally, Evanston is home to famed Northwestern University and the Woman's Christian Temperance Union, resulting in an incongruous mash-up of college-town hangouts and odd liquor laws.

Hotbed for Goodies

Evanston's Central Street is a swath of boutiques and cafés. Serious gourmands stock up at the renowned **Spice House**, reputed for their incredible spectrum of high-quality and unique spices, seasonings, rubs, and mixes. All these flavors will certainly inspire and nurture your inner Grant Achatz. It's also a solid choice for housewarming gifts. Nearby on Central Street is **Rose's Wheatfree Bakery and Café**. A rare and relevant establishment, they've garnered a giant following, all of whom come routinely for a treasure trove of gluten-free goodies including breads, cookies, cakes, cupcakes, and muffins to take home. Also sought after is the café menu of pizzas, salads, and sandwiches. Moreover, they carry the precious Tennessee-style Grampa Boo's Basting and Barbecue Sauce for some thrilling at-home grilling. Evanston and the tony North Shore are also known for **Belgian Chocolatier Piron**—this decadent den features a variety of handmade chocolates and special gift items, and also brings some of the finest and richest Belgian chocolates to Evanston.

Dog Day Delights

On the other side of the spectrum and shunning all things gluten-free and highbrow is **Wiener and Still Champion**, a hot dog stop where National Corn Dog Day is celebrated with the works (*sans* ketchup). When ordering, remember that the Chicago dog is a specific thing: a steamed, all-beef hot dog with yellow mustard, Day-Glo relish, chopped onion, tomato wedges, pickle spear, sport peppers, and celery salt on a poppy seed bun. That neon relish is made with sweet pickles and dyed a bright green (sort of like the Chicago River on St. Patrick's Day). Dunk their deep-fried pickles into sauces that reach as high as "truffle-mushroom" or as low as "bacon-bacon." Another inordinately famous and faithful hot dog and burger base is **Poochie's** in Skokie. For a more retro experience, approach the iconic **Superdawg**, with its dancing hot dogs dressed in spotted gear. This family- owned and-operated drive-in will make you feel as if you've just entered the set of *American Graffiti*. With its super menu of super-dogs (made with pure beef), burgers, sandwiches, beverages, and soda fountain specialties including floating scoops of ice cream in bubbling root beer, this is as much a family tradition as it is a landmark since 1948. True fast foodies pay homage to the golden arches at the McDonald's Museum in Des Plaines. The building is a re-creation of the original store, with massive displays of fresh potatoes being peeled and root beer drawn from a barrel by a uniformed crew of mannequins, fashioning a diorama that is as visually authentic as it is weird. It is no surprise that Chicago has its fair share of highway fast food stops. After all, the concept was virtually invented here when the Fred Harvey Company (which Hollywood immortalized in Judy Garland's *Harvey Girls* film), went from catering to railway passengers to a constant roster of motorists. It partnered to build the visually imposing series of mid-century "oases" stretching over the Illinois Tollway now catering to modern-day travelers.

Ethnic Enclaves

In such a diverse cultural urban center, it is no wonder that other ethnic enclaves are also thriving. Along Devon Avenue, you will find one of the country's larger South Asian communities. This corridor of South Asia showcases sincere and genuine restaurants (*desi* diners included), shops, and grocery stores serving a largely Indian and Pakistani clientele. Come for terrific *tandoori* and leave with an elaborate sari. Presenting everything Japanese under one roof is **Mitsuwa Marketplace** in Arlington Heights. This enormous supermarket carries everything from top-notch beef and sashimi to Japanese groceries, baked goods, books, and cosmetics. Also housed within this marvel is their version of Restaurant Row replete with restaurants offering everything from traditional Japanese dishes to fast-food Chinese and Korean selections. Journeying from Asia to the Middle East and closer to Park Ridge, Des Plaines, and Niles, find an array of ethnic supermarkets filled with Greek and Middle Eastern specialties. The influence of a massive Mexican population is found here as well within deliciously authentic tacos, tortas, and other foods at the many taquerias dotting these sprawling suburbs. There is a new generation of casual eateries and fast-food concepts booming here—**bopNgrill** is frequented for its fantastically messy burgers and Korean fusion foods. Interesting choices may reveal bop plates like *bulkogi, bul dak,* and *loco moko* or signature patties like the umami featurng truffled mushroom duxelle, sun-dried tomato confit, *togarashi* mayo, bacon, and smoked gouda. Meanwhile, **Buffalo Joe's** is *the* go-to spot for chicken wings on Clark St.; **Rollin' To Go** is a pearl among Northwestern students; and **Al's Deli** is a neighborhood fixture. With fast-food forgotten, end a day here at **Amitabul**. This fusion Korean restaurant prepares delicious and healthy items. Also on the menu are Buddhist delicacies with organic vegetables and spicy sauces for a vegan-friendly meal that, somehow, couldn't be more American. It is truly a gem that transcends all traditional tastes.

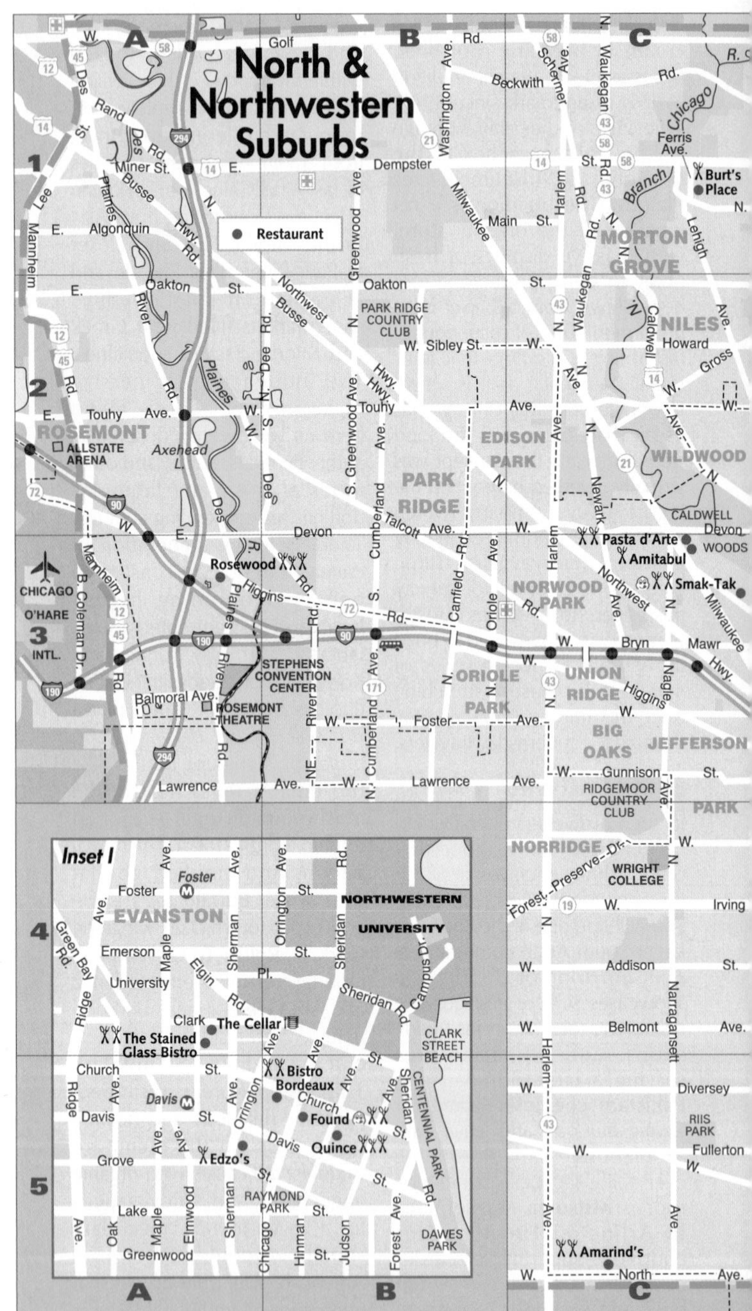
North & Northwestern Suburbs
Restaurant
Burt's Place
Pasta d'Arte
Amitabul
Smak-Tak
Rosewood
Amarind's
ROSEMONT
ALLSTATE ARENA
CHICAGO O'HARE INTL.
STEPHENS CONVENTION CENTER
ROSEMONT THEATRE
PARK RIDGE COUNTRY CLUB
PARK RIDGE
EDISON PARK
NORWOOD PARK
ORIOLE PARK
UNION RIDGE
BIG OAKS
JEFFERSON PARK
RIDGEMOOR COUNTRY CLUB
NORRIDGE
WRIGHT COLLEGE
MORTON GROVE
NILES
WILDWOOD
CALDWELL WOODS
RIIS PARK
Inset I
EVANSTON
NORTHWESTERN UNIVERSITY
CLARK STREET BEACH
CENTENNIAL PARK
DAWES PARK
RAYMOND PARK
The Cellar
The Stained Glass Bistro
Bistro Bordeaux
Found
Quince
Edzo's
Foster
Davis

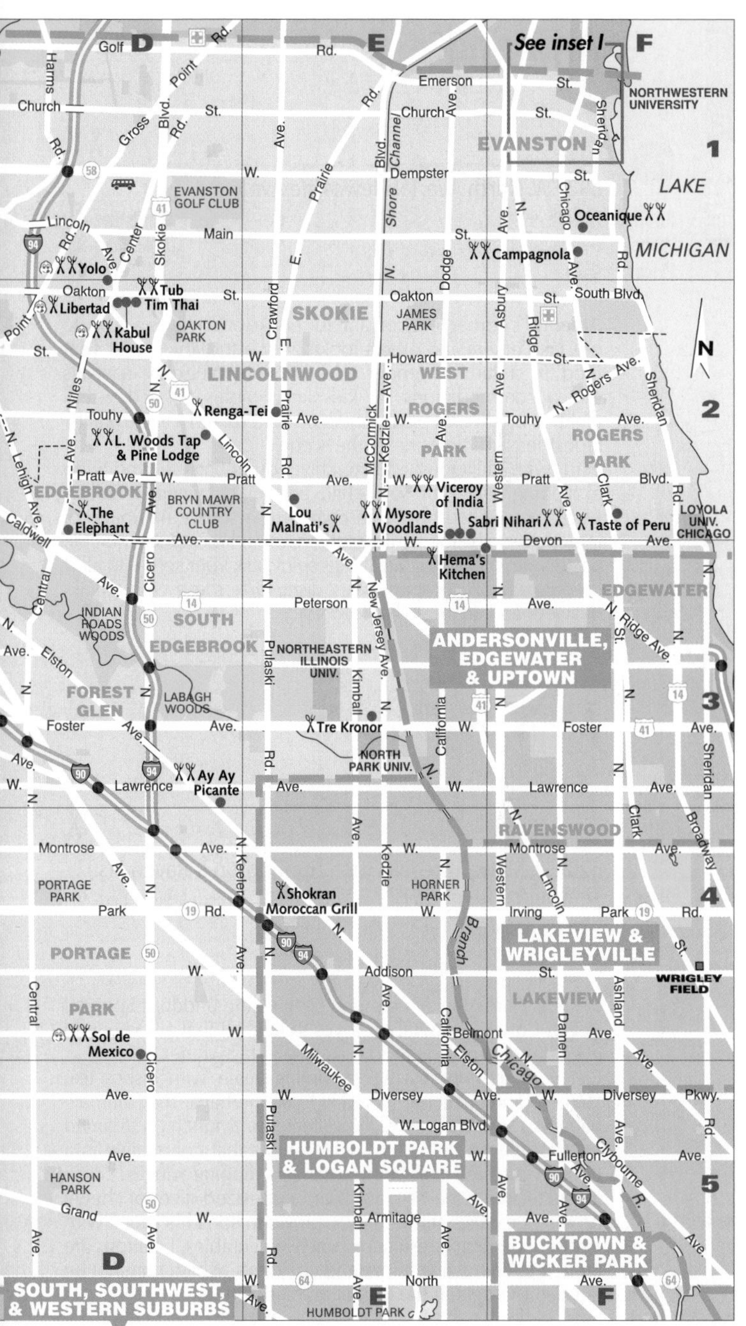

See inset I
D
E
F
1
2
3
4
5
NORTHWESTERN UNIVERSITY
EVANSTON
LAKE MICHIGAN
EVANSTON GOLF CLUB
Oceanique
Campagnola
Yolo
Tub
Tim Thai
Libertad
Kabul House
OAKTON PARK
SKOKIE
JAMES PARK
LINCOLNWOOD
WEST ROGERS PARK
ROGERS PARK
Renga-Tei
L. Woods Tap & Pine Lodge
EDGEBROOK
BRYN MAWR COUNTRY CLUB
The Elephant
Lou Malnati's
Mysore Woodlands
Viceroy of India
Sabri Nihari
Taste of Peru
LOYOLA UNIV. CHICAGO
Hema's Kitchen
EDGEWATER
INDIAN ROADS WOODS
SOUTH EDGEBROOK
NORTHEASTERN ILLINOIS UNIV.
ANDERSONVILLE, EDGEWATER & UPTOWN
FOREST GLEN
LABAGH WOODS
Tre Kronor
NORTH PARK UNIV.
Ay Ay Picante
RAVENSWOOD
PORTAGE PARK
Shokran Moroccan Grill
HORNER PARK
LAKEVIEW & WRIGLEYVILLE
WRIGLEY FIELD
PORTAGE PARK
LAKEVIEW
Sol de Mexico
HUMBOLDT PARK & LOGAN SQUARE
HANSON PARK
BUCKTOWN & WICKER PARK
HUMBOLDT PARK
SOUTH, SOUTHWEST, & WESTERN SUBURBS

Amarind's

Thai XX

6822 W. North Ave. (at Newcastle Ave.)

Phone: 773-889-9999 Lunch Tue – Sat
Web: www.amarinds.com Dinner Tue – Sun
Prices:

Amarind's corner location and turret-like entrance is a favorite of Oak Parkers and others looking for affordable, solid Thai food in a family-friendly environment. Weekday specials and accommodations for kids keep tables filled day and night. A bright and pleasant décor dotted with Thai artifacts, tapestries, and artwork set the scene.

Start with deliciously filled chive dumplings served with a dipping sauce of soy, chili, and black vinegar. Follow with spicy grilled pork loin coated in a savory marinade of lemongrass, shallot, garlic, scallion, mint, lime juice, and chili paste (note that if you like things spicy, ask your server to alert the kitchen). Accompany tasty dishes like these with a glass of sweet and creamy Thai iced tea.

Amitabul

Korean 

6207 N. Milwaukee Ave. (bet. Huntington & Raven Sts.)

Phone: 773-774-0276 Lunch & dinner Tue – Sun
Web: www.amitabulvegan.com
Prices:

With its Korean-inspired menu of "Healing Buddhist Spiritual Vegan Cuisine," Amitabul strives to heal all that ails you (and even if it doesn't, the food is still really tasty here).

Get your immune system humming again with dishes like "Green and Greener Nirvana," or perhaps the ultimate panacea, "Dr. K's Cure All Noodle Soup." Munch on steamed *mandoo* vegan dumplings, with flavors that come alive in a duo of salty red chili and sweet soy dipping sauces. Spice lovers tuck into the "Yin and Yan," coin-sized slices of chewy brown rice cakes stir-fried in a spicy crimson chili sauce with a host of perfectly fresh and crunchy vegetables. Libations are limited to energizing juices and cozy teas, which may not be enough to brighten the lack of ambience here.

Ay Ay Picante

D3 Peruvian XX

4569 N Elston Ave. (bet. Kennicott & Kiona Aves.)

Phone: 773-427-4239 Lunch & dinner daily
Web: www.ayaypicante.com
Prices: Irving Park (Blue)

Incans, Andeans, and conquistadors have shaped Peru's cultural and culinary history, and Ay Ay Picante celebrates them all, bringing flavor to an otherwise bland neighborhood. Murals of mysterious images of the Peruvian desert decorate the dining room, and pan flute melodies play in the background.

Leave the carb-phobic at home; Peruvian staples of corn, potatoes, and rice are all over this six-page menu so vegetarians won't go hungry. Authenticity strikes a chord in classic dishes like crispy fried empanadas stuffed with hard-boiled egg and ground beef; or *tamal Peruano*, steamed banana leaves filled with chicken, nuts, and black olives, and paired with *salsa criolla*. Their signature *aji verde* is so much in demand it's now sold by the bottle.

Bistro Bordeaux

B5 French XX

618 Church St. (bet. Chicago & Orrington Aves.), Evanston

Phone: 847-424-1483 Lunch Sun
Web: www.lebistrobordeaux.com Dinner nightly
Prices: $$ Davis

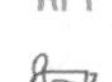

"L'authentique" reads the stencil on one of Bistro Bordeaux's windows, and the décor inside offers a slice of Parisian life for those with champagne dreams but no chips to spare. Pressed-tin ceilings, buttery yellow walls gilded with smoky mirrors, and the requisite trill of Edith Piaf telegraph this French experience in the middle of Evanston.

A staunchly typical menu keeps it authentic with bouillabaisse, steak frites, daily foie gras preparations, and an all-Gallic wine list to match. Pan-roasted wild trout gets a Provençal touch with delicious Meyer lemon-thyme beurre blanc; and heady Pernod accents that addictive herb-and-shallot butter dousing plump, meaty escargot. A rich chocolate terrine wheeled by on a wooden dessert cart deserves a forkful.

Burt's Place

C1 — Pizza

8541 Ferris Ave. (bet Capulina & Lincoln Aves.), Morton Grove

Phone: 847-965-7997 — Lunch Wed – Fri
Web: N/A — Dinner Wed – Sun
Prices: ⊜

If you're dedicated to deep-dish pizza, follow these three rules to guarantee a memorable meal at Burt's Place: make a reservation and place your order a few days in advance, call as soon as or just before the restaurant opens to reliably reach a staffer; and arrive on time to ensure a still-hot and bubbling pizza. Why go to all this trouble for a pizza? Quite simply, because Burt's, a neighborhood favorite that looks the part with its tchotchke-covered, wood-paneled dining room, makes great deep-dish and that's it.

With limited oven space, timing is paramount. But when a generous slice with a thick, caramelized crust, tangy tomato sauce, piles of toppings, and the perfect balance of cheese hits your table, you'll know why you made the effort.

Campagnola

F1 — Italian

815 Chicago Ave. (at Washington St.), Evanston

Phone: 847-475-6100 — Dinner Tue – Sun
Web: www.campagnolarestaurant.com
Prices: $$ — Main

Who says you have to head downtown for a fabulous night out on the town? Campagnola is proof that the suburbs can sizzle. From its sultry and soft lighting to the exposed brick walls and comfortable banquette seating, this Italian jewel seems to be designed with a tête-à-tête in mind.

The subdued sophistication of the dining room is echoed in the kitchen, where the chef ensures that the best designs are indeed simple. You won't find a high-falutin carte filled with adjectives describing fancy ingredients or fussy cooking techniques. Instead, this menu is purely about simplicity where dishes like chicken *al mattone* and linguini tossed with spicy shrimp headline. From start to finish, Campagnola satisfies with every beautiful bite.

The Cellar

A4

820 Clark St. (bet. Benson & Sherman Aves.), Evanston

Phone: 847-864-8678 — Dinner nightly
Web: www.thecellarevanston.com
Prices: $$ — Davis

The Cellar is the younger sib to Evanston stronghold, The Stained Glass Bistro, located around the corner. Though the two spots share a kitchen, they each have distinct personalities—this one's the global nomad who's just finished her *Eat, Pray, Love* round-the-world trip of self-discovery and returned to tell her tales...and share a cool craft beer and plate of tapas with you too.

What the Stained Glass does for wine drinkers, The Cellar does for beer. These far-reaching brews pair seamlessly with the small plates menu divvied into sections labeled A Hint of Europe, All-American, and Worldwide. Dive into varied bites like blue cheese beignets with roasted mushrooms and Port wine syrup, before going whole hog on the fried chicken with sweet garlic gravy.

Edzo's

American

A5

1571 Sherman Ave. (bet. Davis & Grove Sts.), Evanston

Phone: 847-864-3396 — Lunch Tue – Sun
Web: www.edzos.com
Prices: $$ — Davis

A burger joint in a college town seems almost too run-of-the-mill to even mention, but this casual Evanston spot is anything but average. Cafeteria trays and an eye-popping cartoon mural lend a retro '80s sense to the simple, family-friendly space where cooked-to-order plates put more emphasis on fresh than fast. Get your cravings out of the way early in the day, since Edzo's closes up shop every afternoon at 4:00 P.M. Thin griddled or thick charred patties with local grass-fed beef cry out for carefully crafted accompaniments like hand-cut fries, made "angry" when smothered in hot sauce, giardiniera, and jalapeños, or loaded with caramelized onion cream and frizzled leeks. Spoon up thick milkshakes in seasonal combos like maple-bacon and rhubarb pie.

The Elephant

Thai

5348 W. Devon Ave. (bet. Central & Minnehaha Aves.)

Phone: 773-467-1168 Lunch & dinner Mon – Sat
Web: N/A
Prices: ꞩꞩ

BYO

Look closely at the large elephant painting in this cheerful Edgebrook Thai spot: the familiar Windy City skyline peeks out from behind the pachyderms. It's an apt backdrop for a restaurant that's long been a second kitchen for local families, whether dining in or out.

Chef/owner Ann Leevathana brings authentic Bangkok flavor to a menu packed with traditional Thai ingredients like Thai basil, galangal, and Kaffir lime. She turns out spot-on renditions of fan favorites like deeply-flavored *massaman* curry and *nam sod* combining warm ground chicken with a healthy dose of pepper flakes, red onion, peanuts, and cilantro. Specialty dishes like spicy basil duck in an intensely flavored, heat-filled sauce with fresh basil leaves shouldn't be overlooked.

Found

American

B5

1631 Chicago Ave. (bet. Church & Davis Sts.), Evanston

Phone: 847-868-8945 Lunch Fri – Sun
Web: www.foundkitchen.com Dinner Tue – Sun
Prices: $$ Davis

Conventional dining be damned. If the vintage charm of Anthropologie or Etsy strikes your fancy, then Found is your restaurant. An antique-chic vibe dominates this lively no-reservations spot in Evanston, where diners populate the stylish wingback chairs, sofas, and low-slung coffee tables. Waiting patrons edge gingerly around the globes and framed art scattered through the space.

Once you snag a primo seat, couch, or bar stool, choose a few shareable plates on the eclectic menu—from twice-fried wings glazed with smoked chilies, lemon, and honey, to luxe caviar service. The wood oven churns out plump pork chops served with celeriac purée and salsa verde. For dessert, savor every scoop of coffee gelato crowned with homemade ricotta and walnut meringue.

Hema's Kitchen

Indian

2439 W. Devon Ave. (bet. Artesian & Campbell Aves.)

Phone: 773-338-1627 — Lunch & dinner daily
Web: www.hemaskitchen.com
Prices: $$

Bustling Devon Avenue is the go-to neighborhood for Indian and Pakistani vittles, music, movies, clothing, and other delights. And Hema's Kitchen is one of the stalwarts of the area, a favorite of locals (so much so, a second location opened in Lincoln Park), despite the fact that there is no shortage of restaurants from which to choose.

The menu, by Hyderabad native chef Hema Potla, includes some old favorites and twists on the classics. The chicken roll is basically an Indo-wrap, with a kebab rolled in butter-brushed *paratha*, along with verdant green chutney. Lamb *rogan josh* is a mouthwatering curry; sweet, nutty, spicy, and tart, seasoned with cardamom, cloves, and other spices. And pistachio *kulfi* is a creamy, sweet ending to this spicy meal.

Kabul House

Afghan

D2

4949 Oakton St. (at Niles Ave.), Skokie

Phone: 847-674-3830 — Lunch Mon – Sat
Web: www.kabulhouse.com — Dinner nightly
Prices: $$

BYO

Kabul House is the place to sate any craving for kebabs. Chef and owner Abdul Qazi runs this charming operation, in an airy space decked with Afghan artifacts, comfy burgundy booths, and wood floors.

Tables are prepped with shakers of sumac alongside their salt and pepper siblings, and meals kickoff with homemade flatbread and a side of spicy cilantro-garlic *chatni*. Each dish is authentic and downright delicious, from the spiced pumpkin with yogurt sauce to the nourishing lamb stew. Tuck into the heavenly *mantoo*, ground beef and onion dumplings, bathed in tomato-meat sauce and drizzled with mint yogurt. For a mouthwatering meat-a-thon, try the trio of skewered chicken, lamb, and ground beef kabobs served with rice and grilled vegetables.

Libertad

Latin American 

7931 Lincoln Ave. (bet. Niles Center Rd. & Oakton St.), Skokie

Phone: 847-674-8100 — Lunch Sun
Web: www.libertad7931.com — Dinner Tue – Sun
Prices: $$

At Libertad, Chef/owner Armando Gonzalez's free-spirited cooking pairs contemporary Latin American dishes with a multitude of cultural influences. The open kitchen and bar give guests a bit of dinner theater as they watch flames dance around sauté pans, while bartenders shake up Asian pear-cardamom mojitos and margaritas *rojas*, made with the botanical spirit called "Hum."

Liberties are taken with traditional preparations throughout the menu with inspiring results. Vegetarian *albondigas* aren't the expected meatballs, but light, crispy corn fritters over tomatillo-basil sauce; and a *chile relleno* comes stuffed with goat cheese, tofu, wild mushrooms, and epazote. As adventurous as the savory courses are, desserts like apple cobbler are more restrained.

Lou Malnati's

E2

Pizza 

6649 N. Lincoln Ave. (bet. Avers & Springfield Aves.), Lincolnwood

Phone: 847-673-0800 — Lunch & dinner daily
Web: www.loumalnatis.com
Prices:

Lou Malnati got his start in Chicago's very first deep-dish pizzeria. In 1971, he opened his own, and it's been golden ever since. With 30 locations around Chicago (the original is a bit of a time warp), Lou's remains family-owned and operated with great food and devoted service.

They have an extensive menu of pizzas, pastas, and other Italian classics. Portions are colossal: begin with stuffed spinach bread—that great Chi-style garlic, spinach, and cheese combo with tomatoes stuffed into bread—and you'll struggle to stay upright. Then try the "Lou" pizza, a buttery pastry-like crust crowned with spinach, mushrooms, and sliced tomatoes, doused in sauce and slathered with gooey cheese.

Bonus: you can ship Lou's anywhere in the U.S. through their website.

L. Woods Tap & Pine Lodge

D2 — American XX

7110 N. Lincoln Ave. (at Kostner Ave.), Lincolnwood

Phone: 847-677-3350 — Lunch & dinner daily
Web: www.lwoodsrestaurant.com
Prices: $$

Nostalgic for the supper clubs of yore? This cozy Lincolnwood cabin looks the part with oxblood leather booths, wood-paneled walls hung with mounted fish, and a bar with plenty of Wisconsin beers to make any cheesehead feel at home. The only thing (happily) missing is that haze of cigarette smoke. It also feels the part thanks to a menu of family-friendly American classics like pot roast, paired with daily specials: Thanksgiving comes every Monday with roast turkey and all the fixings, and Fridays mean fried lake perch.

Barbecue is a lodge specialty, with baby back and beef ribs served "devil-style" for the fiery tempered; or tangy mahogany-skinned chicken. Portion sizes are hefty, so plan accordingly for a slice of cream cheese-frosted carrot cake.

Mysore Woodlands

E2 — Indian XX

2548 W. Devon Ave. (bet. Maplewood Ave. & Rockwell St.)

Phone: 773-338-8160 — Lunch & dinner daily
Web: www.mysorewoodlands.info
Prices:

There is no lack of authentic Indian food in Chicago, but Mysore Woodlands stands out from the pack thanks to its focus on South Indian vegetarian cooking. Bold, intense flavors make up for the basic banquet hall-style décor at this orange-hued venue set on a restaurant-heavy stretch of Devon.

The Woodlands special *thali* lets diners sample a swath of delicacies without breaking the bank—platters are laden with metal bowls of crunchy *poriyal* like okra with mustard seeds and chilies; and soups like peppery *rasam* with basmati rice. Mysore masala *dosas* filled with spiced potatoes, or pancake-like *uthappams* with tamarind-infused *sambar* and coconut chutney, offer a whirlwind culinary tour; while cashew- and cardamom-flecked rice pudding offers a rich finale.

Oceanique

505 Main St. (bet. Chicago & Hinman Aves.), Evanston

Phone: 847-864-3435 — Dinner Mon – Sat
Web: www.oceanique.com
Prices: $$$$ — Main

Chef Mark Grosz opened this romantic seafood gem in 1989, and loyal clients have been fishing for excuses to make the trip to Evanston ever since. In this soft-toned dining room with hand-painted touches and wavelike fabric billowing from the ceilings, servers treat each meal as a special occasion.

The chef's affinity for French techniques expresses itself on a constantly changing menu that may include tender quail with apricot-chanterelle stuffing; seared scallops with a lobster-soy broth; and dark chocolate cake layered with rich crème Chantilly and chestnut ice cream. If the impressively thorough wine list makes drink decisions difficult, Grosz's son, dedicated wine director Philippe Andre, is happy to guide guests through pairings and selections.

Pasta d'Arte

Italian XX

C3

6311 N. Milwaukee Ave. (bet. Highland & Mobile Aves.)

Phone: 773-763-1181 — Lunch Tue – Fri
Web: www.pastadarte.com — Dinner nightly
Prices: $$

The imposing columns and inviting façade of this Norwood Park trattoria stand out on this otherwise mundane stretch of Milwaukee; while inside, genuine hospitality brings neighborhood couples and families back night after night. A snug dining room with warm, crimson-painted walls leads to a modern granite bar and year-round patio, heated with a fireplace to ensure a cozy feel even during those brutal Chicago winters.

Traditional Italian dishes get modern tweaks here and there—straightforward plump gnocchi bathe in creamy mushroom sauce, while pumpkin ravioli try balsamic sauce on for size. The *piccante* pizza pays homage to the great Italian beef sandwich, loading up a cracker-thin crust with spicy giardiniera and thinly sliced roast beef.

Quince

Contemporary

1625 Hinman Ave. (bet. Church & Davis Sts.), Evanston

Phone: 847-570-8400 Dinner Tue – Sun
Web: www.quincerestaurant.net
Prices: $$$

Quince fits in seamlessly with its surroundings on the ground floor of The Homestead, a historic downtown Evanston inn. Whitewashed wooden walls, a wood-burning fireplace, and quaint enclosed porch speak to the rustic romance of days gone by; though shaded drum light fixtures and cream banquettes lend a contemporary touch.

Depending on the night, the kitchen's reach may exceed its abilities, though effort shows in each artfully composed American dish. The small green *raviolo* atop a medium-rare New York strip steak carries a rich demi-glace that sauces the meat when pierced; and a cloche filled with cherry wood smoke obscures grilled baby octopus in a tangle of purées and garnishes. Balsamic ice cream complements poached strawberries infused with basil.

Renga-Tei

Japanese

3956 W. Touhy Ave. (at Prairie Rd.), Lincolnwood

Phone: 847-675-5177 Lunch Mon & Wed – Fri
Web: N/A Dinner Wed – Mon
Prices:

There's no glitz but plenty of piscine glory at Renga-Tei, set among a nondescript row of businesses in a Lincolnwood strip mall. The first hint that you're getting a genuine Japanese sushi experience comes from the staff's synchronized and punctual greeting announcing your arrival. Behind the counter, Chef/owner Hisao Yamada foregoes a smiling hello to remain focused on working the steel like an old pro.

A bright, clean, and minimalist décor matches the quality of food on the plate. This is not the place for gimmicky rolls smothered in sauce, but pristine fish with sublime sticky rice. Sunomono *moriwase* or *tekka* rolls with julienned cucumber are perfect palate teasers; while a single novelty roll, the Chicago Super Crazy, displays a dash of humor.

Rosewood

Steakhouse XXX

9421 W. Higgins Rd. (at Willow Creek Dr.), Rosemont

Phone: 847-696-9494 — Lunch Mon – Fri
Web: www.rosewoodrestaurant.com — Dinner nightly
Prices: $$$

In a city teeming with giant steakhouses, this independent gem continues to shine bright from the north suburbs for over two decades now. Owner Jim Mandas offers up serious steaks, chops, and seafood—along with warm hospitality—in this clubby, art deco den near O'Hare. Broad-shouldered businessmen and frequent flyers know Rosewood's satisfying spread by heart: they're not about to find any airplane pretzels here. Splurge on the upgrade and get a peppercorn or horseradish crust on your already succulent USDA Prime steak; keep it light with seafood like moist Skuna Bay salmon with cabernet sauce; or go old-school with jumbo shrimp cocktail.

The dessert menu is loaded with nearly a dozen modern faves like key lime tarts or white chocolate bread pudding.

Sabri Nihari

Indian XX

2502 W. Devon Ave. (bet. Campbell & Maplewood Aves.)

Phone: 773-465-3272 — Lunch & dinner daily
Web: www.sabrinihari.com
Prices: ©©

Named for both a signature stew and a famous shop in Pakistan, Sabri Nihari does both inspirations justice within its colorful yet upscale space that's been serving Halal Pakistani, Afghan, and Indian specialties to the neighborhood since 1977. For newcomers to the world of Indo-Pak cuisine and culture, a stroll past the shops on Devon Avenue after lunch is a feast for the senses.

Oversized rounds of fluffy naan are key to sopping up the flavorful sauces of each dish such as the Nihari beef or lamb stew, loaded with crushed pepper and spices; frontier chicken in garlic- and ginger-infused tomato sauce; or fruity chutney served alongside crispy batter-dipped chicken *pakoras*. Traditional menu items also include hearty biryanis and *lahori boti haleem*.

Shokran Moroccan Grill

Moroccan

E4

4027 W. Irving Park Rd. (bet. Keystone Ave. & Pulaski Rd.)

Phone: 773-427-9130 Dinner Wed – Mon
Web: www.shokranchicago.com
Prices: ⊜ Irving Park (Blue)

BYO

Judging by the ordinary façade, commercial surroundings, and hovering highway, you may be tempted to pass right by. But, oh, the delights that would be missed! Arabic for "thank you," Shokran is a scrumptious spot for homemade Moroccan, where rich silk fabrics billow from the ceiling; framed mother-of-pearl artifacts hang on burnt sienna walls; and hookah pipes and copper chargers bedeck the room.

Brace yourself for the couscous royale—melt-in-your mouth braised lamb; juicy merguez (spicy sausage stuffed with ground lamb and beef); tender zucchini, rutabaga, carrots, and chickpeas snuggled into fluffy couscous. Satiate the sweet tooth with handmade cookies—from almond pastries to *fekkas*, each morsel is fresh and irresistible. Thank you, Shokran.

Smak-Tak

Polish

C3

5961 N. Elston Ave. (bet. Markham & Peterson Aves.)

Phone: 773-763-1123 Lunch & dinner daily
Web: www.smaktak.com
Prices: ⊜

BYO

Set on a desolate stretch, Smak-Tak ("taste it" in Polish) and its skilled team of old-world cooks prepare some of the city's best Polish food. With knotty pine paneling covering the walls and ceiling, wood tables, and a faux fireplace, the space resembles a cozy mountain cabin.

Tiffany-style glass lamps bestow a gentle glow on large portions of food. Patrons should plan their ordering so they can try a little of everything including a delicious pickle soup bobbing with chunks of potatoes, cucumber, and fragrant dill; or tender and plump veal meatballs tossed in a well-seasoned mushroom gravy and coupled with a side of creamy carrot and cabbage sauerkraut. Pierogis filled with cheese and potato pancakes served with applesauce are other stomach-busters.

Sol de Mexico 

D4 — Mexican XX

3018 N. Cicero Ave. (bet. Wellington Ave. & Nelson St.)

Phone: 773-282-4119 — Lunch & dinner Wed – Mon
Web: www.soldemexicochicago.com
Prices: $$

Thanks to this hugely skilled kitchen, dishes are bold and authentic, tortillas are made on the spot, and *moles* are the renowned house specialty. Mexican paintings, carved masks and colorful artifacts hang on bright orange walls and splashes of cobalt blue pop against white linens.

Start with freshly made guacamole, then explore the roster of exciting and interesting fare, such as the *chambandongo*, layering fresh tortilla, shredded pork, almonds, pecans, and raisins in deeply flavored *Teloloapense* red *mole*. The *camarones en mole verde* is a delightfully classic sauce combining herbs, tomatillos, pumpkin seeds, and epazote over juicy grilled shrimp, and served with grilled vegetables and rice. Feeling adventurous? Try the five-course chef's choice menu.

The Stained Glass Bistro

A4 — American XX

1735 Benson Ave. (bet. Church & Clark Sts.), Evanston

Phone: 847-864-8600 — Dinner nightly
Web: www.thestainedglass.com
Prices: $$

All are welcome to worship at the altar of the wine grape here, where wines by the glass, on tap, and in flights are served nightly. Exposed ductwork and beams snaking across high ceilings lend an urban-chic feel to the romantic, pendant-lit space warmly lined with wooden wine racks.

Complementing the global drink list is soul-satisfying American bistro fare with eclectic influences, from a foie gras BLT with applewood-smoked bacon and white truffle mayonnaise, to crispy-skinned barramundi paired exquisitely with a creamy pea, artichoke, and *fromage blanc crustade*. Dessert may feature Chocolate^3 or a trio of decadent treats. A true community gem, The Stained Glass Bistro offers deals to Northwestern students and faculty who may inquire.

Taste of Peru

Peruvian

F2

6545 N. Clark St. (bet. Albion & Arthur Aves.)

Phone: 773-381-4540 Lunch & dinner daily
Web: www.tasteofperu.com
Prices: $$

BYO

Don't be put off by the plain-Jane exterior. Inside, wood masks mingle with posters of Peruvian destinations atop desert-toned walls; red tapestries cover the tables; and lively (sometimes live) music reveals the passion of Cesar Izquierdo. This chatty owner has been touting his peppery cuisine in East Rogers Park since 1974.

The menu shows a range of Peruvian food, from the classic *papa rellena* stuffed with tender ribeye cubes, walnuts, and raisins, to a steamed rice- tomato- and onion-combo in *lomo saltado*. If the complimentary *aji verde* tingles the taste buds a little too much, take a swig of cold and refreshing Inca Kola. When choosing a sip to savor with your meal, take note that Chilean *pisco* won't be welcomed—this is a Peruvian place, after all.

Tre Kronor

Scandinavian

E3

3258 W. Foster Ave. (at Spaulding Ave.)

Phone: 773-267-9888 Lunch daily
Web: www.trekronorrestaurant.com Dinner Mon – Sat
Prices: ⊜

BYO

This cheery corner cottage with its hand-painted fairy tale murals and chalet accents is an apt home for Swedish standby Tre Kronor. Named after a Stockholm castle and the three crowns on the Swedish national emblem, this restaurant's yellow-and-blue décor also shows off its Scandinavian heritage. The Sweden Shop across the street lets guests transport a bit of Nordic atmosphere back to their homes.

Breakfast is an all-day affair here, as the kitchen turns out batches of plump iced cinnamon rolls; thick waffles piled high with fruit and whipped cream; and airy Swedish pancakes with tart lingonberry sauce. Swedish meatballs with pickled cucumbers; Reuben sandwiches on toasted *limpa* rye bread; or salmon-and-dill quiche are among their savory standards.

Tub Tim Thai

Thai XX

D2

4927 Oakton St. (bet. Niles Ave. & Skokie Blvd.), Skokie

Phone: 847-675-8424 Lunch & dinner Mon – Sat
Web: www.tubtimthai.com
Prices:

Better than a sauna (and more fun to say), Tub Tim Thai in Skokie serves up its own healthy, brow-soaking dose of spice. Though the friendly servers will look at you askance for ordering anything above level 2 on their four-tier heat ranking, those who like it darn hot will be sniffling with a smile.

Every meal at Tub Tim should start with a plate of aromatic *meang kum*, a DIY appetizer wrapping roasted coconut, peanuts, ginger, dried shrimp, limes, shallots, and Thai bird chillies in a *chabo* leaf, then dipped in a sticky-sweet sauce. Entrées like *pad prik khing*, stir-fried with fresh basil leaves, chili paste, and green beans, showcase the kitchen's mastery of spice, while spring rolls and pad Thai keep with tradition. For dessert, try a fried banana.

Viceroy of India

Indian XX

E2

2520 W. Devon Ave. (bet. Campbell & Maplewood Aves.)

Phone: 773-743-4100 Lunch & dinner daily
Web: www.viceroyofindia.com
Prices:

The periwinkle and lavender walls, sky-blue ceiling painted with clouds, and steely booths lining the spacious dining room at Viceroy of India keep things cool, letting the spice-inflected cuisine churned out by the kitchen provide the heat. White linen-draped tables as well as a full bar and wine list make this West Rogers Park retreat a regal choice.

Though an à la carte menu is available for those who've got to get their fill of tandoori chicken, longtime patrons and lunch regulars make a beeline for the popular lunch buffet, stocked with North Indian standards like *pakoras*, samosas, *saag paneer*, chicken *makhani*, and goat curry. Complimentary naan is available by the basketful.

The grab-and-go café next door lets passers-by get their sweets fix.

Yolo

Mexican

D1

5111 Brown St. (bet. Floral & Lincoln Aves.), Skokie

Phone: 847-674-0987 Dinner Tue – Sat
Web: www.yolomexicaneatery.com
Prices: $$

BYO

Despite what Yolo may mean to abbreviation-friendly Tweeters and texters, it is short for *yolotli*, the Aztec word for heart. This charmingly tiny, under-the-radar Mexican spot located just off Skokie's main drag is simple and clean, save a few stone statues and artwork in brown, burgundy and cream. But, the understated tone of the space belies the colorful food on each table.

Richly flavored, authentically prepared salsas and sauces dazzle first-time guests and are craved by regulars; while *moles* like the chocolate-y pumpkin seed-accented *pipian* on tender shredded chicken and the piquant *mole de tamarindo* slathered on boneless pork ribs are standouts. A wedge of dense, rich, and creamy house flan makes for a fittingly sweet finale.

Your opinions are important to us. Please write to us directly at: michelin.guides@us.michelin.com

South, Southwest & Western Suburbs

South, Southwest & Western Suburbs

With perhaps a few high-profile exceptions (here's lookin' at you, President Obama's Hyde Park), the neighborhoods of the city's west and south sides and the west and south suburbs rarely make the pages of traditional visitors' guides. Instead, they're saved for those residents who work and live in these city environs.

Feeding Families

While it's certainly true that these neighborhoods may not have the museums, hotels, or 24-7 service of those more centrally located, they are a foodie's dream come true, with lesser-known groceries, tasty takeout joints, and other ethnic eateries. Back in the day, some of these neighborhoods, including Back of the Yards, once home to the famous Chicago Stockyards, changed the food industry. Today the Marquette Park neighborhood, where, in 1966, Martin Luther King, Jr. brought his civil rights marchers, may seem questionable after dark. But it is still worth a ride for no reason other than the mighty mother-in-law. No, not visiting a relative. That's the name of **Fat Johnnie's Famous Red Hots'** best dish: a tamale, a kosher hot dog, chili, and (processed) cheese poised on a bun, handed through a window. This may be a shabby and shaky trailer, but Fat Johnnie's hot dogs (a mainstay for over 30 years now) have a reputation of their own and have been luring hungry hot dog lovers from the world over. The rest of Marquette Park (near 63rd St.) features predominantly Mexican storefronts, taquerias, and other food vendors. Film buffs love the fact that Marquette Park (the 600-acre actual green space, not the neighborhood) was featured in the iconic movie *The Blues Brothers*.

Eastern European Eats

Closer to Midway International Airport, near Archer Heights, is a concentration of Eastern European shops mixed among classic Chicago-style brick bungalows. One favorite is **Bobak's Sausage Company**, with its 100-foot-long meat counter. This meat lover's paradise is a Chicago-based organization that caters mainly to food entities, grocery stores, and delis. Shopping here is entertainment in and of itself. Purchase a hot lunch to eat on the spot or buy a range of delicious sausages (Polish-style) and other deli meats to take home for the family. For a bigger and better taste of Chicago, you can also choose to buy from their bulk-pack items, retail-pack items, and imported specialties. Want to try this on your own? They also proffer a list of recipes. For a more Polish and Lithuanian take on deli dishes, try Evergreen Park's **AJ Meats**.

Ireland in Chicagoland

Nearby Beverly is the hub of the city's Irish bar scene, something many people first discover during the raucous South Side Irish St. Patrick's Day parade. But all year long, bars serve corned beef, cabbage, and plenty of cold beers. The **Thai Cafe** in Downers Grove may be located in a strip mall, but it's selection of spicy items (maybe *nam sod*?) is anything but ordinary. Non food attractions in Beverly include a number of Frank Lloyd Wright houses and other significant architectural monuments (not to mention a real castle). Farther north and closer to Lake Michigan, cerebral hub Hyde Park attracts Obama fans, academicians, students, and more architecture buffs. Professors and students at the University of Chicago hover around the surrounding cafés, restaurants, and bars geared towards the smarter set. During the summer months and baseball season, don't miss the White Sox at the U.S. Cellular Field. A lick of the five-flavor ice cream cone from the **Original Rainbow Cone**, a Chicagoland staple since 1926, promises an equally thrilling experience. Housed in a pretty pink building, the original menu has also unveiled a range of splits, shakes, and sundaes; as well as a decadent carte of ice cream flavors such as black walnut, New York vanilla, and bubble gum-banana.

Chicago's Beloved Bites

Those without any health, heart, or cholesterol problems ought to try the beloved breaded steaks (with a mélange of toppings) from **Ricobene's**, which has several locations on both the south side as well as in the south suburbs. Ricobene's also caters to the beefy best in everyone by serving up those Chicago classic pan, deep-dish, or thin-crust pizza pies alongside other delectable offerings like mouthwatering barbecue specialties (try a full slab dinner); Italian-esque sandwiches (imagine the Sloppy Joe and Vesuvio Italian classic sandwich); Chicago-style hot dogs; and char-broiled burgers. Suburban Oak Park may be more famous for its past residents like Ernest Hemingway and Frank Lloyd Wright, but nonetheless, foodies care more about vinegar-maker Jim Vitalo. His amazing, subtle herb-infused **Herbally Yours** vinegars are sold in bulk at the **Oak Park Farmer's Market** on Saturdays in the summer.

Grazing Through the Middle East

Suburban Bridgeview, home to Toyota Park, where the Chicago Fire soccer team usually plays, is one of the region's best stops for authentic Mid-East fare. Throughout this locale, you'll find restaurants fitted with grills and bakeries galore. Visit many centrally located stores, and be sure to take home classic snacks like pita, hummus, and baba ghanoush; as well as fresh groceries for a night of magnificent Middle Eastern munching. In closing, it would be simply blasphemous to end your meal without some sweet. So after you've consumed your fill of falafel and the like, move on to more lush respites in this Middle Eastern Corridor, namely **Elshafei Pastries** for some sticky-sweet baklava and other pistachio-pocked delights. Need additional saccharine satisfaction? Linger at **Albasha Sweet** and **Nablus Sweets**. One bite of these syrupy, nectarous, and creamy pastries will have you smiling for the rest of the evening. Can there be any other way to end such fresh, fun, and divine fare?

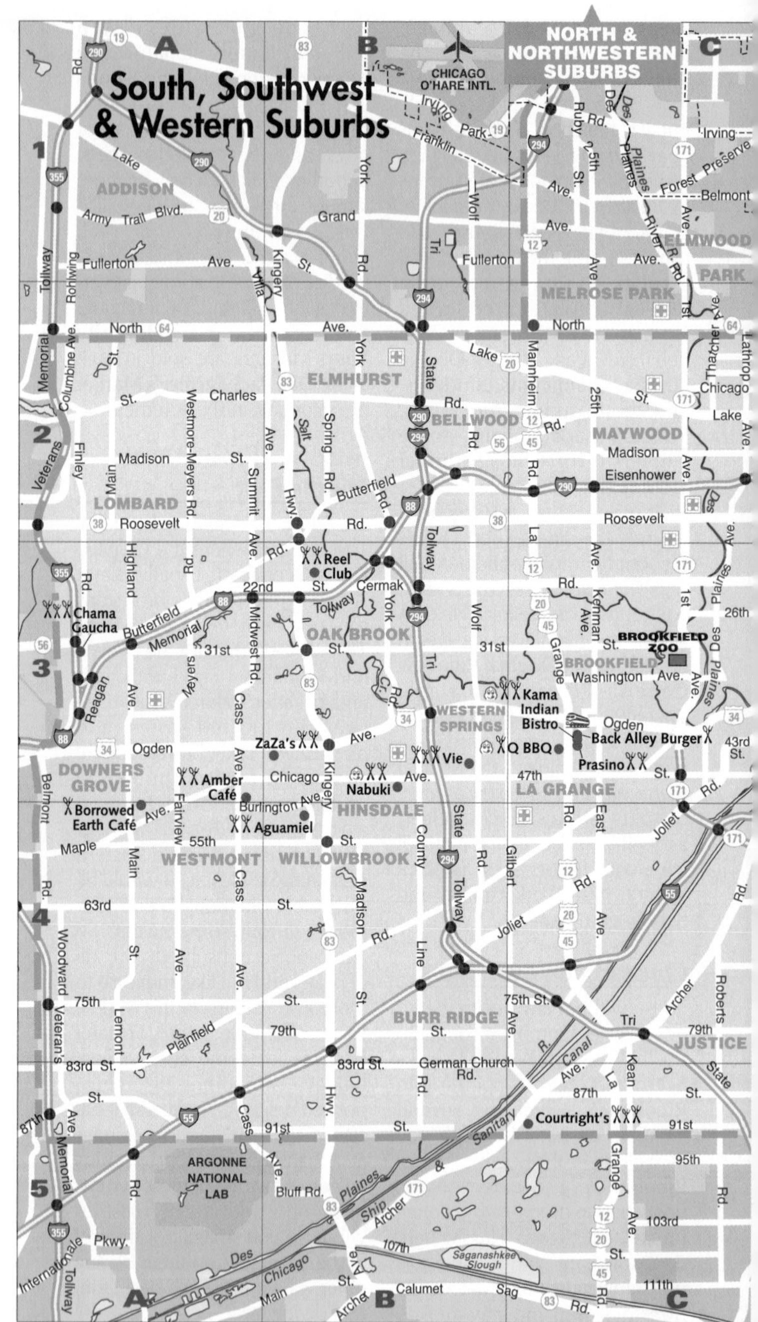
South, Southwest & Western Suburbs
NORTH & NORTHWESTERN SUBURBS
CHICAGO O'HARE INTL.
ADDISON
ELMHURST
BELLWOOD
MAYWOOD
MELROSE PARK
ELMWOOD PARK
LOMBARD
OAK BROOK
BROOKFIELD
BROOKFIELD ZOO
WESTERN SPRINGS
DOWNERS GROVE
LA GRANGE
HINSDALE
WESTMONT
WILLOWBROOK
BURR RIDGE
JUSTICE
ARGONNE NATIONAL LAB
Saganashkee Slough
Reel Club
Chama Gaucho
Kama Indian Bistro
Back Alley Burger
Q BBQ
Prasino
Vie
ZaZa's
Amber Café
Nabuki
Borrowed Earth Café
Aguamiel
Courtright's

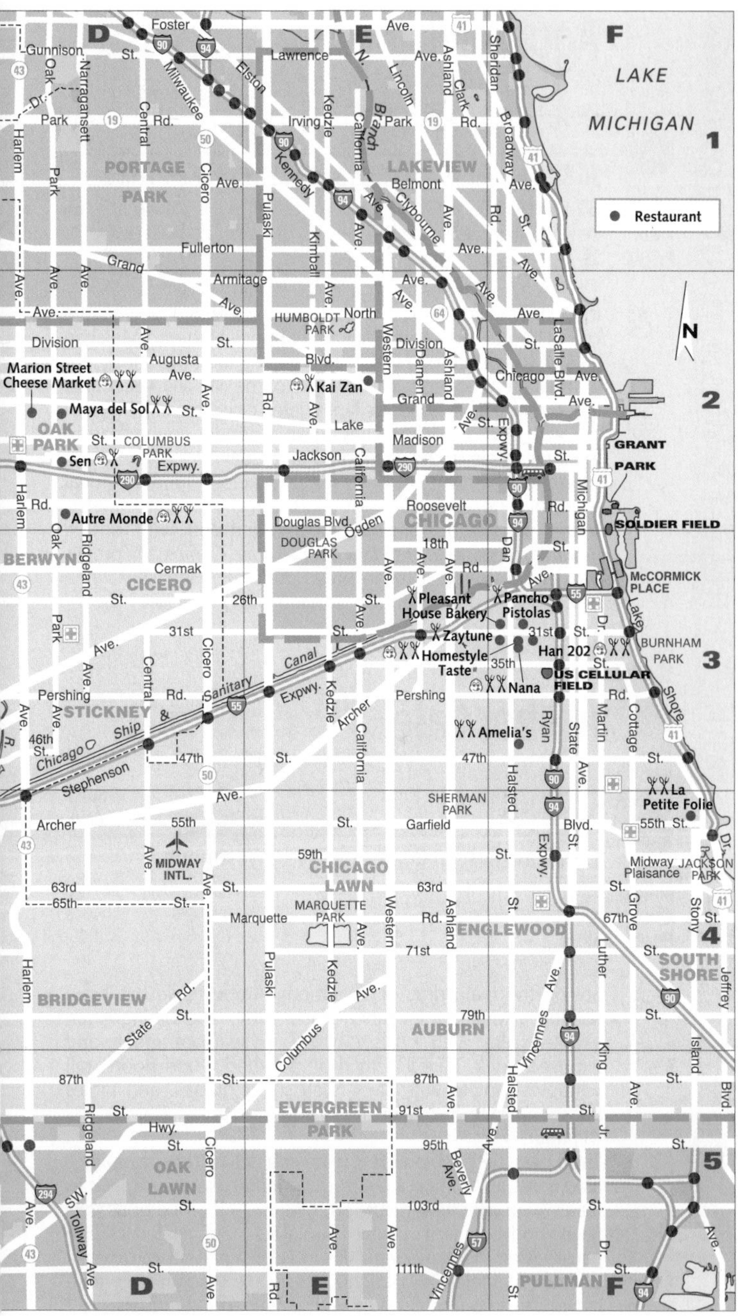

LAKE MICHIGAN
Restaurant
Marion Street Cheese Market
Maya del Sol
Sen
Autre Monde
Kai Zan
Pleasant House Bakery
Pancho Pistolas
Zaytune
Homestyle Taste
Han 202
Nana
Amelia's
La Petite Folie
PORTAGE PARK
LAKEVIEW
HUMBOLDT PARK
OAK PARK
COLUMBUS PARK
CHICAGO
DOUGLAS PARK
BERWYN
CICERO
GRANT PARK
SOLDIER FIELD
McCORMICK PLACE
BURNHAM PARK
US CELLULAR FIELD
STICKNEY
SHERMAN PARK
MIDWAY INTL.
CHICAGO LAWN
MARQUETTE PARK
ENGLEWOOD
JACKSON PARK
SOUTH SHORE
BRIDGEVIEW
AUBURN
EVERGREEN PARK
OAK LAWN
PULLMAN
D
E
F
1
2
3
4
5

Aguamiel

Mexican XX

B4

30 S. Prospect Ave. (at Railroad Ave.), Clarendon Hills

Phone: 630-537-1966 Dinner Tue – Sun
Web: www.aguamielrestaurante.com
Prices: $$

In a striking art nouveau-inspired space glowing with the colors of a desert sunset, Aguamiel brings high-end Mexican cuisine to Clarendon Hills. While settling in at the bar or one of the large wooden tables, try one of the Mexican-accented traditional cocktails like a cilantro julep or lip-tingling mezcal-rita with *chile de arbol*. They make a perfect counterpart to the guacamole or *queso fundido* of the day.

Alongside familiar dishes, family recipes and regional specialties populate the menu. Pork loin *en manchamanteles*, served on corn husks, pairs tender grilled pork with roasted peanuts, pineapple, and dark ancho *mole*. *Capirotada* proves Mexico can make a mean bread pudding, especially when studded with pecans and sweetened with *piloncillo*.

Amber Café

American XX

A3

13 N. Cass Ave. (at Burlington Ave.), Westmont

Phone: 630-515-8080 Dinner Tue – Sat
Web: www.ambercafe.net
Prices: $$

Set on the main drag of Westmont, Amber Café has been serving a touch of elegance since 2004. The dining room exudes calm with walls cloaked in seafoam green and exposed brick. Paved with rosy, polished wood floors, tall windows replete with steel-hued sheer drapes, and tables boasting white linen and fresh flowers, Amber Café is *très* romantic.

Stroll past the pebbled-glass wine cabinet to the cozy micro-tiled bar. Catch dinner here from a menu based on American ideals with Mediterranean sensibilities. Grilled octopus gets flavor and pep from charred tomatoes and pickled chilies; pan-roasted Alaskan king salmon is pristinely plated over a bed of vegetables; and a light cheesecake is balanced with a perky citrus compote spiked with ginger and kumquats.

Amelia's

Mexican XX

F3

4559 S. Halsted St. (at 46th St.)

Phone: 773-538-8200 — Lunch & dinner daily
Web: www.ameliaschicago.com
Prices: ⊜⊜

BYO

Nods to traditional Mexican décor, such as white calla lilies and a terra-cotta roof-tiled awning, perk up the dining room of this South Side south-of-the-border standby just off the Dan Ryan. Ample seating at white linen-draped tables inside the unassuming corner restaurant welcomes neighborhood regulars and newcomers alike.

The menu names its inspiration as the cuisine of Central-Southern Mexico, but nonetheless, Amelia's feels free to incorporate global influences and techniques into its roll of dishes. Ash-layered tamales *judio* are steamed in banana leaves and topped with fruity sesame seed-infused *mole*; and Maine lobster empanadas join pleasantly with grapefruit salad. Homemade corn chips and fresh jalapeño-laced guacamole make a perfect couple.

Autre Monde

Mediterranean XX

D2

6727 W. Roosevelt Rd. (bet. Euclid & Oak Park Aves.), Berwyn

Phone: 708-775-8122 — Lunch Sun
Web: www.autremondecafe.net — Dinner Tue – Sat
Prices: $$

Hint: when a restaurant names its backyard greenhouse, the kitchen takes sourcing very seriously. "Raffy" joins other local farms in growing most produce for this Mediterranean-tinged Berwyn favorite. No sports sully the bar TV screens here; they show foreign films or Star Trek, as if overtly conjuring "another world" (the name's French translation).

A panzanella salad of roasted carrots, squash, and mushrooms with toasted bread showcases the menu's seasonality alongside crispy brick-roasted chicken. Cracker-thin flatbread with creamy Fontina and wild mushrooms brings textural and flavorful harmony. The carefully selected wine list matches the Mediterranean vibe, with choices spanning from Croatia to Greece, along with dessert wines and grappa.

Back Alley Burger

American

1 S. La Grange Rd. (at Burlington Ave.), La Grange

Phone: 708-482-7909 — Lunch & dinner daily
Web: www.backalleyburger.com
Prices: ©©

What started as an alley-wide sliver of a spot in La Grange is now as wide as a boulevard, thanks to a recent relocation. Suspended wooden garage doors and tread-patterned aluminum give a fun nod to this industrial setting, while numerous tables and booths keep it casual for families and big groups of friends.

Grab tons of napkins before ordering at the walk-up counter as they flaunt 30 combinations of half-pound burgers and sandwiches. These feature toppings like pastrami and fried jalapeños, while patty options like crab cakes, Italian sausage, and freshly ground beef, make it easy to go overboard. If you haven't reached your fill, sweet potato fries, hand-spun shakes, and wedges of homemade pie are appropriate pairings with the all-American lineup.

Borrowed Earth Café

Vegan

A4

970 Warren Ave. (bet. Highland Ave. & Main St.), Downers Grove

Phone: 630-795-1729 — Lunch & dinner Tue – Sat
Web: www.borrowedearthcafe.com
Prices: $$

The sign saying this Downer's Grove spot opens at "10:37ish" is the first hint that husband-and-wife owners Danny and Kathy Living are on a free-spirited culinary journey...and you're invited along for the ride. What started as a detox den blossomed into this laid-back café that's seriously devoted to raw, vegan, and organic food made with exceptionally fresh and well-chosen ingredients.

Nothing is heated over 115°F to preserve nutrients; salads like a trio of shredded beet, chayote squash, and cucumber shine and keep company with a mild *chile relleno* dipped in a crispy, delicately dried macadamia nut batter. Pecan turtle cheesecake made with cashew cheese on a toasted nut crust is tall and showy, drizzled decadently with chocolate and caramel sauces.

Chama Gaucha

A3

3008 Finley Rd. (at Butterfield Rd.), Downers Grove

Phone: 630-324-6002 — Lunch Mon – Fri
Web: www.chamagaucha.com — Dinner nightly
Prices: $$

Chama Gaucha is a sort of carnivorous carnival that will have you crying uncle after devouring pounds of delicious skewered meats grilled over the open-fire *churrascaria*. Meals begin at the bountiful salad bar, but save plenty of room for the piping hot and juice-dripping meats. Chicken, pork, sausage, bacon-wrapped filet, lamb—it's all here and ready for the taking. The wine list focuses on reds for a good reason, but go Brazilian and order a caipirinha.

The mood feels theatrical, with *passadores* or gauchos flaunting machismo in slicing spit-roasted meats from long metal skewers, Zorro-style right at the table. Just be sure to have your red and green signs at the ready, so servers know when to stop. This is glorious gluttony at its best.

Courtright's

C5

8989 Archer Ave. (bet Cemetery & Willow Springs Rds.), Willow Springs

Phone: 708-839-8000 — Dinner Wed – Sun
Web: www.courtrights.com
Prices: $$$

If you need a palate cleanser for the contemporary rustic-industrial décor that adorns so many Chicago restaurants nowadays, take a trip outside city limits to Courtright's in Willow Springs, where a classic arts and crafts design reigns. Floral motifs scroll across carpets and walls, mirrored by abundant floral arrangements and views of the Cook County Forest Preserve through the windows.

Delightful French-influenced food reflects the special-occasion feel of the dining rooms. Plump, tender stewed snails in a cast iron crock swim in a buttery tarragon sauce with diced prosciutto; while guinea hen *ballotine* sidles up to shallot compote and balsamic-sautéed kale with smoked almonds. Delicately fried lemon ricotta fritters end the evening on a sweet note.

Han 202

Chinese XX

F3

605 W. 31st St. (bet. Lowe Ave. & Wallace St.)

Phone: 312-949-1314 Dinner Tue – Sun
Web: www.han202.com
Prices: ⊜

BYO

Named after the Han dynasty, most are pleasantly surprised by this restaurant's sparkling clean and minimalist décor. The dining room is replete with white walls, dark wood floors, and red-stained tables. The small, tidy kitchen is partially open and offers a peek at an orderly staff churning out Chinese food incorporating a touch of fusion.

Instead of pulling up a seat at the bar, focus on the $25 five-course prix-fixe showcasing fine product, expertly prepared, which may begin with crispy fries dressed with truffle oil; followed by delicate shrimp tempura garnished with fried candied walnut halves. Meals end on a decadent note—imagine dark chocolate mousse dusted with cocoa powder and neatly plated with a fresh raspberry and blueberry.

Homestyle Taste

Chinese XX

F3

3205 S Halstead St. (bet. 32nd & 33rd Sts.)

Phone: 312-949-9328 Lunch & dinner daily
Web: N/A
Prices: ⊜

BYO

When the winter winds start whipping, step into this family-run restaurant, where the name says it all. Homestyle Taste is authentic, chili-heavy Chinese food that will warm even the most bone-chilled Chicagoan. The dining room's dangling red fabric strands of chilies are harbingers of what is to come. Even the freshly brewed tea verges on scalding, though the hot and sour soup is perfectly balanced with vinegar, white pepper, and full-bodied flavors. Just don't forget to try the ethereally light, "hand pancake" and pull it apart, shred by shred. Chopped spicy chicken is served cold on the bone, bathed in scarlet chili oil that's at once searingly hot, salty, and sweet. Garlicky fried string beans are perfect for those who can't take the heat.

Kai Zan

Japanese

2557 ½ W. Chicago Ave. (at Rockwell St.)

Phone: 773-278-5776 Dinner Thu – Tue
Web: www.eatatkaizan.com
Prices: $$

How small is a restaurant with 1/2 in its address? Pretty darn petite one can assume. However, Kai Zan packs a heap of personality into its narrow footprint on far west Chicago Avenue. Shimmering surfaces like glossy white tiles, mother-of-pearl coasters, and a marble sushi counter impart a pristine feel to this buzzed-about Japanese respite.

Go with the fishy flow and sample from the menu of seared and raw contemporary sushi. Squares of escolar soaked in a soy-truffle sauce with addictive fresh pickled wasabi; salmon slices wrapped around scallops, then seared with a citrus glaze; and tidy one-bite *makimono* walk the line between overly complex and simply inspired. Take note that though the bites are budget-friendly, the register tally can add up.

Kama Indian Bistro

Indian

9 S. La Grange Rd. (bet. Burlington & Harris Aves.), La Grange

Phone: 708-352-3300 Dinner Tue – Sun
Web: www.kamabistro.com
Prices: $$

Kama now offers double the pleasure by relocating from its tiny digs across from the La Grange Metra station, to an expansive dining room. The sultry deep purple- and jet black-color scheme remains from the old stomping ground, as does the hypnotic sitar music stimulating the senses as much as the scent of fresh-ground spice blends churned out of the kitchen.

Owner Vikram Singh takes inspiration from his father, noted Indian chef Manmohan Singh, to compile a creative and diverse Indian menu straight from the family recipe book. Many dishes hail from Goa, the smallest Indian state with the biggest flavors and boldest spices. Lamb tacos arrive as spicy bites dressed in pungent *vindaloo,* tamed slightly by coconut milk, crumbled *paneer,* and *pico de gallo.*

La Petite Folie

French XX

F4

1504 E. 55th St. (at Harper Ave.)

Phone: 773-493-1394 — Lunch Tue – Fri
Web: www.lapetitefolie.com — Dinner Tue – Sun
Prices: $$

French aperitifs and digestifs are at the ready behind their handsome curved wood bar, and white lace curtains on the floor-to-ceiling windows work wonders to transform the tree-lined courtyard of the Hyde Park Shopping Center into picturesque Paris. Owner Mary Mastricola, a Le Cordon Bleu and UIC alumna, has returned to her collegiate roots with this *très charmant* bistro.

Her Gallic palate shines through in elegant dishes showcasing in-season ingredients from local markets. Highlights have unveiled smoked pheasant salad punctuated by dried cherries and earthy walnuts; or hazelnut-crusted salmon atop squid ink fettuccine. The all-French wine list has enough Burgundy, Bordeaux, and Chinon to make a satiated diner burst into song with the *Marseillaise*.

Marion Street Cheese Market 

American XX

D2

100 S. Marion St. (at South Blvd.), Oak Park

Phone: 708-725-7200 — Lunch & dinner daily
Web: www.marionstreetcheesemarket.com
Prices: $$ —  Harlem (Green)

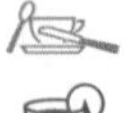

In its mission to bring together nothing less than the best seasonal and local ingredients, this Oak Park *fromagerie* has spawned a bistro that elevates the market's purpose to new heights. Within this cozy space with tin ceilings and warm woods, find affluent droves nibbling on cheese and charcuterie plates. Others can be seen dining on more substantial fare like chorizo quiche or lamb-chestnut stew. A list of purveyors on the menu shares the kitchen's ingredient sources, from local bison to nearby hot sauce producers.

The adjoining market lets you replicate this artisan meal at home with honey, preserves and jams, wine and craft beer, local chocolates; and other specialty foods. Make sure you save your café receipt for a same-day discount in the market.

Maya del Sol

Latin American XX

D2

144 S. Oak Park Ave. (bet. South Blvd. & Pleasant St.), Oak Park

Phone: 708-358-9800 — Lunch Sun
Web: www.mayadelsol.com — Dinner nightly
Prices: $$

Oak Park

Holiday lights may twinkle in the window, but this Latin jewel's inventive and tasty plates lure food lovers year-round. The divided den features an ample bar, tables, and TVs on one side; on the other, exposed brick and sunflower-stenciled lamps surround snug booths. Dusky ochre hues set a calming vibe for a family-friendly feast.

Aloof teens and jubilant toddlers share tables with adults who are here for such *delicioso* dishes as champagne gazpacho finished with *cajeta* and crispy tortilla strips; *calabaza rellena* smothered in a sweet corn-butter sauce; and *crepas de cajeta,* lacy crêpes folded over caramelized goat milk syrup, pecans, and plantains.

The fiery stretch limo parked out front is a thrill, but it's truly the food that steals the show.

Nabuki

Japanese XX

B3

18 E. First St. (bet. Garfield Ave. & Washington St.), Hinsdale

Phone: 630-654-8880 — Lunch Mon – Fri
Web: www.nabukihinsdale.com — Dinner nightly
Prices: $$

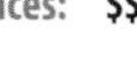

Suburbanites missing the flash of big-city sushi frequently mob this Hinsdale favorite for after-work bites and weekend meals. Find them taking over the bare, glossy white tables strewn throughout the contemporary room for a taste of the fashionable life—as well as creative, clever Japanese fare with tumblers of sake.

Pristine sashimi arrives ornately plated and includes red snapper slices dotted with the chef's special sauce surrounding a haystack tangle of fried onions and shredded daikon. Crispy calamari and rock shrimp are coated in a zippy *furikake-togarashi* veneer; additional crunch comes from numerous tempura options like pumpkin or scallops. Kids balking at raw fish can sample the hot dog roll wrapped in sushi rice, or panko chicken fingers.

Nana

Latin American

F3

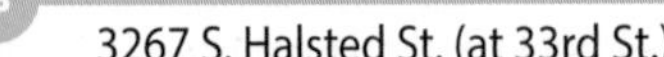

3267 S. Halsted St. (at 33rd St.)

Phone: 312-929-2486 — Lunch daily
Web: www.nanaorganic.com — Dinner Wed – Sun
Prices: $$

Nana Solis raised her kids just up the stairs from this family-run and convivial Bridgeport favorite—thus, the authentic and evocative moniker. With a menu centered on organic ingredients from local farmers, the big "nana" of Mother Nature gets a shout-out too.

Every seat in this deceptively big space between the front coffee bar and rear open kitchen gets a workout. Devoted breakfast droves pile in (sometimes in their jammies during the regular pajama brunch) for creamy grits infused with Latin swagger via chopped poblanos; or a savory-sweet Monte Cristo with thick-sliced ham and smoked cheddar layered between brioche French toast.

Lunch and dinner options like maple-glazed chicken with *tostones* and Cara Cara orange *mojo* sate with flavor and flair.

Pancho Pistolas

Mexican

F3

700 W. 31st St. (at Union Ave.)

Phone: 312-225-8808 — Lunch & dinner daily
Web: www.panchopistolas.com
Prices:

Since 1997, South Siders and White Sox fans have flocked to this red brick building with the pistol-packing Pancho sign for serious steak that's tender and seasoned just so. From carne asada with grilled scallions and peppers to a stuffed skirt steak burrito, the perfectly cooked medium-rare beef can be added to several dishes on the menu and is worth the upgrade.

Beyond just steak in its juicy forms, the lively spot does right by its Mexican fare, which keeps the spice levels low but still tastes great when married with margaritas from the glass-block bar. If you can handle the 17-inch-long Pancho *grande* burrito, it might be wise to arrive with an extra plate—this multi-tortilla wonder is so long, it hangs over the platter upon which it's presented.

Pleasant House Bakery

English 

964 W. 31st St. (bet. Farrell St. & Lituanica Ave.)

Phone: 773-523-7437 Lunch & dinner Tue – Sun
Web: www.pleasanthousebakery.com
Prices: ⓢⓢ

The British royal pie, a rarity in Chicago, has found a home at tiny Pleasant House Bakery—and though U.K. expats go gaga for their savory meat pies, carnivorous Midwesterners can learn to love them too. The jovial staff welcomes everyone at the walk-up counter, bringing traditional British delicacies to marble-topped tables in this wedge-shaped dining room.

A meal of Jamaican meat, or steak and ale pie wrapped in all-butter crust with a side of shucked green peas massaged in butter and fresh mint couldn't be more proper. Until, of course, you add a plate of crispy spud chips tossed with cheese, chopped ribeye and gravy; or *banoffee* pie and snickerdoodles for dessert.

Reservations are only accepted for Sunday high tea with sandwiches and scones.

BYO

Prasino

American 

93 S. La Grange Rd. (bet. Cossitt & Harris Aves.), La Grange

Phone: 708-469-7058 Lunch & dinner daily
Web: www.prasino.com
Prices: $$

Prasino means "green" in Greek and this eco-friendly arena lives up to its moniker by using organic ingredients from local farmers and purveyors. Additionally, its décor features recycled or reclaimed materials where possible. This oversized space in La Grange feels easygoing and cozy with lighting salvaged from corrugated cardboard and wood tables. The same philosophy extends to its sister restaurant in Wicker Park.

Broiled shishito peppers are a game of spicy roulette: most are fairly tame, but white miso-ginger aïoli cools down any unexpectedly searing bites. Sustainably sourced black cod pan-roasted with a soy glaze is tender and brightly sauced; while at dessert, carrot cake with sugar-frosted walnuts walks the line between virtuous and indulgent.

Q BBQ

Barbecue

C3

70 S. LaGrange Rd. (bet. Cossit & Harris Aves.), La Grange

Phone: 708-482-8700 Lunch & dinner daily
Web: www.Q-BBQ.com
Prices: ⓢ

Look for the line snaking out the door and you'll know you've found Q—even city folk walking from the Metra will spot it easily. Once inside this warmly hued lair, gander at their chalkboard listing the daily smoked meats and sides denoting regional barbecue from across the country. Also watch out for the hickory and applewood cords lining the floor.

Chopped Texas brisket is tender and lightly smoky with a well-done crust; Carolina pulled pork is tangy and moist; and Memphis chicken wings get a dry rub with brown sugar for a sweet finish. Don't forget the football-shaped hush puppies for the table, and a jar or two of smoky, spicy, and tangy mustard- or vinegar-based sauces to take home. Grab a six-pack of Minnesota-brewed Hamm's beer while you're at it.

Reel Club

Seafood

B3

272 Oakbrook Center (off Rte. 83), Oak Brook

Phone: 630-368-9400 Lunch & dinner daily
Web: www.reel-club.com
Prices: $$

Mall dining doesn't often provoke chills of excitement, but this splashy seafood spot brings gaggles of well-heeled clients to the Oak Brook Mall for a taste of the ocean and the sleek appeal of a downtown kind of respite. The front Barracuda Lounge caters to shoppers recharging their batteries with a round of Reel Palmers, while the tasteful wood-paneled dining room is a prime-time surf and turf destination.

Along with raw selections like sushi and maki, the succinct menu covers all bases from hearty steaks and fresh fish to hefty salads. Charred cedar planks add smoky flavor to barbecue-basted whitefish fillets; and house-made oyster crackers complement creamy clam chowder.

An abundant seafood and salad buffet is a luxe option for Sunday brunch.

Sen

D2 — Japanese

814 S. Oak Park Ave. (bet. Harrison & Van Buren Sts.), Oak Park

Phone: 708-848-4400 — Lunch & dinner Tue – Sun
Web: www.sensushibar.com
Prices: $$ — Oak Park

It can't be a coincidence that Sen rhymes with Zen. Certainly not at this unfussy bento box of a restaurant in Oak Park, where soothing, neutral tones and textures like gray stone floors, wooden benches, and wafting new age music lend a spa vibe to the space. In lieu of colorful, buzzing distractions, Sen focuses its artistry solely on seafood.

Sip a fruity Sen-tini or glass of sake and put yourself in the sushi chefs' hands for a custom sashimi platter, which may include ultra-fresh kampachi, hamachi, and salmon belly. Or sample an imaginative maki like the Sen with torched scallops and lemongrass reduction. Tangerine-bright kabocha crab soup with large chunks of leg meat is creamy and refreshing; while fried mini wontons offer big satisfaction.

Vie

B3 — American

4471 Lawn Ave. (bet. Burlington Ave. & Elm St.), Western Springs

Phone: 708-246-2082 — Dinner Mon – Sat
Web: www.vierestaurant.com
Prices: $$$

Seasonal American cuisine gets a sleek twist in this tranquil space in downtown Western Springs. Polished concrete floors, abstract black-and-white photographs of rural settings, and metal clipboards that present the menu keep things modern but definitely not pastoral. When he's in the house, Chef Paul Virant is a constant blur of activity, gliding from table to kitchen to ensure every guests' satisfaction.

Midwestern farms and produce take center stage on the farm-to-table-focused menu, accented by Virant's signature pickled vegetables and preserved fruit. Charred Meyer lemons and crunchy pickled green beans bring acidity to grilled scallops with brown butter sauce; and cherry-raspberry jam pairs with peanut butter semifreddo for a whimsical dessert.

Zaytune

Middle Eastern

F3

3129 S. Morgan St. (at 31st Pl.)

Phone: 773-254-6300 — Lunch & dinner daily
Web: www.zaytunegrill.com
Prices: ⊜ — Halsted

Don't dismiss this tiny, value-oriented Middle Eastern lair as just another passable Bridgeport eatery. Zaytune, marked by a black awning and brick façade, is a well-kempt place putting out seriously good eats. Owner Daniel Sarkiss is a graduate of Kendall College's culinary program; his love for and flair with fresh ingredients and bold seasonings keeps Zaytune ahead.

Order at the counter and await carefully composed classics like tabbouleh, hummus, baba ghanoush, and fava bean stew that have more than just the local vegans swooning. The grilled flatbread is something you'll want to wrap yourself in on a cold day. Golden brown falafels and chicken shawarma wraps are a sight to behold; while pistachio *kinafa* and walnut baklava are a teeny splurge.

ZaZa's

Italian

B3

441 W. Ogden Ave. (bet. Richmond & Woodstock Aves.), Clarendon Hills

Phone: 630-920-0500 — Lunch Mon – Fri
Web: www.zazasclarendonhills.com — Dinner nightly
Prices: $$

Looking for ZaZa's among the mix of car dealerships? The wine barrels and bottles outside this Clarendon Hills favorite are a dead giveaway. Inside, black-and-white photos of luminaries like Bogie, Bacall, and the Rat Pack hang on Dijon-yellow walls, while cheery Italian-American tunes from the same bygone era adds to the nostalgic glow. The handsome wood bar makes a great perch for a martini on a Saturday night.

Starters like shrimp scampi change with seasonal availability, but complimentary spicy olives are always offered as a taste bud teaser. Hearty entrées like crisp sautéed eggplant Parmesan give you enough for tomorrow's lunch. And in a place as classic as this, how could you not finish with a scoop of creamy spumoni the size of a tennis ball?

ERTON
OTEL
TOP-TAP

Indexes

Where to **Eat**

Alphabetical List of Restaurants

K

L

M

N

O

P

Q

R

Restaurants by Cuisine

Afghan

American

Asian

Austrian

Barbecue

Belgian

Central Asian

Chinese

Contemporary

Indonesian

International

Italian

Jamaican

Japanese

Korean

Latin American

Lebanese

Macanese

Mediterranean

Mexican

Middle Eastern

Moroccan

Persian

Peruvian

Pizza

Polish

Scandinavian

Seafood

Southern

Southwestern

Spanish

Steakhouse

Thai

Vegan

Vegetarian

Vietnamese

Cuisines by Neighborhood

CHICAGO

Andersonville, Edgewater & Uptown

Loop

Pilsen, Little Italy & University Village

River North

Steakhouse

Streeterville

American

Contemporary

French

Indian

Italian

Mediterranean

Seafood

Steakhouse

West Loop

American

Asian

Contemporary

French

Fusion

Gastropub

Greek

Indian

Italian

Japanese

Latin American

North & Northwestern Suburbs

South, Southwest & Western Suburbs

Starred Restaurants

Within the selection we offer you, some restaurants deserve to be highlighted for their particularly good cuisine. When giving one, two, or three Michelin stars, there are a number of elements that we consider including the quality of the ingredients, the technical skill and flair that goes into their preparation, the blend and clarity of flavours, and the balance of the menu. Just as important is the ability to produce excellent cooking time and again. We make as many visits as we need, so that our readers may be assured of quality and consistency.

A two or three-star restaurant has to offer something very special in its cuisine; a real element of creativity, originality, or "personality" that sets it apart from the rest. Three stars – our highest award – are given to the choicest restaurants, where the whole dining experience is superb.

Cuisine in any style, modern or traditional, may be eligible for a star. Due to the fact we apply the same independent standards everywhere, the awards have become benchmarks of reliability and excellence in over 20 countries in Europe and Asia, particularly in France, where we have awarded stars for 100 years, and where the phrase "Now that's real three-star quality!" has entered into the language.

The awarding of a star is based solely on the quality of the cuisine.

Exceptional cuisine, worth a special journey

One always eats here extremely well, sometimes superbly. Distinctive dishes are precisely executed, using superlative ingredients.

Excellent cuisine, worth a detour

Skillfully and carefully crafted dishes of outstanding quality.

A very good restaurant in its category

A place offering cuisine prepared to a consistently high standard.

Bib Gourmand

This symbol indicates our inspectors' favorites for good value. For $40 or less, you can enjoy two courses and a glass of wine or a dessert (not including tax or gratuity).

Under $25

Brunch

Late Dining

Notes

Michelin

The Michelin Adventure

It all started with rubber balls! This was the product made by a small company based in Clermont-Ferrand that André and Edouard Michelin inherited, back in 1880. The brothers quickly saw the potential for a new means of transport and their first success was the invention of detachable pneumatic tires for bicycles. However, the automobile was to provide the greatest scope for their creative talents. Throughout the 20th century, Michelin never ceased developing and creating ever more reliable and high-performance tires, not only for vehicles ranging from trucks to racing cars but also for underground transit systems and airplanes.

From early on, Michelin provided its customers with tools and services to facilitate mobility and make travelling a more pleasurable and more frequent experience. As early as 1900, the Michelin guide supplied motorists with a host of useful information related to vehicle maintenance, accommodation and restaurants, and was to become a benchmark for good food. At the same time, the Travel Information Bureau offered travellers personalised tips and itineraries.

The publication of the first Michelin road map, in 1910, was an instant hit! In 1926, the first regional tourist guide to France was published, devoted to the principal sites of Brittany, and before long each region of France had its own Green Guide. The collection was later extended to more far-flung destinations, including New York in 1968 and Iceland in 2012.

In the 21st century, with the growth of digital technology, the challenge for Michelin maps guides and digital services is to continue to develop alongside the company's tire activities. Now, as before,Michelin is committed to improving the mobility of travellers.

MICHELIN TODAY

- 69 production sites in 18 countries
- 113,400 employees from all cultures and on every continent
- 6,000 people employed in the Michelin Technology centre
- A commercial presence in more than 170 countries

Moving for a world

Moving forward means developing tires with better road grip and shorter braking distances, whatever the state of the road.

CORRECT TIRE PRESSURE

RIGHT PRESSURE

- Safety
- Longevity
- Optimum fuel consumption

-0,5 bar

- Durability reduced by 20% (- 8,000 km)

- Risk of blowouts
- Increased fuel consumption
- Longer braking distances on wet surfaces

It also involves helping motorists take care of their safety and their tires. To do so, Michelin organises "Fill Up With Air" campaigns all over the world to remind us that correct tire pressure is vital.

WEAR

DETECTING TIRE WEAR

MICHELIN tires are equipped with tread wear indicators, which are small blocks of rubber molded into the base of the main grooves at a height of 1.6 mm. When tread depth is the same level as indicators, the tires are worn and need replacing.

Tires are the only point of contact between vehicle and the road, a worn tire can be dangerous on wet surfaces.

NEW TIRE

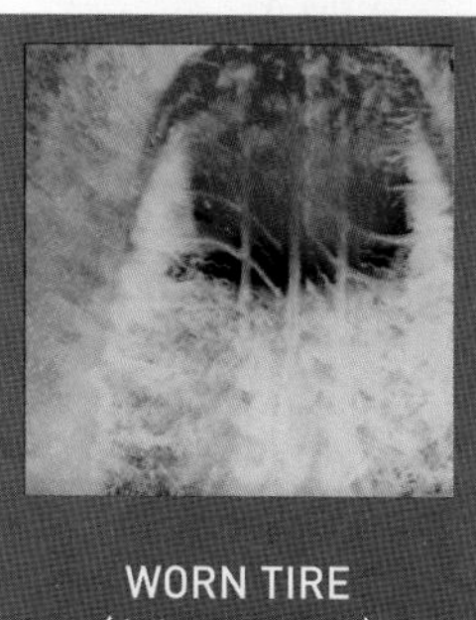

WORN TIRE
(1,6 mm tread)

The photo shows the actual contact zone on wet surfaces.

Moving forward
means sustainable mobility

INNOVATION AND THE ENVIRONMENT

By 2050, Michelin aims to cut the quantity of raw materials used in its tire manufacturing process by half and 99.8% of the company's tires are produced in ISO 14001 certified factories. The design of MICHELIN tires has already saved billions of liters of fuel and, by extension, millions of tons of CO_2.

Similarly, Michelin prints its maps and guides on paper produced from sustainably managed forests and is diversifying its publishing media by offering digital solutions to make travelling easier, more fuel efficient and more enjoyable!

The group's whole-hearted commitment to eco-design on a daily basis is demonstrated by ISO 14001 certification.

Chat with Bibendum

Go to www.michelin.com/corporate/EN/home
Find out more about Michelin's history and the latest news.

QUIZ

Michelin develops tyres for all types of vehicles. See if you can match the right tyre with the right vehicle…

Solution : A-6 / B-4 / C-2 / D-1 / E-3 / F-7 / G-5

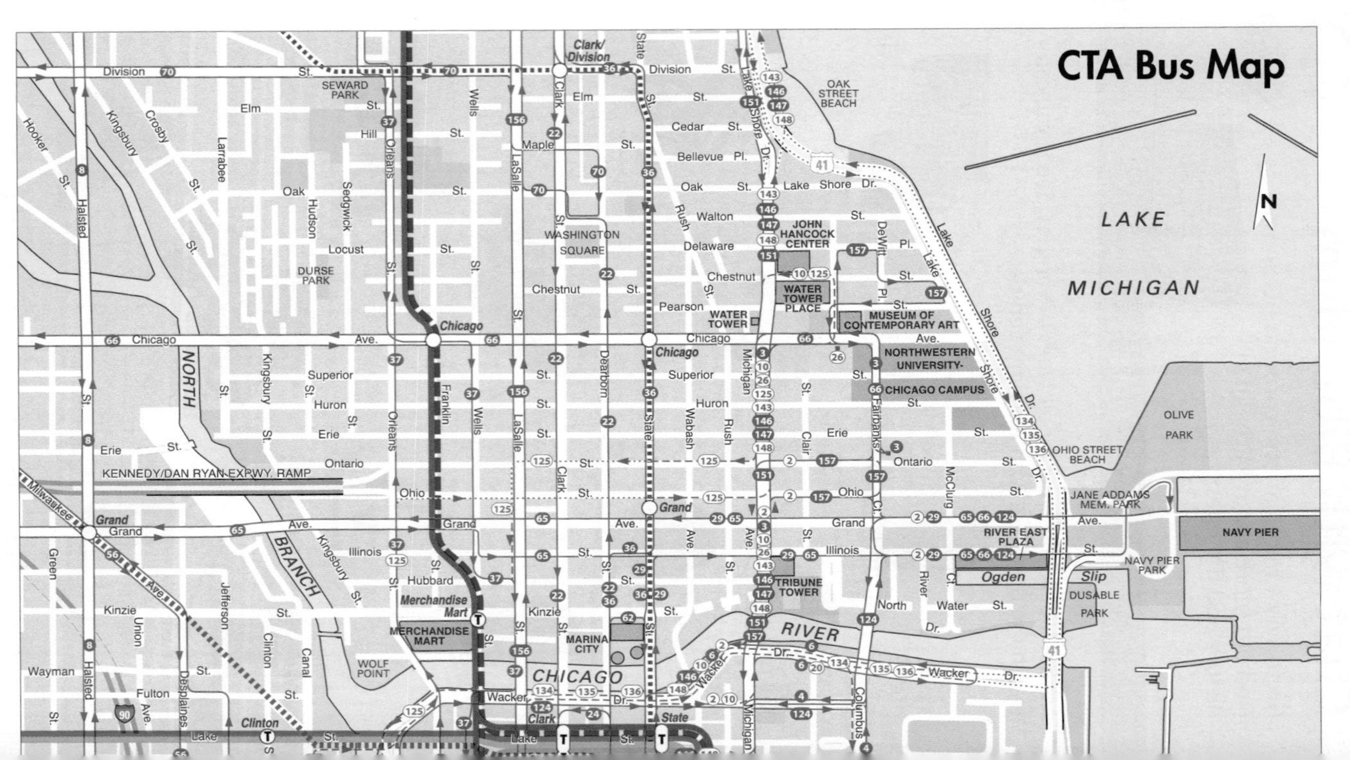
CTA Bus Map
N
LAKE
MICHIGAN
OAK STREET BEACH
JOHN HANCOCK CENTER
WATER TOWER PLACE
WATER TOWER
MUSEUM OF CONTEMPORARY ART
NORTHWESTERN UNIVERSITY-
CHICAGO CAMPUS
OLIVE PARK
OHIO STREET BEACH
JANE ADDAMS MEM. PARK
NAVY PIER
NAVY PIER PARK
RIVER EAST PLAZA
Ogden
Slip
DUSABLE PARK
TRIBUNE TOWER
MARINA CITY
MERCHANDISE MART
Merchandise Mart
WOLF POINT
WASHINGTON SQUARE
SEWARD PARK
DURSE PARK
KENNEDY/DAN RYAN EXPWY. RAMP
NORTH
BRANCH
CHICAGO
RIVER
Clark/Division
Chicago
Grand
State
Clark
Clinton
Division St.
Lake Shore Dr.
Chicago Ave.
Grand Ave.
Illinois St.
Ohio St.
Ontario St.
Erie St.
Huron St.
Superior St.
Chestnut St.
Delaware Pl.
Walton St.
Oak St.
Bellevue Pl.
Cedar St.
Elm St.
Pearson
Michigan Ave.
Rush St.
Wabash Ave.
State St.
Dearborn St.
Clark St.
LaSalle St.
Wells St.
Franklin St.
Orleans St.
Sedgwick
Larrabee St.
Halsted St.
Kingsbury St.
Hudson
Locust
Hill
Maple
Crosby
Hooker
Milwaukee Ave.
Green
Wayman
Fulton
Kinzie St.
Hubbard St.
Desplaines
Union
Jefferson
Clinton
Canal St.
Lake St.
Wacker Dr.
Columbus
Fairbanks Ct.
McClurg Ct.
St. Clair
DeWitt Pl.
Mies van der Rohe
North Water St.
River Dr.
41
90

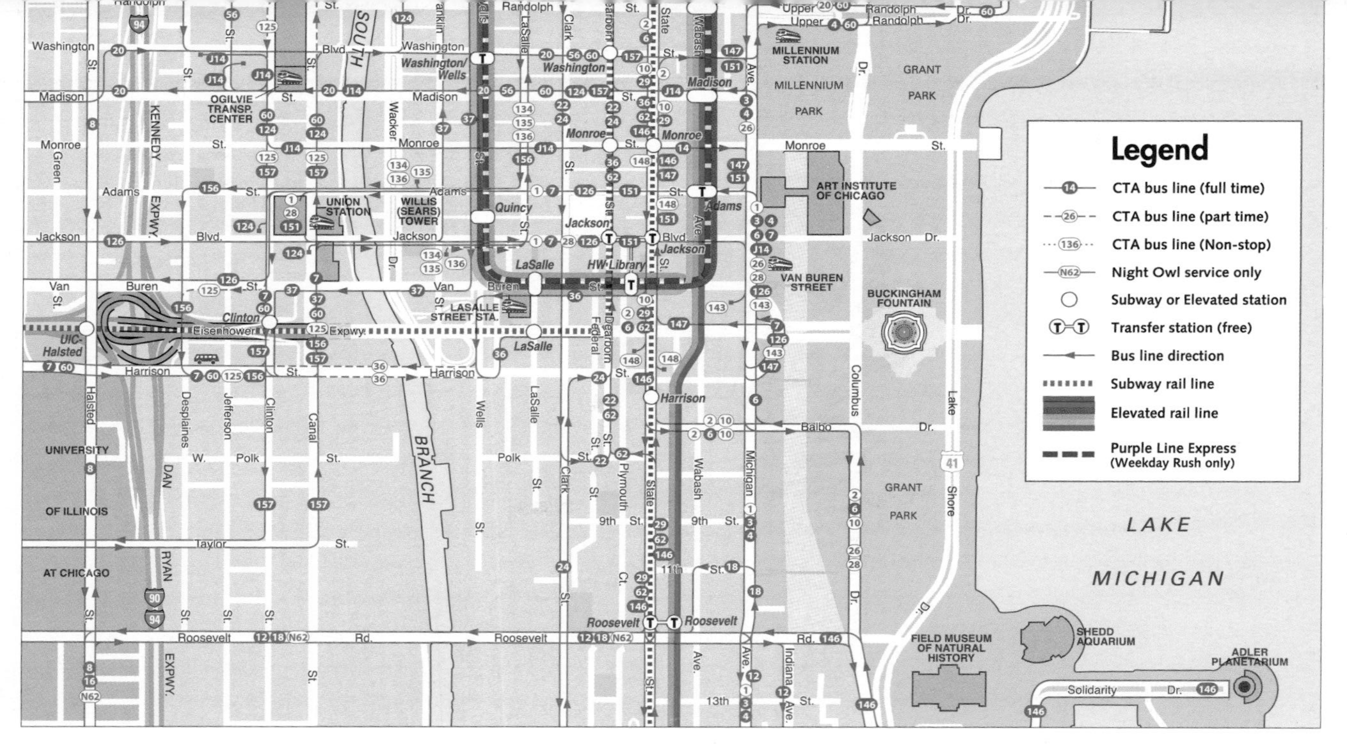

Legend
CTA bus line (full time)
CTA bus line (part time)
CTA bus line (Non-stop)
Night Owl service only
Subway or Elevated station
Transfer station (free)
Bus line direction
Subway rail line
Elevated rail line
Purple Line Express
(Weekday Rush only)
LAKE
MICHIGAN
MILLENNIUM STATION
MILLENNIUM PARK
GRANT PARK
ART INSTITUTE OF CHICAGO
VAN BUREN STREET
BUCKINGHAM FOUNTAIN
FIELD MUSEUM OF NATURAL HISTORY
SHEDD AQUARIUM
ADLER PLANETARIUM
OGILVIE TRANSP. CENTER
UNION STATION
WILLIS (SEARS) TOWER
LASALLE STREET STA.
UNIVERSITY OF ILLINOIS AT CHICAGO
SOUTH BRANCH
KENNEDY EXPWY.
DAN RYAN EXPWY.
Eisenhower Expwy.
Lake Shore Dr.
Columbus Dr.
Michigan Ave.
Wabash Ave.
State St.
Dearborn St.
Clark St.
LaSalle St.
Wells St.
Wacker Dr.
Canal St.
Clinton St.
Jefferson St.
Desplaines St.
Halsted St.
Randolph
Washington
Madison
Monroe
Adams
Jackson Blvd.
Van Buren St.
Harrison
Polk
Taylor
Roosevelt Rd.
Balbo Dr.
9th St.
11th St.
13th St.
Solidarity Dr.
Washington/Wells
Quincy
LaSalle
HW Library
Clinton
UIC-Halsted
Harrison
Roosevelt

Michelin